W9-BTP-080

Beyond the
Iran-Contra Crisis

Beyond the Iran–Contra Crisis

The Shape of U.S. Anti-Terrorism Policy in the Post-Reagan Era

Edited by

Neil C. Livingstone

Terrell E. Arnold

Lexington Books

D.C. Heath and Company/Lexington, Massachusetts/Toronto

This book is published as part of the Lexington Books
Issues in Low-Intensity Conflict series, Neil C. Livingstone, consulting editor.

Library of Congress Cataloging-in-Publication Data

Beyond the Iran–Contra crisis.

Includes index.
1. United States—Foreign relations—1981- . 2. Terrorism—Prevention. 3. United States—National security. 4. Terrorism—Government Policy—United States. I. Livingstone, Neil C. II. Arnold, Terrell E.
E876.B49   1988   327.73   87-45376
ISBN 0-669-16466-6 (alk. paper)
ISBN 0-669-16467-4 (pbk. : alk. paper)

Published simultaneously in Canada
Printed in the United States of America
Casebound International Standard Book Number: 0-669-16466-6
Paperbound International Standard Book Number: 0-669-16467-4
Library of Congress Catalog Card Number: 87-45376

The paper used in this publication meets the minimum requirements of American National Standard for Information Sciences—Permanence of Paper for Printed Library Materials, ANSI Z39.48-1984. ∞™

88 89 90 91 92 8 7 6 5 4 3 2 1

Neil C. Livingstone would like to dedicate this book to his grandmother, Helen "Mimi" Livingstone. Terrell E. Arnold dedicates this book to the memory of Dr. Lawrence Mouat.

Contents

Introduction

This book is a compilation of essays by leading experts regarding the impact of the Iran–Contra scandal on U.S. anti-terrorism policies and institutions. It is an attempt to assess the events leading up to the November 1986 disclosure that the United States had engaged in a secret dialogue with at least one major faction in the revolutionary regime that rules Iran and that U.S. weapons had been transferred to Tehran in exchange for American hostages held by Iranian-backed terrorists in Lebanon. It is not the purpose of this book to recount the actual details of the Iran initiative or to explore the diversion of proceeds from U.S. weapons sales to Tehran to the U.S.-backed Contras fighting the Sandinista regime in Nicaragua. There are many other authors, including some of the participants in the actual events, far better qualified to do so, and a flood of accounts can be expected.

Of much more immediate interest is the need to understand the evolution of U.S. anti-terrorism policy in the Reagan years and to evaluate the pressures felt by U.S. policymakers that contributed to the ill-fated Iran initiative. Only in this way can steps be taken to correct any deficiencies that exist and to reestablish U.S. credibility in the war against terrorism.

In chapter 1, a former deputy director of the State Department's Office of Counterterrorism, Ambassador Parker W. Borg, describes the development of U.S. anti-terrorism policies and initiatives, especially efforts to establish a framework of cooperation with U.S. allies in Europe and elsewhere. Borg focuses on the "anger, disappointment, and cynicism" that greeted the Iranian initiative in foreign capitals and suggests steps needed to put the U.S. anti-terrorism program back on a solid footing, especially against state sponsors of terrorism.

William R. Farrell, a retired U.S. Air Force officer who is on the faculty of the U.S. Naval War College, discusses in chapter 2 the reasons why the National Security Council became an operational rather than a purely consultative unit and attempts to put the recent crisis into historical perspective. Efforts by Congress to micromanage foreign policy as well as congressionally imposed restraints on the president's ability to make policy are assessed as contributing factors to the crisis. In chapter 3, coeditor Terrell E. Arnold, also a former deputy director of the State

Department's Office of Counterterrorism, analyzes how nations that place a high value on human life can find their foreign policies hostage to terrorist groups that seize their citizens. He looks at the impact that the families of hostage victims had on the Reagan administration, especially in view of their access to the media. The extent to which this pressure contributed to the U.S. decision to provide arms to Iran and what can be done about it in the future form the dominant themes of Arnold's chapter.

J. Robert McBrien, who has been involved in the U.S. government's anti-terrorism campaign since its inception, contends in chapter 4 that the U.S. experience in Lebanon, especially the traumas of 1983, had an excessive and unwarranted impact on U.S. anti-terrorism policies and ultimately contributed to a lack of perspective on the part of senior U.S. policymakers in developing strategies for securing the release of hostages. Coeditor Neil C. Livingstone maintains in chapter 5 that the U.S. air raid on Libya in April 1986 represented "the high-water mark of the Reagan administration's war against terrorism" but that its impact and the other successes of the previous five years were wiped out by the clumsily executed Iran–Contra initiative and the "irresistible urge of Congress to play inquisitor rather than physician to a troubled policy." Livingstone contends that the anti-terrorism policy of the United States is adrift and that only time will tell if it can regain the momentum it had only eighteen months ago. Of particular concern is the damage suffered by the CIA and the U.S. intelligence community as a result of disclosures stemming from the various Iran–Contra inquiries and lingering questions concerning the nation's ability to conduct covert operations against terrorists and their state sponsors in the future.

Policy is invariably hostage to means. So it was with U.S. anti-terrorism policies. Following their arrival in Washington, Reagan administration policymakers found that U.S. intelligence and counterterrorism capabilities had been severely undermined by the Vietnam War, Watergate, multiple inquiries into alleged wrongdoing by the CIA, and the defeatist policies of the Carter administration. Before a tough, proactive anti-terrorism program could be implemented by the new administration in the face of growing international threats, it was necessary to revitalize both the U.S. intelligence establishment and the nation's special operations forces. Perhaps no other action since the Vietnam War has had as much impact on the nation's overall anti-terrorism capabilities as the congressionally mandated reforms directed at U.S. special operations forces. In chapter 6, Ross S. Kelly, a major in the U.S. Army Special Forces Reserves and author of a monthly column on special operations forces around the globe, reviews the recent organizational restructuring of U.S. special operations forces and the development and deployment of specialized elite counterterrorism units. Kelly questions the commitment of some in the government to the special operations concept and contends that advocates must maintain a posture of continued vigilance and activism to ensure that the SOF revitalization is ultimately completed.

W.D. Livingstone, press secretary to Senator Peter Wilson of California, in chapter 7 focuses on the growing ability of terrorists to manipulate the media and the Reagan administration's inability to comprehend fully this fact or to respond to it effectively. Contrary to many critics of the media, however, Livingstone believes that the media are often scapegoats for the failure of governments to resolve terrorist crises satisfactorily. Indeed, he suggests that effective media coverage of terrorist outrages, which builds public support for strong countermeasures, represents the best defense against terrorism.

Chapter 8 explores the many infrastructural and technological vulnerabilities that characterize postindustrial societies. The chapter's author, Robert K. Mullen, is an acknowledged expert who has been retained by government agencies and private industry to assess new threats to nuclear plants, primary power distribution grids, transportation systems, computer networks, and dozens of other potential terrorist targets. In the wake of worsening U.S. relations with Iran, Iranian officials and Iranian-backed extremists have repeatedly threatened to carry out terrorist attacks in the United States itself. Should this happen, technological targets are sure to be high on their list.

Nancy Rodriguez Asencio is the wife of former U.S. Ambassador to Colombia Diego Asencio, who was held hostage by M-19 terrorists in the embassy of the Dominican Republic for sixty-one days. Her son-in-law was one of the American hostages in Iran. As a result of her husband's ordeal and other hostage episodes that have affected family members and friends, Asencio has become deeply involved in efforts to develop effective crisis management programs for the families of hostage victims. Asencio believes that families are, in many respects, just as much victims as the actual hostage. Given the pressure hostage families exerted on the Reagan administration, the plight of family members deserves far more attention, and this is the subject of chapter 9.

Yagil Weinberg, a former Israeli Defense official now attached to the University of Maryland Center for International Security, examines in chapter 10 the impact of the Iran–Contra crisis on U.S.–Israeli relations. This is a particularly important subject; some critics in the Congress and the media have suggested that Israel bears a great deal of the blame for drawing the United States into the Iran initiative.

The recent Iran–Contra congressional hearings revealed that private sector firms and individuals had played major roles in the Iran initiative and the Contra resupply effort. Critics charge that by contracting out various support services and operational requirements to private firms and organizations, Lieutenant Colonel Oliver North and his allies were able to avoid congressional prohibitions on aid to the Contras and to circumvent normal oversight channels. In chapter 11, Peter J. Brown and Terrell E. Arnold survey the security industry, believed to be by some "the fastest-growing industry in the world," and examine its role in the Iran–Contra crisis.

Chapters 12 and 13 are concerned with new efforts to use legal prosecutory approaches to combating international terrorism. In chapter 12, Terrell E. Arnold probes the thorny issue of extradition, which has been underscored by Italy's decision not to extradite the Palestinians accused of seizing the *Achille Lauro* and murdering passenger Leon Klinghoffer and West Germany's refusal to send alleged TWA hijacker Mohammed Ali Hamadei to the United States. Arnold also examines questions related to jurisdiction, the collection of evidence, and the need for international cooperation in successfully prosecuting international terrorists. Navy Captain (select) E. Anthony Fessler focuses exclusively on the extraterritorial apprehension and prosecution of terrorists in chapter 13. As this book goes to press, the big news on the terrorism front is that the FBI lured accused Shiite terrorist Fawaz Younis to a yacht in international waters, where he was apprehended and brought back to the United States to stand trial. Fessler's chapter represents a definitive legal statement of this promising new method of bringing terrorists to justice.

Beyond the Iran–Contra Crisis is the second book by the coeditors to explore in a timely manner policy issues related to terrorism; it is part of Lexington Books' Low-Intensity Conflict series. Their first book, *Fighting Back: Winning the War against Terrorism*, which appeared in 1985, was characterized by a wide diversity of opinion as well as an emphasis on practical subjects of interest to policymakers. All of the contributors to this volume have been engaged in one form or another in actual efforts to control and suppress terrorism and therefore write with a sense of immediacy and without the academic detachment from reality common to many other works in the field.

International terrorism represents one of the most serious and intractable problems confronting the United States and its Western allies. How the United States and other democratic countries choose to meet this challenge ultimately will turn on the quality of the debate, both public and private, over the alternatives available to policymakers. We hope that *Beyond the Iran–Contra Crisis* will contribute positively to this debate and help those in the trenches find workable solutions to the problem.

1
The Evolution of U.S. Anti-Terrorism Policy

Parker W. Borg

An International Problem

Anger, disappointment, and cynicism were among the international reactions to the recent U.S. arms deals with Iran, for two reasons: because the Reagan administration had taken the moral high ground on terrorism, becoming one of the strongest critics of efforts by other countries to seek accommodation with terrorist groups, and because the exchanges involved transfers of military equipment (rather than prisoners or money, the normal commodities for such secret transfers) to one protagonist in a brutal war where official U.S. policy was to stem the arms flow.

In pursuing the Iranian connection, the United States followed a well-worn path other nations have trod. When their citizens are being held by terrorists, nations too often tend to think of themselves as standing alone, and accordingly they act unilaterally. While this attitude might be understood in the case of Italian actions toward the Red Brigades or West German responses to the Red Army Faction attacks, it is more difficult to understand in the case of the U.S. concern about hostages in Lebanon. In June 1985, about the time the decisions were made to pursue the Iranian initiative, about thirty foreigners from eight countries had been seized over the course of the previous eighteen months (ten Americans, ten French, five English, and one each of Spanish, Swiss, Dutch, Irish, and Saudi nationality). In June 1987, twenty-eight foreigners from at least nine nations were held hostage in Lebanon. Despite occasional efforts to share information, each government seemed at times to pursue the release of its own nationals without regard to the other hostages and almost as if there were a competition to see whose hostages might be released first.

Separate Perspectives

Governments around the world have approached the problem of terrorism in their own way because each has faced a different variation of the problem, often one

This essay was originally issued by the U.S. Foreign Service Institute, Center for the Study of Foreign Affairs, under the title "International Terrorism: Breaking the Chain of Violence."

form at home and another abroad, based on its particular social, historical, and political circumstances. For the United States, the terrorist problem has been an international one, affecting U.S. citizens and interests primarily in Europe, the Middle East, and Latin America. For most other countries, terrorism has been more of a problem at home than abroad, and the most dangerous terrorists have been domestic rather than foreign. For example, for the British, the problem has been the Provisional Irish Republican Army; for the Germans, the Baader-Meinhof gang and more recently the Red Army Faction; for the French, Action Directe and various separatist groups; and for the Spaniards, the Basque separatists.

As the Germans and Italians learned in the 1970s, actions that free terrorists held prisoner and meet other terrorist demands are likely to be regretted. The freed terrorists are experienced criminals who became available for new violence, and when the principle of no concessions is set aside, terrorists are more likely to seize new hostages each time a state puts one of their colleagues behind bars. Lessons that states may have learned at home, however, have not been applied with similar rigor abroad. When dealing with Middle Eastern terrorist groups, despite a lot of tough talk about no concessions, many states in the West have been prepared eventually to cut a deal. And despite their alliances, there has been little cooperation. Lebanon presents a unique situation because of its political chaos, but it also should have presented a unique opportunity for cooperation because the citizens of so many states have been victims of its political turmoil.

In addition to the Lebanese problem, two other factors have altered the face of terrorism in Europe in the mid-1980s. First, the spillover of Middle Eastern terrorism has changed the equation in a slightly different way for each European state. Not only did the number of Middle Eastern–related incidents double in 1984 and 1985 from the average for 1980–1983, but the focus also shifted increasingly to non–Middle Eastern targets, and the attacks included some of the most spectacular incidents of 1985 and 1986. The second factor—which is related to the first— is the growing evidence of official involvement by some Middle Eastern states. While state support of terrorism by Libya, Iran, and Syria has been a serious Middle Eastern problem for many years, during the latter part of 1985 Libya and Syria, in particular, became increasingly involved in incidents in Europe. Although the growing Middle East connection is an important incentive for the Europeans to work together more closely, the principal concern of each state has continued to be its individual domestic problem.

Martyr Complex versus Statistical Evidence

Americans have a special martyr complex about terrorism. Recalling the attacks against its embassy and marines in Lebanon, the peril of the Americans aboard TWA flight 847, the apparent targeting of Americans during the *Achille Lauro* incident, and several other dramatic attacks, Americans have developed an exaggerated view of the threat to them from terrorists outside the United States. Believing that they are the primary target of terrorists, Americans have altered their view of the rest of the world and demanded better protection from their government when working and traveling abroad. (During the summer of 1986, many Americans cancelled travel plans to Western Europe because of fear of terrorism.) Congress has reflected these concerns with emotional hearings following each major terrorist incident and new counterterrorism legislation in 1984, 1985, and 1986.

Despite the perception of terrorism as an American problem, the facts show a different situation: that terrorism is clearly an international dilemma. While U.S. interests have been targets of some of the most dramatic incidents and American victims have received extensive publicity, statistics show that a wide range of nationalities are victims of terrorism and that a relativley small percentage of the victims are Americans. State Department statistics showed that U.S. citizens and property were victims in an alarming 35 to 40 percent of the international terrorist incidents in the 1979–1983 period. For 1984 and 1985, however, this figure dropped to about 22 percent each year, climbing slightly in 1986 to 26 percent, with the department noting in 1984 that the change reflected both an overall decline and a growing ability to keep track of terrorist incidents not involving U.S. victims or property. What these statistics do not make explicit is that often citizens of other countries are also victims in incidents affecting Americans, such as the Rome and Vienna bombings and the *Achille Lauro* hijacking.

Citizens and property of more than eighty countries were targets or victims of international terrorist incidents in both 1985 and 1986, up from more than seventy countries in 1983–1984. Preliminary casualty figures for 1986 showed 579 people killed and 1,552 wounded in terrorist incidents, but Americans made up a smaller proportion of these totals than one might think: 12 killed (2.1 percent of the total) and 101 wounded (6.5 percent). These figures are down somewhat from the statistics for 1985 and 1984. Americans killed in terrorist actions in these years totaled 38 of 825 in 1985 (4.6 percent) and 11 of 312 in 1984 (3.5 percent). Americans wounded in terrorist incidents were 12 percent and 3.1 percent of the total wounded for each year, respectively. In recent years, only 1983 showed a different pattern: 271 Americans killed (41 percent of the total of 652 deaths), but two incidents, the bombings of the U.S. embassy in April and the marine barracks in September, accounted for 95 percent of these casualties.

Such statistics are not intended to downplay the importance of effective measures by the United States against terrorism but rather to provide a better perspective on the relationship between the United States and the rest of the world in looking at the threat. There is little question that Americans are likely to remain important targets of terrorists in the years ahead. First, because the United States is a superpower, its policies and actions are held responsible for the status quo in many countries around the globe, particularly in those under attack by radical elements. Second, U.S. officials, businesspeople, and tourists are omnipresent around the world, making them easy targets for both random and directed violence. And third, the role of the U.S. press in determining what is important international news and the competitiveness of its networks mean that incidents involving Americans will receive dramatic coverage.

U.S. Responses to Terrorism

As a principal target and major victim of terrorist attacks and as leader of the Western world, whose values are increasingly under assault by terrorists, the United States has an obligation to play a major role in the fight against international terrorism. Too often the United States has sought to pursue this role through unilateral action. It has merely reacted to single incidents, such as the *Achille Lauro* hijacking or the growing role of Libya in terrorism, without developing an overall approach that takes into account the international nature of the problem.

The Force Option

Ask the average American about recent successful actions against terrorists, and almost invariably he or she will refer to the greater willingness to use force, citing as examples the interception of the Egyptian aircraft following the *Achille Lauro* hijacking in October 1985 and the bombing of Tripoli and Benghazi in April 1986. This willingness by the United States to use force added a new dimension to the struggle against terrorism. In addition to higher approval ratings for the president, these attacks bolstered confidence in an otherwise frustrating struggle. They signaled to friends and foes that the United States was serious about taking strong action— and if they persisted in looking the other way, this new willingness to use force could affect their interests.

The military force option has two variations: it is direct when applied against a specific target, as during the two actions, and it is indirect when used to demonstrate force or establish presence, as during the naval maneuvers in the Gulf of Sidra in April 1986, the joint exercise with the Egyptians in the fall of 1986, and the naval task force activities off Lebanon in February 1987. Indirect military action can be effective only if it is backed by a willingness to make use of force. That makes it an important tool in support of friends or against states that support terrorism, as in the case of the confrontation with Libya, but a questionable one when there is no state involvement, as was the case during the naval maneuvers in February 1987 in reaction to the kidnappings in Lebanon. In the fight against terrorism, indirect force, the demonstrations and maneuvers, can be effective only in specialized cases where the confrontation is against a sovereign government linked to the terrorist action. If employed otherwise, as during the shelling of Lebanese hills by the *New Jersey* in 1983, it is more likely to breed new terrorists than to punish any existing ones.

The first requirement for a response involving the direct use of force is good intelligence. It must be known with a high degree of certainty not only who committed—or might commit—the act of terrorism but also where they can be found now or at a particular time in the future. The United States was able to use its direct force option on two recent occasions when this information was available, but in almost every other situation where the use of force might have been considered, the intelligence was neither adequate nor timely. Most frequently, it is vague, from questionable sources, or refers to a location that the terrorists may only have passed through briefly at some time in the past.

Assuming first-rate intelligence, there are important issues to evaluate when considering the use of force: What sort of terrorist act occurred, and what would be a proportionate response? Was the act an isolated one or part of a pattern by a particular group? Have the terrorists taken refuge in a friendly country or one where U.S. forces might take action? What local forces or other foreign forces might be in a better position to respond? What are the other options, overt and covert, for dealing with the problem? What is the capability of the United States to respond in a timely manner? What legal, moral, or practical problems might be raised over the use of U.S. forces? What will be the impact of U.S. force on friends and foes in the region? Are there likely to be innocent victims? What is the risk to the rescue force?

Adding the normal shortcomings in intelligence to the political, logistical, and moral constraints on the use of force, one can understand why there have been and probably will continue to be so few cases where direct force is appropriate. Nonetheless the United States has demonstrated that it can use direct force judiciously against selective targets. Most critics have come around to the position that force is a legitimate option for consideration during terrorist incidents.

The Question of Preemption

The American public, on the one hand protected from the everyday contact with terrorism regularly experienced by citizens of Europe and the Middle East and on the other captivated by a simplistic "Rambo" response portrayed on television and movie screens, seems to place undue emphasis on the use of force as the solution to the problem of terrorism. Although perhaps the most visible of the responses, force represents only one of a range of options. These other measures have received less publicity but have played a much more important role in strengthening the United States in combating terrorism during the past few years.

Following the bombing of the U.S. Marine Corps barracks in Lebanon in 1983 and the subsequent Long commission report, there was an attempt to shift U.S. counterterrorism policy from one that constantly seemed on the defensive, reacting to terrorist events, to one that better anticipated terrorist actions when possible. To contrast it with the previous reactive policy, in some circles this new policy was called proactive, an ill-defined term that to many meant preemption, which in turn implied the use of force. Although the new policy expanded the range of options to include greater use of force, its purpose was to seize the initiative against terrorists by using the entire range of available measures more effectively. These measures include self-defense, intelligence, the law, and diplomacy. Another potential tool, covert action, has played little official part because of continuing disagreement between the executive and legislative branches over its proper role, and evidence of its misuse in the Iran–Contra affair has probably sharply reduced its prospects for the immediate future.

In commenting on the need for stronger action against the growing terrorist threat, Secretary of State George Shultz stated in October 1984, "Our responses should go beyond passive defense to consider means of active prevention, preemption and retaliation. Our goal must be to prevent and deter future terrorist acts." He was criticized at the time by many for being too hawkish. His words were widely interpreted as applicable solely to military force rather than to the whole range of possible actions. Preempting and preventing terrorist acts will be far more easily accomplished through better defense and better use of intelligence than through any possible military act.

Unilateral Actions

Good self-defense must be the first line against terrorism because one can never know when or where a terrorist may strike. The State Department has been upgrading building security at U.S. embassies through supplementary construction programs and increasing personal security among its employees through strengthened training programs. Many private sector organizations have adopted stronger security measures themselves, recognizing that their employees are also vulnerable, and increasingly so in places where U.S. government protective measures have diminished the threat to official Americans.

The United States has upgraded the priority it places on information about terrorist groups among the intelligence community, encouraged other members of the official U.S. community overseas to contribute information on terrorism, and improved coordinating mechanisms in Washington and at embassies abroad in order to respond to specific threats in a more timely manner.

Congress has given U.S. prosecutors and courts new tools to deal with terrorism outside the United States in the last few years, including the following:

The 1984 Act to Combat International Terrorism, which established a program of rewards for information leading to the arrest and conviction of terrorists.

The Foreign Assistance Authorization Act of 1985, which expanded the jurisdiction of the Federal Aviation Administration (FAA) to inspect airports outside the United States and established a procedure for issuing travel advisories for airports that fail to meet minimum security standards.

The Omnibus Anti-terrorism Act of 1986, which among other provisions makes the murder or assault of an American overseas a U.S. crime and prohibits Americans from providing training or other services to foreign authorities that would aid and abet international terrorism.

Diplomatic Actions

Diplomatic tools are more important than generally recognized. Although not effective against individual terrorists or groups, they are probably the most important and widely used of the tools against states that support terrorism. Five countries are on the secretary of state's list of terrorist-supporting states: Libya, Iran, Syria, Cuba, and Southern Yemen. Diplomatic initiatives include such actions as export controls, particularly on military equipment, termination of assistance programs, restrictions on travel to the United States by officials and other citizens of specified foreign states, and reductions in diplomatic presence.

During 1986, the administration twice made dramatic use of these diplomatic tools. In January, the United States responded to Libya's growing support for terrorist groups by halting all business and financial ties, freezing Libyan assets, ordering all U.S. citizens to depart Libya, and calling on friendly governments to take similar actions. In November, following the London trial of those accused of attempting to bomb the El Al flight, the United States supported British efforts against Syria with a reduction in the U.S. diplomatic presence in Damascus, the elimination of trade credits to Syria, and other commercial restrictions.

Except for the U.S. support of the British against Syria, the measures were largely unilateral: from U.S. military actions in the Mediterranean to the better protection of U.S. personnel and facilities and from the improvements in U.S. intelligence gathering to the expanded jurisdiction of U.S. prosecutors. Even the diplomatic measures were essentially unilateral in that they were conceived and executed primarily for their direct impact on the offending state and only secondarily as part of a coordinated effort. Behind these unilateral actions lay the perception by many decision makers of international terrorism as a special U.S. problem that neither its allies nor the host governments were prepared or willing to combat in the manner the United States believed essential. Such new measures were seen as necessary to help overcome the imagined U.S. impotency following the Beirut bombings and spectacles like the TWA flight 847 hijacking. Outside of the State Department and some of the congressional offices dealing with foreign affairs, U.S. decision makers too often downplayed the international dimensions of the problem, seldom acknowledging that long-term success would require careful coordination with other countries.

Recent Achievements in International Cooperation

Levels of Cooperation

Opportunities for action against terrorism on the international front are numerous, but the mechanisms for cooperation are weaker and slower than for unilateral actions. More important, international cooperation has historically had a feeble record, which has served to reinforce unilateralist tendencies among decision makers.

International cooperation against terrorism takes place on three levels: bilaterally on a country-by-country basis, multilaterally in international organizations, and collectively among like-minded states.

The United States has pursued closer bilateral ties on terrorism with other nations around the globe—intensifying links with such friends as Great Britain, Canada, Italy, and Israel and developing new links with countries where political ties have been more complicated, ranging from Greece and some of the countries of the Middle East to the Eastern bloc. Bilateral cooperation permits exchanges in intelligence, sharing information about the movement of suspected terrorists, mutual protection of property, and the adoption of common approaches to terrorist incidents.

In one form or another, the United States has initiated cooperative ventures with some fifty governments, about forty of which have participated in the Anti-Terrorism Assistance Program, which by the end of 1986 had brought nearly 3,000 foreign officials to the United States to participate in counterterrorism training courses similar to those offered to U.S. police and security officials.

Although the United Nations has frequently become bogged down in regional confrontations when considering important issues, the United States and other nations, including the Soviet Union, have succeeded in developing a cooperative approach on terrorism. Through two of the specialized agencies of the United Nations, the world community has also worked to establish better security standards at airports and at sea.

The third area of cooperation has been among like-minded countries. International organizations can develop a consensus on accepted standards, and bilateral links are the best way to exchange intelligence effectively. Nonetheless, there has long been a need for a forum where states might consider common approaches for action against terrorism. Among the like-minded groups that have recently considered terrorism have been the Summit Seven, the European Community (EC), the North Atlantic Treaty Organization (NATO), and the Council of Europe.

Historically, the past two years may stand out as the decisive years for important first steps in the international effort against terrorism. Although this cooperation is still in its preliminary stages, the successes beginning in the latter part of 1985 have been auspicious. Four areas of cooperation stand out: (1) establishing the principle that terrorism is a threat to all nations, (2) improving travel security, (3) strengthening legal actions against terrorists, and (4) initiating common measures against state supporters of terrorism.

A Threat to All Nations. The United Nations broke precedent in late 1985 in taking a strong stand against terrorism. At the U.N. Conference on Crime Prevention in Milan in November 1985, participants approved the principle that terrorism is a threat to all nations and should be considered a crime. In December 1985, the General Assembly adopted nearly unanimously its strongest resolution condemning terrorism, and the Security Council adopted a resolution that condemned the taking of hostages. Although such resolutions lack legal weight, they are important in establishing a consensus on acceptable international behavior. In its 1987 session the United Nations will again have the opportunity to consider the question of terrorism and to determine whether unity on this important issue can be sustained and strengthened.

Improved Travel Security. Improving travel security has been a priority issue for two specialized agencies of the United Nations. The International Civil Aviation Organization (ICAO) approved in late 1985 and began implementing in 1986 tightened civil aviation security procedures for airports around the world. ICAO also adopted a model security clause for insertion in bilateral civil aviation agreements. Following the *Achille Lauro* hijacking, the United States proposed in the International Maritime Organization (IMO) international security measures designed to improve security at ports and aboard ships. The IMO approved these measures in September 1986 and has begun looking at ways to regulate port and maritime security in the same way ICAO regulates air security. In addition, in November 1986, Italy, Egypt, and Austria deposited a draft maritime security convention, which extends the extradite-or-prosecute principle to maritime matters.

Strengthened Legal Action. More effective legal action against terrorists has been achieved through international action and closer bilateral cooperation. On the international front, Interpol, the international police organization composed of 142 member states, agreed in 1986 to extend its cooperation to the pursuit of terrorists who have committed criminal acts. Previously Interpol had looked upon terrorist actions as political and outside its jurisdiction.

Bilaterally, in addition to police and juridical cooperation in the prosecution of suspected terrorists, discussions have focused on (1) more determined pursuit of terrorists who are suspected of crimes against foreigners, to complement the often vigorous action for crimes against their own nationals (such as crimes against U.S. citizens in European states); (2) stronger efforts to control suspected terrorists who find safe haven in one country for terrorist acts committed in another (such as separatists or Middle Eastern terrorists who make easy use of Europe's open borders); (3) better sharing of information about suspected terrorists in order to restrict travel movements and improve data bases; and (4) extradition treaties that close the political offense loophole for serious violent crimes. The U.S. Senate approved a supplementary extradition treaty with the United Kingdom in 1986, which is now in force. Similar modifications in treaties are under discussion with other democratic states.

Congress recently modified U.S. law to permit the prosecution of terrorists in the United States for crimes committed abroad. The existence of these laws has permitted U.S. legal authorities to participate in criminal investigations abroad and provided an important impetus to local prosecution. The Italians successfully prosecuted and convicted the *Achille Lauro* hijackers, and the alleged mastermind of that plot is reportedly under a form of house arrest in an Arab state because of the arrest warrants out for him in several countries. With the participation of a French lawyer representing U.S. interests, a French court convicted Lebanese terrorist George Ibrahim Abdullah in March 1987 for complicity in murder plots against U.S. and Israeli embassy officials and sentenced him to life in prison despite fears that his supporters would repeat the campaign of violence witnessed in Paris in September 1986. The U.S. request for the extradition from the Federal Republic of Germany of Mohammed Ali Hamadei, one of the accused hijackers of TWA flight 847, presents a somewhat different situation. Germany was not a direct party to Hamadei's hijacking of a U.S. plane over international waters, although his prosecution there under the provisions of the Hague Convention is possible.

While new laws give the United States the means to prosecute suspects accused of certain foreign crimes at home, they can best be used to strengthen prosecutions abroad. Their direct use for U.S. prosecutions should be carefully controlled. On the one hand, obtaining convictions of terrorists for overseas crimes could be complicated by U.S. civil liberties, skilled defense lawyers, and the intricate appeals process. On the other, Americans would not be pleased if enthusiastic prosecutions permitted other countries to relinquish their responsibilities to take action against terrorists. Also, the supporters of those convicted might direct even more violence at Americans, as some Middle Eastern groups have done to France and England when their members have ended up in French and British jails.

Opposition to State Supporters of Terrorism. Perhaps the most important international successes against terrorism in 1986 occurred in the effort to develop a strong common front against state supporters of terrorism. The United States has maintained a list of terrorism-supporting states since 1978 and has pursued economic and political actions accordingly, but there was little support in Europe for categorizing states or acting against them in this manner. Arguing that other issues were always more important than terrorism in their bilateral relations with these states, the Europeans effectively avoided taking any strong deterrent actions against such states until mid-1986.

The Case of Libya

When Deputy Secretary of State John Whitehead toured Western Europe in January 1986 to argue the case for joint action against Libya for its involvement in the Rome and Vienna airport bombings, there was only mild interest. When U.N. Ambassador Vernon Walters visited Europe after the Berlin disco bombing in April and it was apparent that the United States was likely to take strong action unilaterally, the Europeans showed greater concern. And when it became apparent that the Americans were going to take unilateral military action against Libya, the Europeans, perhaps hoping to blunt U.S. action, began to act. They took steps that eventually reduced their diplomatic ties, banned arms sales, stepped up surveillance of suspected terrorists, and agreed not to fill in behind departing U.S. companies. The leaders of the seven industrialized democracies followed up with a strong statement against Libyan state support for terrorism at their May summit in Tokyo. While the U.S. military attack may have frightened Muammar Qaddafi into retreating to his tent in the desert, it probably also stimulated Europeans into their first joint action against Libyan state terrorism, including the subsequent expulsion of more than one hundred Libyan officials.

The Case of Syria

While the United States led the initiative against Libya, the British picked up this approach and used it against Syria in the fall of 1986, following the finding by the British court of a Syrian role in the attempted bombing of the El Al flight earlier that year. The British brought the case of Syrian support to the EC allies, who, with the exception of Greece, agreed to adopt strong, though limited measures to downgrade diplomatic representation, end arms sales, and limit aid and trade ties.

These coordinated actions among the Europeans and with the United States against Libya and Syria seem to have resulted in a marked reduction of Middle Eastern terrorist activity in Europe during the last part of 1986 and the first part of 1987. Preliminary statistics for 1986 and for the first three months of 1987 show that terrorist incidents of Middle Eastern origin in Europe may have declined by as much as 50 percent from their 1984 and 1985 levels.

From a position of unwillingness to act collectively against states like Libya at the beginning of the year, the Europeans had come full circle by the end of the year, moving first to joint action in support of the United States and then to actions on their own initiative. Over the course of one year, the Europeans had moved, albeit uneasily, from rejection to acceptance on a case-by-case basis of the concept of branding states for their support of terrorism.

Looking to Like-Minded States for More Cooperation

Although international cooperative ventures have begun scoring some successes against terrorists and their state supporters, there is still a long way to go. The Europeans have demonstrated that they can band together against common terrorist enemies, although these collective efforts have been slow, frustrating, and at times stymied by any one member's unwillingness to act, which reduces collective action to the lowest common denominator level. As Greece demonstrated during the fall of 1986 when the EC was considering taking action against Syria, a state that refuses to go along with others in the group can tone down, block, or weaken any collective approach by withholding consensus.

Collective action is difficult to achieve, but it is clearly worth working for. Acting alone, a state can strengthen its laws and procedures for dealing with terrorists, improve its intelligence-gathering capacity, and develop both its protective and active defenses; however, the impact of the best of these measures is limited outside each state's borders, severely so in a hostile environment. Acting bilaterally, states can provide better protection to each other, share intelligence, synchronize laws and understandings, and develop common diplomatic approaches to terrorism questions. Bilateral approaches, however, are insufficient when dealing with problems that confront more than two states and require coordination. What is the best way to halt Libyan or Syrian state support for terrorism? To improve security at Beirut International Airport? To bring an end to the hostage situation in Lebanon? The United Nations can perform an important role in expressing an international consensus through its resolutions and conventions; it can also develop procedures through its specialized agencies, but it has rarely been effective on specific problems. Coordinating bodies of like-minded states, such as the Summit Seven or the EC working groups, can look at these sorts of questions and provide the important bridge between bilateral and international efforts.

Cooperation among the Economic Summit Seven

The United States has recognized the importance of cooperation among like-minded nations for the past decade but has not succeeded in establishing any effective collective body that includes it as an active member. During most of the early 1980s, the United States looked primarily to the seven industrialized democracies (the United States, Canada, Britain, France, West Germany, Italy, and Japan), which meet annually at the summit level, as the most likely forum for a collective approach against terrorism. The Summit Seven established a group of experts, which has met periodically over the years, discussed possible initiatives, and made preparations for statements at the annual summits. Declarations of intention for joint action against terrorism emanated from the summits at Bonn in 1978, Venice in 1980, Ottawa in 1981, London in 1984, and Tokyo in 1986. Past declarations have condemned a host of evils—hijackings, the taking of hostages, acts against diplomatic personnel, abuses of diplomatic immunity, and state support of terrorism—and they have promised cooperation in all these areas, but to little effect. Occasionally the actions have paralleled those of other bodies, such as the action by the EC against Libya following the Tokyo summit, but in most cases the declarations have served mainly to signal political resolve rather than to endorse specific actions.

At the Venice summit in June 1987, the seven leaders again issued a statement condemning all forms of terrorism and reaffirming their commitment to previous summit statements. The seven also noted again their resolve to oppose state-sponsored terrorism but added a new dimension: their confirmation of the principle of making no concessions to terrorists.

Despite the nearly annual statements, the Summit Seven leaders and their experts have reached agreement to implement only one of the declarations—and then to apply it in only one case. The Bonn Declaration of 1978 resolved that the seven would cease all flights to and from any state involved in hijacking that refused to extradite or prosecute the hijackers or return the aircraft, including halting flights by the offending state's national character. (The declaration did little more than put teeth in the Hague Convention on the Unlawful Seizure of Aircraft, which went into effect in 1971 and which had over 125 signatories, including Iran, Lebanon, Afghanistan, and Syria.) After working out implementing procedures, the seven eventually agreed to take sanctions against Afghan Ariana Airlines in 1981 because of the conduct of the Karmal regime in giving refuge to the hijackers of a Pakistan International Airlines aircraft in March of that year. In subsequent years, despite dozens of potential candidates, the seven have not agreed on a single additional country where these sanctions might be applied.

There are many reasons why the Summit Seven failed to extend the sanctions of the Bonn Declaration to other cases or to develop into a more effective forum of states against terrorism. The sanctions against the Afghanis were flawed; they lacked a time limitation and an agreed termination procedure. Making this first case against Afghanistan, the issue invariably became tied with Western concern over the Soviet presence and what signal would be sent if sanctions were lifted. It was much easier to consider sanctions against a Soviet client state than against any other country where one or more of the seven might have special interests. At Tokyo in April 1986, the seven leaders agreed to make the Bonn Declaration "more effective in dealing with all forms of terrorism affecting civil aviation." New guidelines for an extended Bonn Declaration were approved at the 1987 Venice summit, but the more important question revolves around the will of the seven to implement the new agreement.

Some members of the Summit Seven have had long-standing reservations on the broader question of the seven as a forum for closer cooperation: first, should discussions go beyond general platitudes into practical measures, and second, should political issues like counterterrorism be permitted to dilute the original economic focus of the group? Although not stated in the context of the seven, there seems also to be a fear among the Europeans that signaling public cooperation with the United States on specific counterterrorism questions ties their hands too closely to U.S. policies and actions, especially in relation to the Middle East. Some European members of the seven revealed their uneasiness when they declined to participate in the special meeting on Lebanese hostages called in February 1987 at a time when U.S. ships were cruising off the coast of Lebanon.

Cooperation through NATO

As it became evident in 1985 and 1986 that the Summit Seven would not provide an effective framework for counterterrorism cooperation, the United States turned its attention to other potential groups. Although thought was given to the creation of a new body to concentrate on the problems of terrorism, there was little support for this measure. NATO seemed to be a possible forum—and one that Congress subsequently directed the president to consider—but the United States encountered reservations among NATO members. A standing NATO committee on counterintelligence had begun to look at terrorism questions, but this group represented the counterintelligence community rather than the counterterrorism community and had a separate primary mandate. Efforts by the United States and others to expand NATO's role in counterterrorism met with little success during 1986, but discussions have continued.

Cooperation with the EC

During 1986 the United States turned increasingly to closer cooperation with the EC and its subgroups. Recognizing the importance of cooperation among the like-minded in Europe, several EC bodies had developed their own special agenda to promote intra-European cooperation against terrorism—one group under the justice and interior ministries focusing on police and security matters and another under the foreign ministries on policy issues and diplomatic measures. Within each of these two bodies the Europeans worked out plans for joint actions against Libyan and Syrian state-supported terrorism.

Although key European states seemed wary of developing any direct counterterrorism ties with the United States within a common organization, they seemed prepared to consult with the United States informally through these two mechanisms via the country currently holding the EC presidency. U.S. delegations, headed by Attorney General Edwin Meese, met with representatives of the EC justice and interior ministers in April and December 1986 and again in April 1987 to explore the possibilities for closer cooperation. Although the EC foreign ministries have also agreed in principle to cooperate with the United States, they have moved much more slowly than their police counterparts in developing a consultative approach.

Cooperation between the United States and the two bodies of the EC under this informal structure presented certain inherent shortcomings. Cooperation is first dependent upon the willingness and ability of the country holding the EC presidency for each six-month term, moving ahead rapidly when it served the political interests of one incumbent and possibly slowing down with a successor. Second, while cooperation seems to be moving ahead on the police and security front through the justice and interior ministries, it seems stalled on the policy side working with the foreign ministries. Third, the informal consultative structure presents problems. When faced with a complicated or delicate terrorist problem, the United States could easily have trouble working in any group where it sits on the outside, consulting and coordinating but never included in the direct dialogue. It could be difficult for the United States to take a particular problem, such as the hostages in Lebanon, to an EC group, put forward a U.S. proposal, and be satisfied by the outcome without having been a party to the debate. In addition, while the Europeans seem prepared to talk periodically with the United States about terrorism problems, there is the separate issue of coordinating with other like-minded nations, such as Canada, that have been close allies in the international counterterrorism effort and seem equally anxious to be part of a coordinating group.

Summit Seven–EC Cooperation

A dramatic breakthrough in international cooperation occurred at the end of May 1987 when the justice and interior ministers of the seven industrial democracies met in Paris with their counterparts from the EC leadership troika (those countries representing the past, present, and future EC presidencies, in this case the United Kingdom, Belgium, and Denmark, respectively). The purpose of the meeting was not to formulate new measures against terrorism but to demonstrate the willingness of the EC to extend the cooperation developed through the interior and justice ministries group to the entire group of industrial democracies.

Calling the meeting a "new dimension" in the anti-terrorism fight, Attorney General Edwin Meese, who headed the U.S. delegation, said that this was "the first of what we expect to be a continuing series of meeting of law enforcement officials concerned with terrorism." French Interior minister Charles Pasqua noted that the meeting showed "a willingness to take all the measures necessary," including exchanges of information, advances in technology, and possible new legislation.

Although the meeting was organized by the French and Germans, the press in Paris viewed it as a victory for U.S. efforts to pressure the Europeans for closer cooperation at the highest levels of government. The active involvement of the French government in 1987 in this effort among justice and interior ministries stood in marked contrast to their opposition in 1985 to a German proposal for similar talks among justice and interior ministries in the Summit Seven context. The change in the French attitude might be attributed not only to political change in France between 1985 and 1987 but also to the enthusiasm of the French Interior Ministry for closer transatlantic cooperation and to the concept of a joint forum that combined the concerns of the seven with the activities of the EC so that both groups follow a common agenda. While the Summit Seven leaders in their Venice statement welcomed the progress represented by this initiative, the substance of follow-up meetings will determine whether this combined forum can improve cooperation.

Need for a Common Forum

If the cooperation discussed in Paris between the EC and the seven industrial democracies evolves successfully, it will be the most significant milestone in the international effort against terrorism in the past decade. As an effort among justice and interior ministries, it should strengthen police and security cooperation, of critical importance because most terrorist actions are also criminal actions. Additionally transatlantic cooperation needs also to be extended more effectively to general policy issues and such specific questions as civil aviation and state-supported terrorism. One alternative might be an effort parallel to the current one, which would include the foreign ministries of the EC and the Summit Seven.

Developing an effective body of like-minded states concerned about counterterrorism political questions should clearly be in the long-term best interest of the Europeans. U.S. military actions against Libya in April 1986 stimulated the Europeans to closer cooperation with the United States and with each other. The U.S. attacks occurred in part because of the inability of the United States and the Europeans to reach agreement through bilateral discussions on the growing Libyan threat and the urgency of parallel actions. Even with an accepted procedure for informal consultations, there is a good chance the United States will not be satisfied with the actions planned by the Europeans inside their own forum and will decide to act unilaterally. Over the longer term, North Americans, Europeans, and other like-minded nations will need a forum for joint debate and discussion.

The development of a counterterrorism form to consider political questions would not require the creation of a new bureaucratic structure or new procedures for action. Following the operating style of the EC, a rotating chairperson could host periodic meetings in which members might pose new problems for consideration, review past efforts, reach agreements on joint or parallel actions, and on occasion issue statements. Special meetings could be called to consider crises. The goal of such a group would not be joint declarations but joint or common actions against terrorism. When possible, decisions for joint action might be taken, but the group would try to avoid the lowest-common-denominator approach, possibly through a majority vote that would call for parallel actions rather than identical ones in cases lacking unanimity. When considering security conditions at Beirut Airport, for example, the United States could pursue its travel advisory and ticketing restrictions; other states could take similar restricting measures in accordance with their own laws; but all the participants would be sending a common message. Admittedly such a loose system of cooperation would be less than optimal, but it could provide a basis for stronger joint action than currently exists. As these limited measures began to work, the forum could be strengthened through wider membership and tighter enforcement.

Issues for Cooperation

In addition to the question of a suitable forum for the consideration of more effective diplomatic actions, there are a number of other cooperative areas that like-minded nations need to address in the development of a more effective counterterrorism effort: broader sharing of intelligence, the enforcement of existing international conventions, the alignment of national laws, the possibilities of covert action, and effective military intervention.

Broader Sharing of Intelligence

Recognizing that sensitive intelligence can be shared only on a bilateral basis—and will never be shared on a multilateral basis—there is a critical need for a mechanism to exchange general information about terrorist groups and terrorist actions with more than one country at a time. As is true for most other countries, the United States can exchange information with some countries more easily than with others. This is an unalterable fact of life about the nature of intelligence operations around the world, but when a terrorist group like Abu Nidal or a state like Libya is involved in a terrorist campaign that affects lives in more than one country, there must be a better way than the current bilateral arrangements to share assessments rapidly. Background information about such actions from sources in more than one country needs to be assembled, assessed, and disseminated quickly to as broad a group of nations as possible to assist in the development of solutions based on common assessments. Another topic for consideration is the establishment of a procedure for sharing information following an incident, including the acceptance of a common reporting format to replace the present ad hoc bilateral arrangements.

Enforcement of International Conventions

Various international conventions already make many of the most common terrorist acts international crimes, but none of these conventions contains the enforcement mechanisms that make them effective. It has been argued that we do not need new laws; we need to put teeth into the existing international agreements. For example, the Hague Convention imposes obligations on states to extradite or prosecute air hijackers, the Montreal Convention imposes similar obligations for aircraft sabotage, and the Convention against the Taking of Hostages establishes jurisdiction for the offense of hostage taking. Over 125 states are parties to the first of these two conventions and 25 to the latter more recent one, but no provisions cover what action should be taken when a state fails to meet its obligations. Other similar conventions concern attacks on diplomats and the protection of nuclear material; these similarly lack enforcement mechanisms.

The Summit Seven attempted to put muscle behind the Hague Convention when it issued the Bonn Declaration, but to date misunderstandings within the group have prevented any effective action. Until the international community or a group of like-minded states determines that it will compel the enforcement of existing international law, there is little reason to consider emphasizing new accessions or the creation of additional conventions.

Alignment of National Laws

As countries consider new treaties with each other and develop new local laws to address the problems of terrorism, they should observe how other governments are combating the problem and seek stronger national laws and more compatible legal systems to strengthen international action. Extradition treaties commonly contain a political offense exception, which permits a state to decline extradition for politically motivated crimes. Since these clauses have more than occasionally permitted terrorists wanted for violent crimes to go free, they merit review and revision to exclude violent crimes. The United States and the United Kingdom have recently modified their extradition treaty; they each need to lead the way now in establishing revised treaties with third parties, and other concerned states need to place higher priority on similar revisions.

When modifications in civil aviation agreements are under consideration, states should include the model security clause, developed by ICAO, which strengthens the international acceptance of the extradite-or-prosecute concept. The United States has announced that it is modifying all of its civil aviation agreements to include this clause, but most other states are moving slowly on this question.

Each state needs also to look at its policies on visas and the movement of people across its borders. Tougher visa restrictions are perhaps necessary on the movement of people from countries that cannot seem to maintain control of their passports. The EC has established working groups to look at the questions of visas and expulsions and exclusions. Finally, states need to look more closely at each other's laws and seek closer compatibility. What laws that have been effective in one state might be established elsewhere? Should membership in a terrorist group be considered a crime, as it now is in some countries?

Considering Covert Actions

Covert action is widely regarded in the United States as a dirty word, the sort of action that would otherwise be illegal and that it does badly because, some say, it is not a part of the American character. Recent U.S. problems with covert action have occurred not only because of differing interpretations of the oversight function but also because the operations seemed directly counter to U.S. policy. The fight against terrorism, however, offers a legitimate, high-priority focal point for covert actions.

That terrorism is international is even more reason that covert counterterrorism programs should be developed cooperatively with other governments. Covert actions would have to be planned on a case-by-case basis among the specific parties to a problem; they would never work among a large group of even the most like-minded nations. Covert action need not mean outterrorizing the terrorists or becoming involved in assassination plots against unpopular foreigners (although the comparable morality of an assassination plot and a bombing attack is certainly worth consideration); rather it should encompass developing programs to disrupt terrorist plans and to deliver known terrorists to justice. For example, providing training, funds, and equipment to the intelligence service in a friendly country to prevent terrorist actions directed at U.S. targets would seem a legitimate covert action. If the United States is to establish a more effective covert counterterrorism capability, either unilaterally or in concert with other states, it will have to address more effectively its separate internal problems of proper congressional oversight and frequent press leaks.

Reexamining the Military Force Option

Despite the apparent success of the United States in using military force to bring the hijackers of the *Achille Lauro* to justice and to signal displeasure against Libya, there is widespread misunderstanding of the limited but important role that military force can play in the fight against terrorism. The Israelis have resorted regularly to the force option against terrorists and the Americans have turned to it on selected occasions, but most of the European states have been more reluctant to use this option and are critical of its use by others.

The Israelis demonstrated at Entebbe in 1976 and the Germans in Mogadishu in 1977 that trained counterterrorism forces can bring a particular incident to a successful conclusion. The United States and other Western nations subsequently developed their own special counterterrorism units that confidently exercise their capabilities, periodically engage in competitions with the counterterrorism units of other countries, and regularly ready themselves for potential combat at the time of an incident. These units, however, have not played a major role in resolving any terrorist incident outside their own borders since the German action at Mogadishu. It was conventional U.S. air and naval forces rather than the special counterterrorism forces that operated in Libya and against the *Achille Lauro* hijackers.

What should be the purpose of these highly trained counterterrorism forces in the coming decade? Has the West perhaps developed forces trained to operate in an Entebbe-type scenario that are irrelevant to the present situation? The element of surprise is gone because the existence of counterterrorism forces is widely known within terrorist circles and their possible deployment is a subject of instant press speculation at the time of an incident. Middle Eastern hijackers seem to plan their defenses around the possibility of intervention; for example, the TWA flight 847 hijackers shuttled back and forth between Beirut and Algiers and then moved the hostages into the depths of Beirut supposedly to foreclose any military option. Where might a counterterrorism force be deployed in the future? Each such force is small and dependent upon either a permissive operating environment or encountering no resistance. What chance is there that terrorist groups will consider taking an airplane to a poorly guarded city like Entebbe in the future? What chance is there that any self-respecting and sovereignty-conscious Middle Eastern state will admit its own diplomatic and military deficiencies and permit a Western military force to storm a hijacked plane? These are all important questions, but they tell only part of the story.

The modern state seems to require as part of its military arsenal a highly trained force that can respond skillfully to threats posed by small enemy forces in a hostage barricade situation, hijacking, or similar threat, regardless of the fact that there might not be much of a chance to put such forces to use. Perhaps counterterrorism forces should be seen as a preventative weapon rather than a reactive one. While some Middle Eastern groups may have changed their tactics because of counterterrorism forces, other terrorists may not be so sophisticated and may reflect on their prospects for success because of these forces. Although such a preventative factor cannot be measured, the existence of highly trained forces changes the equation in a confrontation, giving governments a degree of muscle that strengthens their hand in pursuing other measures to resolve the incident.

Nonetheless, given the absence of a single successful assault by a counterterrorism force during the past few years when there have been a record number of dramatic terrorist hijackings, each Western government ought to be considering how these forces are currently structured. Could a multinational force stationed in the Mediterranean area operate more effectively against hijackings? Variations in composition might include an international police SWAT team under the aegis of Interpol, a Western military force under NATO, an international team under the United Nations, or an exclusively Middle Eastern force under an Arab group. Such forces would not represent any nation but would be international or professional policing organizations. For these forces to be effective, participating states would have to subordinate their sovereignty to the controlling authority, which would activate and employ the force upon the request for intervention. The existence of such a multinational counterterrorism force in the immediate area and its more likely acceptance by governments in the Middle East might act as an important deterrent to Middle Eastern hijackers.

Conclusion: Setting Priorities

The United States has achieved some notable successes in the fight against terrorism. It has improved its internal organization, defenses, intelligence-gathering capacity, laws, diplomatic efforts, and national will to take decisive action. While the United States has taken important steps to improve international cooperation, a significant failing of U.S. decision makers has been their tendency to seek unilateral solutions to what they perceive as a special U.S. problem without recognizing the implications of such unilateral actions. While such U.S. initiatives may have spurred the Europeans to closer intra-European cooperation, they may also have created a certain fear among the Europeans about the dangers of cooperating too closely with the United States. The problem feeds on itself: the United States acts unilaterally because it cannot develop a collective approach; the Europeans retreat from proposals for closer collaboration in a common forum because they fear it might tie them too closely to unilateral U.S. actions.

Three priorities for the United States seem most important: first, the prompt reestablishment of a clear and well-articulated policy, one whose rhetoric does not exceed logical options and where actions will be consistent; second, recognition of the international nature of the problem and the way in which unilateral U.S. responses impede international cooperation; and third, a continuing effort to convince Europeans and other like-minded states of the importance of developing joint approaches.

The Europeans have also made great strides in the fight against terrorism in the last few years, particularly in their greater resolve to prosecute and hold terrorists in prison, their actions against Middle Eastern terrorism, and their development of a common approach through the mechanisms of the EC. The Europeans must strengthen this common approach so that terrorists from one state cannot find a safe haven next door and must recognize that the North American problem with terrorism is an international one and therefore requires closer collaboration than might be necessary in other areas. Since terrorism for Americans does not occur at home but does so heavily in Europe and the Middle East, Europeans cannot shut the door on direct cooperation with the United States and expect the problem to go away. Without cooperation between the United States and Europe, the United States is likely to resort regularly to unilateral actions, including military ones. The Europeans may regret this, but unless meaningful mechanisms for consultations can be established, they will have no one to blame but themselves.

Working bilaterally, in international organizations, and as like-minded states, Europeans and Americans have taken important joint steps against terrorism, but much more needs to be done. Individually and collectively, like-minded nations need to address such specific questions as intelligence sharing, enforcement of international conventions, coordination of laws and law enforcement efforts, covert action, and military options. In response to a state that strays from the no-concessions approach, other nations need to reiterate their own firmness. The worst outcome occurs when nations permit the transgressions of friends to serve as an excuse to weaken their own resolve to pursue a tough line against terrorism and to reduce their level of cooperation.

International terrorism is likely to remain a serious dilemma for the rest of the century, and it could easily worsen. Until there is greater recognition of terrorism as an international problem—rather than a national problem or even a regional one—requiring close international cooperation, the terrorists will retain the initiative.

2

The National Security Council and the Iran–Contra Crisis

William R. Farrell

During the final weeks of 1986 and through most of 1987, there occurred a thorough examination of the formulation and execution of national security decision making in the Reagan administration. Although the central focus was the sale of weapons to Iran and the clandestine transfer of funds to the Nicaraguan Contras, the entire decision-making process came under close scrutiny. Fundamental flaws, which centered on individuals as well as the process itself, were identified. Some deficiencies allowed for quick repair; others, more the result of institutional and political dichotomies, will continue to be the subject of debate for years to come.

The special review board appointed by the president and composed of former Senator John Tower, former Secretary of State Edmund S. Muskie, and former national security adviser Brent Scrowcroft determined that the National Security Council (NSC) process had failed to "prevent bad ideas from becoming presidential policy."[1] The so-called Tower report took issue with the way President Reagan used the NSC, observing that the "NSC system will not work unless the President makes it work."[2] Policy was not forced to undergo the rigorous review that the NSC was designed to bring about: "Had the President chosen to drive the NSC system, the outcome could well have been different." Rather, Reagan's leadership resulted in a detached management style that allowed free-lancing by key NSC staff members. Such activity was seen as depriving the departments concerned of a thorough policy review of key issues, resulting in incomplete advice and subsequent ineffective and dangerous policies. Despite the time-consuming efforts required, it is only when the built-in tension between the president and the executive agencies is worked through completely that sound policy options emerge. In skirting the organizations involved, the execution of policy depended upon private individuals outside government. The Tower report cited the dangers of such privatization of policy, which could well lead those outside government to gain powerful leverage and influence over NSC policymakers.

The views expressed in this chapter are those of the author and do not necessarily represent those of the U.S. Naval War College or any other organization.

One of the key problems that arises when the NSC, a policy-coordinating body, becomes also an executor of policy is that objectivity is lost. People become too wedded to their own ideas and thus are less able to detect when to change or abandon certain courses of action.

The debate over the NSC has been interesting and informative but somewhat incomplete. A more thorough analysis would require a review of the reasons why there was first established a coordinating organization such as the NSC, how it has evolved over the years, and how the problems of the Reagan administration are not unique.

Origins and Evolution of the National Security Council

As World War II drew to a close, a great debate took place among the offices of the executive departments and the Congress concerning the formulation of national security policy. One result was the passage of the National Security Act of 1947, which established the NSC "to advise the President with respect to the integration of domestic, foreign and military policies relating to national security so as to enable the military services and other departments and agencies of the Government to cooperate more effectively in matters involving the national security."[3] The statutory members of the council are the president, vice-president, secretary of state, and secretary of defense. The president, and not, as many believe, the national security adviser, is the head of the NSC. Over the years, presidents have invited the heads of other agencies to become members of or advisers to the NSC, among them, the director of central intelligence, the chairman of the Joint Chiefs of Staff, the ambassador to the United Nations, and key domestic policy advisers. The NSC thus enables the president to bring into government without congressional approval people whom he considers important.

The NSC is a function of the president it serves as the Tower report pointed out:

> The NSC is going to be pretty well what a President wants it to be and what he determines it should be. Kennedy—and these are some exaggerations and generalities of course—with an anti-organizational bias, disestablished all [the Eisenhower-created] committees and put a tight group in the White House totally attuned to his philosophic approach. . . . Johnson didn't change that very much, except certain difficulties began to develop in the informality which was [otherwise] characterized by speed, unity of purpose, precision. . . . So it had great efficiency and responsiveness. The difficulties began to develop in . . . the informality of the thing.[4]

The Tower report observed that the Nixon administration returned to use of the NSC as a principal forum of national security advice, and this pattern continued through the Ford, Carter and Reagan administrations: "Such presidential trust and reliance on the NSC can be understood if it is realized that the staff of this policy advisory system is structured on a basis, primarily, of loyalty to the President."[5] This is most noticeable in the early days of a new administration as it "sets upon the path of 'undoing the wrongs' of the previous incumbency, [and] reliance can be placed on a small body largely responsive to presidential desires, and not necessarily subject to the policy orientation of previous bureaucratic structure."[6] A brief historical review of the postwar administrations and their use of the NSC system will shed necessary light on the importance of the advisory body.

Truman Administration

President Harry S Truman saw the establishment of the NSC as part of the continuing institutional battle between the Congress and the executive.[7] Having served under a particularly strong president, Franklin D. Roosevelt, Truman viewed the legislation establishing the NSC as an attempt to limit executive power. Of the first fifty-six meetings, Truman presided over only eleven. This, coupled with serious personality differences among key advisers, limited the effectiveness of the NSC. Truman seemed more willing to turn to members of the NSC and cabinet members individually for advice rather than to the NSC as a corporate body. But the Korean War forced the need for coherent policy development, and Truman ordered weekly meetings of the NSC and required that "all major national security recommendations . . . be coordinated through the Council and its staff."[8]

During 1950 it became apparent to Truman that the NSC was becoming too large. As the year progressed, the number of persons attending meetings decreased, and the role of the council increased, becoming the main body for handling national security matters. By the time Truman left office, he had reverted to seeking advice from key individuals rather than the NSC as a unit.

Eisenhower Administration

When Dwight D. Eisenhower came to office, he was leery of the "bureaucrats" in the Department of State and other agencies. He believed that their professional views were politically tainted because the Democrats had been in office so long, and thus he turned to his own advisers and the NSC for guidance. It was during the Eisenhower administration that the role of a principal security adviser emerged.

A former general, Eisenhower sought thorough staff work. He relied heavily on the NSC staff secretary to deal with current security matters and used the chief of the NSC staff as his chief planner. An elaborate staff system was created that served as a consensual decision-making group. Eisenhower described the NSC as

a corporate body, composed of individuals advising the President in their own right, rather than as representatives of their respective departments and agencies.

Their function should be to seek, with their background of experience, the most statesmanlike solution to the problems of national security, rather than to reach solutions which represent merely a compromise of departmental positions.[9]

Eisenhower attended most NSC meetings. The meetings were opportunities for an extensive exchange of ideas and met the staff needs of a president with Eisenhower's background.

Kennedy Administration

President John F. Kennedy judged the Eisenhower system to be overly rigid and formal.[10] He radically changed the organization for formulating national security policy that had evolved since 1947 and restructured the NSC staff to serve him and not the NSC. During his administration, "Power shifted signficantly to the State Department and the Pentagon, and annual reviews of basic national security policy were subsumed into a system that introduced yearly military posture statements prepared by DOD [Department of Defense] and presented by Secretary of Defense [Robert S.] McNamara personally to Congress."[11]

Kennedy had a highly personal style of reaching decisions. At times he would deal with cabinet members individually, requesting that they address an issue and provide recommendations. At other times he formed a committee of principals or appointed an interdepartmental task force to address key regional matters. He used the NSC not as a forum for policy development but as a sounding board for ideas. The State Department's influence during the Kennedy presidency increased significantly.

Johnson Administration

President Lyndon B. Johnson's approach was not much different from Kennedy's, though he did seek to reduce the role of his predecessor's "brain trust."[12] Johnson performed most of his security policy coordination during the so-called Tuesday lunch with Secretary of Defense McNamara and Secretary of State Dean Rusk. By the end of his administration, he had reassembled the NSC to meet every other week in an effort to coordinate decision making among the government departments. On the whole, however, the Johnson era saw national security policy formulated outside the NSC environment.[13]

Critics have charged that Johnson's informal decision-making process was in great disarray, but defenders claim that "this chaos was functional, was efficient in terms of the Constitution, precisely because it guaranteed that no flunky—to use one of LBJ's favorite pejoratives—"play President."[14] Johnson had approximately a dozen aides, and the director of the NSC staff, Walt Rostow, was listed as special assistant to the president. There was no formally established hierarchy; all key advisers had a direct line to the president. Johnson believed, as FDR had, that as long as several people claim jurisdiction over the same turf, no one can bottle up vital information. "As long as the barons are engaged in turf fights, [the president] will see all the options and be the only president in town. No one else can or will make the final decision."[15]

Nixon Administration

The arrival of President Richard M. Nixon saw a return to a more formal NSC structure similar to the Eisenhower years. The intent was to ensure that policy issues were thoroughly studied and that comprehensive alternatives and options were developed before a matter was brought to the White House for a decision. Henry Kissinger emerged as the administration's principal spokesman on national security issues.[16]

Although the NSC was not used as a forum to make decisions—Nixon made them based on information from a variety of sources—during the first Nixon administration it rose in stature and importance, primarily because of Kissinger.[17] One commentator on the NSC system seriously wondered "whether the NSC would function as effectively without Kissinger, and whether it can bequeath a heritage of accomplishment to be absorbed by the permanent machinery of government."[18]

The role of the NSC at this time was to serve as a forum for discussion in which the interested departments and agency representatives stated the issues, presented alternatives, and discussed the implications of particular policy recommendations. The intent was to ensure that distinct options, with all the pros and cons, were elevated for consideration. As a result, numerous committees and groups were established covering issues of defense, intelligence, energy, strategic arms matters, crises, and foreign policy.[19] Critics of such an elaborate system noted that Johnson's NSC had a staff of thirty-five, a budget of $628,000, and an adviser who occupied an office in the basement, had no press spokesman and held no press conferences, and never tried to "play President." Kissinger, on the other hand, moved out of the basement, hired 155 professionals, had a budget of $2 million, and held numerous (sometimes daily) press conferences, allowing ample time to "play President."[20]

As the problems of the Watergate scandal began to take up Nixon's time, the national security decision process was decentralized, and the NSC met less and less frequently; during 1973, it met only twice. Although the committees and groups remained largely intact, the decision-making process centered more and more on key subordinates such as Kissinger and Secretary of Defense James R. Schlesinger. Those who were most critical of this period commented that national decision making in the Nixon White House had deteriorated to a repetition of Johnson's "Tuesday lunches," only without the president and not on Tuesdays.[21]

Ford Administration

Gerald R. Ford continued many of the organizational aspects of the Nixon years; however, his national security adviser, Brent Scrowcroft, played much less of a public role and concentrated more on policy coordination than had Kissinger.[22] President Ford's personality was such that he enjoyed the give and take of meetings with his key staff. The number of NSC meetings increased, and as a result of extensive congressional investigations (the so-called Church committee hearings) into the uses and abuses of U.S. intelligence agencies, the overall policy determination for intelligence activities was placed squarely on the NSC.

Carter Administration

Concern for the role and function of the NSC system confronted Jimmy Carter when he came to office in 1977. Initially the system was designed with multiple channels of access to the president and a relatively weak NSC. This process was found wanting as time progressed, and criticisms increased that the Carter administration was less than effective in making policy. In response, Carter attempted to strengthen the NSC and the role of the National Security adviser, recognizing that the system needed centralized strength and authority if it was to be able to coordinate policy among powerful bureaucracies.[23]

Carter's national security adviser, Zbigniew Brzezinski, was of the opinion that the cabinet, as such, was not designed to make foreign policy in an environment of "institutional flexibility and inherent ambiguity."[24] Taken with Carter's concern that there be no "Lone Ranger" in his administration, Brzezinski proposed a series of committees, which the president rejected, requesting a leaner organization. Two committees emerged: the Policy Review Committee (PRC) to deal with foreign policy issues, defense policy issues, and international economic matters, and the Special Coordination Committee (SCC), which would focus on intelligence, arms control, and crisis management. Brzezinski recommended to Carter that the SCC not be chaired by a department head since the issues to be considered would pose jurisdictional conflicts and touch on the president's own political interests: "It followed that the Assistant for National Security Affairs should chair the Special Coordination Committee."[25] Brzezinski, not unlike Kissinger before him, chaired the key committees that would have a major impact on the implementation of policy. Carter also gave his National Security Assistant (NSA) cabinet status in efforts to increase his power to coordinate policy.

Brzezinski also ensured that although the PRC meetings were chaired by a secretary from one of the departments, the minutes of such meetings and a listing of options were prepared by the NSC staff and submitted to the President through the NSA. Despite the criticisms of the "Lone Ranger" of the previous administrations, Brzezinski was well aware of power politics and the need to exercise control: "I was determined to maintain active and personal dialogue with the President . . . because only then could I assert my own authority in a manner consistent with his views."[26] Brzezinski also insisted that only he provide the president with the morning national security briefing; he did so for the entire administration.

During the Carter years the Central Intelligence Agency (CIA) was "held under strict control by the NSC." The director of the CIA had relatively limited access to the president—initially once a week and later only twice a month and always in the presence of the NSA.

Brzezinski described the Carter decision-making system as perhaps the most centralized in the postwar era. The president was actively involved and stated at the end of his administration, "There have been Presidents in the past, maybe not too distant past, that let their Secretaries of State make foreign policy. I don't."[27]

Reagan Administration

According to Robert C. McFarlane, the former NSA, President Reagan rejected the idea that the NSC system should dominate the policy process. Rather, the cabinet departments and agencies concerned with the four main aspects of security policy—diplomatic, military, economic, and intelligence—should play a lead role in policy development: "Although a NSC-centered system can be very responsive to a President's desires, the alternative, a cabinet government, ensures that the President is not isolated from political and institutional realities."[28] Cabinet government allows the president to extend his control throughout the policymaking process without undercutting the authority of key department heads who can more readily act in the president's name. The function of the NSC is to ensure that members of the cabinet present their views directly to the president, "the final policymaker," while still providing sufficient central guidance and control.[29]

The roles of the NSA identified by McFarlane were not too different from those set forth during previous administrations: the hottest broker of advice from outside the White House and an independent adviser and policy manager. The NSA must be able to present the views of each department to the president so that the president appreciates the substantive debates within his administration. At the same time, the NSA must provide central direction and be an independent adviser who can present issues to the president from a perspective that "transcends individual agency perspectives to encompass the policies and concerns of the administration as whole."[30]

Senior interagency groups (SIGs) focusing on diplomatic, military, economic, and intelligence policy were established to assist the NSC process. Each SIG was to be chaired by the department head most closely concerned with the matter involved. In the area of arms control, however, an issue "involving particularly complex and sensitive interdepartmental relations," a special group headed by the NSA was created. It is interesting to remember that during the first days of the Reagan administration, Secretary of State Alexander Haig made strenuous efforts to obtain chairmanship of all the key committees that affected foreign policy. An individual long familiar with the concentration of power in the White House, Haig strongly believed that without control of these committees, his impact on policy would be weakened. But strong counterviews were offered by Reagan's political and policy advisers sensitive to turf battles. In a compromise announced from the White House (and as a surprise to Haig, who was not personally informed), crisis decision making would be assigned to the vice-president.[31] This Special Situation Group was to ensure that White House guidance needed for policy execution under severe time constraints was available and imposed over any committee system.[32]

Concerning relations with the Congress, McFarlane pointed out:

> In fact, one of the key lessons of national security policy learned over the past decade is that close contacts with the Congress must be established and nurtured throughout the policy process. One of the key functions of the NSC staff is to work with the White House office of congressional relations to ensure that these requirements are met. At a broader level, the staff also ensures that congressional concerns are considered in the policy development process, that the Congress is kept informed of policy decisions, and that the Congress has the information and arguments it needs to judge adequately the administration's recommendations on security issues.[33]

There has been more similarity than disparity concerning the roles and functions of the NSC and the NSA over the years regardless who is occupying the White House at the time. Difficult policy issues, such as responses to terrorism, need to be addressed in an environment where the "correct answer" is very much a function of ideological and bureaucratic interpretations. There is a need for centralized control in the executive branch especially given the separation of powers and differing executive departments with overlapping jurisdictions.

Comments made during the Iran–Contra hearings charged that the NSC had become too powerful and thereby disregarded the will of, if not laws passed by, the Congress. In fact, the opposite is true. An NSC system with five national security advisers in a six-year period during the administration of a delegating president such as Ronald Reagan allows cabinet departments a stronger hand and, further, allows Congress more influence than usual. The problems faced by the Reagan administration will most assuredly be faced by others in the years to come. They center around the role and functions of the NSA and the NSC and the long-standing institutional concerns by the Congress and the executive coupled with the politics of the day in an open democratic society.

Functional Roles of NSC Members

Individuals working on the NSC are holding down a job. They will have a description, which indicates the work the individual should be doing, if only in the broadest sense. Beyond this there exists the concept of role, which is more than a job description and consists of how the work is done, or a pattern of behavior. Bosses are expected to behave in a fairly standard way; the same can be said for new employees, old veterans, accountants, lawyers, and the like. All such descriptions can then be compounded. One might have a young woman–new employee–receptionist or perhaps an NSC staffer–marine–workaholic–patriot. What emerges is a clear indication of very complex roles that people can find themselves filling at different times in their career.

The expected behavior of the employee—how he or she is supposed to act—may be quite different from performance—how the employee actually behaves. Expectations may not in any way be universal. How an NSA may expect a subordinate staff member to behave in a given situation may be very different from what a congressional committee might expect of that same person. Tensions between individuals and within one's self often result when there are differences in expected and actual behavior.[34] The subsequent conflict and strain that emerge can be very costly to an organization as well as to individuals directly involved. This strain often results from a lack of clarity and consensus about the role an individual is expected to fulfill.

A historical review of the responsibilities of the NSA discloses a continuity independent of the political persuasion of the incumbent president. The core responsibility of every NSA has been to ensure that the decision-making process provides the president with the issues and assessments needed to make the best policy decisions.[35] How this job has actually been performed over the years has varied with the personalities and capabilities of those appointed. Additionally, since the NSA and his staff must meet the needs of the president, presidential definition of how the role is to be fulfilled is equally important. A lack of definition and a failure to specify exactly what is expected allow the NSA and his staff to define their own expected behavior.

There has been a good deal of competition over the years between the secretary of state and the NSA as to who is the nation's spokesperson for national security policy. The example of Secretary of State Haig is not unique. Brzezinski had differences with Secretary Cyrus Vance, Kissinger with Secretary William Rogers, NSA McGeorge Bundy with Secretary Dean Rusk. Even in administrations where there is initial agreement regarding who is to play what role, it is inherently difficult for the NSA to remain a neutral coordinator of others' views and equally difficult for a secretary of state not to have his organization's views accepted as the prevailing opinion in a national security or foreign policy debate.[36]

When President Reagan came to office, there existed a considerable amount of ambiguity as to the role of the NSA. Although it was apparent that Reagan and his advisers knew what they did not want, it is not all that clear that they understood what they did want.[37] Richard Allen, Reagan's first NSA, was not to be a reincarnation of a Brzezinski or a Kissinger; he was to report to the President through the White House counselor, Edwin Meese. It was said that Allen was to be removed from day-to-day operational responsibilities, yet he led an interagency task force that took the lead to persuade Congress to sell AWACS aircraft to Saudi Arabia. Allen described himself as White House coordinator of national security policy;

Meese described him as "just a note taker." Further, it was said that Allen was not the White House spokesman for national security affairs, yet he gave numerous briefings to the press, spoke to foreign leaders, and gave speeches to interested groups.

Additional indications of conflict between managerial and advisory responsibilities can be found during the Nixon administration with actions and results that bear striking similarities to the Iran–Contra affair. NSA Kissinger privately advised Nixon in 1970 to approve a South Vietnamese secret offensive into Laos, which seriously affected the North's ability to mount an offensive. Kissinger, as related in his memoirs, initially relied on his deputy, Brigadier General Alexander Haig, and other NSC staff members for advice. Eventually a series of cabinet meetings was held to try to co-opt any opposition from key officials such as Secretary of Defense Melvin Laird, Secretary Rogers, and CIA director Richard Helms:

> "So much time, effort, and ingenuity were spent in trying to organize a consensus of senior advisers that there was too litte left to consider the weakness of the plan. . . . There was no role for the devil's advocate." . . . Perhaps most ironic, at the meeting of top advisers . . . Secretary of State Rogers made, in Kissinger's own words, an "extraordinarily effective presentation" which argued that the U.S. plan was already known to the enemy, was beyond the capabilities, of the South Vietnamese, and would destroy the fragile gains of "Vietnamization" should the operation fail. In retrospect "Rogers was right on target," but Nixon and Kissinger had so thoroughly discounted his advice that he was no longer a credible advocate, at least to them.[38]

It is not surprising that when those who as NSA or members of the NSC staff see themselves as policy coordinators, policy advocates, action officers, public spokespersons, and policy implementors, opportunities for thorough policy review become fewer as the time needed for competing responsibilities increases. Such can be a recipe for failure in any administration, whether the topic under consideration is terrorism or peace in the Middle East.

Institutional Concerns of the Congress and the Executive Branch

One of the key members of Congress during the Iran–Contra hearings was Congressman Lee H. Hamilton (D–Indiana), chairman of the House committee. As the hearings progressed, Hamilton revealed, "I have been asking myself what is the central issue we have been dealing with? I think that the central issue is, can you make the constitutional system of shared power work in foreign policy, in a dangerous world? We're not dealing with a new problem. The Constitution is not clear."[39]

The problem, however, is not new; it has been debated since the founding of the nation. The great debates between Alexander Hamilton and James Madison focused on the powers of a strong executive versus a strong representative body such as Congress. The Constitution gave to Congress the right to declare war, raise an army, investigate wrongdoings of the executive branch, and, if necessary, impeach the president. Additionally, the Senate has to approve the appointment by the president of senior officials by a simple majority and to ratify treaties by a two-thirds vote. Congress can easily meld domestic politics into foreign policy by pledging support for a key matter, such as the sale of weapons to an ally in exchange for a promise by the president to support a farm bill, a large public works project, and the like. Congressional staffs have also grown over the years, giving members the personnel and expertise necessary to take on the executive branch in matters of foreign policy. Several of these staff positions are filled with former military and intelligence officials. Robert McFarlane is a prime example of an individual who retired from the U.S. Marine Corps and accepted a position on the staff of the Senate Armed Services Committee. He subsequently assumed a high-level position in the State Department, followed by appointment as assistant NSA and finally NSA.[40]

The increased congressional staff size allows a more concentrated scrutiny of the executive branch and its activities. Since the early 1960s the number of professional staff working for congressional committees has increased 240 percent. There are approximately 14,700 employees on both the personal and committee staffs, which, coupled with the approximately 5,500 employees of the General Accounting Office, provide Congress with extensive capabilities. The much smaller Congressional Budget Office and the Congressional Research Service are also useful tools of the Congress.[41] However, the size and membership of Congress (100 senators and 535 Congressmen and women) makes unified policymaking in the area of national security difficult. Because of the numerous committees and subcommittees, power is not centralized but diffused. Rarely is the institution able to speak with one voice except at moments of great import. For a bill to become a law, it must pass through hearings by committees and subcommittees in the House and the Senate before going to the floor of either house. Often it must then be refined by a joint committee to ensure the interests of both parties and houses are melded. After all this, a bill may be delayed or defeated by a simple majority vote.[42]

It is difficult to discern a congressional viewpoint on any topic, let alone on national security and terrorism. All would agree that terrorism is wrong and must be stopped, but many would differ on the best way to go about stopping it. Many differing views emerged from a review of the lessons learned from the Iran–Contra hearings. Senator David L. Boren (D–Oklahoma) stated, "The President should have learned some lessons out of this—he's got to work out a partnership with Congress, and he's got to supervise his own staff. I hope Congress has learned some lessons as well: We can't all be Secretaries of State. . . . The war the American people would like to see ended is the war between the two ends of Pennsylvania Avenue."[43] Senator George J. Mitchell (D–Maine) indicated that "the major danger [of enthusiastic legislative reform] is in overreacting. It is clear that the President and his associates ignored the law in many respects. There's always the tendency to tighten the laws to prevent [a recurrence]. The danger is that we may deprive a future President of flexibility."[44] Senator Orrin G. Hatch (R-Utah) was blunter in his assessment: "How terribly overblown this affair has become. We have elevated the art of beating a dead horse to new heights."[45]

Certainly institutional battles take place between Congress and the executive, but much of the blame for unsatisfactory policy development lies within the executive branch itself. As the history of the NSC indicates, the difficulties between the State Department and the NSC are not new. To read in the press that a secretary of state "with unusual bluntness" indicated that he was unhappy with the current NSC system and would like to see his position as the principal foreign policy adviser strengthened should not be surprising. However, because the secretary of state in this case is George Shultz and because the interview took place after the Tower report and the Iran–Contra hearings makes these statements most interesting.[46] A revised NSC system, a new NSA, and congressional concerns appear to have done little to mitigate the continuing battle for control of foreign and national security policy.

Governmental policy on terrorism and other national security issues takes place in an environment fraught with built-in tensions. Our democratic system and federated government has ensured a division of power among branches of government and between agencies dealing with complex problems. Interest groups, think tanks, and the media ensure that significant events are kept before the decision makers. Additionally, many problems in the national security arena have no clear-cut solution. There is a great deal of uncertainty as to what response is the correct one. Does one articulate, much less pursue, policy in the same way with a Soviet official, an Iranian official, or a representative of a terrorist group? Policy decisions are often the result of the best-argued case by the more articulate advocate before the final decision maker.

Persons in positions as secretary of state, NSA, secretary of defense, and others possess power and prestige. It is through the exercise of influence based upon power and prestige that they attempt to formulate policy and see that it is implemented. Therefore personal relationships with a president are critical. The NSA sees the president on a daily basis and maintains an office in the White House. If a powerful secretary of state and secretary of defense are at odds over key policy matters (arms control, technology transfer, terrorism), often the NSA will forge policy options for the president. A strong NSA can help bring order out of conflict. A relatively weak NSA and NSC staff may well give up on getting the agencies and key individuals together and develop their own solution to a problem. This decision could well lead to freelancing by the NSC itself since the government organizations concerned would have opposed such policy. This explanation goes a long way in showing why such dedicated and talented people as may be found on the NSC could wind up before congressional committees attempting to defend their actions:

> In any administration, a president's confidence is gained through demonstrated loyalty and competence, which normally come only through daily interaction with

the president. . . . Secretaries [of state] themselves must be responsive to the chief executive's confidence, but they confront a dilemma. They can either distance themselves from their own department, thereby setting it adrift, or become State's advocate at the risk of being suspect themselves.[47]

Secretary Cyrus Vance was initially successful in balancing the two competing roles until battles with Brzezinski intensified. President Carter concluded that "Cy Vance mirrored the character of the organization which he led. He was . . . extremely loyal to his subordinates, and protective of the State Department and its status."[48] He was also allowed to resign in a policy dispute over the Iranian rescue attempt.

Conclusions

Secretary of State Shultz was asked to comment during the Iran–Contra hearings as to why he had not resigned in a policy dispute with other members of the Reagan administration. He made it quite clear that in his opinion policy battles do not cease just because a presidential decision has been made. "Nothing ever gets settled in this town, [and so] you can say, 'I'll give up and leave' or 'I'll stay and fight.' "[49] This in essence is how policy is formulated by the U.S. government.

Although some members of the opposing party may wish to make it appear that the failings of the Reagan NSC are particular to his administration, a historical review discloses that the circumstances may differ, but the potential for failure is constantly present, no matter who is in the White House.

Such terms as *centralized policymaking* and *decentralized execution* have been used to describe the dilemma confronted by a president. There is no formula ensuring that X number of parts centralization added to Y number of parts decentralization will ensure policy success. The very term *dilemma* implies choice between unsatisfactory solutions in an environment where outcome prognostication is an arcane art mastered by no one. Thus, pundits and commentators will continue to have much to write about in describing the successes and failures of presidential administrations. The same may also be said for former presidents and former NSC members.

Personalities, institutional differences, and the exercise of influence contribute to the development of national security policy. The interaction of these forces rarely occurs in a neat, predictable way or in a fashion that would allow prescriptions for success. At a minimum, one can only hope to mitigate failures in an uncertain world. At best, the president can endeavor to use the NSC apparatus to monitor implementation of effective policies.

The U.S. government was created to preserve freedom and a democratic way of life. To date, the system has stood the test. Yet leaders and policymakers continue to differ in their interpretations of what is right for the United States. The NSC, NSA, and NSC staff are in positions to promote the competition of ideas and to advise the president on successes and failures of his policies. They are simultaneously powerful by virtue of responsibilities assigned by the president and constrained by the Constitution, the separation of powers, the requirements for bureaucratic competition, and human fallibility. Their performance, however, is always critical. National security, from arms control to countering terrorism, is a high-stakes enterprise.

Notes

1. Dick Kirschten, "Towering Indictment of the Boss," *National Review*, March 7, 1987, p. 561.

2. Ibid. See also *The Tower Commission Report* (New York: New York Times, 1987), pp. 62–94.

3. U.S. Congress, National Security Act of 1947, sec. 101 (a).

4. *Tower Commission Report*, pp. 7–8.

5. John E. Endicott, "The National Security Council–Formulating National Security Policy for Presidential Review," in Endicott and Stafford, eds., *American Defense Policy*, 4th edition (Baltimore: Johns Hopkins University Press, 1977), p. 314. Though a bit dated, this is one of the best concise analyses of the roles and functions of the NSC.

6. Ibid.

7. This historical overview is based primarily on the material found in ibid. Additional material can be found in Stanley L. Falk, *The National Security Structure* (Washington, D.C.: Industrial College of the Armed Forces, 1967); Robert H. Johnson, "The National Security Council: The Relevance of Its Past to Its Future," *Orbis* 13, no. 3, (Fall 1969); John P. Leacacos, "The Nixon NSC: Kissinger's Apparat," in *American Defense Policy*, pp. 379–389; Robert C. McFarlane, "The National Security Council: Organizing for Policy Making," in *The Presidency and National Security Policy*, ed. R. Gordon Hoxie (Center for the Study of the Presidency, 1984), pp. 261–273; Henry Kissinger, *The White House Years* (Boston: Little, Brown, 1979); Zbigniew Brzezinski, *Power and Principle* (New York: Farrar, Straus, Giroux, 1983).

8. Endicott, "National Security Council," p. 316.

9. Ibid.

10. McFarlane, "National Security Council," p. 263.

11. Endicott, "National Security Council," p. 317.

12. McFarlane, "National Security Council," p. 263.

13. Endicott, "National Security Council," p. 317.

14. John P. Roche, "Taming the NSC," *National Review*, March 27, 1987, p. 40.

15. Ibid.

16. McFarlane, "National Security Council," pp. 263–264.

17. Endicott, "National Security Council," p. 317.

18. Leacacos, "Nixon NSC," pp. 379–380.

19. Endicott, "National Security Council," p. 318.

20. Roche, "Taming the NSC," p. 42.

21. Endicott, "National Security Council," p. 318.

22. McFarlane, "National Security Council," p. 264.

23. Ibid.

24. Brzezinski, *Power,* p. 57.

25. Ibid., p. 58.

26. Ibid., p. 64.

27. Ibid., p. 74.

28. McFarlane, "National Security Council," pp. 264–265.

29. Ibid.

30. Ibid., p. 266.

31. Brzezinski, *Power,* p. 58.

32. McFarlane, "National Security Council," pp. 270–271.

33. Ibid., p. 269.

34. David J. Lawless, *Organizational Behavior* (Englewood Cliffs, N.J.: Prentice-Hall, 1979), pp. 337–338.

35. David K. Hall, "The Role and Conflicts of the National Security Assistant" (Newport, R.I.: National Security Decision Making Department, Naval War College, 1984). This well-documented reading contains detailed information on numerous role problems facing the NSA.

36. Ibid., pp. 3–4.

37. Ibid., p. 5.

38. Ibid., p. 8.

39. Christopher Madison, "It's Congress's Move," *National Journal,* August 8, 1987, p. 2019.

40. David Hall, "Private and Public Participants in the National Security Process" (Newport, R.I.: National Security Decision Making Department, Naval War College, 1987), pp. 14–15.

41. Ibid., p. 16.

42. Ibid., p. 17.

43. Madison, "It's Congress's Move," p. 2015.

44. Ibid., p. 2017.

45. Christopher Madison, "Curtain Falls on an Instructive Play," *National Journal,* August 1, 1987, p. 1981.

46. Michael R. Gordon, "At Foreign Policy Helm: Shultz vs. White House," *New York Times,* August 26, 1987, p. A-1.

47. Duncan L. Clarke, "Why State Can't Lead," *Foreign Policy,* no. 66 (Spring 1987):131.

48. Ibid.

49. Dick Kirschten, "White House Notebook," *National Journal,* August 8, 1987, pp. 2042–2043.

3
Hostage Taking: Restoring Perspective After the Iran–Contra Crisis

Terrell E. Arnold

I n his writing on the political processes of his time, Thomas Jefferson once complained that the effect of coercion was "to make one-half of the world fools and the other half hypocrites."[1] His comment remains relevant, describing the chemistry of runaway desperation and overcharged emotion that surrounds the modern crime of political kidnapping. Most generously explained, terrorism is a desperate act of desperate people, but the kidnappings in Lebanon, which collectively amount to nearly forty years of confinement for innocent people, are surely desperation run amok. Most compassionately interpreted, the confinement of loved ones eventually generates an abiding, unshakeable misery, but if it leads to the kinds of bargaining with terrorists that has occurred in the past two years, the misery clearly has been allowed too much to govern our actions.

How is it possible to achieve a balanced response to kidnapping or hostage taking that is nationally and personally self-interested yet capable of dealing with both immediate and long-term elements of this problem without paying too high a price for relief? Analysis of the immediate cases in Lebanon does not offer a full set of answers, but many of the elements are there, and other elements are supplied by cases outside the Middle East context.

The Lebanon Cases

At the time of this writing, twenty-four hostages are being held in Lebanon by groups associated with the loose cluster of terrorists that calls itself Islamic Jihad, or Islamic Holy War. Beginning with kidnappings in March 1984, this cluster, mainly the Shiite fundamentalist group called Hesbollah (Party of Allah), has kidnapped and confined nearly forty people, some of them for more than twenty-four months. Four of these hostages (Terry Anderson, American; Alec Collett, British; and Marcel Carton and Marcel Fontaine, French) have been held since March 1985. Five Americans have been released or have escaped: CNN Beirut bureau chief Jeremy Levin; a Presbyterian minister, the Reverend Benjamin Weir; a Catholic priest, Father Lawrence Martin Jenco; hospital administrator David P. Jacobsen; and journalist Charles Glass. Two American hostages have died in captivity: Peter Kilburn, who apparently was murdered in April 1986 as retaliation for the U.S. raid on Libya, and William Buckley, who appears to have died from accumulated effects of torture and confinement.

Most of the media coverage in the United States focuses on the Americans, but at least two-thirds of the hostages in Lebanon have been of other nationalities. In July 1987 there were nine American, three British, six French, one Indian, one Irish, one Italian, one South Korean, and two West German hostages.

The makeup of the list of hostages shows clear patterns. Some nationalities—Irish and South Korean, for example—appear out of place at first, but the professions of these two hostages—one is a teacher and the other a diplomat—make their captivity explicable. The present list of hostages contains the following professions: teachers and other academic professionals, nine; journalists, writers, and electronic media, seven; clerics, one; diplomats, three; and businessmen, three.

An analysis of this list and of the professions of other hostages who have been freed or have died in captivity reveals that, as a rule, they had five properties in common:[2]

1. The hostages or their organizations have a long-term presence in the Middle East.
2. In the main, they are associated with private organizations, not with governments.
3. Each is in significant measure devoted to improving, explaining, or changing the economic and social conditions of the region.
4. Each is a carrier of outside ideas and influences, mainly Western.
5. Each in his profession is a communicator.

It is an ironic twist that Islamic fundamentalists and power seekers bent on exploiting Islamic fundamentalism consider the qualities of all these hostages to be threatening. It is a double irony for critics who would like to pin the entire Middle East turmoil on U.S. support of Israel that the rejection of Western influences, which impels Iran to support these terrorists, would probably continue its violent course if the Arab–Israeli dispute were to go away.

The Kuwait Bombings

The irony grows even greater when one considers that the central objective of the terrorists in taking these hostages relates to an episode of the Iran–Iraq war, not to the Arab–Israeli dispute. This whole series of kidnappings began with six bombings in and around the city of Kuwait in December 1983. The principal targets were the U.S. and French embassies and Kuwaiti airport, port, and power production facilities. The attacks were carried out by seventeen or more people, most of whom were captured, tried, and imprisoned by Kuwaiti authorities. Members of the group principally were from the Iraqi Dawa party, an Iran-sponsored Shiite group opposed to the Iraqi government of Saddam Hussein, but three members proved to be Lebanese, members of families in Hesbollah.

The attacks in Kuwait were considered by U.S. and other intelligence authorities at the time to have been carried out under Iranian direction in an attempt to jolt Kuwait out of support for Iraq in the war. How this attack was set up has not clearly emerged, but given the involvement of Hesbollah, a clear path for Iranian direction and support exists via Iran's embassy in Damascus, to Iranian Revolutionary Guard elements stationed in Lebanon's Bekaa valley, to Hesbollah headquarters at that time near the pre-Roman temple town of Baalbek in the Bekaa, and through Hesbollah members to the Dawa leadership in Kuwait. However the plan may have been delivered, among the individuals captured and imprisoned by Kuwait were the Hesbollah members.

Kuwaiti authorities acted quickly to bring the bombers to trial for murder and other criminal acts. By the end of February 1984, their fate was known: the prospect was that all the culprits would remain in prison for a long time. Six had been sentenced to death, three of them in absentia.

Hesbollah began the current series of kidnappings in March 1984 with the abduction of CNN Beirut bureau chief Jeremy Levin, followed within a week by the kidnapping of U.S. embassy political officer William Buckley. Hesbollah's demand for the release of the Kuwait bombers appeared shortly after in a Paris-based Arab-language newspaper. This demand has been renewed frequently: on a videotape of July 1984 in which Levin, Buckley, and Benjamin Weir linked their own fate to the fate of the Kuwait bombers; in a second videotape released later in 1984 in which Levin and others reiterated the demand; in the initial demands of the TWA flight 847 hijackers; and most recently in a videotape sent to a Western news agency by the kidnappers in late August 1987. On that tape, French hostages Jean-Paul Kauffmann and Marcel Carton said, "France knows well that our fate is tightly connected with the prisoners in Kuwait." Behind them as they spoke were two posters in French that read: "The seventeen Combatants Imprisoned in Kuwait Must Be Freed" and "The Combatants Do Not Forget the Oppression of the Superpowers."[3] Despite the demands and the lofty rhetoric, the bombers remain in prison in Kuwait. Although they have yet to carry out any of the death sentences, Kuwaiti authorities to date have adamantly refused to release the prisoners.

The government of Kuwait and Hesbollah seem to be locked in bootless struggle. Kuwait, quite rightly, sees no benefit and considerable political liability in letting convicted criminals go. Hesbollah has never stated any higher purpose than getting its friends out of jail; for that reason alone it continues to hold innocent people. In the process, however, Hesbollah has scored political gains that can have the effect of entrenching kidnapping among the instruments of modern terrorism.

The Outlook for Hostage Takings

"Kidnapping," say Brian Jenkins and Robin Wright, "has become a weapon of choice," for several reasons.[4] First, it is a cheap attention getter. In the Middle East, it has been a remarkably successful bargaining tool. Large, powerful armies or police forces cannot prevent it. Hardening of institutional targets has made the unprotected individual a preferred target. And that category of targets is limitless and largely defenseless. Thus, although many experts, including Jenkins, tend to see large events such as nuclear terrorism in the future, terrorists themselves seem likely to stick with simple, proved, comparatively safe devices like kidnapping for making their point.[5]

A Guaranteed Attention Getter

The attention-getting ability of hostage taking is practically guaranteed and unlikely to diminish. A kidnapping, particularly in the Middle East, can be counted on to secure immediate headlines and prime-time electronic media coverage, no matter who the victim or kidnappers are. The soul searching done by the media since the TWA flight 847 hijacking in June 1985 has led to some guidelines for individual networks on terrorism coverage, but the prevailing view in print and electronic media is that such stories should be covered. On the public side of the equation, intense encounters like a hostage taking are gripping human interest stories.

A major requirement of kidnapping as an attention-getting instrument of terrorism is the necessity to sustain the pattern of media and public attention. Just holding a hostage is not sufficient. That fact, no doubt, has prompted the occasional release of videotapes using the hostages themselves to renew demands by their kidnappers in Lebanon. To keep Western eyes on them, Hesbollah recently claimed that Kuwait has mistreated Shiites imprisoned for the bombings in that country.[6] On a videotape released in August 1987 obviously to get such attention, the leaders of Hesbollah asserted that their mistreatment of hostages is a quid pro quo for Kuwaiti treatment of the Kuwait bombers.[7] Recent rumors that one or more hostages may have been taken to Iran from Lebanon were probably part of that same attention-getting tactic.

Kidnapping as a Bargaining Tool

The success of kidnappings as a bargaining tool is a key factor in Hesbollah's continued hostage takings. Since the series of Hesbollah–Islamic Jihad hostage takings began in March 1984, Shiite fundamentalists have leveraged millions of dollars worth of weapons out of the United States and Israel for Iran; they have achieved the release of hundreds of prisoners from Israel; they have persuaded France to release funds frozen after the Iranian revolution that brought the Ayatollah Khomeini into power; and they have hazed the West Germans into refusing to extradite accused

TWA flight 847 hijacker Mohammed Ali Hamadei to the United States. As sponsor and protector of Hesbollah in Lebanon and as the ultimate user of the U.S. embassy takeover in Tehran by members of the Revolutionary Guard, Khomeini could easily say that he has used hostage takings to undermine the presidencies of both Jimmy Carter and Ronald Reagan.

There are limits to this strategy, as evidenced by the fact that Hesbollah's successes have been principally in bargaining with foreigners and not with other Arabs. Jenkins and Wright indicate that according to reports of local relief agencies, as many as "2,000 local Muslims, Christians and Jews have disappeared" in a decade or so of low-level warfare in Lebanon.[8] It is hard to see that there are any local political or territorial gains from that pattern of human coercion and intimidation. Rather, the principal yield seems to be fuel for communal disputes that can rend Lebanon for generations to come.

From the viewpoint of Hesbollah, the most frustrating aspect of the hostage-taking strategy must be its apparent inability to move Kuwait. Hesbollah finds itself locked into a failed strategy, but unfortunately for Western hostages, Hesbollah may be itself caught in a vortex of the Iran–Iraq war in that Iran probably would not agree to any Hesbollah move that would lessen pressure on Kuwait. Unmoved by the continuing captivity of hostages, as well as by direct approaches by the United States and others to release the bombers, the Kuwaitis have remained adamant. Thus, despite the impressive record of achievements attributable to kidnappings by the group and its sponsors Iran and Syria, Hesbollah's prime objective remains beyond reach.

Achieving a Perfect Defense

The continuing kidnapping of foreigners in Lebanon, including the abduction of Charles Glass in June 1987, underscores the difficulty any government has in denying would-be hostage takers their access to potential victims. If foreigners still have not gotten the message that Lebanon is a risky place to be, the chances appear slim that any less threatening area of the world would ever be lacking in foreigners to abduct. Putting aside for the moment the availability of potential victims, however, the probability is very low that any open society could array itself absolutely to prevent terrorist kidnappings.

For the democracies, there are at least four major impediments to achieving such success. First is the matter of public tolerance for interference with privacy and daily living. The security systems and procedures involved, as well as the amount of street-level intelligence activity needed, would demand too high a public acceptance of overt police presence in exchange for protection from a threat that is far less imminent than the risk of accidental death.

Second is the matter of constitutional rights. Unless there exists significant evidence of a kidnapping threat from a specific source, authorities generally have no legal basis for interfering with people's conduct. Even patterns of close surveillance in such circumstances are challengeable on grounds of harassment.

Third is a question of resources. The probable human and financial resource costs of developing a reliable screen against kidnappings would make the funding of a project like the Strategic Defense Initiative a relatively simple matter. To illustrate, Jenkins estimates that $50 billion to $60 billion will be spent annually on security systems and services by the year 2000.[9] Security experts generally would argue that even at those costs, the security screen will be porous and imperfect, and it will provide little protection, if any, from small, random terrorist attacks against elements of society at large.

The fourth impediment lies with human habits. In the absence of a visible threat, few people seem able to sustain highly disciplined security postures or maintain elaborate security systems and procedures. The whole effort would be obviated by inattention.

The Future Targets

Future security expenditures are likely to go mainly for hardening institutional targets and for protecting highly threatening facilities and people. The public will get some benefit from that process in the form of heightened security at airports and in other public and many private facilities.

In the main, private citizens will be on their own. In the current pattern of cultural, political, business, and tourist travel, foreigners are everywhere, and they will remain the most fertile field of potential victims for terrorist kidnappings.

What Can Be Done?

Kidnapping is a random, unpredictable event that is likely to harm very few people personally. And like other crimes against persons in our increasingly crowded society, the individual cannot do much to prevent it. The most constructive effort may be to put it in perspective.

Very few people are significantly at risk; the chance that someone might become a terrorist kidnap victim appears to be several million to one. If one avoids high-risk areas like the Middle East, and a few countries such as Columbia, the chance of being kidnapped diminishes greatly. Because this possibility is so remote, it should not radically alter the way people live and work. That order of risk should not lead to paranoid responses to this or other low-level threats in the environment. It should not prompt individuals or groups to make demands of their own government or of others for substantial adjustments in policies, programs, or courses of action that can have only marginal effects on the exposure to the threat of possible kidnapping. It should not provoke requests for orders of protection that the system, viewed objectively, will not be able to deliver.

How do people cope with the dramatic and emotionally charged fact of unjust human confinement once an episode begins? Part of the answer can be drawn from other bodies of experience with severe personal crises. For example, the families of the victims of the August 16, 1987, Northwest airline crash near Detroit appeared to handle the accident and their personal losses with great composure and self-control. Partly that appears to have been due to recognition of accidental death as an environmental risk to everybody. There was no point in railing about an unjust selection of victims; their presence on that flight was a consequence of random choices.

Increasingly, the victims of terrorist kidnappings have been chosen in a manner also at random. The passengers of TWA flight 847 became hostages because they happened to be on that airplane on that day. Most of the passengers were not Americans. On the face of things, Hesbollah seems to have chosen its kidnap victims in Lebanon in a more targeted way, picking largely on foreigners of Western nationalities, but the individual selections look like a random choice from among the available potential foreign victims.

The Chemistry of Political Kidnappings

Given the remote prospect that any person may ever be a terrorist kidnap victim, one must ask why we have such trouble with the event when it does occur. Partly the answer is that we have allowed ourselves to be bedazzled by the politics of terrorist kidnappings, specifically the Middle East ones. *Bedazzled* is the correct term because if any or all of the kidnappings that have preoccupied us so deeply in the past three years had been the work of criminals without political motive, our responses would have been a good deal more clear-cut and a great deal less confused.

A comparison of policies toward criminal kidnappings versus policies toward terrorist kidnappings makes the confusion quite apparent. The basic rules applied by law enforcement agencies and supported by the public regarding criminal kidnappings include:

Dialogue with the kidnappers to obtain release of the victims without harm to them.

The use of force to restrain or deter kidnappers in the event it appears likely that harm can come to victims, bystanders, or law enforcement officers.

The killing of the kidnapper in the process of resolving an incident if it appears that the kidnapper may kill or harm other people.

The courts have so interpreted the conditions for use of deadly force in such situations that society is largely comfortable with them. People seem to accept the consistency of such uses of force with a system of constitutionally guaranteed personal liberties.

It seems odd that coming out of this tradition of law enforcement we thought it necessary to formulate a different policy for poltical kidnappings. The best effort to deal with the problem to date is to get stuck about midway between treating terrorist kidnappings as politics and treating them as crime.

A Reverence for Politics

To say that an action is political means usually that the individual or group engaged in that action is on some errand related to the organization or management of the community or the state. In American practice, things seen to be political are considered legitimate through a broad but significantly undefined range of human behavior. Stating that a kidnapping is political, therefore, puts the event in a field of motivation that many people feel duty bound to consider. Some people seem impelled by the force of their own political training to look at the motives of the terrorist. In those circumstances, it is practically instinctive to seek dialogue.

The Policy of No Concessions

Coming at the problem with such reverence for politics and desire for dialogue, it was easy to make a bed of nails with the policy of no concessions to terrorists. The issue arises only when someone or something is held hostage. There is no negotiating with a terrorist after an assassination or a bombing; what the terrorist wanted to say was said, and the message itself was nonnegotiable. A no-concessions policy is exposed to no stress in assassinations and bombings; the rhetoric of the position is as freestanding as the message of the terrorists because there is no need for dialogue or direct communications. Moreover, failure to seek contact with the terrorist excites no criticism.

On the other hand, when terrorists choose kidnapping, they announce the intent, indeed the need, to negotiate. Hostages matter to families, friends, the media, and government. Thus, making no apparent effort to discover what is needed to obtain release of a hostage does not make sense. This scenario is not radically different from the one that arises in an ordinary kidnapping; the reactions of those affected are no different, and the requirements of the case, stripped of political overtones, do not seem different.

There are differences, however, in responses, and one of the most important is that in a criminal kidnapping, negotiators try to find out what is on the kidnapper's mind. They ask what the problem is and what the kidnapper wants. Such a dialogue is normal for kidnappings and hostage barricade situations. Law enforcement officers or other authorities may not feel bound or in a position to do what the hostage taker or kidnapper wants done when they ask what the problem is, but negotiators have found that knowing the problem can lead toward the solution.

Some Refinements of Policy

In this context, it is evident that the policy of no concessions needs some refinement. A policy that announces that the United States will not yield to blackmail is needed, but the Middle East hostage cases have demonstrated frequently that a policy that says the United States will not talk, listen, or respond in any way cannot be sustained. There is no need to be stoic in the face of a terrorist challenge, nor is there any need to be more adamant when the criminal is a terrorist than simply engaged in common crime. Rather, in these situations, the pressure from families, friends, the public, and media to find a way out is intense, and the issues as well as the process are always more complex if the politics of the case are allowed to obscure the fact that a crime is in progress.

The Other Hostage Cases

Kidnappings outside the Middle East could shed important light on solutions to the problems experienced in this field. A key fact to note is that the public generally does not know much about the other kidnappings and hostage cases. For example, between 1981 and 1985, there were nearly ninety kidnappings, hostage takings, and hijackings around the world that involved Americans. Fewer than a third of these incidents occurred in the Middle East. During 1984–1985, when the Hesbollah kidnappings were in their early stages, there were eight kidnappings of Americans in Latin America, six in Sub-Sahara Africa, and four in the Asian region. In the first eight months of 1987, hostages were freed from captivity in the Sudan, Mozambique, the South Pacific, and Lebanon. There was so little publicity in the majority of these cases, however, that the names of the victims of those kidnappings are not generally known; few people, moreover, know where the incidents occurred, and hardly anyone has any real sense of the reasons behind the kidnappings. The name many people are likely to be aware of is former ABC correspondent Charles Glass, who was taken at Beirut International Airport in June 1987 and released two months later.

Several qualities distinguish the cases in other regions of the world from the Middle East ones. First, the incidents tended to grow out of local disputes; U.S. officials could assert persuasively that the United States had nothing to do with the dispute between Muslim leaders in Khartoum and black separatists in the southern Sudan. They could argue successfully that Americans were not involved in the internal politics of Mozambique. Official and nonofficial Americans could refuse to be drawn into the dispute between Tamils and Senhalese in Sri Lanka. Second, because there was little or no publicity, U.S. authorities could pursue quiet efforts to determine what was at issue and how to deal with it on a case-by-case basis. Senior officials did not get drawn into broadside public declarations of no concessions to terrorists. Third, negotiators were able to deal with the cases without escalating the process to top levels of leadership. Fourth, the American media and the public did not get caught up in intense soul searching about U.S. policies and motives toward the kidnappers, or their countries, or their enemies.

The Political Kidnapping

The contrast between handling of Middle East kidnappings and the approach to cases outside that region exposes a crucial juncture in the psychology of political kidnapping: people's feelings about the cause of the kidnapper erode perspective about the event itself. There is at best a remote possibility that the crime of political kidnapping will be treated as an ordinary crime in these circumstances. Moreover, as shown often in the Middle East kidnappings, policies of governments become central issues in the resolution of the incident, and people who oppose those policies find themselves siding with the kidnappers against their own government. Thus, the more kidnappings are dealt with as political events the more the penalties mount. Hostage cases get elevated to the status of central, national policy issues. The mere fact of a hostage taking becomes a vehicle for critics to condemn public policy. Debate over policy undermines the moral authority of leadership at a time when that authority is most needed by the leader to be effective in negotiations.

The contrast in treatment erects a costly contradiction in responses to the crime of kidnapping. A criminal kidnapping of an individual on the domestic level is handled by local law enforcement officials and the professionals of the FBI, and the political risks of the incident are generally few. But a political kidnapping of an individual on the international level quite suddenly can, and usually does, engage top leadership. It can challenge the authority and prestige of the presidency.

The reason is that labeling the act political ensures that a terrorist kidnapping will engage government policy machinery directly and probably at high levels. As a result, negotiating room is lost by escalating the issues immediately to the top. Jimmy Carter made this error early in the Iran hostage case. Ronald Reagan allowed himself to be similarly boxed in by centralizing management of hostage negotiations in the National Security Council, tying them in both appearance and reality to the Oval Office. The resultant trap, as terrorism analyst Jeffrey Simon describes it, was to "let United States foreign policy become subservient to the resolution of a terrorist incident."[10]

The culprit is the no-concessions policy as commonly portrayed in official rhetoric. That policy invites leadership to verbal excess. President Reagan's famous Rose Garden speech on greeting the returned Iran hostages, Alexander Haig's upending of the priorities as between terrorism and human rights, and the continuing tough talk, particularly of the president and Secretary of State George Shultz, all tend to pit the will of U.S. leadership against that of small terrorist groups mainly in the Middle East.

In the minds of the terrorists, the rhetoric indicates that the United States thinks terrorism is very important and therefore that the terrorists' actions are significant. In the end, it probably suggests to the terrorists that the United States will bargain because U.S. leaders consider terrorism too important to ignore.

In a perverse sort of way, application of the no-concessions policy boxed U.S. negotiators into a position where they more than likely would have to make concessions to resolve the Lebanon kidnappings. The terrorists clearly knew how much the resolution of these cases meant to media, hostage families and friends, and some government officials. As the Iran arms deals developed, Iranian leaders also learned that despite tough rhetoric, the return of the hostages was so improtant to top U.S. leaders that they would bargain covertly. The Iranians undoubtedly could sense easy prey; U.S. covert signals sharply contradicted publicly stated U.S. policy. That had immense potential for embarrassment, and it raised the stakes.

The Impact of Scandal

It is not yet clear that the Iran–Contra experience has altered behavior very much. During the last days of his tenure as assistant to the president for national security affairs, Robert C. McFarlane wrote in his foreword to *Fighting Back*: "In national security terms, terrorist attacks place leadership in a quandary. The nation is not in any immediate sense threatened." However, he said, "The attacks must concern us. The casualties and the human distress caused by such acts are a worry well beyond their numbers. We cannot forget."[11] With those words he identified the trap that he, Lieutenant Colonel Oliver North, and Admiral John Poindexter were to enter in succeeding months, following the policy imperative of a compassionate president: get the hostages back.

Since the Iran–Contra scandal broke in November 1986, the administration has kept a comparatively low profile, largely as a result of the congressional Iran–Contra hearings and the investigation of special counsel Lawrence E. Walsh. Still, a basic pattern of giving the Middle East hostage cases a high-policy profile remains unchanged. In June 1987, President Reagan proposed in a letter to President Hafiz Assad of Syria to send U.S. ambassador to the United Nations Vernon Walters to Damascus for talks on U.S. hostages. Walters paid his visit during early July 1987 and while in Damascus reportedly asked Assad "to do everything he could to bring about release of these hostages."[12] Meanwhile the State Department's Bureau of Near Eastern and South Asian Affairs vigorously pushed for the return of U.S. Ambassador William L. Eagleton, Jr. to Damascus as a gesture following Syria's reported expulsion of radical Palestinian terrorist Abu Nidal.[13] Both of these actions signaled clearly that concern for the hostages and the battle against terrorism remained central policy issues. On the private side, among hostage families and friends, the talk was growing once again of the "forgotten hostages," a precursor for future pressure on the administration to do something to get the hostages released. The incipient trap described by Jeffrey Simon remained in place.

There were indications, however, that the public may be learning more from the Iran experience than Washington has. In June 1987, an editorial in the *San Diego Union* bluntly asserted that West Germany's caving under terrorist pressure and refusing to extradite Mohammed Ali Hamadei to the United States was "to blame for the capture of four additional hostages."[14] Writing of the kidnapping of Charles Glass, the *Chicago Tribune* echoed the State Department spokesman's position: "We will not yield to terrorist blackmail."[15] Commenting that there was a new realism demonstrated in the public reaction to the Glass abduction, *New York Post* columnist Eric Breindel commented that "the country didn't stop." The public did not "demand that the U.S. Government negotiate."[16] Noting that three videotapes of the hostages had been sent out by the terrorists in as many months, Breindel suggested that the terrorists might decide to hurt a hostage if they did not get some attention, but he concluded that the correct response was "stand firm."[17]

That kind of public gathering of the will has happened before. In *The Army of the Potomac: Glory Road*, Civil War historian Bruce Catton notes almost with disbelief that following the chain of Union military disasters that dogged the footsteps of the Army of the Potomac from the first battle of Bull Run to Chancellorsville, the people of the North decided they were going to stay with it and win the war. The aspect of this state of mind that mystified Catton the most was that the public seemed undeterred by accumulated failure and undismayed by the ineptitude and too frequent displays of stupidity on the part of military leadership. Despite those negative signs, they seem to have decided on the cool, unshakeable approach that is essential to victory in a long fight.

An attitude of this sort is needed to deal with hostage situations; anything less leads into a wilderness, like the scene around Chancellorsville, where both vision and judgment become easily impaired. If the experts are right in their sense of the future, people need to develop that coolness in the face of terrorist challenge because hostage takings are the most common terrorist attack to be expected in coming years, and hostage takings demonstrably are the point of greatest vulnerability to terrorist manipulation. The fact that public feeling seems to have moved toward that calm approach provides a better basis for recasting national policies on terrorism than any merely Washington-based reaction to the Iran–Contra affair. There now appears to be a genuine public resolve to put terrorist kidnappings in their proper context.

Given that opportunity, how should policies be revised? The list of suggested changes is short:

Restate the policy of no concessions to terrorists as a policy of no giving in to blackmail. This keeps the essential policy in place, but it removes the element of inflexibility because it does not appear to mean no dialogue.

Hew to a policy of making no concessions of substance, but neither discuss it nor explain it. Rather, adopt a position similar to U.S. policy on comment about ships carrying nuclear weapons: do not comment one way or the other about how a specific case would be handled, and do not respond to questions about hypothetical ones.

Turn off the tough rhetoric, but go ahead and act, including uses of force, where action is deemed appropriate and feasible.

Hold no victory celebrations on the return of hostages. Events such as Rose Garden receptions, calls on the president by hostages, and other acts that glorify and underscore the political character of the hostage experience should stop.

Try to deal with foreign, political hostage takings at the same levels of tone, urgency, and response that are applied to a domestic kidnapping. To respond differently to an international crime elevates the crime.

Structure the management of terrorist incidents in the federal government to keep the negotiating process as far as possible from the Oval Office. The president should be informed and consulted on any issue of consequence, but he should not become involved in any negotiation except in extreme circumstances.

Bring the executive and the Congress together on restoring and sustaining a bipartisan policy toward terrorism.

Strengthen and institutionalize approaches to victim and victim family assistance to make it easier for them to find out where to go for help and who to talk to about problems.

National policy should treat political kidnappings in a manner that reflects the seriousness of the crime against individuals but does not exaggerate the potential impact of such crime on the interests or the safety of the country. The policies of the other Western nations now affected by kidnappings should be the same. The crime of political kidnapping is an affront to democratic societies. It is not in any real security sense a significant danger.

Notes

1. Jefferson's actual quotation is, "What has been the effect of coercion? To make one-half of the world fools and the other half hypocrites." Thomas Jefferson, *Notes on Virginia* (1782).

2. These conclusions appear in Terrell E. Arnold and Moorhead Kennedy, *Terrorism: The New Warfare* (New York: Walker, forthcoming).

3. "Kidnappers Claim Torture in Kuwait, Threaten Others," Associated Press, August 21, 1987.

4. Brian Jenkins and Robin Wright, "Why Taking Hostages Is a Winning Terror Tactic," *Washington Post*, July 12, 1987, p. C1.

5. Brian Michael Jenkins, "The Future Course of International Terrorism," *The Futurist* (July–August 1987):8.

6. Following a series of six bombings, including attacks on the U.S. and French embassies in December 1983, the government of Kuwait arrested and convicted twelve members of the Iraqi Dawa party, a Shiite fundamentalist group, of carrying out these attacks. At least three others were found guilty and sentenced to death in absentia. Hesbollah has run its entire pattern of kidnappings since the March 1984 kidnapping of CNN Beirut bureau chief Jeremy Levin for the primary purpose of obtaining release of the Kuwait bombers.

7. "Kidnappers Claim Torture in Kuwait."

8. Jenkins and Wright, "Why Taking Hostages."

9. Jenkins, "Future Course," p. 11.

10. Jeffrey D. Simon, "The Need to Avoid a Terrorist 'Trap'," *New York Times*, August 17, 1987.

11. Robert C. McFarlane, foreword to *Fighting Back: Winning the War against Terrorism*, ed. Neil C. Livingstone and Terrell E. Arnold (Lexington, Mass.: Lexington Books, 1986).

12. "Walters Hopeful on Hostages," *New York Times*, July 17, 1987, p. 7.

13. Ambassador Eagleton was withdrawn from Damascus in early 1987 in support of Britain's break in diplomatic relations with Syria. Britain broke relations following intelligence and court findings in the Nazer Hindawi case that Syria's ambassador to Britain had taken part in a plot to blow up an El Al aircraft en route from London's Heathrow airport to Israel. Following a mode of operations applied in other aircraft bombing attempts, Hindawi intended to send the bomb on board the El Al flight in the luggage of his unsuspecting girlfriend.

14. "Lessons from a Terrorist," *San Diego Union*, June 26, 1987, p. B-6.

15. "The Hard Truth about Hostages," *Chicago Tribune*, June 21, 1987, p. 22.

16. Eric Breindel, "Hostages and Terror: The New Realism," *New York Post*, July 7, 1987, p. 33.

17. Ibid.

4
Lebanon, Terrorism, and Future Policy

J. Robert McBrien

Beirut International Airport—July 15, 1958. On a sunny afternoon in July 1958, Company F of U.S. Marine Battalion Landing Team (BLT) 2/2 rolled ashore on the Mediterranean beach immediately adjacent to Beirut International Airport. Greeted by sun bathers, young boys, soft drink vendors, and local horsemen, the first contingent of what would become, within the brief span of two weeks, a U.S. military force of 14,298 marines and soldiers secured the airport without incident.[1]

In an explicit exercise of the Eisenhower doctrine, the objective of the U.S. intervention was to "support the legal Lebanese government against any foreign invasion," in this case, the Syrian First Army with 40,000 men and over 200 Soviet-built medium tanks. The Syrian army force was the principal, although only the potential, adversary against whose presence the U.S. military planning had to be focused. The irregular forces of the various Lebanese confessional factions totaled about 10,000. Dispersed throughout Lebanon "in bands of 400 to 2,000 men and lightly armed," they were not viewed as likely to provide effective resistance to the marines.[2]

Beirut International Airport—October 23, 1983. In the early hours of a pleasant Lebanese Sunday morning, a quarter of the U.S. Multinational Force (USMNF) contingent of 1,250 U.S. Marines were asleep or otherwise engaged inside the Battalion Landing Team Headquarters at the airport. Without warning, a yellow Mercedes-Benz stake-bed truck carrying one person accelerated through the public parking lot south of the headquarter's compound. Crashing through both barbed wire and concertina fence, it sped past marine guardposts, through an open gate, around barriers, and over the sand-bagged booth of the sergeant of the guard. Driving straight into the lobby of the building, it detonated with a force equivalent to more than 12,000 pounds of TNT. The toll was 241 U.S. military personnel killed and more than 100 others wounded.[3]

The mission of the marines has been stated several ways. Only a month prior to the catastrophe, a Joint Chiefs of Staff alert order provided a mission statement to

The opinions expressed are the author's and do not necessarily reflect the opinion of any government agency or of the Center for Strategic and International Studies.

the commander in chief of the U.S. European Command that read, "To establish an environment which will permit the Lebanese Armed Forces to carry out their responsibilities in the Beirut area."[4] Only a short time before that message was sent to clarify the situation for the U.S. forces in Beirut and their chain of command, an assistant secretary of state testifying before the Senate Foreign Relations Committee placed the "presence of the Marines in a policy context" and stated the principles underlying U.S. policy toward Lebanon: "The withdrawal of all external forces; a sovereign Lebanon under a strong central authority, dedicated to national unity and able to exercise control throughout the territory; and security for Israel's nothern border."[5]

Testifying at that same September 1983 hearing, marine commandant P. X. Kelley stated that the marines' "mission at this time is presence. . . . Their current mission, as it did in 1958, remains one of presence."[6] Little more than a month later, General Kelley, who clearly did not create the assigned mission for the marines, was now describing the tragedy in terms of that mission:

> Well, first let me tell you that presence as a mission is not in any military dictionary. It is not a classic military mission. . . . I guess the best description is that we are a visible manifestation of U.S. strength and resolve to Lebanon and the free world. . . . It should be clearly understood that this was basically a diplomatic/political mission.[7]

Without debating whether the U.S. military mission in 1958 was to effect a presence, we might recall the brief dimensions of the environment that the 14,000 U.S. marines and soldiers faced: internal strife of the sort that had troubled Lebanon in various forms from long before its twentieth-century emergence as an independent nation; a threat of internal chaos that would destroy Lebanon as a nation and render it susceptible to Syrian–United Arab Republic (UAR) incursion and control; the loss of another Middle East state friendly to the West, particularly in the wake of the assassinations and coup d'état in Iraq; and the concomitant feat that Soviet influence and power would be strengthened in the Middle East. But within that turmoil, the U.S. forces faced a ragtag assortment of factional militias, perhaps 10,000 none more than 2,000 strong, and lightly armed. As for the Syrian–UAR threat (to which the U.S. forces were structured), "direct intervention from the United Arab Republic as a result of the American landings was unlikely."[8]

In contrast, the 1,250 men of the U.S. Marine contingent in the tripartite MNF faced an assemblage of confessional militias, Palestinian "stay behinds," radicalized Lebanese Shiites, Iranian Revolutionary Guards, and assorted terrorist groups (both autonomous and state backed) that were not only well armed in many cases but were also practiced innovators with field-expedient means of murder from simple urban ambushes to vehicle bombs. Although accurate head counts are difficult to achieve, this potpourri of armed, irregular forces appears to have numbered between 35,000 and 50,000. The evacuation of nearly 12,000 Palestinian forces in August and September 1982, in which the first U.S. Marines MNF contingent of 800 participated, simply reduced the range of possible adversaries that the second MNF would eventually confront.

In addition, the terrible civil war that had consumed Lebanon since 1975 was exacerbated by the invasions of Israeli and Syrian forces, the Israeli siege of Palestinian forces in Beirut, the assassination of Lebanon's President-elect Bashir Gemayel, and the massacre of hundreds of Palestinian civilians in two refugee camps by Christian militiamen. Lurking darkly on the horizon since 1979 was the fervid expansionism and anti-U.S. hatred of Iran's radical Shiism under the Ayatollah Khomeini.[9]

When the last of the U.S. forces departed Lebanon in late October 1958, the internal situation in Lebanon had stabilized without the need for U.S. forces to engage in provocative or seemingly partisan actions. In that process, the U.S. forces suffered only two casualties from hostile fire—one U.S. army sergeant killed and another wounded from factional militia gunfire. The one hundred days of U.S. intervention in strength (14,298 men and nearly 100 tanks) had succeeded; it had done no harm, and the Lebanese had for the movement resolved their own differences, achieved their own political equilibrium, among themselves.

By contrast, as the small contingent of U.S. Marines completed their withdrawal from Beirut in late February 1984, their exposure to the intense and convoluted factionalism of Lebanon in the 1980s had born witness to a failed disengagement proposal, to the approaching disintegration of President Amin Gemayel's government, to the seizure of West Beirut by an assemblage of the Druze and Shia militias, to more than 400 of their own casualties, and soon after reassertion of Syria's role in modifying the internal struggles of the Lebanese. Nothing in Lebanon had been improved by the U.S. presence. Certainly the only impact on terrorism was to expose the United States and its marines and diplomats to deadly radical Shiite, Iranian-inspired terrorism. If the Department of State was correct—that "any kind of withdrawal would be a devastating blow to the Government of Lebanon and to American policy"—then the failure of the United States to join with France in that rarest of occurrences, a combined reprisal against Syria (which had, at the minimum, acquiesced in the attacks on the U.S. and French MNF forces), had compounded the devastation and further exhibited the ambiguity of U.S. policy.[10]

Fall–Winter 1986–1987

As the Iran initiative of the Iran–Contra affair began its inexorable unfolding in late 1986 and early 1987, the American people watched the simultaneous development of yet another twist in the confusing relationship and impact of terrorism and Lebanon on U.S. foreign policy and Washington's perceptions of what events constitute vital interests and U.S. National security crises. While American hostages Father Lawrence Jenco and David Jacobsen, both victims of Hesbollah kidnappings in 1985, were released in 1986, two other victims of the Islamic Jihad's kidnapping flurry in 1985 remained in captivity. Frustration over their plight was heightened by the knowledge that William Buckley, identified by the Tower commission as the CIA station chief in Beirut, had been tortured and executed since his seizure in 1984 and that the highly effective U.S. raid on Libya had resulted in the retaliatory killing of Peter Kilburn by his captors, the Revolutionary Commando Cells, a group with apparent links to both Libya and Iran.

Hostage concern was escalating further as more Americans and other innocent foreigners in Beirut fell victim to kidnapping. In September and October, Americans Frank Reed, Joseph Cicippio, and Edward Tracy were kidnapped by groups identified as the pro-Libyan Arab Revolutionary Cells (Reed) and the pro-Iranian Revolutionary Justice Organization (Cicippio and Tracy). This time the terrorist captors did not bother to make demands.

The pitch of tension rose when in January 1987, amid the crescendo of Iran-Contra revelations and speculations, two West Germans, four more Americans, Anglican Church envoy Terry Waite, one Frenchman, and two West Germans were kidnapped, with all the terrorists except those holding the French hostage having links to radical Shiite organizations and, probably, Iran. The names of the claimant organizations were elaborate: the two Germans were grabbed by the Organization of the Oppressed on Earth and the four Americans were snatched by the Islamic Holy War for the Liberation of Palestine.

All of these events lay in the shadow of the June 1985 hijacking to Beirut of TWA flight 847 and the subsequent spectacle of Americans held hostage and a U.S. sailor murdered by the radical Shiite terorrists before the powerful Amal faction gained some control of the spectacle. In fact, the events of January 1987 were inextricably tied to the kidnappings of the two Germans, Rudolph Cordes and Alfred Schmidt, actions carried out by brothers and friends of the two Hamadei brothers under arrest in West Germany. Mohammed Hamadei's extradition has been sought by the United States for his role in the hijacking of TWA 847 to Beirut and the murder of U.S. seaman Robert Stethem aboard the flight. (Instead of extradition, however, he will be tried in Germany for other terrorism-related offenses.) Cordes and Schmidt were grabbed off the streets of Beirut to force his release. And in another twist, the Bonn government arrested his brother, Abbas Hamadei, for involvement in other terrorist operations in Germany. At least two of the 1987 kidnappings in Beirut were the work of the other five Hamadei brothers, who were associated with Hesbollah, the Shiite terrorist movement in which Abbas Hamadei is a security official. Thus, brotherly love added to the Beirut scenario a kind of warped Hatfields-versus-McCoys confrontation between the Hamadei family and the governments of the United States and West Germany.

In response to these events, as well as simultaneous expansion of the gulf shipping war between Iran and Iraq, two carrier-battle groups from the U.S. Sixth Fleet with at least twenty-two warships moved into the eastern Mediterranean, positioning themselves off the Lebanese coast. From that vantage point, they were to provide a variety of military response options to the death threats and other contingencies that the multiplicity of terrorist groups, heavily armed militias, newly returned Palestine Liberation Organization (PLO) forces, and Syrian and Iranian regional ambitions might produce. The European allies, however, feared a U.S. military strike of some sort after the April 1986 raid on Libya. Concerned that a U.S. raid in the Middle East would probably cause the deaths of hostages and further undermine Western interests in the Middle East, they declined to convene a high-level multilateral conference on terrorism that had been scheduled for early February in Rome. The United States, while reasserting its no concessions to terrorists policy under the flood of criticism that was accompanying Iran deal disclosures and the forthcoming release of the Tower commission report, gradually stepped away from the threatening posture, the administration's Middle East focus shifting even more closely to the Persian Gulf and away from the intractability of Lebanon.

Parallel Facts and Possible Futures

Outside of the policy context, there are some tentative lessons and perspectives to be gained relative to terrorism and Lebanon and the kidnappings that have captured the world's attention. Thus, it is not a digression here to speculate briefly on what the statistics of terrorism combined with the character of terrorist events and other significant political developments may mean in the future.

The various kidnappings, however terrible and dramatic the plight of the captives, do not represent the much broader array of international terrorism incidents that the United States and other nations face and to which U.S. anti-terrorism policy is equally addressed. Thus, although terrorist kidnappings nearly doubled in 1985, that tactic, even with the inclusion of hijackings and hostage-barricade cases, still ranked only fourth in the list of favorite international terrorist techniques. Bombings and armed attacks clearly dominated the statistics, and arson came in third, slightly ahead of kidnapping and hostage taking.[11]

Outside of Lebanon, Shiite terrorism, although often deadly and of formidable potential, has not been the grimmest of the reapers. In 1985, the year for which U.S. statistics are most up to date and accurate, Palestinian groups accounted for a third of all international terrorist incidents. The Palestinian terrorists managed to reach that level of activity despite the fact that approximately 12,000 Palestinian fighters had been expelled from Lebanon in late 1982 and dispensed to eight other Arab states. (Incidentally, Palestinian terrorist groups spent much of their lethal energy on killing fellow Middle Eastern nationals.) Interesting developments in 1986 and 1987 may show a major change occurring, although the statistics of terrorism tend to be deceptive in the short run. Unofficial State Department data for 1986 show a 47 percent decline in incidents of Middle East origin occurring in Western Europe, and preliminary data for the first half of 1987 suggest that the decline in Middle East–origin terrorism could be as much as 71 percent.[12]

This drop in Palestinian terrorist actions, as well as the near absence of either Libyan or Syrian sponsorship of terrorist attacks since late 1976, means that France's discovery of an Iranian embassy employee's connection to the bloody "red September" bombings of 1986 is likely to combine with the hostage kidnappings in Beirut to push Iran back to the top spot for being a state encourager, if not sponsor, of terrorism.

During roughly the same time that the United States and other Western nations were suffering through the infliction of multiple Beirut kidnappings, the PLO was managing to reintroduce itself into Lebanon in reduced strength despite the grim and very bloody resistance of the Muslim militias and the Israeli attacks on reconstituted Palestinian bases. In addition, the increasingly influential radical Shiites of the Hesbollah were, in classic Lebanese fashion, engaging in shifting alliances with other Muslim factions and militias, embarking on autonomous campaigns, engaging the Israeli Defense Forces and Christian Lebanese forces, and all the while threatening and assaulting Western interests in Lebanon.

Within this same time frame, the United States bombed Libya, an act that appears to have had a singularly successful impact on Qaddafi's propensity to sponsor terrorism. Other, perhaps subtly compelling, influences on the activities of Libya and Syria are to be found in the success of sustained U.S. efforts to develop a concerted and persistent international front against terrorism. Long-established bilateral and multilateral institutional interests among friendly powers—particularly intelligence services, law enforcement agencies, and criminal jutice authorities—have begun to bear fruit. Combined pressures of greater border vigilance, successful arrests and prosecutions, breaks in relations and diplomatic expulsions, economic and trade sanctions (even if mainly symbolic), and intelligence successes have worked independently and in combination to preempt and deter state-backed terrorism. Although a cohesive and uniform system of international opposition to terrorism has not suddenly burst upon the scene, the confluence of measures in 1986 has had a salutary effect.[13]

This is not to say that wild cards and deadly potential do not exist. The reunification of the PLO under Yasir Arafat in April 1987 produced a more radically anti-Israel organization and an organizaton that, at least in principle, is more willing to engage in anti-U.S., anti-West violence. If events proceed well for them, the reunified PLO should produce a substantial decline in the intramural violence that has previously occupied the Palestinian terrorist groups and kept them from concentrating their energies on Israel and the West. In theory at least, the restoration of Palestinian solidarity (which had never been long lived) will enable their combined energies to be focused externally on Israel and other targets. Furthermore, whether Syria's favorite terrorist surrogate, Abu Nidal, expelled from Damascus in

June and reportedly in residence in Libya, will cooperate with the reunified PLO or instead choose to operate in some autonomous or otherwise deniable fashion is another troublesome unknown.

Iran and its adherents and surrogates from the Hesbollah have been on center stage of the terrorism review since the United States announced its intention to reflag and protect Kuwaiti oil tankers, and predictions of Iranian-backed terrorist attacks against U.S. interests have been prominent. Iranian-connected terrorism, a serious danger, has been raised to a new level of concern. But Iranian-connected terrorism has been with us prominently since 1983 (1979 if we call the embassy takeover and 444 days of captivity for Americans terrorism) and in that time— outside the hotbed of Lebanon—it has been Palestinian and non–Middle East acts of terrorism that have caused the most U.S. casualties.

Observations

Assessments of the U.S. role in Lebanon between 1982 and 1984, particularly the policies and decisions that placed 1,200 U.S. Marines in the cauldron of Beirut, have not been kind. Even before the marines were withdrawn from Beirut, the Long commission, which examined the October 1983 suicide bomb destruction of the Marine compound, concluded that there was "an urgent need for reassessment of alternative means [to U.S. military involvement] to achieve U.S. objectives in Lebanon."[14]

Roy Gutman, in describing President Reagan's decision to return the marines to Lebanon following the massacre of hundreds of Palestinian civilians at the Sabra and Shatila refugee camps, was especially tough:

> It was the quintessence of policy based on public relations gestures, not calculations of interests, purposes and means. Fundamental steps were not taken. [National security adviser William] Clark failed to require the most basic preparations—position papers from around the government laying out the consequences of the move.[15]

Brookings Institution scholar and former senior National Security Council officer for the Middle East William Quandt has been gentler but no less pointed:

> The mistakes made have not been of intention, but rather of analysis, judgment and execution. A better sense of priorities, a feel for the importance of time, a commitment of Presidential leadership, a more coherent public posture, a deeper knowledge of local Lebanese realities, a strategic understanding of Syrian and Israeli motives—all these would have vastly improved the conduct of US policy in Lebanon.[16]

The United States did not become involved in Lebanon in 1982 because of terrorism; instead it appeared to be conducting a poorly conceived and badly executed emulation of its successful 1958 intervention. Its withdrawal, however, was in large measure because of terrorism and the ability of its tactical employment to achieve ends of ostensible strategic importance. Since that time, U.S. policy toward terrorism has been enmeshed with the plight of hostages in Lebanon, and policy on Lebanon has been inextricable from the issues of terrorism and hostages.

The lack of control by the United States over political events in Lebanon from 1982 forward has not of itself been a policy failure; it is simply a reality—a preexisting and sustained condition—that has been bound to affect profoundly the U.S. role then as it now continues to be. It did not have (nor does it now) leverage, commitment, or identified political interests of sufficient regional or strategic gravity. The totality of conditions and their projected effects is not enough to justify serious efforts to obtain leverage and to take the considerable risks that then would accompany its application. Quandt has stated the case in this manner: "The United States does not have vital interests in Lebanon per se. If interests are literally vital, one must be prepared to pay a very high price to defend them. This is not the case in Lebanon."[17] An even more succinct appraisal was expressed by Gutman: "The fact that the republic [of Lebanon] has survived this setback [the U.S. withdrawal] proves Lebanon was never the vital interest it was declared to be."[18]

The U.S. policy failure in 1982–1984 occurred in the confusion of and the absence of connections among the hopes of decision makers, the expressed purpose of the U.S. involvement, the expectations of what would be achieved, the actions taken and omitted, and the illusion that all of this derived from a vital interest of the United States. In the case of the U.S. Marines' presence between 1982 and 1984, the United States could not establish that its objective of helping to induce internal political stability in Lebanon by effecting the withdrawal of foreign regional military forces was either vital to the United States or achievable in the environment that confronted it and with the methods and assets that it was committing.

In the case of terrorist hostages from 1984 to the present, the same type of exaggerated sense of U.S. interests and its ability to control events came into play. In this instance, however, there was not simply an improvisational policy on terrorism and hostages where none previously existed or where policy was exceedingly ambiguous. On the contrary, there was an established national policy of no concessions to terrorism and of punishing state support of terrorism.[19] This was augmented by the U.S.-inspired Tokyo summit declaration on terrorism that included as its lead-off measure the "refusal to export arms to states which sponsor or support terrorism."[20]

We do not have to reevaluate the precise wisdom of the U.S. declared policies on terrorism or reexamine the as-yet-incomplete record of the Iran arms deal to find the discontinuity between the policy rhetoric of what the United States should or should not be doing and the methods chosen to save the Beirut hostages. Whether conceived and intended as a deliberate, expedient deviation from declared policy or viewed as tactical measures within a best-case regional strategic objective (but an objective without a framework), the Iran initiative discernibly ran afoul of declared national policy. The obsession with the Beirut hostage tragedies and a probably inchoate sense that the return of the hostages would be not only a humane achievement but also a telling blow against terrorism appear to have accelerated the process of converting an event-specific, improvised policy into an operation at odds with the well-understood goals of U.S. anti-terrorism policy. In his August 12, 1987, address to the nation, President Reagan himself aptly stated the sentiment that makes the Iran initiative so similar in the confusion and vagueness of its origins and implementation to the decisions and subsequent actions that accompanied the involvement of U.S. Marines in Lebanon between 1982 and 1984:

> Our original initiative [a strategic opening to Iran] got all tangled up in the sale of arms, and the sale of arms got tangled up with hostages. . . . I let my preoccupation with the hostages intrude into areas where it didn't belong. . . . I was stubborn in my pursuit of a policy that went astray.

Another element of the Iran arms deal deserves comment. Although it has only limited procedural similarities to the Beirut-82 decisions, it was critical to the outcome of the Iran initiative: the entire Iran initiative was an out-of-process approach from policy conception, to implementation, to evaluation and analysis. In contrast, however, the Libya raid—which, interestingly, involved many of the same key actors operating over parallel periods of time—worked as well as it did partly because it had a coherent relationshp to national policies, because the decisions were made within the context of those policies combined with an understanding of regional dynamics (particularly Qaddafi's general isolation), and because the full decision-making process, albeit a highly restricted one, was involved throughout.

Although the policy of objectives and events that led the United States into its debacle in Lebanon in 1983 did not have a direct correlation with the attention given to the hostages thereafter, a pattern of incompleteness and miscalculation is present in both cases. Just as in 1982 the confusion of hope with objective expectation led the United States to introduce forces and leave them there, at a time and in such numbers that they could not moderate the situation, the emotionalism and intensity of concentration on the hostages' terrible personal tragedies turned the U.S. no-concessions policy on its head. In both cases, the process of policy development and execution mistook high hopes and good intentions for hard facts and limited expectations.

Clearly, one vital lesson is that the United States cannot afford to indulge in what journalist Roy Gutman has called "the practice of allowing rhetoric and impulse to dominate the decision-making process.[21] Ultimately we must recognize that although it is hard to think of terrorism outside the context of the most recent or the most vexing crisis, we have no other option than to view it from a perspective that will sometimes subordinate our fondest hopes and best intentions to the cold realities of a sustained conflict. That is exactly what long-term policy and strategy development to meet national security interests demands; it is a lesson we should not have to learn again through more hard experience.

Notes

1. Jack Shulimson, "Marines in Lebanon: 1958" (Washington, D.C.: History and Museums Division, Headquarters, U.S. Marine Corps, 1983).

2. Ibid., p. 12.

3. U.S. Department of Defense, "Report of the DOD Commission on Beirut International Airport Terrorist Act, October 23, 1983" (Washington, D.C., December 20, 1983) (commonly referred to as the Long commission report).

4. Ibid., p. 35.

5. Testimony of Nicholas A. Veliotes in U.S. Senate, Committee on Foreign Relations, *Hearings on Events in Lebanon,* 98th Cong., 2d sess., September 13, 1983, p. 2.

6. Testimony of General Paul X. Kelley, commandant, U.S. Marine Corps, in ibid., p. 5.

7. Remarks by General P.X. Kelley, USMC, SASC Conference, October 31, 1983.

8. Shulimson, "Marines in Lebanon," p. 39.

9. See, for example, Yehuda Bar, *The Effectiveness of Multinational Forces in the Middle East,* International Essays (Washington, D.C.: National Defense University, 1986), p. 53; Trevor N. Dupuy and Paul Martell, *The Arab-Israeli Conflict and the 1982 War in Lebanon* (Fairfax, Va.: Hero Books, 1986); and *Hearings on Events,* pp. 24–28.

10. *Hearings on Events in Lebanon,* p. 5.

11. Department of State, "Patterns of Global Terrorism: 1985" (October 1986).

12. Incidents of Middle East origin in Western Europe:

1985	1986	Percentage Change	First Half of 1987 (Preliminary)	Percentage Change
74	39	−47	8	−71

13. Department of State, Current Policy No. 947, "Terrorism and the Rule of Law," address by L. Paul Bremer III, ambassador at large for counterterrorism, before the Commonwealth Club, San Francisco, April 1987.

14. Long commission report, p. 8.

15. Roy W. Gutman, "Battle over Lebanon," *Foreign Service Journal* (June 1984):31. See also former Under Secretary of the Navy Robert J. Murray interviewed in "Retreat from Beirut," Frontline 3, a PBS Broadcast, WGBH Educational Foundation, 1985: "You need someone . . . who will look at it and say, 'Um, smells like three-week-old fish to me, Buddy.' You need somebody who's gonna keep a weather eye on it so that people who are advocates don't get too far out of hand. People who've got too much of themselves."

16. William B. Quandt, "Reagan's Lebanon Policy: Trial and Error," *Middle East Journal* 38, no. 2 (Spring 1984):250.

17. Ibid.

18. Gutman, "Battle," p. 33.

19. The report of the vice-president's task force on combatting terrorism describes these elements of policy: "The U.S. Government will make no concessions to terrorists. It will not pay ransoms, release prisoners, change its policies or agree to other acts that might encourage additional terrorism. At the same time, the United States will use every available resource to gain the safe return of American citizens who are held hostage by terrorists.

"U.S. policy is based upon the conviction that to give in to terrorists' demands places even more Americans at risk. This no-concessions policy is the best way of ensuring the safety of the greatest number of people.

States that practice terrorism or actively support it will not do so without consequence. If there is evidence that a state is mounting or intends to conduct an act of terrorism against this country, the United States will take measures to protect its citizens, property and interests." See *Public Report of the Vice President's Task Force on Combatting Terrorism*, (Washington, D.C.: U.S. Government Printing Office, 1986).

20. May 1986. The Summit Seven are the United States, United Kingdom, France, West Germany, Italy, Canada and Japan.

21. Gutman, "Battle," p. 33.

5

The Raid on Libya and the Use of Force in Combating Terrorism

Neil C. Livingstone

> Superior force is a powerful persuader.
> —Winston Churchill[1]

Shortly after 2 A.M. on the morning of April 15, 1986, U.S. warplanes conducted air strikes against Libyan airfields, Libyan strongman Muammar Qaddafi's headquarters, and other targets, including suspected terrorist training and coordination facilities near the cities of Tripoli and Benghazi. One U.S. F-111B fighter bomber and its crew was lost in the raid. President Reagan described the action as "a single engagement in a long battle against terrorism."[2]

The raid purportedly was in retaliation for Libyan involvement in the bombing of a West Berlin disco on April 5, 1986, that killed a U.S. serviceman and a Turkish woman and injured 204 other people, 64 of them Americans. In retrospect, it is clear that this was simply the public justification for a U.S. decision that had, for all intents and purposes, already been made. Indeed subsequent evidence indicates that Syria's complicity in the bombing was more significant than Libya's.

Whether the principal or subordinate perpetrator of the West Berlin bombing, Libya was clearly "headed for a fall," in the words of one U.S. policymaker.[3] President Reagan explained in a televised address on the evening of April 15:

> Colonel [Qaddafi] is not only an enemy of the United States. His record of subversion and aggression against the neighboring states in Africa is well documented and well known. He has ordered the murder of fellow Libyans in countless countries. He has sanctioned acts of terror in Africa, Europe and the Middle East as well as the Western Hemisphere.[4]

In addition to a long history of support for international terrorism, in the week before the U.S. response, defense officials reported that Libya was planning terrorist attacks against U.S. diplomatic missions in ten African countries, as well as in areas of the Middle East and Latin America. Authorities had preempted an attack on the U.S. embassy in the Philippines only a short time earlier. In one African country, moreover, it was reported that three Libyan agents were planning to bomb the U.S. embassy and kidnap the U.S. ambassador. Secretary of State George Shultz indicated on April 15 that the United States had information that Libya was targeting thirty U.S. embassies for attack.

From the standpoint of U.S. policymakers, Washington had exhausted all peaceful remedies for dealing with Libya and curtailing its support of international terrorism. It was time to act. And although Syria and Iran were perhaps even more aggressive supporters of terrorism, neither was as vulnerable to U.S. military power as Libya, which was within easy striking distance of U.S. bases in Europe and the U.S. Sixth Fleet. Unlike Syria, which boasted a formidable air defense system and a military assistance treaty with the Soviet Union, Libya's defensive capabilities were no match for the United States. It had been learned from the Israelis that the Libyan air defense system shut down at midnight when the duty officer left his station. Libyan pilots did not fly at night, and the only real threat came from a squadron of MiG-21s manned by Syrian pilots twenty-four hours a day. The Syrian interceptors, however, needed clearance from either Qaddafi or his deputy, Abdul Salam Jalloud, to sortie and therefore were not operationally independent.

Perhaps most important, Libya had been demonized sufficiently for most Americans to feel few pangs of conscience in attacking it. In his seventeenth-century travelogue, John Leo described Libyans as being "principally adicted unto Treason, Trecherie, Murther, Theft and Robberie. Their Nation, because it is most slavish, will gladly accept of any service among the Barbarians, be it never so vile or contemptible."[5] In terms of public perceptions, Leo's description of Libya has a decidedly contemporary ring. Its erratic leader, Colonel Qaddafi, is the man everyone loved to hate, and even his Soviet allies keep him at arms length. The late Egyptian president Anwar Sadat once described Qaddafi as "100 percent sick and possessed of the demon." Israeli, U.S., and French intelligence assessments portray him as schizophrenic, swinging back and forth between a warm and even personality one moment to a cold, aggressive, and meglomaniacal personality the next. According to former Sudanese president Jaafar Nimeiry, Qaddafi has "a split personality— both evil." In view of its military weakness, political isolation, and the fact that all of its high-priority targets and population centers were spread along the Mediterranean littoral, Libya presented a vulnerable and inviting target.

Although many in the administration felt that the Ayatollah Khomeini's Iran was the terrorist sponsor most deserving of U.S. retaliation, Iran presented a number of logistical and strategic problems that National Security Council and Defense Department planners had not been able to overcome. Not only was it far from U.S. air bases and open water where U.S. warships could safely operate, but the question of secondary and tertiary consequences arising from military strikes against Iran raised the risks to unacceptable levels. There was concern that open hostilities between the United States and Iran would drive Tehran into the Soviet camp. It was also feared that Iran might hit back at either Kuwait or Saudi Arabia, especially the oilfields in the eastern part of the country, or even launch a massive worldwide terror campaign that might reach to the shores of the United States.

Besides, the administration had already embarked on secret negotiations with a faction of the Iranian government headed by the Speaker of Iran's parliament, Ali Akbar Hashemi Rafsanjani, and had delivered two shipments of arms to Iran in addition to two other shipments provided by the Israelis.

Thus, after years of rising frustration over the growth of international terrorism and the failure of the Western alliance to take meaningful cooperative steps to deal with the problem, the Reagan administration decided to strike back forcefully and unilaterally against one of the principal state sponsors of terrorism. The April 15 raid was a watershed in the war against terrorism, yet many questions remain. Was the raid successful? What did it accomplish? What does it mean for the future, particularly in the light of the subsequent crackup of the Reagan administration's anti-terrorism policy on the shoals of the Iran–Contra affair?

Genesis of the Raid

The Reagan administration had come to power on the heels of the 444-day Iranian hostage ordeal, a period that former Carter administration official Steve R. Pieczenik disparagingly described as a time of affirmative action negotiations with terrorists involving Muhammad Ali, Andrew Young, and Ramsey Clark. It was a period where there was no real policy for dealing with terrorism, and new initiatives for addressing the problem were usually met with skepticism or disinterest by the administration's human rights activists and third worlders. Nevertheless, it was the Carter administration's seeming lack of resolve and ineptitude in dealing with the hostage crisis that, more than any other reason, resulted in the Reagan landslide of 1980.

Although the Reagan administration came to power with tough talk about swift and effective retribution against terrorists, little substantive action occurred until the traumas of 1983: the bombings of the U.S. embassy and embassy annex in Beirut, the suicide bombing of the U.S. Marine barracks with the loss of 241 U.S. military personnel, and the bombing of the U.S. embassy in Kuwait. What had seemed a mere irritant suddenly became the administration's top foreign policy priority as more and more coffins bearing dead Americans were returned to the United States and the flags lowered to half-staff. Like the Carter administration before it, the Reagan White House suddenly found itself with a major credibility problem as members of Congress, reporters, and the general public demanded to know what the administration was doing about terrorism.

Although the 1983 attacks produced a fragile consensus within the administration that tougher measures had to be taken to combat terrorists and their state supporters, retaliation was slow in coming. Initially Defense Secretary Caspar Weinberger and Chairman of the Joint Chiefs of Staff (JCS) General John W. Vessey opposed retaliatory strikes against terrorist camps and installations in the Bekaa valley out of fear that such a response would only prompt more attacks on the U.S. Marines in Lebanon. Once the marines were pulled out, Weinberger and the JCS contended that retaliation by the United States would place U.S. allies in the region in jeopardy.

Despite public statements—viewed in some circles as an excuse for inaction in the face of serious provocation—by senior administration officials that the United States lacked evidence as to the individuals and nations behind the 1983 bombings, Western intelligence agencies possessed detailed and irrefutable evidence that the Shiite terrorist organization Hesbollah, in league with Syria and Iran, was the principal culprit. The specific location, in the city of Baalbek in the Bekaa valley, where several of the explosive devices had been constructed, was known, along with the location of a number of Hesbollah dormitories and other facilities. Indeed, the United States engaged in the planning of joint reprisal raids with the Israelis and the French but in both instances failed unltimately to take action. The French, weary of U.S. indecision, carried out their own unilateral reprisal in November 1983. The United States made a halfhearted attempt to bomb Syrian antiaircraft positions and a radar site in Lebanon on December 4, 1983, but the loss of two aircraft further dampened the Pentagon's enthusiasm for anti-terrorist strikes. The pilot of one aircraft was killed and the administration publicly humiliated by the release by the Syrian government of the captured bombardier-navigator to the Reverend Jesse Jackson.

The United States Goes on the Offensive

Despite opposition from many in the administration to adopting a more proactive policy against terrorism, by early 1984 it was clear that the momentum was shifting in favor of those calling for the use of military force against terrorists and their state sponsors. President Reagan was growing increasingly fustrated by U.S. impotence in the face of repeated terrorist attacks on U.S. citizens and interests. There had been too many funerals of Americans and too few of terrorists, the president was known to believe. Indeed he had always favored surgical retaliatory strikes in policy meetings but had deferred to the correlation of views expressed by his principal advisers.

By 1984, however, a number of key personel changes were beginning to have an impact on administration policies. Robert C. McFarlane had become the president's third national security adviser and was deeply committed to developing the capabilities and devising the policies necessary to protect the United States from terrorist attacks and to strike back at terrorists and their state sponsors. To this end, he was one of the principal authors and chief proponents of national security decision directive 138 (NSDD 138), which amounts to a declaration of war against international terrorism. Although classified, NSDD 138 took the place of the purely passive strategy that had previously existed and, while not spelling out the policy in detail, specifically endorsed preemptive and retaliatory military action against terrorists. "We cannot and will not abstain from forcible action to prevent, preempt or respond to terrorist acts where conditions merit the use of force," McFarlane explained.[6]

McFarlane found an important ally in Secretary of State George Shultz who, like himself, had been a former marine officer and had seen marines die on his watch in Lebanon. According to former Pentagon official Noel Koch, Shultz's "greening" on the subject occurred during a day-long session at the Department of State on March 24, 1984. In addition to the secretaries of state and defense, present also were FBI director William Webster, White House counselor Edwin Meese, top CIA, Defense, and State Department officials, and a small number of outside experts on the subject of terrorism. In the wide-ranging informal discussion that ensued, U.S. options for dealing with the problem of terrorism were explored, including the use of force, and the strengths and weaknesses of each approach were debated. Although it was not the purpose of the session to reach any conclusions, it was clear to all present that the president's frustration was shared by many other members of his administration and that there was a growing predisposition to use force against terrorists when the right opportunity arose.

Less than two weeks later, on April 3, 1984, Shultz said the issue was not whether the United States would retaliate "but rather when and how and under what circumstances."[7] Shultz vowed to educate the public as to the reasons that would justify the use of force and the realities and risks involved. He also worked to resolve the so-called tough issues relating to what one expert called the "standards of proof and degrees of association" needed to make a direct connection between specific terrorist atrocities and various states that aid and abet such activities.[8]

While the secretary of state rapidly became the chief public proponent in the administration of the use of force to combat terrorism, behind-the-scenes it was CIA director William Casey who was the real architect of some of the Reagan administration's most significant anti-terrorism policies. To Casey, terrorism was the greatest evil of the time and demanded a firm and unwavering response. As he told an American Bar Association conference in London on October 14, 1985: "The reality—the bottom line—is that terrorism aims at the very heart of civilization. We have no realistic choice but to meet it, and that means head on. Nothing else will work."[9] Casey was generally the strongest proponent of using military force in cabinet and National Security Council (NSC) meetings, and under his leadership the CIA initiated a rapidly expanding covert war against terrorists and their state sponsors. Acting on improved intelligence, the United States carried out a number of successful preemptive operations against terrorists, including the 1982 arrest in Rome of would-be Arab hijackers of a TWA flight bound for Tel Aviv. Most preemptions, however, never received publicity. The United States also set up a number of counterterrorist proxy groups in foreign countries skilled in preemptive and punitive actions. One such group, going well beyond its charter, planted a bomb in a Beirut suburb in March 1984 that killed more than eighty people. The target of the bombing was Hesbollah leader Mohammed Hussein Fadlallah, who had been implicated in the 1983 bombing of the U.S. Marine headquarters and dozen of other atrocities in Lebanon.

At the Pentagon, men like Noel Koch and Admiral James D. Watkins, commander of naval operations (CNO), added their voices to the growing chorus of those advocating the prudent use of force. Watkins too had been profoundly affected by the bombing of the marine headquarters; nevertheless, he wrestled for months with the issue of the morality of retaliation. However, he finally concluded that "we should work to make terrorist acts so counter-productive and costly, or seem so costly, that potential perpetrators will think twice before conducting, or threatening to conduct, terrorist acts. In this context, even a retaliatory act carried out for its deterrent effect may, under carefully controlled circumstances, be moral."[10]

The seizure of U.S. hostages in Lebanon, especially the abduction, torture, and death of CIA chief of station William Buckley, produced still more bitterness and frustration throughout the administration. The president constantly inquired after the hostages, and their release, especially Buckley's, became almost an obsession in some quarters and was one of the major preoccupations underlying the ill-fated Iran initiative. In 1984 and 1985 occurred a string of other terrorist incidents—bombings and airline hijackings, especially the seventeen-day ordeal of TWA flight 847—that made the United States appear to be a muscle-bound giant, unable to strike back at its Lilliputian tormentors. Reagan's anger seethed to the surface after four U.S. Marines were slain by terrorists in a café in San Salvador during the TWA 847 incident. "Our limits have been reached," announced the president, who vowed that the United States would consider responses "military and otherwise" to combat terrorism.[11] The following day, a visibly upset Reagan told the nation: "They say the men who murdered these sons of America disappeared into the city streets. But I pledge to you today, they will not evade justice on Earth any more than they could escape the judgement of God. We and the Salvadoran leaders will move any mountain and ford any river to find the jackals and bring them and their colleagues in terror to justice."[12]

The United States won its first significant, if incomplete, public victory in the war against terrorism in October 1985 with the bold midair interception of the Palestinian terrorists who had seized the cruise ship *Achille Lauro* and murdered a wheelchair-bound American, Leon Klinghoffer. Although it was opposed by Secretary of Defense Caspar Weinberger and his deputy, William Howard Taft IV, on both procedural grounds and because of the alleged impact the interception would have on U.S. relations with Egypt and the rest of the Arab world, President Reagan gave his blessing to the operation, which was the brainchild of Lieutenant Colonel Oliver North and Admiral John Poindexter. The Egyptair jetliner bearing the terrorists was ultimately forced down by the U.S. F-14s at Sigonella Air Base in Sicily, but the Italian government, in a cowardly and venal move, cut a secret deal with the Egyptians and the Palestine Liberation Organization (PLO) to permit the mastermind of the operation, Mohammed Abbas (Abu Abbas), to escape. Following a tense standoff by U.S. commandos and Italian carabinieri at the air base, Abbas was spirited away and put on board a chartered Yugoslavian plane.

His four companions, however, were detained by the Italian government and ultimately forced to stand trial. Magid al-Molqi, the Palestinian who confessed to the actual murder of Klinghoffer, was handed a thirty-year sentence, and two of his confederates were given prison terms of twenty-four and fifteen years. A fourth hijacker is scheduled to be tried separately as a minor. Abbas and two deputies, Ozzudin Badratkan and Ziad el-Omar, were tried in absentia and sentenced to life imprisonment, although the gesture by the court had a hollow ring considering the complicity of the Italian government in effecting Abbas's escape.

Despite the failure to apprehend Abbas and the relatively light sentences given to his confederates, the *Achille Lauro* interception was a dramatic and precedent-shattering operation that demonstrated U.S. military power could be used effectively against terrorism. Potential media and congressional criticism of the operation was stifled by the public's overwhelming approval of the administration's initiative, although a few members of Congress, including Senate Intelligence Committee chairman David Durenberger (R–Minnesota) continued to insist that the White House had violated the War Powers Act. The president's popularity soared to 68 percent, and the country was swept by a wave of pride and patriotism.

The United States Reaches the End of its Rope

In spite of the success of the *Achille Lauro* interception, even in late 1985 the administration had not yet reached a decision on the direct employment of force against state sponsors of terrorism. There had been no retaliation for the 1983 attacks in Lebanon or the death, by now confirmed, of William Buckley. Although many U.S. policymakers still shirked from the use of force, especially those in the Pentagon chastened by the Vietnam experience, a gradual consensus was developing that military force might well be the only remedy for the plague of terrorist incidents gripping the globe. Nothing else had worked. Cooperation among Western nations was as elusive as ever. Terrorists and their state sponsors, confident of Western indecisiveness and inaction, openly boasted of their atrocities and taunted their victims. Proponents of using force believed that a military strike against terrorism was the best way to give credibility to nonviolent alternatives for dealing with the problem such as political and economic sanctions. Even Defense Secretary Weinberger was showing more flexibility on the issue of striking back militarily against terrorists, going so far as to describe the TWA 847 incident as the "beginning of a war."[13] He was joined in this assessment by other senior officials who called for treating attacks on U.S. diplomats and airliners as acts of war.

The use of force was predicated on a number of preconditions being met, and by late 1985 there was reason to believe that all was ready. The successful application of force, for example, had to await the prepositioning of the necessary military forces. It required improved intelligence, an understanding of the terrorist threat by the American people, and better defensive measures in place to rebuff possible reprisals. The United States had needed time to build its case against terrorists and their state sponsors and to exhaust all peaceful remedies for addressing the problem before resorting to military force. Finally, the right incident was needed to trigger the U.S. reaction, and that occurred at the La Belle Disco in Berlin.

The decision to go forward with a strike against Libya, however, was made in the immediate aftermath of the December 27, 1985, Rome and Vienna airport attacks, the deadliest terrorist incidents of the year. Palestinian gunmen opened fire with submachine guns and grenades on holiday travelers crowded around the El Al check-in counters at Rome's Leonardo da Vinci airport and Vienna's Schwechat airport. The attacks left fourteen people dead and more than one hundred injured. One of those killed at the Rome airport was an eleven-year-old American girl, Natasha Simpson, one of five Americans who died in the coordinated attacks. President Reagan was especially outraged and saddened by the young girl's senseless murder and the pictures of her grieving parents.

The attacks were confirmed to be the work of Abu Nidal's Black June organization, perhaps in retaliation for the Israeli raid on the PLO's headquarters in Tunis in October 1985. A report by the U.S. Department of State issued in January 1986 placed some of the blame squarely on Qaddafi's doorstep. "Libya has provided sanctuary, training assistance and financial support to the Abu Nidal organization," the report contended, "and there are reliable press and other reports that its headquarters have been moved to Libya."[14] The president and his top advisers concluded that the United States had little choice but to strike back at Qaddafi, not only to prevent future attacks but to make it clear that Americans could not be murdered with impunity.

A global program against Libya was launched; it involved a number of elements, including covert efforts to destabilize the Qaddafi regime, to enlist European support in adopting comprehensive political and economic sanctions against Libya, and a commitment to challenge Libyan adventurism at every opportunity. In addition, the United States virtually suspended all economic ties with Libya and froze Libyan government assets in the United States and in U.S. bank branches overseas. In view of the potential threat that U.S. citizens working in Libya would be taken hostage in retaliation for future U.S. actions, U.S. passports were invalidated for travel to Libya and all Americans residing there ordered home. In explaining U.S. actions, President Reagan announced, "Qaddafi deserves to be treated as a pariah in the world community."[15] He also described the Libyan leader as "not only a barbarian, but he's flaky."[16]

It was evident that the United States and Libya were on a collision course. In March, U.S. naval forces sank two Libyan patrol vessels in the Gulf of Sidra and attacked onshore radar installations. A week later, a midair explosion rocked a TWA jetliner en route to Athens, killing four Americans, including an eight-month-old infant. While evidence pointed at several terrorist groups with links to Libya, no conclusive determination as to the perpetrators had been reached when the bomb went off in the Berlin disco.

Criticism of the Raid

With only a few significant exceptions, the European reaction to the U.S. raid on Libya was one of chagrin and outrage or simply silence. Although Margaret Thatcher's government had permitted the United States to launch its F-111s from bases in Great Britain, the decision was generally unpopular; polls showed that only about one in four British citizens supported the action of their government. In West Germany, where the newspapers were largely critical of the U.S. raid, public opinion was equally divided among supporters and opponents of the air strikes against Libya. Ironically only in France did the raid receive strong public support. The French government, along with that of Spain, was widely criticized in many quarters in the United States for its failure to permit its territory to be overflown by U.S. warplanes, necessitating a 2,800 mile round-about route over water. In reality, as one policymaker put it, "the French neither did so much as we would have liked, nor as little as reported."[17] In another irony, the French embassy in Tripoli was heavily damaged by an errant bomb.

The French government, which had been engaged in a protracted war with Libya in Chad for over a decade, was roundly assailed at home for its decision not to grant the United States overflight rights, whereas Thatcher's government, which had provided assistance to the raid, was roundly assailed at home for having done so.[18] Some observers believed that the fate of eight French hostages in Lebanon played an important role in the French decision, although the Thatcher government was not deterred by the same consideration. The Kohl government in West Germany tried to stay above the fray by condemning the U.S. resort to force but expressing understanding of why the Americans felt compelled to act. In Italy, Prime Minister Bettino Craxi's coalition repeated its performance in the *Achille Lauro* affair by cringing on the sidelines and distancing Italy, and its $4 billion a year trading relationship with Libya, from the U.S. decision.

There was the usual deafening roar of denunciation from many third world and Soviet-bloc nations. A resolution condemning the U.S. air strike was introduced in the United Nations Security Council, although it was vetoed by the United States, France, and Great Britain.[19] The U.S. ambassador to the United Nations, Vernon Walters, angrily rebuked critics of the raid, especially Cuban foreign minister Isidoro Malmierca, who had compared the Reagan administration's policies to those of Adolf Hitler, and Indian Foreign Minister Bali Ram Bhagat, speaking on behalf of Prime Minister Rajiv Gandhi, chairman of the Nonaligned Movement. "Alignment against the United States is not new," thundered Walters, mocking the supposed neutrality of the Nonaligned Movement. "But rarely has it been as brazen as it was in this chamber this afternoon."[20]

Public opinion polls in the United States demonstrated strong approval of the raid, although there were some dissident voices. Former CIA director Stansfield Turner wrote a critique of the raid published in the *Washington Post,* full of fears that the United States had offended its European allies and alienated the Arabs.[21]

After rejecting any notion that the raid had been effective, Turner, in a complete about-face, proceeded to suggest that if the United States was going to use force against Libya, it should mine Libya's harbors and cut off its commerce by sea, a sure formula for provoking a donnybrook with Washington's allies in Europe or, worse, an outright confrontation with the Soviet Union. Turner's former boss, president Jimmy Carter, also joined the chorus of naysayers. At an Atlanta symposium, the former president empathized with Qaddafi over reports of the purported death of an adopted daughter in the raid, despite the fact that it appeared to be a ploy by the Libyan strongman to win international sympathy. "If 17 years ago somebody had killed Amy, I would not have rested until her killer was punished," Carter was quoted as saying. "No, I don't think it [the raid] was the right thing to do. . . . I think in the long run it will be a mistake."[22] Among the other critics were the leaders of a number of Protestant denominations, including the presidents of the United Church of Christ and the Presbyterian church, the Reverend Jesse Jackson, and former Attorney General Ramsey Clark. Clark, writing in the *Nation*, called for President Reagan's impeachment:

> Reagan's raid, called a surgical strike, killed at least twice as many Libyans in one night as all Americans killed by terrorists world-wide in 1985. The President seems to be proud of what he ordered and of the "heroes" who carried it out. His one-liners are vintage Hollywood: "We didn't aim to kill anybody." He should tell that to a judge.
>
> Unless it is lawful for the President to use military bombers in a attempt to assassinate a foreign leader and to kill and mutilate scores of human beings sleeping innocently in their homes thousands of miles and many days from any claimed act of provocation, of which they probably were never aware, then Ronald Reagan must be impeached and tried for high crimes and misdemeanors.[23]

Such statements, however, were the exception rather than the rule. On the whole, there was very little criticism in the United States. In the U.S. Congress, few voices were lifted in protest, and what criticism there was was muted. The American public, according to one goverment official, wanted "to see the terrorists bashed" and would have been unhappy if they had not been.[24]

Aftermath of Operation El Dorado Canyon

In the immediate aftermath of the raid, U.S. officials braced for Libyan reprisals. However, it soon became clear that the Qaddafi regime was in disarray, if not fighting for its life, and therefore too preoccupied to launch a new wave of terrorist attacks at the United States and Great Britain. The United States also made it clear to the Libyan government that reprisals were likely to provoke another attack. A senior Reagan administration official said the continued U.S. sabre rattling in the months following the raid was designed "to warn elements of the Libyan leadership that their country will pay a price if [Qaddafi] engages in new episodes of adventurism."[25]

Despite such warnings, there were several terrorist incidents where Libyan involvement was suspected following the bombing raid. The most serious was the execution in West Beirut, one day after the raid, of two British and one U.S. hostages held by a Hesbollah splinter group controlled and financed by Qaddafi. A note found with the bodies of the slain men indicated that they had been killed in retaliation for the U.S. raid on Libya. Initially it was believed that all three men were British citizens: Leigh Douglas, a lecturer at the American University in Beirut, Philip Padfield, director of a private language school in West Beirut, and freelance journalist Alec Collett. Later it was learned that the body believed to be Collett's was in reality the remains of American Peter Kilburn, a sixty-year-old librarian at the American University.

According to Western intelligence reports, a Major Halifa, the Libyan military attaché in Damascus, received direct instructions from the Libyan intelligence headquarters in Tripoli to travel to Beirut and see to it that the three hostages were killed. Halifa made appropriate arrangements with Syrian authorities and traveled to Beirut in a two-car convoy, arriving three hours after his departure. The first car, a British-made Land Rover, was loaded with Syrian security personnel who facilitated the movement of the Libyan military attaché through Syrian-controlled territory, after which they returned to Damascus. The second car, also a Land Rover, was equipped with radio telephones, and protected by Libyan security guards, who took Major Halifa, dressed in civilian clothes, to his destination in West Beirut.

After meeting with Hesbollah leaders, it was agreed that the executions would take place that evening on a dark, narrow, deserted street in the Shiite section of West Beirut. In order to confirm the deed to his superiors, Halifa brought a camera to the execution site so that pictures could be taken of the actual murders. After the three men were killed, their bodies were dumped on a pile of garbage, and Major Halifa traveled to offices rented by the Libyans in West Beirut to make certain that local reporters were notified of the location of the bodies. The following morning, the energetic young Libyan military attaché was on his way back to Damascus, and two days later he left Syria for Libya.[26]

In the weeks that followed, one U.S. diplomat was shot in Aden, South Yemen, and another in Khartoum, the capital of the Sudan. In the first two months following the raid, the United States experienced eleven terrorist attacks that plausibly could be linked to the action against Libya. The only direct military action by Tripoli occurred when Libyan patrol craft fired two Scud missiles at the Italian island of Lampedusa, both of which missed their target.

Evaluation of the Raid from a Military Perspective

The joint U.S. Navy–Air Force military operation was aimed at the removal of Qaddafi from power and the destruction of key targets in Tripoli and Benghazi; however, the operation turned into a far more complicated mission than originally planned.

What initially was viewed by planners as a preemptive counterterrorist strike was changed by the JCS and the Pentagon into an elaborate air raid involving the massive use of U.S. military power against highly sophisticated targets in the dead of night. Although some of the navy pilots had combat experience, none of the air force crews had ever been in combat before.

From a strictly military point of view, the main difficulties stemmed from the decision to carry out the attack at night, which added an operational complication to an already complex mission. The planners had settled on a night attack because they were fearful of early detection of the F-111s by Soviet satellites and submarine patrols. This forced the F-111 and A-6 and A-7 pilots to carry out their bombing runs without "eye contact with the targets" and increased the likelihood of misses and target misidentification. The decision to attack at night was also predicated on the desire to avoid combat with the Libyan Air Force during the bombing.

The night attack also increased the demands on the electronic sweeping planes that guided the approaching warplanes to their targets since the attacking planes were forced to maintain a fixed approach, relying solely on their flight and navigation instruments and their laser guiding and infrared target identification systems. The decision to launch a night attack also forced the U.S. Air Force to expose the extraordinary capabilities of the EF-111 Ravens to the watchful eyes of the Soviet Navy.

Other problems were a direct result of the decision to use both navy warplanes from the Sixth Fleet and air force bombers based in Great Britain, involving nearly fifty planes over the target areas and another forty tankers. The planners were therefore forced to coordinate the arrival of the F-111s with the attacking aircraft catapulted from the heaving decks of the U.S. aircraft carriers in the Mediterranean. Instead of a quick in-out navy air attack, the joint navy–air force operation demanded split-second coordination, the highly complicated midair refueling of the F-111s at night, and subjected the F-111 crews to difficult levels of stress and fatigue.

A daylight attack would have deployed only the carrier-launched planes from the Sixth Fleet and reduced the built-in risk of failure, so why were the F-111s employed? Sources within the JCS admit that the decision to use a joint operation, involving both navy and air force contingents, can be attributed in large part to rivalries within the armed services. The navy could have done the job, but the air force wanted to share the glory and test some of its newly acquired weapons systems. There was also a desire to involve Great Britain in the mission so as to give the impression of Western solidarity.

In addition, Admiral William Crowe, chairman of the JCS, had demanded more firepower and flexibility over the battle zone. Crowe's concerns were based on the fear that the situation might escalate into a major confrontation that could exceed the Sixth Fleet's military capabilities. Crowe and his advisers reasoned that a scenario could develop where navy interceptors would be so busy defending the fleet and the returning A-6s and A-7s that the Sixth Fleet would have insufficient air power to launch a second bombing attack aimed at neutralizing the Libyan Air Force. Moreover, he warned that the initial wave of attackers might lose planes, compelling the fleet to engage in major rescue operations to save survivors. The addition of a third carrier, the use of the F-111s, or the introduction of different armaments on the navy planes would provide the cushion needed, Crowe maintained. Even given such considerations, the deployment of the F-111s is still difficult to defend.

Despite public pronouncements by the Defense Department and other administration officials expressing satisfaction with the accuracy and results of the bombing operation, others were not so favorably impressed. After studying satellite photos, a senior intelligence official admitted that the "final results were rather poor."[27] Few planes, it turned out, hit their precise targets. The air force planes missed the Libyan intelligence headquarters, which serves as the actual command and control center for Libyan-backed terrorist operations.

Another close miss was the Azzizia Barracks, where Qaddafi lived and worked. The air force was instructed to assign "enough planes to the Azizzia barracks" to turn the facility "into dust," but the attempt failed. Although some bombs did hit the barracks, most did not, and Qaddafi escaped serious injury because he was in a fortified bunker underneath the barracks built by the West Germans. Apparently the barracks had been targeted by six F-111s. Three of the planes dropped their bomb loads on what they believed to be the barracks, causing the damage that was reported. Two other planes suffered from malfunctions and could not identify the target and, consequently, jettisoned their bombs over water. The sixth plane missed the target altogether.

During the many hours of meetings and planning sessions preceding the raid, the question of whether Qaddafi himself was a target came up repeatedly. In his study of the raid, Seymour M. Hersh maintains that "the assassination of Qaddafi was the primary goal of the Libyan bombing."[28] Those present in the actual planning of the raid, however, contend that the United States was not trying to kill Qaddafi. But it was also noted that if Qaddafi were killed by a bomb, no one would shed any tears for him. "We did not try to kill Qaddafi," former NSC aide Oliver North recalled. "There was no Executive Order to kill him, nor was there an Administrative Directive to go after him. If he was killed in the process, 'c'est la vie,' but there was no deliberate intention to kill him."[29] The NSC, in an internal document prepared during the many planning sessions and discussions prior to the raid, describes the rationale for targeting the Azzizia Barracks. "The facility contains command and communications centers for use in conducting terrorist attacks and other subversive activities," states the document. "The compound is heavily guarded by elite Jamahiriyah troops, Qaddafi's personal guard. The target was selected in an effort to disrupt Qaddafi's ability to stage additional terrorist attacks and to vividly demonstrate Qaddafi's limited capacity for response to his adversaries, who oppose his terrorist and subversive activities."[30]

As a counterterrorist preemptive strike, the mission must be judged, to some extent, a failure because neither Qaddafi nor his regime was eliminated. Despite exact intelligence and the highly sophisticated weapons used in the attack, the F-111s sent against the Azizzia Barracks either failed to drop their bombs or for the most part missed the target. And while there has been some diminishment of Libyan-sponsored terrorism following the raid, it probably is a result more of internal problems than any formal decision by Libya's leadership to renounce their support of terrorism as an instrument of national policy. Even in the light of these facts, however, as Blundy and Lycett conclude,

> There is no doubt that the raid had some military success. Soviet-built Ilyushin transport jets were wrecked at Tripoli military airport, a severe blow to Qaddafi's ability to move troops and equipment. Benghazi airport, which like Tripoli is both civilian and military, was severely damaged and a new Sam 5 missile site destroyed. The Jamahiriya military barracks in Benghazi received direct hits and so did a naval training academy, a frogmen's training school and a camp for training Palestinian guerrillas, just west of Tripoli.[31]

Nevertheless, as a political counterterrorist operation, the raid was highly successful. While the Reagan administration found that it was "easier to condemn Carthage than destroy it," the United States turned the tables on Libya's erratic strongman; the hunter became the hunted. The raid shook the Qaddafi regime to its very foundations, and although the Libyan strongman survived, he immediately went into hiding in the Libyan desert. Apparently in the confusion that followed the raid, Qaddafi was wounded, but few details are known about the attack. Whether he was wounded by a disenchanted Libyan Army officer, a hired assassin, or a crazed bodyguard is still unknown, but apparently Qaddafi became so paranoid that he subsequently moved his military capital to Sabhah, some 420 miles into the desert on the edge of the Sahara.

Two days after the attack, on April 17, fighting was reported at two Libyan military camps, and the situation became so bad that the Libyan Air Force was called in to strafe rebellious army units. In spite of the best hopes of Casey, Oliver North, and the other administration planners, the mutiny within the Libyan Army was brutally suppressed, with a high loss of life. Although none of the military uprisings was successful, it was clear that Qaddafi's grip on the Libyan military and intelligence establishments had been weakened.

In retrospect, it was perhaps remarkable that Qaddafi survived at all. As Blundy and Lycett have observed, "Qaddafi had received a blow which few Western leaders could have survived. He had been caught pathetically unprepared; his defences had failed abysmally. His armed forces had performed badly in a crisis. There was little to show for the billions of dollars he had spent on his armoury. A canyon emerged between Qaddafi's rhetoric and reality."[32] Not only did the raid make clear to Qaddafi the unmistakable fragility of his regime but Libya's almost complete isolation. The Soviet Union did not raise a hand to assist its ostensible ally and in fact moved its warships out of Tripoli harbor in advance of the attack so they would not accidentally be hit. Neither Syria nor Iran came to Libya's defense, and the halfhearted clamor of disapproval from the Arab League quickly dissipated. Most important, the United States had proved its readiness and ability to strike, far from its own borders, at the state sponsors of terrorism, a message that surely did not go unrecognized in Tehran and Damascus, not to mention Tripoli. The U.S. raid was also aimed at Washington's timorous European allies as a clear demonstration that the United States was prepared to go it alone, if necessary, to protect its citizens and national interests. It was an unmistakable warning to the Europeans that the United States would consider additional military operations, wherever and against whomever it deemed appropriate, unless they began to cooperate more fully on measures for combating terrorism short of the use of force.

The Europeans Get the Message

Within days of the raid, the foreign ministers of the European Community (EC), meeting in Luxembourg, agreed to a number of cooperative measures designed to undermine Libya's ability to carry out terrorist operations. In addition to an agreement to expand the exchange of intelligence information with the United States and other friendly nations, the twelve EC states pledged:

1. To reduce significantly the size of Libya's diplomatic missions in Europe and review the size of their own missions in Tripoli.

2. To reduce the freedom of movement of Libyan diplomats by requiring them to obtain special permission to travel outside the cities to which they were accredited.

3. To limit the number of other Libyans residing in EC countries. This provision was targeted chiefly at Libyan students, airline employees, and trade mission representatives. Western intelligence organizations suspected that Qaddafi was utilizing the country's national airline, and a European hotel chain and bank owned by the Libyan government, as part of the infrastructure of terrorism.

4. To prohibit Libyans expelled from one country from being admitted to any other EC nation.

5. To seek additional ways of preventing Libyan abuses of diplomatic immunity.

In the weeks that followed, the EC countries carried out a wave of arrests and deportations of suspected terrorists. A former Libyan diplomat was arrested in Italy for allegedly plotting to kill the U.S., Saudi Arabian, and Egyptian ambassadors, and some twenty-four other Libyans were expelled from the country over the next four weeks. Great Britain deported another twenty-one Libyans, mostly students, for suspected involvement in "revolutionary activities" in late April and banned between 200 and 300 Libyan students from aviation-related training courses. Even

Greece, which under the Papandreou government had turned a blind eye to Middle East terrorist operations on its territory, expelled a number of Libyans believed to have been involved in recruiting other Arabs for terrorist activities.

At the May 5 economic summit meeting in Tokyo, the leaders of the seven largest industrial democracies condemned terrorism and vowed to fight it "relentlessly and without compromise" by means of "determined, tenacious, discreet and patient action combining national measures with international cooperation." Although there was no specific statement of approval of the U.S. air raid three weeks earlier, Libya was singled out for condemnation as a source of state-sponsored terrorism. Meeting with the press, Secretary of State Shultz spelled out the meaning of the joint declaration as it related to Muammar Qaddafi: "The message is: you've had it, pal. You are isolated. You are recognized as a terrorist."[33]

Against a backdrop of other expulsions and arrests of suspected terrorists throughout Europe, on June 24 the United States and Italy signed a bilateral anti-terrorist agreement to improve intelligence cooperation. In late September, EC interior ministers, the Trevi group, adopted still further measures to improve their anti-terrorist cooperation, especially regarding communication between law enforcement agencies and the pooling of information about the identities, operations, and venues of known terrorists.

In short, something remarkable occurred in Europe in the wake of the U.S. bombing raid: the once-circumspect and cautious Europeans were galvanized into taking unilateral as well as concrete cooperative steps against terrorism in general and Libya in particular. Rationalizations and whitewashing aside, there is no explanation for the "born-again" anti-terrorism of the Europeans other than the U.S. raid on Libya and the fear that Washington would take additional unilateral military steps against terrorists and terrorism-sponsoring states unless effective cooperative measures short of using force could be found.

The Use of Force against Terrorism

While U.S. policymakers conceded that the air strike would not stop Libyan terrorism unless Qaddafi was removed from power, they nevertheless believed that it was time to strike back, as both a catharsis and a signal of U.S. resolve and determination to hold accountable nations that sponsor terrorism around the world. Gone in an instant was the U.S. policy of equivocation and vacillation, the shortsighted European-like weakness of the Carter years. The raid on Libya, moreover, signaled a new maturity in U.S. thinking on the subject of terrorism. Rejected was the notion that terrorism could be defeated with good intentions. Reagan administration officials realized that without some kind of potential sanction, such as the use of military force, peaceful and cooperative measures for combating terrorism would lack teeth. More than anything else, the Libyan raid stimulated an effort on the part of U.S. allies to find answers to the problem of terrorism short of the use of military force. It also jolted the purveyors of terrorism out of their insouciant disregard for the consequences of their actions; no longer could they be certain that the United States would not strike back with vengeance in the wake of a terrorist attack.

The Reagan administration had shown remarkable restraint in combating terrorism prior to the Libyan raid and chose to act only when the moral and legal issues surrounding retaliation could be satisfactorily addressed. Indeed in connection with the Libyan raid, it may well be that the United States had more latitude morally than legally to do what it did. Over the years the United States has been characterized by its belief in a moral order and its discomfort in using force to achieve its international goals. Nevertheless, since the earliest days of the Reagan administration, there was recognition that international terrorism represents the ultimate abuse of human rights. Thus the answer to the question often posed by ethicists as to whether more good than evil will arise from a particular set of actions (even taking into account unintended consequences) was clear: a real case could be made for the fact that the Libyan raid was preemptive and therefore served to prevent future outrages and, hence, to save innocent lives.

Among the notions discredited by the Libyan raid was that U.S. retaliation against the state sponsors of terrorism and their proxies would endanger U.S. citizens even more by setting off a cycle of attack and counterattack from which no one would emerge the winner. The fact remains that there is overwhelming evidence that military retaliation will deter terrorism. Terrorists respect very little, but it is clear that they respect superior force. For a nation beset by enemies, Israel is victimized by precious little terrorism, not only because of the skill demonstrated by the Israelis in preempting terrorist attacks but because of the ruthlessness they exhibit in conducting reprisals against those responsible. Although there was a smattering of violence linked to Libya in the aftermath of the U.S. air raid, the fact remains that Libya has been remarkably quiescent on the terrorism front since April 1986.

Military force is certainly not the answer to every terrorist challenge. It represents one of the most useful options that policymakers must have to choose from. It gives credibility and currency to all other potential options, and the prudent and systematic use of military force on an intermittent basis keeps terrorists and their state sponsors off balance and forced to devote far more attention and resources to their own protection instead of to the conduct of terrorist operations. Just as unpredictability is critical to the survival of a threatened individual targeted by terrorists, so too is unpredictability a useful characteristic for nation-states to exhibit on occasion.

This is not to say that there are no risks in retaliating against terrorists and their state patrons. Air crews and special operations forces may suffer casualties or be captured during retaliatory operations. Innocent civilians may be killed or wounded. The use of military force, no matter how justified, can be a source of contention between allies and adversaries alike. Finally, there is always the risk of failure. Short, decisive, and ultimately successful military actions are all the United States has patience for. Anything else too rapidly becomes a media donnybrook and the subject of frenzied political debate, especially if the operation is anything less than an unqualified success. Military operations are inherently hazardous and require not only expert skills and careful planning but a good measure of luck. In recent years, all too often military failures have been treated as the product of misconduct or stupidity and scrutinized by commissions, panels, and boards in an exercise—similar to that in the Soviet Union—more designed to affix blame than fix the problem. This, in turn, has imbued the Pentagon with a pervasive sense of caution and placed a premium on inaction rather than action.

Today most of the gains scored in the Libya raid have been wiped out by the Iran–Contra debacle. The Reagan administration, which had for so long railed against the capitulation of other nations to terrorist demands, was suddenly and dramatically shown to have been conducting behind-the-scenes diplomacy with one of the chief terrorism-sponsoring nations and even trading arms for hostages. Gone was the moral high ground on which the United States had staked out its anti-terrorist position. If that were not enough, Washington was once again gripped by an orgy of vituperation and allegation as congressional committees competed for headlines and television time in the name of ferreting out wrongdoing. The administration's anti-terrorism decision-making procedures and actual operations were laid bare, providing a treasure trove of information to hostile intelligence services. Many of those responsible for the strides that had been made in improving U.S. anti-terrorism capabilities or had been key advocates of proactive anti-terrorist operations were held up to public ridicule and even threatened with criminal prosecution.

It can be anticipated that there will be a return to the days when U.S. anti-terrorism efforts were hobbled by bureaucratic infighting, institutional caution, and little clear sense of the threat or what to do about it. Congress and the media, not to mention the public, remain largely ignorant as to the often dark and frequently unsavory realities of this kind of conflict, and the recent joint hearings by the Senate and House select committees investigating the Iran–Contra scandals have probably served less to educate than to make the situation more confusing. Promising new initiatives such as the extraterritorial apprehension of terrorists and the expanded use of proxy forces are no doubt dormant for the time being, and covert operations against international terrorists and their state sponsors are being scaled back rather than expanded. Indeed, shortly after he succeeded Admiral John Poindexter as the president's national security adviser, Frank Carlucci announced that the administration was shutting down at least one-third of ongoing covert operations.

Nowhere is the problem more acute than at the Pentagon, where the JCS and the civilian bureaucracy have combined to undermine the special operations reforms mandated by Congress, which are critical to the creation of effective U.S. anti-terrorism capabilities. A 1986 Pentagon study concluded that the U.S. military establishment is structured to fight either a nuclear war or a conventional war in

Europe but is ill prepared to deal with a world in which there is neither war nor peace. According to the report, "Our current defense posture reflects our inability to understand the form and substance of this direct challenge [terrorism] to our interests." It goes on to say that "our lack of understanding is manifested in a lack of unity of effort; lack of doctrine, training, organizations, and materiel to execute operations; and lack of a sustaining support system. Short of war, we have no strategy or comprehensive plan to address the challenges of political violence."[34]

If U.S. anti-terrorism policy is a vacuum, it also represents an opportunity. It is an issue, for example, that over the years had been co-opted to a large extent by the Republicans, and for the most part the Democrats ignored the problem or found that effective measures for addressing it invariably collided with the antidefense posture and outdated global perspective embraced by many in the party. The Iran–Contra hearings presented congressional Democrats with an opportunity to capture some sense of momentum in the eyes of the public with respect to the shape and form of the nation's anti-terrorist policy. But without exception, the Democratic members of the panel were more interested in uncovering the alleged sins of the Reagan administration than offering any new thoughts and initiatives of their own. Nevertheless, the 1988 presidential contest represents yet another chance for the Democratic candidates to breath new life into what is now, but unlikely to remain, a moribund topic.

The raid on Libya represented the high-water mark of the Reagan administration's war against terrorism. It was demonstrated that there is profit in retaliation and that it is sweet. For a while it seemed that the nation's enemies were in retreat and its allies capable of acting in concert. The gains of the past five years, however, have been wiped out by ill-conceived and clumsily executed initiatives on the part of the White House and the irresistible urge of Congress to play inquisitor rather than physician to a troubled policy. The challenge to U.S. national security posed by the sponsors and perpetrators of international terrorism will not disappear, and by almost every indicator the threat can be expected to grow. If recent events contain any lessons, it is that there is an urgent need for bipartisan agreement and frequent consultation between Congress and the executive on a firm and resolute anti-terrorism policy for the United States that picks up where the Libyan raid left off.

Notes

1. Winston Churchill, note to the First Sea Lord, October 15, 1942.
2. President Ronald Reagan, statement quoted in *New York Times*, April 16, 1987.
3. U.S. policymaker to the author, 1986.
4. "Transcript of Address by Reagan on Libya," *New York Times*, April 15, 1986, p. 7.
5. John Leo, on Africa, in *Purchas His Pilgrimes* (1625).
6. Robert C. McFarlane, "Deterring Terrorism," *Journal of Defense and Diplomacy* (June 1985).

7. George Shultz (speech to the Washington Plenary Meeting of the Trilateral Commission, April 3, 1984).

8. Former U.S. government official to the author, 1986.

9. William Casey (speech to the American Bar Association, London, October 14, 1985).

10. James D. Watkins, "Concern Not for Self, But for Others."

11. President Ronald Reagan quoted in "U.S. Has Reached 'Limits' on Terrorism, Reagan Says," *Washington Post*, June 21, 1985.

12. Ronald Reagan, "Statement in Honor of the Four U.S. Marines Killed in El Salvador," June 22, 1985.

13. "Weinberger Calls It 'Beginning of a War,' " *Washington Times*, June 25, 1985.

14. U.S. Department of State, "Libyan Sanctions," January 8, 1986.

15. Ronald Reagan, press conference, January 7, 1987.

16. Ibid.

17. U.S. policymaker to the author, 1986.

18. See "Raid Revives British Resentment of U.S. Muscle," *International Herald Tribune*, April 28, 1986.

19. The resolution was also opposed by Australia and Denmark, and Venezuela abstained from voting. The resolution, which made no mention of Libya's support of terrorism, was supported in the Security Council by Bulgaria, China, Congo, Ghana, Madagascar, Thailand, Trinidad and Tobago, the Soviet Union, and the United Arab Emirates.

20. "U.S. Rebukes 'Brazen' Foes of Libya Raid," *Washington Post*, April 25, 1986.

21. See "Second Thoughts about Libya," *Washington Post*, May 11, 1986.

22. "Carter Empathizes with Qaddafi 'Loss,' " *Washington Times*, April 18, 1986.

23. Ramsey Clark, quoted in *American Spectator* (September 1986).

24. U.S. policymaker to the author, 1986.

25. "U.S. Warns of New Bombing If Libya Resumes Terrorism," *Washington Post*, August 26, 1986.

26. I am indebted to David Halevy of *Time* magazine for his insights into the murders in West Beirut.

27. Senior intelligence official interviewed by David Halevy, 1986.

28. Seymour M. Hersh, "Target Qaddafi," *New York Times Magazine*, February 22, 1987.

29. Lieutenant Colonel Oliver North interviewed by David Halevy, 1986.

30. Internal National Security Council document.

31. David Blundy and Andrew Lycett, *Qaddafi and the Libyan Revolution* (Boston: Little, Brown, 1987), p. 11.

32. Ibid., p. 14.

33. George Shultz, quoted in "7 Summit Leaders Condemn Terror, Citing Libyan Role," *New York Times*, May 6, 1986.

34. Pentagon report quoted by the Associated Press, "Pentagon to Address the Challenges of Political Violence," September 28, 1986.

6

Special Operations Reform in the Reagan Administration

Ross S. Kelly

The U.S. military's special operations forces—Green Berets, SEALs, Rangers, and others—after over a decade of postVietnam orphan status have been making a comeback. The Reagan administration has found their utility in a muscular foreign policy attractive, as did the special operations forces' (SOF) original patron, John F. Kennedy, in the early 1960s, and for much the same reason: to thwart Soviet expansion and destabilization activities targeted against the third world. At the same time, there has been increased emphasis in two other special operations–related areas, counterterrorism and increased human intelligence collection capabilities. Secretary of Defense Caspar Weinberger stated in the fiscal year 1985 (FY 85) Annual Report to Congress: "Recognizing that the value of these forces transcends the limited investment in resources they represent, we have given high priority to revitalizing Special Operations Forces."

This revitalization has been well (some would say overly) publicized, with the attendant consequences: the degree to which force development reality has kept pace with the administration's rhetoric has become the subject of considerable debate within the U.S. special operations community and in Congress. Given the powerful constituencies within the individual service staffs and on Capitol Hill for more conventional force structures, missions, and weapons programs, it is unsurprising that serious questions remain concerning the services' commitment to increasing SOF capabilities. It was the questioning of that commitment, in fact, that led congressional SOF supporters in 1986 to create a unified special operations command and a new assistant secretary of defense for special operations and low-intensity conflict position (still unfilled a year later). However, it is also true that substantial progress has been made over the past four years in SOF arming, manning, training, deployment, and sustainment.

Why Maintain Special Operations Forces?

Before addressing that progress and the many remaining challenges, it may be useful to review what special operations are and why dedicated forces are maintained to perform them. There is, of course, some diversity of viewpoint. Some analysts exclude counterterrorist operations on friendly ground (whether ours or an ally's) by considering them police operations. Others exclude counterinsurgencies or assistance to friendly resistance movements, which limits their definition of special operations to nothing more than grand raids. Such exclusions are far too restrictive and in any case do not reflect most national policies, in particular that of the United States. The Department of Defense defines special operations as military operations conducted by specially trained, equipped, and organized forces against strategic or tactical targets in pursuit of national political, military, economic, or psychological objectives. They may support conventional military operations, or they may be prosecuted independently when the use of conventional forces is either inappropriate or infeasible. They include guerrilla and counterguerrilla operations, counterterrorism, intelligence collection, psychological operations, and foreign internal defense training, as well as raid and sabotage operations. They may be conducted during hostilities or in peacetime.

Various types of special operations can be and have been carried out by elite troops not specifically designated as SOF. The Israeli rescue operations at Entebbe, for example, involved not only the General Reconnaissance Unit but paratroops and members of the Golani Brigade as well. The *Mayaguez* operation was carried out by marine forces available in the South China Sea. Why then does the United States, or any other nation, organize and maintain dedicated SOF?

Special operations in the generic sense address a spectrum of challenges, many of which occur in peacetime, that may not be appropriate for the regular armed establishment. Threatened and stung by terrorism, the United States, like other nations, has felt the need to develop capabilities specifically targeted against that threat. Nations with complex overseas commitments and interests, such as the United States, the Soviet Union, and to a lesser degree Great Britain and France, have seen special operations in the guerrilla-counterguerrilla, mobile training team, and strategic reconnaissance roles as offering minimum-exposure options in a variety of politically sensitive situations. Certainly special operations may support conventional military operations. In such cases they provide a means of circumventing enemy strengths to attack its weaknesses, stimulate resistance and choas in rear areas, and acquire otherwise unobtainable intelligence. But they are also available for circumstances requiring military skills in peacetime, such as counterterrorism, when declarations of war, or the possible exacerbation of a crisis through introduction of conventional forces, are undesirable.

SOF are therefore established and maintained by nations that recognize the requirement to be able to implement whatever range of special operations–related policy options may be applicable on an other than ad hoc basis. A paratroop or marine company may be able to conduct or participate in a raid, but a surgical rescue operation or counterguerrilla deep reconnaissance campaign may require other skills and, more important, a different planning and execution mind-set. The usual thrust of conventional force training is the achievement of consistent performance of routine tasks to the highest attainable average standard; the emphasis in SOF is on direct-ing individual skills to the accomplishment of functions unique to a given mis-sion. Improvisation and independent thinking are essential. Special operations are not based on sets of exotic operational principles that differ substantially from those of normal combat operations. However, the politico-military frames of reference, the national versus tactical orientations of their reasons for being, and the neces-sity for psychological self-sufficiency on the part of SOF planners and leaders, as well as the mission goals and constraints associated with special operations (par-ticularly in peacetime), require significantly different priorities in the application of common operational principles.

It is to have the capability to conduct special operations on demand, without extensive additional training and orientation, with personnel psychologically at-tuned to a broad spectrum of unconventional requirements, that the United States has developed and maintained its SOFs.

Revitalization and Reorganization

The impetus for the first major event in SOF reorganization, consolidation, and revitalization was conceived in the blood and flames of the failed Iranian hostage rescue attempt and given birth in the Holloway commission report detailing the contributing causes for this disaster at Desert One. Principal among the several recommendations was an institutionalized command and control structure for joint contingency opera-tions and dedicated forces from the several services. The Carter administration re-sponded, setting in motion the organization of the Joint Special Operations Command (JSOC), which would serve as a command and control headquarters for sensitive overseas contingency operations, and an administrative headquarters for such dedicated counterterror and contingency strike force as might be assigned. The word-ing is important, for in the birth of the first manifestation of SOF consolidation, there remained the element that somewhat emasculated succeeding organizational efforts and led ultimately to a congressionally mandated command structure. In effect, the services could vote on whether they would assign forces to JSOC. Thus, in its first few years, JSOC grew into a large headquarters that did contingency planning and coordinated joint exercises but actually commanded very little.

Still, it was a start, and with the Reagan administration came policy planners, both civilian and military, prepared to go much further. Noel Koch, the principal deputy assistant secretary of defense for international security affairs, was also direc-tor of the Office of Special Planning. He was given cognizance over SOF revitaliza-tion, which he approached single-mindedly and energetically, so much so that he was ultimately considered overzealous, and allowed to step down. Before that hap-pened, however, he was able to make considerable progress on a number of SOF reorganization and revitalization initiatives despite less-than-enthusiastic coopera-tion from the services and the Joint Chiefs of Staff (JCS). Among them were:

Requiring the services to provide time-phased master plans in which agreed-upon SOF upgrades to meet validated theater mission requirements would receive specified budgetary, manning, and procurement support.

Creating a Joint Special Operations Agency, headed by a general officer, out of the old JCS Special Operations Division, which had been headed by an army colonel.

Creating special operations commands out of theater unconventional warfare planning cells to upgrade and institutionalize theater commanders' involvement in SOF deployment planning and command and control.

Increasing the numbers of army special forces and Ranger battalions and navy SEAL platoons and special boats.

Apparent progress notwithstanding, however, intraservice and interservice squabbling over SOF asset ownership, service insistence on budgetary autonomy and prioritization authority, and in particular air force mismanagement and lack of support of SOF airlift enhancement programs led Koch to become increasingly critical of the services and insistent on action at the deputy secretary of defense level. When the deputy was Paul Thayer, Koch had a receptive audience; but by mid-1985, William Taft, and his new assistant secretary of defense for international security affairs, Richard Armitage, were disinclined to press the services with the same confrontational enthusiasm that Koch was, and Thayer had been.

With Koch's departure, pressure on the services from the Office of the Secretary of Defense (OSD) for adherence to master plan goals lessened. However, it increased tremendously from Congress. Dan Daniel, (D–Virginia), chairman of the Readiness Subcommittee of the House Armed Services Committee, had established a Special Operations Panel under Earl Hutto (D–Florida). They found allies in two senators, Sam Nunn (D–Georgia) and William Cohen (R–Maine), already determined to end the harmful effects of interservice rivalry through legislation designed to give greater power to the chairman of the JCS and the theater commanders. Together they manifested deep skepticism that the services, the Joint Staff, or OSD would provide the necessary push for seeing the master plan enhancements through or ensuring—and protecting—consolidated SOF funding, training, career development, doctrine, and operational employment. Accordingly, over OSD and JCS objections, in late 1986 they drafted and succeeded in carrying legislation through Congress mandating an all-service special operations command, an assistant secretary of defense for special operations and low-intensity conflict, and a Low-Intensity Conflict Board at the National Security Council (NSC).

A number of issues have not been resolved, new questions have been raised, and Congress is unhappy with how the Department of Defense (DOD) has implemented the legislation. Those aspects, as well as the fundamental problems, will be detailed; at this point, however, it is appropriate to look at the net impact on SOF organization and force structure of the OSD, service, and congressional actions taken thus far, their missions and capabilities, and how the administration has—or could—put them to use.

Forces, Missions, and Capabilities

Special Operations Organizations

The services, the unified and specified (U&S) commands worldwide, and the JCS have on their own or under congressional mandate made much progress in centralizing SOF command and control, unit training management, doctrinal development, and operational planning. The army took the lead in 1982 in developing its First Special Operations Command out of a previous special operations parent organization, the JFK Center for Military Assistance. (All of the individual special forces, psychological operations, civil affairs, international studies, and military assistance training courses and schools have been split out to a resuscitated JFK Special Warfare Center.)

The air force followed suit in creating the Second Air Division at Hurlburt Field, Florida, long the home of air force special operations units and training. The navy for some time was the sole service exception. With two major special operations units assigned to the Atlantic and Pacific fleets, the navy had no centralized parent SOF organization but rather managed training and doctrinal issues from a dedicated section of the navy staff in the Pentagon, through the major subordinate commands, to the units. Recently, with the creation of the new U.S. Special Operations Command (USSOC), the navy created the Special Warfare Center to centralize doctrine and training and a small Special Warfare Command to interface with USSOC on navy SOF deployment. Finally, the SOF units on both coasts were, in mid-1987, placed under USSOC command.

Most of the U&S commands have had staff elements responsible for special operations planning for some time. They have now been reorganized as cadre special operations commands. This peacetime planning entity can be augmented with active and reserve personnel during a crisis or in wartime to provide effective theater command-and-control organs for such SOF units. The services maintain rosters of individual ready reserve officers and noncommissioned officers who are assigned as individual mobilization augmentees.

At the JCS level, the Joint Special Operations Agency (JSOA) was activated on January 1, 1984. JSOA was intended to provide JCS cognizance over, and advise the chairman of the JCS in, all special operations and related activities, including strategic planning, resource programming and allocation, joint doctrine, exercise and readiness evaluation, employment of forces, and interoperability with allied special operations and doctrines. JSOA was to also serve as DOD's focal point for interagency counterterrorism planning and provide JCS supervision over multiservice counterterror forces.

The personnel to pay for JSOA and what few additions accrued to the U&S Commands came from the old Joint Special Operations Support Element (JSOSE), based at MacDill Air Force Base, Florida. JSOSE served as a mobile, ready augmentation package for theater commanders requiring speedy establishment of a working joint special operations command-and-control function. However, although there was only one JSOSE, each U&S Command previously factored it into command contingency planning. The disbanding of JSOSE at the end of FY 84 removed this unrealistic crutch and forced the U&S Commands to orient on in-place or dedicated mobilization assets. However, JSOA's limited success in fulfilling its charter as its creators (and congressional supporters) had hoped provided much of the rationale for Congress's rejection of JCS assurances that it would take care of SOF on its own, and passage of the legislation creating USSOC.

The new USSOC, activated in April 1987, is located at MacDill AFB, Florida. Spaces to pay for its creation came from terminating the U.S. Readiness Command, also located at MacDill. It has assigned to it, or will, the army's First SOCOM and the JFK Special Warfare Center at Fort Bragg, North Carolina; the air force's 23rd Air Force, and the special operations training establishment at Hurlburt Field, Florida; the navy's new special warfare center and Special Warfare Command; and the JSOC. Its mandate replicates JSOA's original charter and in addition includes actual SOF command and control in peacetime; selected contingency command and control; joint training and doctrine authority; and, possibly most important, budgetary authority.

Army Special Operations Forces

The U.S. Army's SOFs consist of Special Forces (Green Berets), Psychological Operations (PSYOPS), Ranger, and Civil Affairs (CA) units. Those in the continental United States are grouped into the First Special Operations Command (SOCOM), headquartered at Fort Bragg, North Carolina. There are nine major units deployed throughout the United States.

- Fifth Special Forces Group—Fort Bragg, North Carolina and Fort Campbell, Kentucky
- Seventh Special Forces Group—Fort Bragg, North Carolina; one battalion in Panama under operational command of Southern Command
- Tenth Special Forces Group—Fort Devens, Massachusetts; one battalion in Germany under operational command of European Command
- First Special Forces Group—Fort Lewis, Washington; one battalion in Okinawa under operational command of Pacific Command
- Fourth Psychological Operations Group—Fort Bragg, North Carolina
- Ninety–sixth Civil Affairs Battalion—Fort Bragg, North Carolina
- First Battalion, Seventy–fifth Rangers—Fort Lewis, Washington

- Second Battalion, Seventy–fifth Rangers—Fort Stewart, Georgia
- Third Battalion, Seventy–fifth Rangers and Headquarters Seventy–fifth Ranger Regiment—Fort Benning, Georgia

There are additionally a Special Forces detachment in Korea, several other small Special Forces elements in Europe, and a dedicated special operations helicopter unit at Fort Campbell, Kentucky.

The army also has four reserve components special forces groups. Two are army reserve groups and the other two national guard units. The reserve components are also where the preponderance of the army's PSYOPS and CA units are located. Two PSYOPS groups, a CA brigade, and a host of independent battalions and companies back up the more limited active-duty capabilities.

The reactivation of the First Special Forces Group (it was the last of the post-Vietnam Special Forces cuts) was the first major step in Army SOF revitalization. The Third Ranger battalion, and the Ranger regimental headquarters were also activated.

Yet another Special Forces Group, the Third, is on the books for activation in a year or two, and First Special Operations Command has developed a mobile signals element to give the command a field operations support capability.

This seemingly bright picture is somewhat clouded by the realities of manning the new units. The manpower to accomplish these increases in SOF is not coming from any dramatic increase in army active-duty end strength but rather from forces command through the personnel savings realized in converting several active army divisions to light divisions, the likelihood is that neither the new SOF units nor the light divisions will actually attain their authorized manning levels. Other "savings" have also been realized through Signal Corps slots eliminated by adoption of Mobile Subscriber Equipment (MSE). So, while the army has made progress in fleshing out the new First Special Forces Group and the Third Ranger Battalion, increased authorizations for SOF force structures have not always been matched by commensurate increases in actual personnel assignment allocations. The army's adherence to its current manpower ceiling may be politically popular, but it renders fixures of "X" number of Special Forces teams illusory. In one extreme case, a unit actually expanded its "paper strength" in numbers of teams while projecting a *decline* in anticipated personnel loss versus gain ratio. This problem is, of course, beyond the scope of the small section on the army staff (which itself has grown) attempting to keep faith with its service's commitments; and throughout most of the army's SOF establishment, measurable staffing upgrades are taking place.

Navy Special Operations Forces

The navy's SOFs are formed principally into two multifunctional naval special warfare groups (NSWGs) under the commanders of the Atlantic and Pacific fleets. NSWG 1 is located in Coronado, California; NSWG 2 operates out of Little Creek,

Virginia. Each group consists of SEAL (Sea-Air-Land) teams and special boat squadrons. NSWG 1 has three SEAL teams, the first, second, and fifth; NSWG 2 has two that it "owns," the second and fourth, plus administrative control over SEAL Team 6, the Navy's national contingency operations element. Additionally, naval special warfare units (NSWUs) with SEAL and special boat detachments are located in Scotland, Puerto Rico, and the Philippines.

Reserve SEAL and special boat squadrons make up a portion of an active NSWG's total strength, much as a round-out national guard brigade does for several active army divisions. There are, of course, advantages to the round-out concept. Since most of the SEAL reservists tend to be clustered near an active group's location, they are able to train with their active counterparts on a reasonably regular basis. However, the extremely low active-to-reserve SEAL turnover (due in part to high retention on the active side), the navy's only means of manning its reserve SEAL units, has left many unfilled slots in reserve SEAL ranks, particularly the enlisted billets. Accordingly, DOD has included an increase of active SEAL platoons (the sixteen-man basic SEAL element) in the SOF revitalization program. In four more years, there should be seventy SEAL platoons, up from the current forty-one. Three years ago, there were fewer than twenty platoons; the "increase" came about as a result of merging the old underwater demolitions teams (UDTs) with the SEALs. Moreover, the navy is bringing a new family of multimission patrol boats into the inventory and meeting its deliveries of SEAFOX surface SEAL delivery craft and submersible SEAL delivery vehicle.

In support of SEAL operations, though not directly subordinated to the NSWGs, are one reserve light helicopter attack squadron on each coast. These squadrons train often with SEAL elements and are skilled in off-carrier and night flight operations.

Air Force Special Operations Forces

The air force created a new unit, the Twenty–third Air Force, to serve as an umbrella command for its special operations elements worldwide. These consist of six MC-130 Combat Talon aircraft, ten AC-130 Spectre gunships, nine HH-53 Pave Low, and several HH-60 Blackhawk helicopters grouped into the First Special Operations Wing at Hurlburt Field, Florida; four MC-130s each in special operations squadrons (along with other aircraft) in Germany and the Philippines; and four helicopters in Panama. All of these are active units.

The air force reserve has another ten Spectre gunships, and the Pennsylvania Air National Guard has four EC-130 aircraft utilized for aerial PSYOPS missions. Also assigned to the special operations aircraft organizations are combat control teams, which parachute into denied areas either alone or with army special forces elements to survey potential drop zones and landing fields and to control airflow.

The Combat Talon and the HH-53 Pave Low are used in long-range infiltration, exfiltration, and rescue operations. There are too few of them, and they are aging. The air force has received only one new Combat Talon in the past four years. As part of its plan for recognizing the emphasis being placed by the administration on SOF, the air force originally proposed to buy ten more Combat Talons. DOD told it to double that figure.

The air force also had the task of developing a replacement for the HH-53s, but limits on funding have led to greatly reduced capabilities of the prototye HH-60D Nighthawk. This program was to have been given to the army in exchange for the Patriot air defense missile system, but the entire SOF aircraft mission question became an issue of major proportions defying sensible resolution. Thus, the army set about increasing its own capabilities.

In the past two years, however, the air force has turned completely around; it is funding improved HH-53s, the new CV-22 "Osprey," and not only new MC-130s but AC-130s as well.

Counterterror Operations

Dedicated multiservice forces specifically trained for counterterrorist missions have greatly expanded since the ill-fated rescue attempt in Iran. Although specific capabilities are classified, they address ground and maritime threats. The units train regularly with other federal counterterrorism forces and allied counterparts.

Of perhaps more importance is the collection of elements into a single whole, commanded by an institutionalized headquarters with extensive operational and intelligence links. This step, born out of recognition that the command arrangement prevailing at Desert One contributed to mission failure, has provided consolidated training and mission planning management, intelligence tasking and analysis, and multiservice doctrinal development. In addition, some theater commanders have tasked their own special forces and marine force reconnaissance units with a contingency counterterrorism or counterterrorism-support role, and the marines recently activated their own anti-terror security battalion.

Missions and Capabilities

The principal army SOF elements are the Special Forces groups and the Ranger battalions. Special Forces are charged with training and assisting friendly resistance forces; training and assisting friendly counterinsurgent forces; conducting basic tactics and weapons training for friendly armies; carrying out pinpoint sabotage operations and rescue and recovery and "snatch" raids; and conducting strategic reconnaissance operations. Rangers provide a large-scale strike capability, as well as an additional rescue potential; both dimensions were demonstrated in Grenada. Rangers are organized and trained as elite light infantry battalions, in a modified TO&E familiar to most soldiers. Where they differ is in their readiness, level of training and motivation, shock mission, and the Ranger qualification prerequisite for its leader personnel.

Special Forces perform either as self-contained intelligence, sabotage, or raid elements or as cadres for training and advising indigenous personnel. They require training not only in employing weapons, guerrilla and conventional tactics, and supporting arms but also in the language and instructional skills necessary to teach foreign pupils of varying levels of sophistication. They also need solid grounding in the elements of revolutionary and counterrevolutionary warfare principles, intelligence collection, evasion and escape, and special demolitions.

The challenge to Special Forces unit training managers is obvious, and it is a challenge that is both partially met and somewhat compounded by the nearly constant demand for special forces mobile training teams. For example, the special forces troopers based in Panama have had disproportionately high levels of experience in foreign internal defense (counterinsurgency, with an ample measure of PSYOPS) training of late in El Salvador and Honduras. However, there has been scant time for those units to train in other special forces tasks. The same is true in lesser degrees for the other Special Forces groups; nonetheless, the similarity of mobile training team missions to much of the classic wartime requirements of Special Forces units, to say nothing of providing a showcase for Special Forces capabilities, is perceived as a counterweight to areas of adverse training impact.

PSYOPS and CA units are intended to preempt and co-opt adversary motivational themes and to reinforce a friendly power's (or, temporarily, U.S. force's) civil administration capabilities. They are organized primarily to support conventional task force and theater commanders but work closely with Special Forces in most of the latter's roles, particularly the foreign internal defense operations.

All army SOF suffer in some degree from a common malady, one for which the ongoing DOD revitalization program provides only a partial cure: the authorized manning levels, operational missions, scope of training requirements, and limited training funds and resources cannot help, when placed against each other, but result in serious capabilities shortfalls. Even were the operational detachments (or A teams) fully manned and fully trained in their specialities, the number of teams available, active and reserve, still fall short of worldwide validated wartime requirements by a significant margin.

The reactivation of the First Special Forces Group and planned reactivation of the Third does make inroads on the total force requirement deficiency, but it also exacerbates to some degree the individual manning and specialty training problems. Some active duty PSYOPS and CA units also remain understrength and undertrained, though improvements in both areas have been and continue to be made.

Some of the same problems are true of the navy SEAL elements. The extensive training required for full SEAL qualification and individual specialties makes manning the additional authorized SEAL platoons as great a challenge as the fleshing out of army SOF. SEALs conduct harbor defense and obstacle reconnaissance, amphibious sabotage, and underwater demolitions. They can conduct limited guerrilla warfare operations and provide maritime patrol and commando training in foreign internal defense programs. The SEAL platoon shortfall is not as serious as the Special Forces Operations Detachment deficiency, and the planned increases will help further, but expanding the training and skills base is another matter.

Air force special operations aim mainly at long-range insertion into, and extraction or rescue of personnel from, denied areas. For these missions, they use MC-130 Combat Talons, HH-53 Pave Low, and HH-60D aircraft, and special operations low-level crews flying conventional MAC C-130s. Equally important are the AC-130 Spectre gunships, which can deliver automatically sighted 20mm, 40mm, and 105mm fire with exceptional accuracy. These are used for ground special operations support and in support of other joint task force elements in a low- to mid-intensity conflict environment. Finally, the EC-130s of the Pennsylvania Air National Guard have a unique airborne television and radio broadcasting capability in support of psychological operations.

The significant shortage of long-range insertion-extraction platforms greatly limits the speed with which Special Forces units could be delivered into denied areas. This forces many theater special operations commanders to choose between scrapping their wartime plans' infiltration schedules or dangerously lowering survivability by relying on conventional C-130s.

Isolated operations could be supported out of the current SOF aircraft inventory but not a full-scale theater unconventional warfare campaign. DOD recognition of air force neglect in this area led to the pointed demands to get more MC-130s. In the interim, the air force is also increasing the number of MAC C-130s and crews designated as special operations low level.

SOF Roles in the Reagan Policy Environment

Anti-Terrorism and Counterterrorism

Terrorists' periodic bludgeoning of the public peace has been attended by increasing sophistication and lethality of their means, an impossible diversity of ends toward which they employ those means, and, infinitely more sinister, the sponsorship of terrorists by states desiring surrogate vengeance or destabilization tools.

Nations facing threats by terrorism—most of the noncommunist countries of the world but particularly the United States, Western Europe, and pro-Western third world countries—have in the last two decades identified a need to develop capabilities targeted against those threats. The Reagan administration has fielded its military counterterror forces in response to hostage situations a number of times. The large deployments and their attendant nonuse frustrations have been well publicized; the smaller, more successful technical assistance activities in support of other countries' response operations have not. Nor have the countless proactive anti-terror training and survey missions carried out both by dedicated counterterrorist forces and by other special operations units.

Discussion of SOF roles in anti-terrorism and counterterrorism presupposes a national strategy. The degree to which such a strategy does or does not exist, and elements that might be incorporated, are more than competently addressed elsewhere. For our purpose here, we will isolate and review some general strategy elements and then examine actual or potential SOF roles in each.

First is problem identification. What constitutes the major potential threats? What do we know about them? What is their casus belli? How do we arm against them?

Second is co-option. This includes domestic and foreign policy options that can remove a particular group's reason for striking a particular government and reduce or eliminate that group's appeal and potential public support. The Anglo–Irish Accords and the Salvadoran land reform programs are examples.

Third is a collection of interrelated elements I will call the proactive elements, which include:

• Prevention through preparation
• Prevention through deterrence
• Prevention through detection and preemption

These involve organizing and planning to meet a threat, at home or overseas, conducting the necessary prevention and response training for crisis management, detection, intelligence, and tactical personnel, and then ensuring a potential aggressor knows that the capability exists to bring his or her efforts to grief. There is not unanimity on this last point; but it is also worth remembering the statement of Doctor Strangelove, who said, "You don't have a deterrent if nobody knows you've got it." By the same token, detection can, but may not necessarily, lead to preemption; preemptive action by a principal or a surrogate depends on a variety of factors, including perception of cost-benefit ratio in terms of lives and political capital and confidence in the intelligence effort. But while it is true that detection may or may not result in preemption, it can at least result in interception or defense.

Finally, there are the reaction elements, which include relief and rescue operations for in-progress incidents and retaliation operations for incidents that have already occurred. The objectives of the last elements, other than the obvious life-saving and punitive ones, are demonstrative—to a national public and to other potential adversaries that they may be assured of the government's ability and will to protect, rescue, and punish. Both elements also depend on reliable, real-time intelligence. Intelligence has not been considered a functional strategy element, chiefly because it—along with national mood and governmental political will—forms the essential environment in which those functional elements exist. Without intelligence, the abstract capability to operate any element cannot become translated into meaningful policy options, as we have seen in the case of the TWA hijacking and with regard to other Americans taken hostage in Lebanon.

These elements, then, and the capability to carry them out, are part of a national strategy. The additional ingredients of will to act and the informed decision making that implements that will and gives it direction are what operationalize that strategy.

Special Operations Roles

Reaction and retaliation are the roles that spring most readily to the popular imagination when one considers SOF roles in the fight against terrorism. Forces organized for these roles must be trained in a wide variety of weapons, equipment, operational scenarios, threat characteristics, and close combat techniques. A truly adequate training and preparation period is lengthy (and costly) and must be followed up with extensive simulation and field exercises if those skills are not to atrophy. Identifying personnel and buying some equipment does not translate into functional capability. Doctrine, and intense training oriented to that doctrine, does.

Another critical component in using SOFs for such highly charged and politically sensitive operations as rescue and retaliation is the requirement for a working command-and-control structure. This includes not only a streamlined communications link from national command authorities but a combination of maturity, technical and tactical proficiency, and understanding of the incident environment, meaning the flow of intranational or international events affecting or potentially affecting an operation. Let us consider some public record revelations concerning the flexing of America's own counterterror muscle overseas.

At Desert One, only the army force involved was a self-contained, dedicated counterterror element. The air force and navy-marine aviation elements were not and for security reasons had not trained with the other actual participating elements. The resulting failures to carry out basic premission inspections for such forbidden items as marked maps, photos, and agents' names, and the plan itself—a complex one chosen over several other feasible options—were all indicative of an inadequate command-and-control setup. That was admitted by the government and addressed by the Pentagon in setting up the JSOC. No institutionalized, professional counterpart yet exists at the national command level, however, though many in the community have been pushing for that for some time; and in the wake of the Iran–Contra scandal, the outlook is for a lower, not higher, operational profile at NSC. As it is, the signals that come from different sources—DOD, State, the NSC—can sometimes conflict. A case in point is the TWA hijacking in 1985. A window of opportunity appeared at one point in the plane's odyssey; U.S. forces were positioned to go; a go-ahead was apparently given and then rescinded; and while the confusion was resolved, the window closed, never to open again. With regard to ground leadership, the precipitate decision to go ahead with a poorly intelligenced, hastily planned raid on Richmond Hill prison in Grenada in 1982, and the near debacle between U.S. forces and the Italian carabinieri at Sigonella airbase in the course of the *Achille Lauro* incident are cause for concern. It should be stated here for the record, however, that whatever shortcomings may yet exist in American counterterror forces' top leadership and national C&C links, the troops and the greatest majority of their leaders are highly skilled, highly dedicated, and utterly professional.

Less visible and less viscerally satisfying but infinitely more important in the long run are the co-optive and proactive strategy elements. Co-option attempts to remove terrorism's raison d'être. As most hard-core terrorists have generally adopted the means of their original cause as the foreseeable end, they cannot usually be successfully targeted, but potential support mechanisms can. Where PSYOPS capabilities exist, they can usefully assist in spreading word and rationale for government actions, denouncing terrorists, portraying the inhumanity of terrorism, and so on. Appropriate behavior and civil and medical assistance operations by SOF elements in military training teams can materially assist in such co-option efforts at the grass-roots level. Concurrently personnel on these teams who treat their charges and the civil populace with condescension and cynicism can only help enrich the terrorists' potential support base.

The proactive elements are those that, if implemented effectively, will seldom be evident to the population at large unless the government chooses, for political or civil morale building purposes, to make them so.

The first, preparation, is the most broadly based in scope and the most difficult to measure in terms of effectiveness of implementation. In the United States, SOF are, have been, or could be involved in these several activities that go into preparation:

Civil threat awareness: SOF elements are involved here only to the extent that their masters choose to showcase response and prevention capabilities as a part of overall discussions on the nature of the threat and the country's response.

Planning for prevention and response to attacks on critical facilities: SOF elements can and have in the United States participated in domestic multiagency contingency planning and exercises, relative to critical energy and weapons production facilities, vulnerabilities, and recovery planning for U.S. embassies and major headquarters overseas and as standby intervention forces at both the 1980 Lake Placid Winter Olympics and the 1984 Summer Olympics in Los Angeles.

Anti-Terrorism Training and Assistance: Beyond the training that law enforcement and military forces do internally and with each other, there are international programs in which the military forces can contribute. These include protection training for U.S. diplomats, their drivers, and guards overseas; training for protection details and anti-terror forces of other countries; and joint exercise training with major counterterrorism forces of one's allies. It can also include some pinpoint assistance to other countries' forces during the resolution of incidents or participating as observers. U.S. SOF have performed in all these roles, as have the British, French, Israelis, and West Germans.

Another proactive element is deterrence. This is manifested in two ways. One is the example to be drawn by terrorists and those who support them from the implementation of other elements, such as recovery, preemptive, and retaliation operations. The other is in building awareness of capabilities specifically for the benefit of would-be attackers.

There is divergence of opinion here, and not without reason. On one hand, if all response and prevention capabilities and actions are kept secret, no deterrent factor can exist. On the other, revelation of techniques, personnel, tactics, and movements can give adversaries who are determined to act, information that can potentially be used against the counterterrorist forces. The German's GSG-9, the Austrians' Cobra Unit, and the U.S. FBI Hostage Rescue Team have all gone public in varying degrees, while the SAS (Special Air Service) continues to refuse public comment on its British counterterrorist plans and activities, and the DOD refuses even to acknowledge counterterrorist unit designations, though they have been matters of public record for years. This disparity in policy between the Justice Department and DOD resulted in some loss of what had originally been a close working relationship between the HRT and the DOD counterterrorist forces. Its existence can only be traced to noncentralized policy development and cannot be said to reflect any true approach to deterrence, unless it is to let the terrorists draw their own conclusions.

To be effective, preemption, the next proactive element, is dependent on accurate intelligence, as well as timing, positioning, and common sense. Preemption can take one of several forms:

Raid in Response to Discovery: This can range from relatively low-level police raids with or without U.S. involvement on safehouses or caches, in countries where police forces are cooperative, to full-scale over-border assaults on terrorist havens in sympathetic areas. SOF can serve as advisers or technical equipment supporters in the former and will figure largely in the latter.

Operations to Minimize Capability: These include raids on training camps, transportation centers, and means of sustainment in nations that harbor terrorists. SOF can be utilized in these roles, though they must generally operate covertly. The United States has operated these elements, though without use of SOF, in Libya and in the Contra raids on Nicaraguan refinery and port facilities.

Preemption can also include elimination or "fingering" (intelligence collection) for later elimination, seizure, or "turning" of terrorists or of those who support them. The United States has thus far officially resisted calls to take out terrorist leaders, for a variety of reasons both moral and pragmatic, though there continues to be a call for it from several quarters. The United States does, however, train SOF in a variety of target-designation roles, and they could be utilized in that capacity.

A possibly more palatable use is suggested in Secretary Shultz's (and the president's) assertions that the United States would act to have extradited or, if cooperation were not forthcoming, would recover unilaterally known terrorists who have acted against U.S. citizens, to the United States for trial. Certainly SOF could be utilized in such actions, presuming that the necessary intelligence and coordination with affected allies are there. For example, when the United States intercepted the *Achille Lauro* terrorists, the plane they were on was forced to land at Sigonella, Sicily, where the air base is under Italian legal jurisdiction except in those areas covered under status of forces agreements. This instance was not such an area, and absent any high-level coordination, the Italian carabinieri rightfully asserted themselves. The U.S. commander's understandable but unwise anger and heavy-handed threats nearly resulted in an intraallied incident.

SOF have received renewed emphasis in part due to their potential utility in countering the terrorist threat. Translating policy emphasis into credible capabilities, however, depends first on having a clear strategy and the will and resources to implement it.

Other Low-Intensity Conflict Roles

Anti-terrorism and counterterrorism is but one mission area in the spectrum of special operations. Many others fall into a category of conflicts now called low-intensity conflict. *Low intensity* as a term is useful only in the strategic vein; at the level of SOF troopers, the light division soldiers, and marines who are expected to fight in these conflicts, a platoon-sized firefight or an ambush can reach higher intensities than any policy writer ever dreamed of.

SOF figure largely in the Reagan administration's foreign policy. The June 10, 1984, *Washington Post* had this interpretation:

> The Reagan Administration is systemically laying the foundation within the Pentagon for increasing military involvement in Third World conflicts. . . . The new emphasis in many ways recalls the early 1960's when President John F. Kennedy commissioned the Green Berets to stop what he called the "communist tide" in poor countries of Asia, Africa, and Latin America. Once again, the Defense Department is beefing up its Green Berets and other special forces, troops trained to kill guerrillas and to teach other armies to do the same.

U.S. security assistance and training programs targeted against externally sponsored insurgencies (or potential insurgency situations) recall the initial surge years of U.S. security assistance programs oriented against insurgencies, those of the Kennedy-Johnson era. A principal element in those programs and those of today is that much of the field implementation of both consists of small teams drawn from SOF units or individuals with SOF backgrounds and skills. A great many other elements provide direct or indirect support, particularly in Central America, where activities in several countries relate to a U.S. strategy for the region. Those activities are backed up by application of airborne and stationary intelligence and target acquisition platforms, large-scale logistics infrastructure development, and covert (or more appropriately, formerly covert) operations. The common thread throughout the direct U.S. assistance efforts is the promotion of tactical skills and grass-roots psychological and political efforts to enable a host country to defeat an insurgency, both on the battlefield and in the popular heart and mind, and for the most part, those who implement these efforts have been U.S. SOF elements or SOF-qualified individuals. Why SOF personnel have long been involved, and today have a preeminent role, in what has in effect for the United States become a regional low-intensity conflict campaign goes to the heart of U.S. strategy in that region and a recognition of domestic and regional political realities.

Much of the policy-driving rationale for the recent prioritizing of U.S. SOF programs could have been written with the special operations role in low-intensity conflict in mind. Secretary Weinberger wrote in the 1985 Annual Report to Congress:

> Buttressed by their massive buildup of strategic and conventional forces, the Soviets have undertaken, both directly and through surrogates, a global campaign of destabilization, focused on the Third World, that seeks to obtain their objectives without direct confrontation with the United States. This is, and will continue to be for some time, the most prominent direct threat to U.S. national security interests. . . . U.S. special operations forces are being employed to counter these destabilization efforts. . . . By assisting others to prepare their own defenses, we enhance the Free World's ability to cope with Soviet expansionism, reduce the likelihood that U.S. forces will become involved in combat, and demonstrate our determination not to default on our commitments.

In most of the third world, and certainly in Latin America, Weinberger's expressed preference for the security assistance, training, and advisory efforts over direct conventional force intervention is more than matched by similar preferences of the countries involved. And quite apart from the onerous symbolism that would be attached to conventional intervention in the eyes of the U.S. public, there are sound doctrinal reasons for avoiding commitment of U.S. ground combat forces. If a sponsor (in this case, the United States) must employ its own troops against guerrillas indigenous to another country, then the counterinsurgency effort will appear to have been preempted from that country's government. The resistance movement can then denounce the host country government as "imperialist puppets" and redirect its own appeal to the populace as one of driving out "foreign invaders."

Army and PSYOPS and CA personnel, navy SEALs, and air force special operations crews are trained to be trainers as well as operators, and the array of skills that would be applicable to their missions of supporting guerrilla warfare behind enemy lines is also applicable to the counterinsurgency mission. For some time, these U.S. SOF have been involved in training conventional Latin American, Asian, and some African and Middle Eastern forces in small unit counterinsurgency tactics, as well as providing more specialized training for reconnaissance and quick-reaction units. They have also carefully, through PSYOPS instruction and the examples set by CA unit deployments, attempted to alter some traditional military and political establishment views of the peasantry in Latin America. Although some personnel are drafted from conventional U.S. units for this work, in some cases that does indeed occur; in specialized areas of wide-net communications, technical intelligence collection, engineering, schools curriculum development, and so forth, assets beyond those normally available to SOF are required. The U.S. Southern Command (SOUTHCOM), which implements and coordinates all U.S. security assistance and other military activities throughout Latin America, draws on the inplace U.S. infantry brigade in Panama and resources in the U.S. for many requirements. Indeed, that brigade has been reorganized as Task Force Bayonet, specifically to serve the security assistance/low-intensity mission.

For basic counterinsurgency training, the use of special operations personnel makes the most sense because they have received training in counterinsurgency and have been trained as well to organize and assist resistance movements. Knowing what the insurgent will be trying to accomplish militarily and psychologically, the task-organized, multicapable SOF training team can or should be able to train at the appropriate levels in the tactical, psychological, and local political measures that can preempt the insurgent. It is worth noting that since fiscal year 1979 there has been more than a 200 percent increase in overseas mobile training teams (MTTs), which support various U.S. security assistance efforts. Of these, special forces have been involved in over 30 percent and have accounted for more than a fourth of the man-days, all with 1/10 of one percent of the army's manpower, and with other missions competing for training time.

The degree to which such goals are actually attained is greatly dependent on not only the skills base that the SOF personnel bring with them but also the receptivity of the host country. Established local attitudes regarding warfare, how the peasantry should be treated, and how to integrate military operations into an overall strategy with a realistic chance of finding and crushing guerrilla units in the field and preventing their regrowth through preemption of the population are not easy to alter. Moreover, most political entities in the third world that receive significant U.S. support are sensitive to being seen as too dependent on that support.

Thus, program manifestations vary greatly, and the United States has been been ingenious, as well as persistent, in adapting to the realities it cannot change while pushing for the changes that have been possible. When the fifty-five-man ceiling placed on trainers in El Salvador during the Carter administration proved inadequate for the total training task, the United States encouraged establishment of the Regional Training Center in Honduras (also largely staffed by SOF personnel), which could put whole battalions through a regimen hard to duplicate with the small team in El Salavador. When Honduras raised objections to the number of Salvadoran battalions being sent through versus the number of Honduran, much of the initial surge requirement for El Salvador had already been accomplished. Thus the United States has continued battalion and cadre training at Fort Benning, Georgia, and Fort Bragg, North Carolina, with follow-on efforts by the in-country team.

In Honduras, a virtually nonstop stream of exercises designed to show the flag and build actual regional operations experience for a number of U.S. conventional units also provide several local long-term benefits to the security assistance program. First, the continuing nature of the exercises has necessitated a virtually full-time U.S. support infrastructure, which would otherwise have been almost impossible to establish as an overseas base or as a permanent augmentation to the U.S. military assistance effort operating in Tegucigalpa. That base supports operations in El Salvador as well as training for Honduras. Second, Honduran forces have a regular opportunity to conduct field training on a scale and against sufficient numbers of "enemy" that would otherwise be impossible to duplicate. Third, the conventional forces deployed by the United States for such exercises have armament and equipment levels similar to those of the Sandinistas across the border and thus graphically, and continually, bring home to Honduras what they may have to face. And fourth, the rotating presence of various support elements does ensure the capability of rapid buildup for U.S. forces if required or of provision of rapid support for Honduran forces. This capability was illustrated when U.S. CH-47 Chinook helicopters were diverted from exercise tasks to lift Honduran troops into the area of Sandinista "incursion" in the spring of 1986.

In Costa Rica, admission by the government that the fighting on its borders between Sandinistas and Contras could have consequences beyond its National Police's capabilities has resulted in increased U.S. weaponry aid and a small special forces mobile training team.

In Panama, though the "School of the Americas" has departed for Fort Benning, the special forces battalion there (in addition to providing cadres for training missions elsewhere) routinely conducts courses for Panamanian and other Latin American forces in small-unit counterinsurgency-related operations.

In El Salvador, while trainers still cannot actually accompany small units in the field, major units have operations, plans, and training (OPAT) advisers or advisory teams at their base camps, while air force and navy SOF advisers work closely with their Salvadoran counterparts.

In addition to the direct assistance counterinsurgency missions, the SOF are performing or could perform others should circumstances so require. One such mission area is counterterrorism. SOF assets have been used to good effect in such activities as critical facility "black-hat" penetration surveys, development of reentry and relief support plans, and training for host country antiterror forces.

Another element of SOF utility often overlooked by U.S. officers charged with training conventional units for operations in nonconventional circumstances is in utilizing SOF troops familiar with a region or country for the kind of area familiarization that formal area studies cannot match. SOF can look at the conventional force from the adversary perspective, provide grass-roots advice in what to expect, train in adversary tactics and weaponry, and serve as credible opposition forces in exercises.

Classic special operations missions are, of course, those in denied areas. President Reagan's declared intention to utilize SOF to train the Contras (outside Central

America) addresses but one of the potential missions that might be assigned to SOF were the president to so direct. They include most of the publicly acknowledged SOF mission spectrum, such as long-range reconnaissance and selective interdiction operations, rescue operations for stranded or detained Americans, amphibious reconnaissance and raids, and psyops. Air force gunships are routinely employed in Latin America and Caribbean exercises and would doubtless find employment over Nicaragua once the air defense systems were neutralized. Certainly, none of the above missions is currently authorized or being undertaken but the continuing nature of the other SOF activities in Central America would greatly facilitate SOF transition into such missions.

Should another country fall into civil chaos, where introduction of conventional forces was planned or even contemplated in protection of U.S. interests, some or all of the measures mentioned might be appropriate. In such circumstances, SOF cadres are also useful as assessment teams and to link up with parties friendly to the United States. They can also be utilized as liaison teams deploying with a conventional force on a contingency mission to effect contact with resistance and/or other U.S. SOF elements on the ground.

Conventional Warfighting

SOF missions in support of general war scenarios are in fact what give them their most powerful constituencies within the services, the theater commanders in chief. Here SOF are envisaged as providing critical strategic reconnaissance, interdiction, and target designation services far behind enemy lines, with the classic mission of guerrilla warfare being relegated to secondary importance.

Issues, Challenges, and Trends

The sheer diversity of SOF missions affects all decision making about force structure, training, equipment, communications, and so forth. First, all SOF elements must be able to operate in a variety of climates, cultures, and terrains. Second, while air force, Ranger, PSYOPS/civil affairs, and SEAL missions do not normally need as many distinct doctrinal orientations as do army special forces, the fact that they must support a variety of theater SOF employment philosophies has some effect on their planning. The major element of the diversity factor is the several distinctive operational mission orientations that compete for special forces doctrinal development and training priorities.

Many NATO and U.S. European Command planners see dedicated special forces assets as theater-directed collectors of essential information in enemy rear areas, providing human eyes and ears at a time when a conventional onslaught may have greatly impaired allied technical collection capabilities. A secondary mission would be sabotage and selected interdiction. Guerrilla warfare would be conducted primarily after the conventional fighting had stabilized, by follow-on assets. What this means from a training standpoint is that active component special operations units—which have both home station and annual European exercise opportunities to play guerrilla warfare scenarios—have had to reorient training priorities to the strategic reconnaissance mission. Meanwhile, reserve units, whose training time and resources seldom permit involved guerrilla warfare scenarios, have been given increased responsibility for that end of the special operations spectrum.

Another school of thought holds that no matter what the mission, rural-oriented skills are passé, at least in Europe. The reduction of European forests, coupled with the sophisticated, multilayered, internal security infrastructure common to Warsaw Pact states, has led to emphasis in some U.S. units on urban guerrilla techniques, which can service both unilateral and resistance-support operations. The success of this technique depends on extensive prehostilities cultivation of potential in-place assets, a condition that special forces training includes but no working-level special operations planner assumes.

Still another school holds that conventional warfare use of SOF behind enemy lines would be dramatically attritive and that special forces' most telling and most likely future contributions will be in the collection of disciplines (counterinsurgency military operations, small unit training, psychological and civil affairs operations, political warfare, and intelligence) known as foreign internal defense (FID). The array of skills required for FID operations is virtually the same as those necessary for organizing and training a guerrilla movement; the difference is the stabilization versus destabilization orientation of security assistance programs.

FID proponents believe the only means of countering an insurgency against a friendly foreign power is through advice and assistance to internal elements. Those who would like to see the emphasis kept on guerrilla warfare skills note that most potential U.S. adversaries have restive (and therefore potentially exploitable) minorities comprising a significant proportion of their population, particularly in key border areas.

The problem is that none of these mission considerations can be denied. Strategic reconnaissance, direct action, FID, and guerrilla warfare remain generic special forces tasks. One theater commander may demand that "his" dedicated active component elements train primarily in one area, to serve his perception of the primary SOF mission, while another will see entirely different needs and priorities. It is a commander's prerogative—indeed his duty—to establish such priorities, but when those assets are shared between commands or given actual security assistance missions that have little to do with wartime tasks, the obstacles to intelligent unit-level resource allocation and training planning are obvious.

Training

The unique nature of SOF missions presents equally unique training challenges. SOF require intensive training on a wide variety of individual skills, training on imparting that knowledge to foreign regular or irregular combatants, and actual overseas opportunities to put into practice what has been learned. Moreover, running a special operations base overseas is a complex task, which can be only partially addressed in a command-post exercise environment. One does not develop guerrilla forces or the preparation of an unconventional operational area, complete with intelligence nets, opposition forces, and civilian participation, overnight; such training is in fact, virtually impossible for the reserve components to organize with their limited active duty time and resources. The heavy commitment lately of SOF elements to military training teams and overseas exercises has, on one hand, provided a wealth of training opportunities. On the other hand, however, it has placed a severe strain on understrength units insofar as maintaining any progressive individual or unit training program.

The diversity of potential missions, the need for mission area orientation and language skills, the desires of owning theater commanders, and contending with the increasing sophistication of both friendly and adversary equipment compete for training prioritization. Particularly difficult to achieve and maintain are the language skills. Yet a three-month course with refreshers takes up so much training time that not all who need it receive it.

Where unit training is aligned to a given theater's area of emphasis, some skills are being learned very well. However, others (including, in some cases, what used to be considered survival skills related to operating with local nationals in denied areas) suffer as a consequence. Moreover, reassignment of a trooper who has become familiar with one mission-area orientation to a unit with a different emphasis has placed both the trooper and his new unit at a disadvantage.

It is in the army's special forces units that this problem has been most pronounced, though the SEALs experience it to a lesser degree. To combat it, the army is attempting to apply its experimental regimental system (a soldier spends all his or her troop duty in U.S. or overseas elements of the same unit) to the special forces groups. Thus, a soldier assigned to the Tenth Special Forces Group at Fort Devens would spend most of his troop duty time either at Fort Devens or with the Tenth's forward-deployed battalion at Bad Toelz, Germany. Attainment of this goal, if achieved, will go far toward minimizing area and language orientation training (and training retention) challenges. The army has also begun a program to build stability on its A teams through assignment of warrant officers as team executive officers, replacing the senior first lieutenants previously authorized but seldom available for that position. Finally, the army has made special forces a separate career branch, further ensuring assignment homogeneity, particularly among officers.

Another positive factor is an increasing trend toward realism in major unit training exercises. Emergency deployment readiness exercises (little- or no-notice deployments), development of hostile environments in which local law enforcement agencies and other opposition forces actively seek out friendly SOF, and involvement of (and support for) reserve SOF on a major scale in the guerrilla warfare scenarios they have previously had scant opportunities to practice are representative of efforts at the unit and theater levels to overcome the impact of externally imposed training constraints.

Command and Control

A number of those who determine how SOF can fulfill the diversity of assigned tasks believe that the solution lies in task organizing existing special forces, Ranger, PSYOPS, and CA units in the army into special operations groups, which would then be supported overseas in the usual fashion by naval and air force special operations elements. They believe existing special forces assets should be grouped into specialist elements, such as a strategic reconnaissance battalion, an unconventional warfare battalion, and a strike battalion. Although this concept probably has little future at the unit table of organization level because it not only magnifies unit-level training problems but flies in the face of centralization of Ranger command and doctrinal authority, it does reflect reality at the theater level. There, cadre special operations commands have been created out of operations staff sections that previously oversaw theater special operations planning. These special operations commands will when fully constituted serve as the theater staff for all SOF forces assigned. These SOF forces may be further assigned directly or in support of a forward operations base with a given functional orientation.

The dark cloud on this horizon is that none of the theater special operations staffs has the equipment, communications, or personnel assigned on a full-time basis that they would require to operate in war. They all require augmentation from outside resources. For a limited-scope, low-intensity operation or campaign limited to a single theater, most such augmentation would come from raiding special operations headquarters and units elsewhere in the active components, with obvious effects on those elements' readiness should they be required suddenly. Here some service and theater self-help initiatives are being developed in response.

For a general conflict scenario, other problems emerge. The active component units would move to their overseas wartime deployment bases immediately upon initiation of hostilities, and preferably prior to that time. Yet the establishment of the sustaining, receiving, and deployment infrastructure depends on reservists, who must be called up, deployed, and worked into their wartime roles. The services have made some headway against this problem by preidentifying individual mobilization augmentees for theater special operations staffs, and some effort is being made to have such augmentees perform their annual training in their wartime roles and locations. At the joint level, the JSOA in 1984 began investigating means of refining the various services' means of calling up selected reservists in short-of-war, short-of-mobilization conditions.

Despite the energy and thought that had been applied to resolution of organizational issues, SOF command and control remained the most important issue into 1986. That it was such as issue stems from more than just interservice turf battles. It was also an issue because of residual concern by professional special operations officers and DOD and congressional SOF advocates that the services were still not wholeheartedly in favor of the program. This was what led to congress's seizure of the revitalization baton from OSD.

Revitalization: Commitment or Cosmetics?

That the service staffs did not embrace the scope of the SOF revitalization program with enthusiasm is a matter of record. Response to an initial draft guidance circulated by DOD in early FY 83 objected to the specificity of the proposed measures and essentially opined that the services should set their internal priorities. Since this approach could conceivably give a theater commander a wealth of army special forces teams upon which to base planning, but not the air force MC-130 Combat Talons to deliver them, or vice-versa, or neither, DOD correctly realized it would have to spearhead a coordinated approach to SOF program development and mandate the program to the services. This was accomplished in a series of specified force upgrade urgings covered by a directive from deputy Secretary of Defense Paul Thayer in October 1984, which effectively established upgrades as policy. It also told each service to provide a time-phased master plan by which it would carry out assigned upgrades.

Noel C. Koch appeared in mid-1985 before Congressman Hutto's special panel on special operations, where he reviewed service actions to meet their respective master plan goals. Koch cautioned that continuous, applied pressure was necessary to prevent loss of momentum once the principal advocates of SOF revitalization had passed from the scene. He noted some service diversion of supplies originally ordered for SOF units, despite DOD directives assigning SOF a high priority. He was concerned over whether service commitment of resources would serve the goals of their respective plans; in many cases they have not.

Koch's major concern was not with the symptoms but the causes of residual service reluctances to support SOF revitalization fully. He observed that most theater commanders continued to view SOF operations as adjuncts to conventional operations and not in their additional, nonconventional, national-strategy-serving separate dimensions. He feared that unless such revisiting of strategic thinking regarding low-intensity operations not tied to general conflict scenarios takes place, SOF would fail to achieve the long-term service constituencies necessary to make SOF truly competitive in resource allocation.

This was the general concern that helped drive creation of the JSOA and motivated Congressman Dan Daniel (D–Virginia), chairman of the House Armed Services Committee's Readiness Subcommittee, to establish Hutto's special panel. In fact, it further moved Congressman Daniel to propose creation of a separated rate service for SOF.

In the August 1985 *Armed Forces Journal*, Daniel opined that "the [SOF] readiness enhancements and force structure increases now under way, while essential, are, in reality, treating the symptoms but not the disease. The heart of the matter lies not in the forces themselves, but in the way in which they are integrated into the national security structure." He went on to cite the unique nature of SOF missions, equipment, and people reviewed the history of service neglect of SOF, and concluded that SOF would not find a legitimate constituency in either their own services or in a single existing service. He ended, "One point is clear. If the United States is serious about special operations, SOF must have a home. That, in fact, is a lesson our friends and foes alike—at least those who are successful at such operations—learned long ago, but one that has yet to soak into our national consciousness."

Daniel's position was modified and incorporated into a compromise bill that he sponsored along with Earl Hutto in the House of Representatives and Senators Sam Nunn and William Cohen in the Senate. This legislation, signed into law in late 1986 over OSD and JCS objections. It created an umbrella command structure for all U.S. active and reserve SOF and an accompanying assistant secretary of defense for special operations and low-intensity conflict.

The motivations and intentions of the SOF legislation's authors were clear. Long dismayed over perceived shortfalls in the services' actions versus their official statements of intent with regard to improving and sustaining SOF capabilities, they saw existing and promised DOD and JCS measures as well meaning but insufficient. They noted that the DOD official formerly assigned responsibility for SOF oversight, Noel Koch, had been eased out of office for his zeal in holding the services to account, that the Joint Special Operations Agency's charter had been diluted since its original conception, and that its director lacked sufficient rank or positional clout vis-à-vis the JCS to do more than some high-level in-house lobbying.

The legislation also authorized raising some of the special operations command positions in the worldwide unified commands from colonel to general officer level and envisaged a board for low-intensity conflict at the NSC. The legislation provided some powerful budgetary authority for the new assistant secretary and the commander of the new U.S. special operations command, and gave them responsibilities for training, doctrinal development, and readiness previously shared not only by the service staffs but by different commands within the services.

That was the intent. What does the reality look like? Both optimism and pessimism have been expressed inside and outside the Pentagon. The secretary of defense's Special Operations Policy Advisory Group, composed of distinguished retired senior officers with matchless special operations credentials, took OSD to task for several indications of less-than-enthusiastic implementation of the congressional legislation. Specifically they cited:

Delays in designating a commander for USSOC (finally, General James Lindsay was named).

Delays in designating the new assistant secretary.

Locating USSOC at MacDill AFB, despite the "sensitivity and political/military" character of USSOC's mission.

Locating the new assistant secretary's office and staff completely out of the Pentagon, in commercial office space nearby.

Insufficient staffing for the assistant secretary's office.

The fact that they had not been consulted when counsel on such measures was the ostensible reason for SOPAG's existence.

Congress also reacted angrily to the position nomination delays and stationing decisions.

Of perhaps more substantive concern than who fills the new positions or where they are located are both lingering scope-of-responsibility questions and new ones occasioned by the legislative acts intended to resolve them.

The first question has to do with day-to-day and operational relationships between the new SOF commander, the existing JSOC, the separate service commands that "own" active special operations forces, the reserve and national guard chains of command that own reserve component SOF, and the theater commanders, whose own roles in commanding and controlling forces in their areas were strengthened in other DOD reorganization legislation passed by Congress. It is probably not too inaccurate to assume that in relation to the theater commanders, the command's role will be somewhat analogous to that of the U.S. Readiness Comand, which it dispossessed at MacDill: that is, training and deploying forces to be utilized by others. There may be some potential for conflict though, as there are contingency provisions for "COMUSSOC" exercising operational command. Logic, however, suggests that forces deployed for any operations chopped to a theater commander might come under his command, while nationally directed contingency operations would be the province of the "COMUSSOC." Other lines of authority questions are still being resolved.

The second major question has to do with the scope of the new assistant secretary's responsibilities regarding intermeshing programs that are strictly special operations and those that are not. The position clearly states "special operations and low-intensity conflict." Does this mean the new office will also have supervision responsibilities over force development and sustainment for the army's new light infantry division? If not, then what influences will the new office have on the troops who must actually operate in a low-intensity environment versus the special operations personnel who operate principally as trainers and advisers? There is cause for concern here. Notwithstanding some excellent new doctrinal initiatives for conventional units operating in a low-intensity environment that have been promulgated by army and marine combat developers, many people in and out of the army believe the original justification for the light divisions—rapid deployment to third world trouble spots—is being subsumed by conventional commanders who continue to operate with a conventional combat mind-set. This critique is somewhat fueled by such events as an assertion by a senior light division officer that loss of most of his helicopters on a recent exercise to a special forces–led guerrilla raid was an "annoyance" and that his "battle focus" was the conventional enemy.

Perhaps the new assistant secretary position should have some role in verifying that low-intensity concepts and doctrines are finding their way into training for all forces that have primarily (or at least ostensibly) low-intensity conflict deployment missions.

Another area of concern is that of special activities or covert (generally intelligence) activities. At the national level, interagency coordination and policy direction in the past was accomplished by several committees, with actual operations by the military, largely service directed. The alleged covert activities by the army staff's Special Operations Division, which came to well-publicized grief in 1985, and the intelligence support activity, directly or indirectly may have involved special operations and/or low-intensity conflict, yet they have not always been integrated with overall Defense Intelligence Agency requirements or coordinated with other national agencies. Consolidating and coordinating anti-terror, counterinsurgency, and other special operations or low-intensity conflict intelligence-related operations and directly monitoring those performed by military elements may be an appropriate role for the assistant secretary, operating closely with the Defense Intelligence Agency. It may now be even more appropriate, in fact, than when the legislation was passed. The increased supervision and involvement foreseen by the legislation for the NSC predated the Iran–Contra arms problems and the attendant rejection (at least publicly) of future operational roles by the national security adviser. While it is to be hoped that Frank Carlucci has not actually entirely abandoned coordinative supervision of foreign policy and intelligence activities related to special operations and the "shades of grey." The degree of involvement in such areas as operational tasking and coordination is likely to be much less than it would have been prior to the recent events.

It is also unclear what role the new assistant secretary will have in security assistance, which falls both within special operations forces' activities, and those of other elements. Currently security assistance training has its own chain, involving the State Department, the Defense Security Assistance Agency, and U.S. military assistance offices in the countries involved. It may be appropriate for the office of the assistant secretary to serve as the action agency for coordinating security assistance training between the countries and federal agencies involved and the military commands from which the trainers must come.

What is clear is that the potential for improvement of SOF status and readiness has been greatly increased without the self-defeating extreme of creating a new service of federal agency.

Doctrine versus Hardware

Equipment is a major consideration. The uniqueness and diversity of SOF missions have caused their small, highly specialized equipment needs to disappear in individual service budgets. High-profile weapons systems and high-density procurement economics were attractive to congressional constituencies and conventional or nuclear warfare planners alike, while SOF found their needs "validated but un-funded." Although the effects of over a decade of neglect are slowly being reversed, nobody involved in SOF operational or resource planning believes that progress thus far or the upgrades finally funded for fiscal year 1988 will provide a lasting solution.

In special operations, perhaps even more so than in conventional operations, validated missions should drive doctrinal development. Doctrine, in turn, should drive equipment development, procurement, and issue. All too often the situation in SOF has been quite the opposite. Limitations on equipment quantity and quality impose limitations on doctrinal practice, in both training and combat. How has and is the revitalization of SOF dealing with some of the equipment issues?

Airlift. The sophistication of air defense systems throughout most of the regions of the world where SOF would be employed in unconventional warfare, direct action, or strategic reconnaissance roles has long been a source of concern for U.S. army and joint command SOF planners. Agreeing that the use of aircraft without specialized infiltration-assist electronic countermeasures (ECM) and counter-countermeasures (ECCM) and beacon-homing capabilities for behind-the-lines insertions was an obsolescent technique, the air force over fifteen years ago began searching for alternatives. The proving ground was Vietnam; standard C-130 aircraft were rigged with various combinations of jamming and detection modules and used to support classified cross-border operations. Similarly, the H-3 helicopter, of rescue and recovery fame, was fitted out with ECM equipment. Both were employed successfully in special operations during the war, with the result that standardized production models were introduced: the MC-130 Combat Talon and the HH-53 Pave Low.

With the end of the war, however, also came an end in air force procurement priorities for SOF-related aircraft. Most of the various gun platforms developed by the air force for special operations and low-intensity conflict support passed into legend and the boneyard. The sole survivor was the AC-130 Spectre gunship.

Although the air force did not similarly phase out its SOF delivery platforms, it did curtail procurement. In mid-1987, only fourteen MC-130s and nine HH-53s were available to meet validated wartime infiltration-exfiltration requirements, which are many times that number.

Perhaps the SOF-related issue that in 1985 and 1986 generated the most heat on Capitol Hill, in fact, was this insufficiency of aircraft designed to move SOF safely into denied areas and dissatisfaction with perceived air force footdragging and mismanagement of efforts to redress the shortcomings. The issue that received the greatest attention (with least justification) was the on-again, off-again proposed transfer of the long-range SOF helicopter role from the air force to the army. The more important issue was and is the tremendous disparity between validated lift requirements and the numbers of specially designed and equipped aircraft (both rotary and fixed wing) available or projected to meet those needs.

Even with programmed MC-130 upgrades, a significant shortfall in employment aircraft will remain. The aerial alternative is a standard C-130 with some radar upgrades and specialized crew training, acceptable in low-air-defense-threat environment but ranking only marginally above suicide against more sophisticated protection. Currently twenty additional MC-130s are programmed in the air force SOF revitalization package. Those MC-130s were historically among the first items offered up by the air force when budget cuts were mandated, and program management was criticized in both the House and the Senate. At last, however, seven MC-130s and five AC-130 Spectres are in construction.

As for the HH-53, the air force has for some time been less than enthusiastic about dedicating its helicopter assets for special operation other than those associated with pilot rescue and recovery. Accordingly, when tasked with development of new helicopters for army SOF support, the air force addressed the responsibility halfheartedly. Funding cuts led to specifications modification, and the result, the HH-60D, was transformed from the all-weather, daytime-nighttime insertion-extraction platform it was supposed to be into a fair weather, daytime-only mutant virtually useless originally for long-range SOF operations, though some modifications and pilot night-sight goggle training have been carried out.

The issue of transferring the rotary-wing role began with acrimony disguised as harmony. The army, dissatisfied with air force reluctance to add to its small fleet of aging HH-53 Pave Low helicopters and its less-than-enthusiastic pursuit of a new long-range replacement, expressed a desire to assume the long-range helicopter mission. As a part of thirty-one army–air force initiatives agreed upon in principle by the respective service chiefs of staff in 1984, Initiative 17 proposed such a transfer. Almost immediately, however, those on the air force staff who opposed the transfer began questioning army ability to manage and absorb Pave Low operations, maintenance, and staffing and training requirements. The army countered by pointing out that Pave Low would remain in service until a replacement had been developed and fielded and that the army had for years been maintaining a sizable rotary-wing inventory and was used to managing the men and machines involved. The debate moved to Capitol Hill and became even more zestful as some legislators saw in the original transfer proposal the first step in a presumed dumping of all air force SOF airlift responsibilities on the army. In December 1984, Deputy Secretary of Defense Taft deferred any action on the proposal until he could be assured that the transfer would not open the door for near- or long-term degradation of existing (minimal though they are) SOF airlift capabilities. That decision was in practice made moot by the USSOC legislation. In the meantime, the army continued to develop its short- and mid-range SOF helicopter support capabilities.

Sealift. Not all means of long-range infiltration are airborne. At one time, the navy maintained two diesel submarines with interior compartments modified specifically for the housing and launching of SEAL, marine reconnaissance, and special forces elements via SCUBA apparatus or rubber boats. After Vietnam, the number dwindled to one, and a few years ago that submarine too was decommissioned. The navy still accepts the validity of sublaunched SOF missions but for some time expected to perform them with nuclear attack submarines. The availability of such vessels for training was highly limited. Many SEALs and virtually all special forces troopers have gone through their careers making amphibious insertions from short-range boats or coast guard cutters simulating the sub role (the coast guard, with its extensive missions and slim resources, has nonetheless proved consistently enthusiastic in its support for amphibious operations planners of all services). Lately, however, the navy has committed to conversion of old Polaris submarines and some diesel boats to expand on the previous capability level.

To support more close-in operations, the navy has procured increased numbers of its high-speed, all-weather Seafox SEAL delivery boat, SEAL delivery vehicles (SDVs), and has confirmed its budget commitment for fielding the new patrol boat family throughout the late 1980s.

Communications. SOF elements deployed in any one of their several behind-the-lines missions have always had specialized communications requirements. First, the equipment must have long-range transmission and reception capabilities. Second, it must be capable of instantaneous burst transmissions of coded messages if it is to defeat enemy direction-finding and decryption capabilities. Third, it must be amenable to airborne or waterborne insertion and mobile enough to move quickly.

Historically, meeting all three requirements has been elusive for army SOF; with no dedicated SOF procurement element available, army SOF had to rely on World War II–vintage equipment or what non-SOF procurers could find. The AN/GRC-109, the special forces' mainstay for years, was reliable for long distances but bulky (several components). Moreover, it had no voice capability. The AN/PRC-74, which replaced the 109, was a single-component, portable voice-and-code unit.

The new unit could have been the answer to the operational detachments' dreams, but it had reliability problems and still could not be netted with conventional forces' radios. After nearly two decades of work, special forces have recently been issued a reliable, multicapability radio, the AN/PRC-70. Its main drawback is that it weighs forty-five pounds, hardly making it portable in any operational sense of the word. Other weight additions exist due to high battery drainage, which requires that excessive numbers of batteries be carried. A number of units on their own rejected usage of the AN/PRC-70 in favor of the much lighter HF-only AN/PRC-104, supplementing that with hand-held commercial VHF units for internal communication. Recently the army accepted the 104 as an interim SOF-wide HF radio until another radio is tested and accepted.

Special forces and naval special warfare groups have recently been issued satellite communications equipment and found it extremely reliable, especially in dead zones too far for tactical FM base-to-detachment communications and too close for sky-wave transmissions. There are potential problems; in a general war situation, satellite survivability is doubtful, and in any case, channel preemption by multiple mobilized theater headquarters is all too likely. It is also somewhat bulky for field use. Still, it is an innovative approach to a long-standing need.

An even more fundamental concern in the communications area is the insufficiency in quantity, particularly in base radios. Special forces groups are supposed to be able to field a special forces operations base and multiple forward operations bases, and the requirements on the group signal companies' tables of organization and equipment reflect that mission. Their authorization level, however, has prevented them in the past from fully supporting that mission or maintaining sufficient stockage to sustain even those base organizations that can be fielded.

Rare is the group that can consistently field the communications gear required for simultaneous deployment of anything beyond the SOF base and one forward operations base. Similarly, a naval special warfare group is tasked with creation not only of a naval special warfare task group (NSWTG) but subordinate task units (NSWTUs). In reality, a deployed group can operate and maintain an NSWTG and one NSWTU only with difficulty.

Thus, as SOF planners consider qualitative communications upgrades, they must also press for quantitative improvement. Parts and components resupply is a problem throughout the services, and even more so in SOF, where the low-density, specialized nature of their communications equipment coupled with low authorized stockage levels magnifies the impact of any equipment loses.

Weapons. Specialized weaponry for SOF is usually considered only in counterterrorism or raid terms (and the counterterrorism forces are well supplied with state-of-the-art weaponry). But other needs also exist. While special forces and SEAL elements are required to know (and teach other) how to use mortars, few are available for training and none are assigned at the unit level. Similarly, while both wartime operational requirements and many mobile training team missions include use and/or training others to use TOW antitank missiles, Stinger antiaircraft missiles, and their Soviet counterparts, no tracking simulation equipment (let alone actual missiles) is assigned.

Special forces units at Fort Bragg and Fort Lewis can train with infantry division equipment and trainers, but other units have much more difficulty. Inclusion of a few of each of the above systems in special forces and naval special warfare group inventories for training purposes would greatly add to overall capabilities and training standardization.

Air force SOF weaponry, as represented in the 20mm, 40mm, and 105mm systems aboard the AC-130 Spectre gunship, are sufficient in guns-per-airframe terms, but the systems are aging. Moreover, with only twenty of these systems available between active and reserve components, the air force cannot meet the majority of its validated theater support requirements. There is no question that the air force's first SOF support priority has to be the MC-130s for which it is now committed. However, with not only increased army SOF forces but that services's turn to light divisions as well, the tremendous additional firepower represented by the AC-130 is more necessary than ever. The AC-130 operates at altitudes too high for most tactical air defense systems to be guaranteed a hit; Spectres were, in fact, ever-present life-savers throughout the six-week-long battle of An Loc in Vietnam, and none was lost, though several other lower-flying aircraft were. They were also used over Grenada. Thus, their use in support of light units in a moderate air defense threat is a proved tactic. That the air force has now recognized the need for additional AC-130s is reflected in aircraft now being constructed and those programmed over the next three years.

Many SOF units have successfully undertaken to improve their own mission area survivability by developing sufficient stores of weapons and other equipment used in that area to equip most individual troopers.

PSYOPS Equipment. PSYOPS equipment deficiencies were once legion (and they paralleled manpower shortfalls), but many improvements have been implemented and more are on the way. The heavy printing presses used by Fourth PSYOPS Group at Fort Bragg are nondeployable, and produce less-than-state-of-the-art posters and leaflets. Progress is being made in procuring more modern, modular equipment, and this equipment, when and if fully fielded, will provide increased mobility and quality to PSYOPS printing efforts.

The obsolete MI29El leaflet bomb, used in Vietnam, is scheduled for replacement. Development of a new leaflet artillery round is also in the works. Video production capabilities have also improved, and have been used to good effect in programs in Latin America.

The Air National Guard Coronet Solo EC-130 PSYOP aircraft presents a formidable potential. Equipped for television broadcast, they are usually set for bands used in North and Central America. In a European, African, Middle East, or Asian conflict, they would require reconfiguration.

A great many improvements to SOF parachute delivery, weaponry, target location and designation, position location, and transportation are in development or operational testing. Increasingly the budget dollars are going toward off-the-shelf, nondevelopment issue items for which the R&D has already been accomplished by another agency, service, or country.

The Future

The expansion and upgrading of U.S. SOF has been a direct function of perceptions of SOF utility in antiterrorism and counterterrorism and counterinsurgency. Certainly SOF have a significant role in the Reagan administration's posture on state-sponsored terrorism and the spread of Soviet-inspired political destabilization. But the continued improvement and sustainment of SOF capabilities must depend on more than a given administration's third world–oriented security assistance enthusiasm. It is unlikely, for example, that a Democratic administration will perceive the regional conflict in Central America in quite the same activist frames of reference as Reagan's.

By the same token, world realities cannot be denied, and it is significant that SOF have found their most energetic advocates in a Democratic-controlled Congress, an institution that will survive a change in executive leadership and in which the necessity and utility of SOF are, at least for key members of the Armed Services Committees, obvious.

The congressional constituency for SOF is a critical one to maintain, but it is not the only one. The peacetime antiterror and counterterror and counterinsurgency assistance roles are the ones most relevant to Congress and to some senior uniformed theater commanders. But SOF's in-service constituency rests largely with those who have historically understood SOF least: conventional commanders with theater war-fighting responsibilities in a general conflict.

Mr. Koch, Congressman Daniel, and others have looked at the U.S. commanders' understanding of SOF as part of the total strategy and found it wanting. It is true that the stand-alone, low-intensity dimensions of SOF capabilities must be factored into theater strategy and that theater commanders and operations deputies may not have advanced their thinking as far as may be desirable from a strategic planning standpoint. They have, however, devoted considerable thought to exploiting the conventional-operations-related force multiplier virtues of SOF. It is that thought process, imperfect as it is, that drove the validated theater SOF requirements, which in turn provided much of the ammunition for Koch, Daniel, Hutto, Deputy Secretary Taft, and JSOA in urging further SOF resource allocations from the services. Critics of the conventional military mind-set are correct in believing that SOF's virtues must ultimately be seen in a nonconventional frame of reference for their ultimate potential in national security planning to be achieved. But for some time before USSOC was created, the most persuasive lanaguage to Joint Staff operations deputies and to the service staffs was the one they understood most, and that came from theater commanders who demanded more SOF assets.

More immediately critical is where SOF goes beyond the organizational restructuring. Lip-service to low-intensity conflicts must end; they have been and are likely to continue being the most probable confrontation arena for the foreseeable future. It must be replaced with fresh assessments of how SOF can be utilized in the shades of gray conflict scenarios, which will surely bedevil theater and national planners in the coming years. Progress has been, and continues to be, made in developing forces and doctrines to deal with such conflicts; it must now be matched with progress in conceptualizing SOF (and other low-intensity conflict capable units such as the light divisions) use in nonwar strategies.

Probably the degree to which this rethinking can occur is limited; those who must do it are by training and inclination attuned to those conventional combat scenarios least likely to occur. Its genesis must be in the staff colleges and war colleges where these officers begin professionally to consider joint command operations, theater strategy, and national strategy; and some increased attention to the most likely scenarios is indeed underway in those institutions, though not nearly in enough scope and detail.

The continuing ability of U.S. SOF to play a significant role in thwarting state-sponsored terrorism and destabilization, as well as maintain general war force-multiplier capabilities, will depend on continued vigilance by SOF advocates in and out of uniform, vigorous execution of their charters by the new assistant secretary of defense for special operations and low-intensity conflict and commander, USSOC, and an end to service relegation of special operations to "nice to have" status. To some degree, the last is inevitable: nobody trusts an elite in a democracy, and it was to reduce the effects of the inevitable that Congress forced the enabling legislation. But mandated change addresses only symptoms. The attitudinal shift that sees SOF as major peacetime actors in national security policy and as wartime force multipliers must come from within the services themselves if SOF revitalization is finally to reflect commitment and not cosmetics.

7

New Media Strategies for Addressing Terrorism

W.D. Livingstone

T he heightened awareness of terrorism in the United States comes not as a consequence of any new strategy or wizardry devised by armed guerrillas so much as it is the product of extensive coverage by the media of a handful of widely publicized attacks.

The means of terrorism—kidnappings, hijackings, bombings, assassinations—have changed little over time. Even the frequency of such attacks against Western nations remains fairly constant.[1] But the intensity and the way with which they are now reported by the media have changed radically, altering the threat posed to society.

In years past, attacks by extremist groups gained at most a front-page article or a possible mention on an evening network news program. Today terrorism directed against Americans can trigger an extravaganza of news reporting such that the story monopolizes all television, radio, and newspaper coverage for days or even weeks. A spate of bombings or kidnappings, given sufficient media attention, can cause severe economic disruptions as tourists rush to alter their travel plans to locations free from the threat of violence.

The media move into a frenzy of news gathering. Networks interrupt regular broadcasts with special reports, repeating vivid and often horrifying pictures of violence, communicating a message of fear and intimidation. During interviews, media personalities relentlessly press officials on what actions the United States may be contemplating, propelling the issue forward in directions that may be premature or unwise.

Such exposure by the media proportionally far exceeds the relevance of the event's threat to society. The enormous amount of news generated by an attack inflames public emotion, which in turn places immense pressure on government leaders to act swiftly against the perpetrators.

The feverish attention given to terrorist events by the media has elevated the public's understanding of the threat posed by extremist groups. But in so doing, the media have come under increasing attack because of the way they report on such incidences. This is especially true for the television industry, which at times has been painted as an accomplice for the inordinate level of attention it seems all too willing to provide to terrorists. Such is the zeal of broadcast journalists to report a news story ahead of their competition that reporters have readily violated basic rules of professionalism, pitting hooded criminals against elected officials as if there were no moral distinction. News anchors recklessly have ventured beyond the recognized boundaries of journalism in a vain attempt to help arbitrate an ongoing crisis, complicating already confusing and dangerous situations. During recent attacks, the media broadcast sensitive military information, potentially compromising U.S. counteractions to free hostages.[2] And in what columnist George Will calls "pornography of grief," reporters have given bad taste new meaning by crassly exploiting the private lives of hostage families, recording every fear and tear.

Since terrorists depend heavily on publicity to achieve their political goals, how—and how much—the media report on attacks has become a growing concern in efforts to halt terrorism. To stem the tide of violence, it has been suggested that laws be passed to limit media coverage, even going to the extreme of mandating a blackout of all news reporting. Others, wary of weakening the First Amendment protections of free speech, believe the media's excesses are best corrected through self-discipline and professionalism. Still others observe that the media have generally offered excellent news coverage of attacks given the circumstances and, when criticized, are merely a scapegoat for inadequate government policies, which they argue must be strengthened to battle terrorism.

Are the media but the messenger of ill tidings and should not be held in contempt for doing what they are suppose to do—report the news, good or bad? Or can a case be made in this unique instance that the media are an integral part of the problem and should be restricted in their efforts to report on terrorist strikes?

Media Strategies of Terrorism

British historian E.H. Carr subdivided the elements of political power into three categories: military, economic, and public opinion.[3] A band of terrorists seeking political power cannot hope to field massive armies to compel opponents to accept their will nor can they tap a state's full financial resources to promote their cause. But clearly terrorists can and do exploit public opinion. Where they fail with the might of their guns, they hope to succeed with the forcefulness of their propaganda.

As a general rule, the more media attention a terrorist group can attract, the greater is its political power and leverage upon events. Strategies for gaining access to the world press have taken many forms and depend on many variables. Some terrorist strikes are designed solely to announce to the public certain demands or political statements. In most cases, a violent attack itself is the message. In other instances, attacks are orchestrated as a means to win specific concessions such as the release of jailed comrades or to prevent the extradition of comrades to other countries for prosecution.

In the spring of 1987, Chilean leftist guerrillas coordinated raids on eight radio stations, forcing them to broadcast a statement declaring an end to a cease-fire that earlier had been announced in anticipation of a visit by Pope John Paul II.[4] In this instance, the airwaves were commandeered to transmit information to fraternal rebels and to the public at large. Targeting eight stations not only guaranteed saturation coverage of their views but communicated an ominous warning about the society's vulnerability to attacks in urban centers by the rebels.

Temporarily seizing control of a radio or television station allows guerrillas to broadcast a message directly to audiences in the immediate area. To communicate the text of a revolutionary manifesto or a political communiqué to the general public, terrorists have relied on blackmail and extortion.

As an example, Croatian terrorists in 1975 hijacked a TWA jetliner and threatened to kill all fifty hostages unless the *Washington Post* and other major newspapers published prepared documents. Editors, fearing they would be blamed for the death of the hostages, reluctantly consented to the terrorists' demands. For its part, the *Washington Post* cleverly minimized any publicity by printing the Croatian statements in the smallest type possible and restricting to just thirty-seven the number of copies where it appeared.[5]

Forcing the Western media to print the communiqués, as in this case, accomplished little if anything for the attendant risk undertaken by the terrorists. At most this tactic can be seen as a vain exercise in futility that reflects a naive understanding of persuasive communications. It is pure fantasy to believe the public, especially in the United States, will be persuaded to act in the terrorist's behalf after reading a statement published in several national newspapers.

While terrorist groups generally seek publicity as a means to further their political goals, not in every instance have they sought to achieve maximum media attention. In the case of reporter Jeremy Levin, a former hostage held in Lebanon, months went by without any public statement by the Hesbollah on the conditions for his release and that of the other hostages. The Hesbollah even videotaped a message by Levin to Cable News Network owner Ted Turner, restricting its availability to the U.S. government.

Seven months were to pass before Levin's wife, frustrated by a lack of progress, broke silence by publicly announcing the conditions for freeing her husband. Shortly after the Hesbollah went public and released photographs of six hostages to an Arabic newspaper in Beirut, along with a statement demanding that Kuwait release seventeen jailed comrades convicted of the 1983 bombings of the U.S. and French embassies.

Bombings

Direct assaults on news-gathering facilities and extortion to force access to the media are rare occurrences when compared to the number of bombings undertaken by terrorists, the preferred method of attack. It was Marshall McLuhan, the media visionary, who observed that "the medium is the message."[6] In this context, bombings are in themselves a medium. Inherently they communicate powerful images and ideas.

A bombing provides immediate credibility to all subsequent threats and demands made by a terrorist organization and focuses attention on their grievances. A bombing foreshadows the possibility of future violence against innocent victims, calling into question a government's ability to protect the public's welfare. It jars the individual's psyche, causing emotional tension and fear. And importantly for terrorists, it attracts the media like moths to light. The more heinous and bloody the crime, the bolder are the headlines and the more time is given to the story on television and radio programs.

One of the more gruesome attacks in memory occurred in late summer 1982. The Queen's Household Cavalry were parading through London's Hyde Park. As they passed a blue Morris sedan parked on Carriage Road, an Irish Republican Army bomb hidden inside exploded, hurling hundreds of four- and six-inch spike nails through the air. *Newsweek* reported, "Horses fell in a writhing mass, dying soldiers bled into tatters of their ornate uniforms and a woman passer-by, her face shredded, screamed, 'Help me! Help me!' "[7] The blast, which took the lives of four cavalrymen and injured twenty-two guards and civilians, struck at the heart of Britain. The horror seemed to call into question: Is nothing sacred? If terrorists are willing to commit the most egregious of crimes imaginable, can anything or anyone be safe?

Although bombings such as this one communicate horrifying images, their impact on the public dialogue is usually short-lived. In most cases, a single explosion generates but a single series of headlines. Like a shooting star, the news accounts burn brightly but then quickly fade away. Journalists and broadcasters convey in their stories the horrid details of maimed and bloodied victims; when nothing remains to be explained, they switch their attention to more newsworthy events, in turn shifting public attention.

Kidnappings

While bombings account for about 70 percent of all terrorist incidents, kidnappings and hijackings generate an avalanche of media attention. One needs only to recount the Iranian hostage crisis to realize the power of such an attack. For 444 days, reporters spewed forth a continuous stream of information about the plight of the fifty-three Americans held hostage, focusing daily the public's attention, molding public opinion. Again in the summer of 1985, Americans had a front-row seat when the Hesbollah hijacked TWA flight 847. From the opening moments of terror to the negotiated release of the thirty-nine passengers seventeen days later, journalists reported each harrowing episode as if it were a miniseries produced for prime-time television. Even a farewell dinner with the hostages and their captors seemed choreographed for the world's television cameras to record.

Hostage-taking incidents that involve large numbers of people open the flood-gates of news due to the scale of the threat against human life and the fact that such stories remain open-ended, fueling additional interest and coverage by journalists. Any word about a hostage will be prominently displayed in the press, which translates into unlimited access for terrorists to the media. Each day of a crisis, gripping news stories splash across newspapers in banner headlines, kindling intense interest. More and more journalists begin focusing on the story, reporting each and every facet, bombarding the public with dramatic details, until the event over-shadows all other news. "The longer the terrorists can string out the hostage situation," columnist David Broder confesses, "the easier access we allow them to our cameras and microphones, the greater the power they gain over their hostages—and over us."[8]

The media understandably give prominence to reporting such hostage incidences given the political stakes. Everyone can remember the damage caused to Jimmy Carter's presidency as it grappled with the Iranian crisis. It could easily happen again, reporters realize. Hostage incidences are a high-risk gambit. From the point of view of the media, such stories are also a self-generating prophecy. Believing a terrorist kidnapping can have major political consequences, reporters deluge the public with news stories and editorials. They focus opinion, magnifying the events of the story such that the attack becomes a major political dilemma with far-reaching consequences.

A hostage incident also produces a mountain of media for reasons beyond its structure. Another factor contributing to the intensity of such stories concerns the enormous and heart-wrenching publicity generated by family members of hostages. Frustrated by the inability of government officials to secure the freedom of their loved ones, family members often turn their rage against the government. They hope public pressure will persuade officials to make concessions, no matter if it undermines long-term policies for the protection of all Americans. Not surprisingly, news stories about families of hostages usually play into the terrorists' hands. Family members rarely vilify the terrorists for fear it could push them to the brink, causing the death of hostages. By contrast, when bombings kill innocent victims, grieving families join government leaders in viciously lashing out at the terrorists, blaming them for their ruthlessness and inhumanity.

One of the outspoken advocates for the plight of the "forgotten hostages" is Peggy Say, whose brother, Associated Press newsman Terry Anderson, was captured March 16, 1985. She repeatedly has criticized the State Department for not doing what she believes is enough to free Americans held captive. During the TWA 847 incident, the State Department contacted Say to request that she not link the release of her brother and the other six hostages directly with the negotiations to free the passengers aboard the plane. Say not only turned down the request but went on the offense, organizing a media campaign with the other hostages' families.

To the chagrin of the State Department, Say flew to Washington, D.C., appearing on numerous television programs, where she charged that the administration had forgotten her brother and the other hostages. The news stories ultimately pressured Secretary of State George Shultz to ask for the release of all the hostages held in Lebanon, not just the thirty-nine still aboard the TWA jetliner. According to Say, the media "turned it around for us and almost got them out. More pressure would have brought them home."[9]

News Theater

An element unique to kidnappings and hijackings not to be overlooked when examining the reasons such attacks cause a furious outburst of news coverage relates to their inherent drama and excitement. Journalists routinely struggle to make interesting for the public news items they must write about in the course of their day-to-day jobs. Such is not the case when covering a hostage incident. As reporters often say, such a story writes itself. A kidnapping incident by definition contains structural parallels to dramatic art—hence the all-too-familiar axioms comparing terrorism to theater and the world stage.

Like a classic, well-made play, a conflict is locked in the opening scene when terrorists storm a jetliner, taking passengers hostage. Not knowing what will happen next creates heightened suspense and tension. The human element—the hostages and their families—weighs heavily in everyone's mind. At stake are their lives and the fate of government leaders, whose actions are carefully scrutinized and evaluated. The cast of characters includes unsung heroes such as John Testrake, the level-headed pilot of TWA flight 847, and faceless antagonists—killers dressed in black ski masks toting machine pistols. The plot unravels scene by scene in a live drama, fusing elements of art with news reporting, creating what has been uniquely termed terrorvision.

In a reversal of this phenomenon, motion pictures have been produced, recreating the tense moments of an attack from the perspective of the hostages, not unlike what might actually have occurred during the 847 episode. The structure of such films need not be altered from reality to heighten the viewer's level of interest or anxiety. In both cases—the real and the imagined—terrorist kidnappings attract large audiences, selling newspapers as readily as theater tickets.

It was a high-stakes hostage incident that first catapulted the issue of terrorism into the consciousness of the modern world. During the 1972 Munich Olympics, eight Palestinian terrorists stormed an Israeli dormitory, killing two athletes in a pre-dawn attack. It was the congregation of media assembled to cover the Olympic games that had drawn the Black September terrorists to Munich. The whole world was watching. Some 4,000 reporters were present—at that time "the largest team of reporters and commentators for any sports event in history."[10] Hours after the initial assault, television networks began sending reports via satellite to an estimated 1 billion viewers.[11] ABC reporter Peter Jennings managed to set up a camera within the perimeter of the heavily guarded sports village, providing pictures of the Palestinian terrorists, whose "floppy hats and stockinged faces popped regularly out of doors and windows and into view."[12] The historic event climaxed in a shootout at a military airfield outside Munich in which fifteen more people died, including all the Israeli hostages and the Arab gunmen.[13]

The Munich massacre sent shock waves around the world. It was the first live, international broadcast of a terrorist raid. It demonstrated not only the potential political power of terrorism but the power of television. Trying to put the attack into perspective in a *Newsweek* editorial, Shana Alexander posed the questions: "Were we watching a game, a sport, a melodrama, a new event? . . . Is this an adventure drama?"[14] Fifteen years later, these paradoxes remain. But now terrorists no longer must seek out the location of television cameras. Because of new technology, news stations can cover terrorist strikes wherever they may happen.

Watching the Making of History

From the beginnings of television, technology has defined in large part the limits of news gathering. Broadcasters always have sought to provide live pictures of important events, but the burden of electronically transmitting a television signal from a remote location back to the main studio for rebroadcast has restricted the opportunities for such coverage. During the early years of television, live broadcasts mainly featured sports contests. In 1947, NBC telecast the World Series for the first time, sending a signal to four cities: New York, Washington, D.C., Philadelphia, and Schenectady. Not until 1952 did the three networks converge in Chicago to report on the presidential conventions, reaching an audience estimated at 70 million viewers. In both instances, truckloads of electronic equipment had to be set up at the remote locations, a time-consuming and costly undertaking.

Since then the technological barriers limiting news gathering gradually have been eliminated to the point that live broadcasts are now an everyday event. These innovations have changed the way news is presented and caused the amount of news made available by networks and local stations to increase. The most recent advancement is the advent of the portable uplink station, a device to transmit video signals from earth to a stationary satellite orbiting some 22,000 miles overhead. This technology replaces the cumbersome microwave relay, which is limited in application since it must be arranged in line of sight to transmit a television signal. Portable uplink stations now make it possible to send live broadcasts over long distances; before, a series of carefully placed microwave relays were required for a remote broadcast beyond the horizon because of the earth's curvature.

All the equipment needed to make a live broadcast now fits into the back of a van with a satellite dish mounted on top. News crews drive to the location of a news story, set up a camera, align the satellite dish, and begin transmitting live pictures. The same technology can fit aboard a Lear jet or as baggage in a passenger plane. As expressed by NBC News president Lawrence Grossman, "We have an incredible capacity to originate where anything is happening."[15] With the new technology, reporters can now broadcast live reports from the jungles of Central America or a remote tarmac where terrorists have commandeered a jetliner.

Satellite technology has also revolutionized the syntax of news. Programs such as "This Week with David Brinkley" and "Nightline" regularly bring together experts from around the world to discuss current events. It is not unusual for a program to include a journalist in the Middle East at the scene of a story, a NATO spokesman in Europe, a Soviet official in New York, and a politician from Washington, D.C., all discussing a single topic.

In addition to vastly improving the wealth of information and the breadth of material networks can bring to bear on a story, satellites have fundamentally altered the way we gather news and the speed with which we are able to get visual information. Radio used to be the preferred medium people turned to when they wanted information on a breaking story. Now, increasingly they switch on the twenty-four hour television satellite news channel CNN to see as well as hear events unfold. No longer is the public dependent on the networks to interrupt their regular programming to broadcast special reports, nor must they wait until the evening news programs to see what happened earlier in the day. The establishment of CNN reflects both a growing interest in news and the capability of technology to gather news as it occurs.

These many technological strides in newscasting have worked to the advantage of terrorists. More news programming translates into increased competition and a larger news hole for terrorists to exploit. Television news programs must fill their allotted time with news stories of the day, and terrorism is hot news.

As the global audience has expanded, so has the power of terrorists. CNN now reaches a potential audience of 39 million households in fifty-four countries.[16] A news story reported on CNN about a terrorist attack can quickly become an international event. The fact that CNN broadcasts news twenty-four hours a day puts tremendous pressure on the other networks to interrupt their regular programming when a terrorist event occurs. If one network offers a special report, showcasing the top news anchor, the others are obliged to do the same or forfeit a share of the market. Live broadcasts by all the networks quickly elevate the issue in importance such that it dominates all other news stories, setting the political agenda.

The fact that competition is so intense among the networks to broadcast the story means they will scramble to provide live reports at the scene of an attack. This in turn heightens the drama and news value of the event, again playing into the hands of the terrorists. General guidelines adopted by news agencies prohibit live broadcasts of terrorists except under the most extreme circumstances. Still, hooded rebels need only provide a little action or drama, such as threatening a pilot with a machine pistol, to ensure their place on the evening news. Such incidences will be recorded on videotape that is beamed around the world by satellites minutes later.

The immediacy as well as the amount of the information generated by the media gives little time for officials or news editors to reflect on the facts. There used to be a delay of up to twenty-four hours before news was disseminated. Now information flows instantaneously. Decisions must be made in a matter of minutes about what to cover, increasing the chance for mistakes and creating more opportunities for terrorists to exploit.

Videoterrorism

A new era in terrorism communication can be precisely dated to January 29, 1985. On this day, the media ran stories on a videotape about kidnapped U.S. diplomat William Buckley. A photograph taken of the videotape that was reproduced in the *Washington Post* shows Buckley standing against a wall holding a January 22 copy of the Beirut newspaper *L'Orient-Le Jour*.[17] In the fifty-six-second videotape message, Buckley gives a short statement on behalf of himself and two other hostages, Benjamin Weir and Jeremy Levin. "We ask that our government," Buckley said, "take action for our release quickly."

What makes this event noteworthy is the fact that the media showed little, if any, reticence in widely reporting the contents of the cassette, which was made available by Visnews, an international television news service. Without prodding or threat, television and radio networks broadcast portions of the cassette on their news programs. Newspapers, which in the past had resisted blackmail tactics, without hesitation reprinted Buckley's political statements and demands.

The videotape has since become the preferred method of communication by terrorists. As an example of its power, in May 1987 the Islamic Jihad for the Liberation of Palestine released a four-minute videotape of Alann Steen, a journalism professor abducted earlier in the year from Beirut University College. Sitting against a blank wall, Steen is shown reading a one-page statement. The camera zooms in to a close-up to emphasize a particular point. "Remember that our issue will be always related to the release of prisoners in the prisons of Israel that occupies the land of Palestine," he says, his firm voice loudly echoing in what seems to be an empty room.[18] Steen chastises the "traitors" in the United States for prolonging the detention of the eight Americans held hostage in Lebanon and claims the administration wishes them "a longer absence and even death."

These words and images—almost certainly spoken under duress—were gobbled up by a press seemingly unconcerned about the larger issue of media manipulation and terrorist propaganda. It is obvious that this videotape and others showing hostages are designed by terrorists as propaganda to put pressure on the government to make concessions. Still, the media report the information regardless of its veracity and political consequences.

The cassettes are simple to produce and from a propaganda point of view are far more effective than techniques previously used. Compare a videotape message to a photograph released by the Red Brigades in 1981, showing Brigadier General James Dozier holding a billboard covered with political slogans, one of which reads: "The capitalist crisis breeds imperalistic war."[19] In both the videotape of Alann Steen and the photograph of General Dozier, pictures reveal evidence about their health and state of mind. Both transmit ideological statements. But the videotape adds a heightened degree of emotionalism. Audiences watching real pictures of a hostage more readily empathize with the individual's dilemma, a pawn caught in a life-and-death struggle. It is difficult to turn away from the tragic situation, to close one's eyes and forget the pleading for help. The videotape supplies pictures and audio for television and radio stations to assemble into a story, without which, it is arguable, they would otherwise not report the story. The images and voice are dramatic and hence capture the public's attention.

The Big Event

Political campaigns and conventions used to be the premier events to showcase a network's new technology and talent. Now, according to Roone Arledge of ABC News, it is a crisis or disaster such as a terrorist hijacking or the tragic explosion of the *Challenger* space shuttle.[20] During emotional times such as these, Arledge explains, a bonding occurs between viewers and news anchors, which can dramatically affect the ratings of news programs.

NBC's top anchor, Tom Brokaw, was vacationing in Africa when militant Shiites hijacked TWA flight 847. The network, in a decision that has been severely criticized, decided not to put second-string anchor Roger Mudd on the air. As might be expected, NBC viewers flipped their channels to the familiar faces of ABC's Peter Jennings and CBS's Dan Rather to get information. Media circles considered NBC's handling of the situation an embarrassment. They blamed top management for poor judgment and for damaging the already weak ratings of the "Nightly News."

When the big event hits, the sheer magnitude of information television can generate is overwhelming. A crisis atmosphere ignites everywhere, especially in the newsrooms, where the air becomes electrified as reporters scramble after the story. In the dog-eat-dog world of television reporting, there is intense competition to get on the air first. During the TWA flight 847 hijacking, the media pulled all the stops to keep viewers "up to date on all the developments." No angle in the story was left unturned. In between news stories of the unfolding events, reporters interviewed every imaginable expert on terrorism, government official, and family member of a hostage. The volume of information quickly catapulted the event to a high pitch, prompting columnist David Broder to write: "Many of us watching felt television crossed the line between covering the story and hyping it."[21] The real problem was the surfeit of news. "Our senses were overwhelmed and our minds were drowned in the coverage."[22]

About the excesses of the media, veteran print journalist Michael O'Neill called its performances an "orgy of overkill that exploited the hostages, their families, and the American people."[23] The *Washington Post* lashed out at the journalists: "There were excesses in taste, and they cannot be condoned no matter that the First Amendment certainly permits them."[24] Editors at the paper said the access the media provided to the terrorists "undermined or at least burdened" President Reagan's efforts to resolve the crisis.

State Department counsel Abraham Sofaer excoriated the news media during a panel discussion on terrorism: "The hijackers sought publicity, and they got it. The world was treated to a media extravaganza that gave irresponsibility and tastelessness a new meaning."[25]

Jody Powell blamed the circus atmosphere created by the media on competition for ratings: "The media obsession with the hijacking of TWA flight 847 has had much more to do with the love of ratings and the resulting revenues than any feelings one way or the other about Ronald Reagan."[26]

While agreeing that the media often "overdo it," veteran ABC reporter Sam Donaldson defended the way the broadcast journalists covered the story: "We overdo it not because primarily we want to steal a competitive march on NBC or CBS or ABC, but because we want to get there with the news. And that leads to maybe going on [the air] twice more during the day than we really had the news to justify."[27]

Government Response

In welcoming back the fifty-three Americans held captive in Tehran, President Reagan sounded a warning of swift and effective retribution against any terrorists planning to attack Americans. The United States, he stated, would never be held hostage again. Although the country had witnessed the power of terrorism almost daily for more than a year as journalists reported on the Iranian crisis, few people in government had a comprehensive knowledge of this new threat to society.

As one of his first actions, Secretary of State Al Haig created an "interdepartmental group" on terrorism to examine ways to prevent future incidents. The group reviewed "embassy security, contingency planning and incident management, training, and international initiatives."[28] To gain a "deeper understanding of the sources and dynamics of international terrorism," the State Department also brought together in May a group of academic and government experts to discuss the terrorism phenomenon.

Equal concern about this new and unexplained threat to the United States was expressed on Capitol Hill. Senator Strom Thurmond (R–South Carolina), chairman of the Judiciary Committee, established the Subcommittee on Security and Terrorism. Its freshman chairman, Senator Jeremiah Denton (R–Alabama), set into motion a series of hearings to "identify the terrorists, their resources, their origin, and their motivations."[29] By answering these questions, he believed the United States "might be in a position to make a careful, thoughtful, measured and effective response to future acts of terrorism."[30]

By year's end, the State Department had in place the beginnings of a comprehensive strategy to fight back. As broadly defined by Frank Perez, acting director of the Office for Combatting Terrorism, "We will resist terrorist blackmail and pursue terrorists with the full force of the law. We will not pay ransom, nor release prisoners, and we will not bargain for the release of hostages."[31] The hard-line policy contained elements to improve intelligence, the security of diplomats and embassies, and international cooperation.

Conspicuously absent in the debate on ways to counter international terrorism were any discussions on the relationship between terrorism and the media. The lack of any systematic analysis can be explained in part by fears that such an examination would wrongfully be perceived as an assault on freedom of speech. Also although the media had played a crucial role in the Iran crisis, coverage of terrorist events in the period immediately following proved nothing out of the ordinary. Not until TWA flight 847—the first sustained crisis—did the role of the media again surface as an integral element of terrorism demanding scrutiny by government officials.

One of the few statements about the media in the early years of the Reagan administration merely recognized the terrorists' desire to publicize their attacks and the ability of terrorists to command worldwide media attention. In an address before a conference on terrorism in Madrid in 1982, Frank Perez, deputy director of the Office for Combatting Terrorism, pointed out that diplomats were often the target of terrorism because of the publicity such attacks generate. "All terrorist attacks," he said, "involve the use of violence for purposes of political extortion, coercion, and publicity for political cause."[32]

The first comprehensive overview of the administration's position on media and terrorism appeared in the Public Report on the Vice President's Task Force on Combatting Terrorism published in 1986. "Terrorism," the report explains, "is a form of propaganda, demanding publicity to be effective."[33] It lists numerous media practices that can lead to problems during an incident, among them saturation television coverage, political interviews with terrorists and hostages, coverage of staged events, participating in negotiations, payments to terrorists for interviews or access, and divulging military actions. The task force rejected any government-imposed restraints that would conflict with the First Amendment and emphasized that the "media must serve as their own watchdog."[34]

The most detailed investigation by any arm of the government to date of the symbiotic relationship between the media and terrorism can be found in a hearing by the House Foreign Affairs Subcommittee on Europe and the Middle East convened several weeks after the TWA flight 847 incident. As described by Congressman Edward Feighan (D–Ohio), the hearing focuses on the dilemma the media face when covering "acts of war against the United States in which their role is itself a critical dimension."[35]

Representatives from television networks, who testified before the subcommittee, defended their coverage of the incident, arguing that it was professional, accurate, and responsible. "Some have criticized the press for presenting too much information to the American public during the hostage crisis," Jack Smith, vice-president and Washington bureau chief at CBS News argued. "We respectively disagree. We believe that our coverage played a constructive role in ensuring the well-being of the hostages and perhaps in facilitating their release."[36]

The congressmen at the hearing uniformly expressed their abhorrence of any measures that would encroach upon the First Amendment. But to find ways to improve coverage by avoiding past mistakes, Congressman Thomas Luken (D–Ohio), called on the leaders in television to "roll up their sleeves and seek common ground for agreement to protect hostages in the next crisis."[37] He proposed a meeting of broadcasters to consider mutual guidelines and self-regulation to avoid mistakes in the future. Each of the networks, while acknowledging the importance of restraint during a crisis, declined to participate in such a meeting.

To the credit of the committee members, the hearing provides a comprehensive look at the problems relating to media coverage of a terrorist incident. Still, it shies away from any examination of sensitive issues such as possible government-media cooperation to prevent the unauthorized disclosure of military information and intelligence. One of the few documents to date even to explore the "triangular media-terrorist-government" relationship was written by Robert Oakley, head of the State Department's recently renamed Office for Counterterrorism and Emergency Planning.

Oakley's paper, intended to stimulate discussion, considers the possibility of putting the government "more on a wartime footing than the present permissive approach."[38] To prevent the unauthorized disclosure of sensitive information, Oakley suggests the media as a whole consider adopting guidelines when reporting on terrorist incidents similar to those that already exist for a number of television, radio, and print outlets. "The guidelines," he puts forward, "could be monitored for compliance by a panel whose official members would be from the media with unofficial members or observers from the American Bar Association, Justice Department/FBI and State Department to provide advice, perspective and factual background."[39] If reporters violate the guidelines established by the media, he proposes that they be privately reprimanded by the panel. Frequent offenders would be publicly criticized. "If stronger sanctions were needed," he explains, "they could be developed in the light of experience."[40]

In addition, Oakley offers the idea that the panel be used to "assist in investigating the unauthorized publication of classified, sensitive intelligence information on terrorism or other national security matters such as military movements."[41] The oversight panel would assist in determining whether information published or disclosed was in fact sensitive or damaging to national security. To help prevent leaks, he suggests the implementation of a procedure whereby reporters would ask government officials at the beginning of an interview whether they were authorized to divulge certain information. If any material turned out not to be specifically authorized for disclosure, the reporter would be in a position to reveal the name of the source to the FBI. As an alternative to the creation of an oversight panel, Oakley suggests passing legislation that "would be a modification of the UK Official Secrets Act, making illegal the publication of certain classified information which would be very carefully defined."[42]

Oakley's views are by far the most controversial offered by a U.S. government official. Although they do not represent an official position of the State Department and are only suggestions for discussion, they reflect a growing concern about the political and military problems caused by the unauthorized disclosure of information.

Government Media Strategy

Just as terrorists have devised strategies to gain access to the media to influence political events, the U.S. government has developed media counterstrategies to try and deny terrorists their objectives. From the outset of the Reagan administration, officials have communicated through speeches, press releases, and press conferences their views on terrorism and what ought to be done to counteract the threat. Officials understand that a broad public consensus is essential to the success of their policies for prevention, preemption, and, if necessary, retaliation. "Our nation," Secretary of State George Shultz stressed in 1984, "cannot summon the will to act without firm public understanding and support. . . . Public support for U.S. military actions to stop terrorists before they commit some hideous act or in retaliation for an attack on our people is crucial if we are to deal with this challenge."[43]

One of the first counterstrategies implemented by the State Department was the establishment of a public affairs working group to assist in the dissemination of material on government policies, including actions taken and contemplated. To help educate the press about the threat posed by terrorism, officials now regularly participate in seminars and produce background papers.

The administration also has examined the interaction between the executive branch and the press to determine how it could be improved, especially during an incident. "If you're going to create a sense of a policy which you are then going to draw upon in a crisis situation, then you've got to do that on a continuing basis," Charles Redman, assistant secretary of state for public affairs, explained.[44] The better the media are informed on the issue, he stresses, the more appreciative they will be of the government's difficult position while managing an incident and the need to put information into the proper context.

After the European backlash to the U.S. air strike against Libya, the government's outreach program was expanded to include audiences overseas. The reason a coordinated program of speeches, papers, and contacts with the press is essential was described at the time by Robert Oakley: "Instead of reacting to individual terrorist incidents in a piecemeal fashion, we must make a much more concerted effort to convince public opinion in friendly countries on the need for cooperation."[45]

While information distributed by government public affairs offices establishes a general framework of understanding over the long run, a whole series of varying media strategies come into play during a crisis. Each terrorist incident involves unique factors—governments, airports, demands, timetables, and number of citizens. Consequently no general policy or public stance can be applicable when handling every incident. "Generally we do try to follow the line that we put out absolutely as much information as we can," Redman stated. "Because the extent that we do that, we defuse wrong information and speculation."[46]

When a crisis occurs, there are always people in government who are willing to talk to the media about terrorism but who know few details about an ongoing crisis, a high-ranking official at the State Department acknowledged. These spokespersons' speculations about ongoing events are then picked up by the media, and suddenly their views become "informed government responses." The information may be completely erroneous, fueling the crisis, or possibly accurate, undermining ongoing plans to rescue hostages. Consequently the strategy of the State Department is to make available as much information as possible to eliminate rumors and speculation. Still, Redman argues, there are times during an incident when the government must remain silent: "There may be points in a crisis when you don't want to do any media at all. You don't want to be forced into saying anything further under any circumstances."[47]

When the White House refuses to provide more than a trickle of information, it is referred to as a "grayout" by reporters, who often will turn to other sources of information to get a story, as happened during the TWA flight 847 incident. Near the end of the crisis, the White House severely reduced the amount of information released during the daily briefing for the press. As a consequence, the administration forfeited the opportunity to get its views on the evening news. "Thus, the pictures needed for television came from Beirut, where Berri and his men were more accommodating," Eleanor Randolph, a journalist at the *Washington Post* reported.[48]

A third aspect in the government's media strategy involves public announcements by officials to communicate information to terrorists and foreign governments. Because it is impossible to send a demarche to an extremist organization, officials must rely on the media to communicate certain facts, such as the administration's willingness to talk with terrorists or warn them of certain consequences if hostages are harmed. President Reagan and Secretary of State Shultz repeatedly have made clear in statements to the media that the United States will not negotiate with terrorists, hoping such declarations will deter extremists from taking Americans hostage.

There are no textbooks to explain all the problems journalists can encounter when covering a terrorist incident. Conversely the government is still learning what methods are effective or inappropriate when managing a terrorist crisis. On one hand, there is a built-in reluctance of government officials to provide much information. "General reaction from someone on the inside is, 'don't say anything,' "

Redman explains. "It's hard to get them to recognize that they help themselves by getting a lot more information out in public."[49]

Officials want to ensure the public is fully informed, but at the same time, they hesitate to promote the terrorists' agenda. When faced with a choice between these two conflicting goals, the State Department generally has restricted the disclosure of information. It repeatedly has discouraged families from speaking out, fearing such attention might endanger the lives of the hostages or upset behind-the-scene discussions. But withholding information can create the wrong impression that the government is not doing enough to help secure the release of hostages. "Administration officials have rarely offered more than boilerplate assurances that they are doing what they can," Laurence Zukerman, associate editor of the *Columbia Journalism Review*, points out.[50] Officials maintain that publicity will only reinforce the captors' position, making it more difficult to resolve the problem. "I do think that the tendency to focus almost obsessively on things of this kind does give a handle to those who we are combatting," Secretary of State Shultz explained. "It's better if we can work at it more quietly. But we haven't been able to do so."[51]

But critics contend that quiet diplomacy is an excuse to limit political pressure and hides the fact that little is being done to free the hostages. "In the end, what many of the families want is the same saturation coverage given the TWA hijacking and the embassy hostages in Iran—or at least substantial coverage of their hostage crisis," Zukerman concludes.[52]

Strategic Deception

The media tend to report any unusual movement of military forces during a crisis, whether it is the cancellation of leave for navy personnel or the deployment of aircraft and ships. Mindful of the media's close scrutiny of its every movement, in the summer of 1986 the U.S. government coordinated a series of signals that it was preparing some action against Libya's Colonel Qaddafi in hopes of keeping him preoccupied and off balance. In a flurry of activity, the United States deployed aircraft and ships, joined the Egyptians in military exercises near Libya, and dispatched a number of high-level officials to European capitals.

Officials correctly predicted the press would report their suspicious activity, but they did not foretell the press would print a story that the Pentagon was completing plans for a "new and larger bombing of Libya in case the President orders it" and that the administration was considering military action against Libya via Chad. The news story, which first appeared in the *Wall Street Journal*, was embraced by national security adviser John Poindexter and called "authoritative" by White House spokesman Larry Speakes. CBS quoted sources in the administration that Qaddafi was "planning new terrorist attacks against Americans in Europe."

In fact the United States was not contemplating military action, which raised questions about the government's credibility. When the truth came out, the administration was berated for deceiving the press. Stories about the disinformation campaign scuttled the whole operation and proved a major embarrassment to the administration. Charles Redman acknowledges the government's plan to deceive Qaddafi but rejects the accusation that the media were purposely deceived. "Regardless what the media says about being misled," he said, "they all had the right story within 24 hours."[53]

The episode illustrates the risk involved when using the press to send false signals to foreign governments that support terrorist activities. The United States can act tough by threatening to use its military forces. But for its policies to be taken seriously, it must involve more than words. Otherwise the United States risks being merely a paper tiger.

Double Standards

When four Palestinian terrorists hijacked the *Achille Lauro* off the coast of Egypt in October 1985, it looked as though it would be a replay of the TWA flight 847 crisis. Palestinian extremists threatened to blow up the ship, including the more than 400 passengers and crew, unless Israel agreed to release fifty prisoners held in their jails. The media were in the process of mobilizing their extensive resources when the incident came to a sudden end. Just two days after taking command of the Italian luxury liner, the terrorists surrendered to representatives of the PLO.

Initially the ship's remote location in the Mediterranean Sea limited photo opportunities for the television networks. Still, the story gained front-page attention, quickly eclipsing all other news and putting pressure on the administration to resolve the crisis. When seven F-14 Navy Tomcats from the U.S.S. *Saratoga* successfully intercepted the hijackers in the darkened sky over Syria, everyone was taken by surprise. The dramatic capture breathed new life into the story. The final chapter came when Italian Premier Bettino Craxi allowed PLO leader Mohammed Abbas, the mastermind of the attack, to escape unharmed, thereby evading U.S. authorities.

The media eagerly reported each nuance of the story just as they had during the TWA 847 hijacking. But this time they received little if any criticism from pundits for their excessive news coverage. For once, the terrorists had lost, and government officials were showered with praise. It was a public catharsis and celebration. The capture proved that terrorists were not invincible.

The absence of any criticism of the media's coverage is reflected in public opinion polls. According to a Times-Mirror poll, 55 percent of the American people considered the news reporting of the *Achille Lauro* incident to be "excellent." This compares with only a 23 percent "excellent" rating for the media in their coverage of the TWA flight 847 crisis.[54] The disparity of views leads to the inevitable question: are critics of the media only concerned about the attention given to attacks when the news is bad? Is there a double standard? So long as terrorists fail to achieve their demands, it would appear the media can violate the rules of professionalism with impunity, freely sensationalizing stories. But if terrorists win embarrassing concessions, the media better tread carefully, for they will be blamed in part for the government's failure to catch and punish the terrorists.

Media: A Double-Edged Blade

There exists a general perception that media attention given to terrorism actually prolongs an incident or will work only to the advantage of the extremists. Following the TWA 847 crisis, Henry Kissinger suggested the media refuse to cover press events organized by terrorists: "I think what the media ought to consider is not to carry anything, including the terrorists. If the terrorists didn't see in this the means of getting their message across, there would be less dog and pony shows like this one."[55]

Kissinger's view is supported by British Prime Minister Margaret Thatcher, who called on the news media to adopt a "voluntary code of conduct" that would "starve the terrorists and the hijackers of the oxygen of publicity on which they depend."[56] Under a media agreement she proposes, journalists "would not say or show anything which could assist the terrorists' morale or their cause."[57]

The views of Kissinger and Thatcher are based on a flawed syllogism, however: Terrorists depend on publicity to achieve their goals; if they are denied publicity, the incentive to commit violent attacks will be removed, leading to a decline in terrorism. Actually the opposite may occur. If the media enter into a conspiracy to black out all reporting on terrorism, extremists may escalate the severity of their violence to the point that publicity cannot be withheld. It also ignores the adverse consequences to inhibiting free speech.

Just because terrorism generates a great deal of media attention, it does not follow that everything or anything reported will be considered gospel by the public. Those who would muzzle the media fail to give sufficient credit to the public to determine what is right and wrong. The media provide officials and the public with information to assess the full extent of an attack. "Given the world today," Charles Redman explains, "the communication networks that exist, the media are going to have people on the ground faster than we are. And they are going to know as much if not more."[58] When a terrorist incident happens, the administration convenes a special task force to monitor and coordinate government responses. Redman confessed that the "task force keeps CNN on because you sometimes find out for the first time things via the media."[59]

Critics of the media's coverage often point to the "contagion factor" to illustrate the dangers of going overboard when reporting on a terrorist incident. Massive coverage, it is argued, stimulates others to commit the same crime. As evidence, they point to a string of "parachute hijackings" following a widely reported incident in 1971. A man who had smuggled aboard a parachute hijacked an Air Canada jetliner and attempted to extort $50,000 before being overpowered by the crew. Two weeks later, in a similar incident, a 727 jetliner was hijacked in Portland, Oregon. This time the hijacker escaped from the plane with four parachutes and $200,000. In the next six years, twenty-five hijackings were documented that involved attempted parachute escapes.[60]

Obviously the media's attention of the first hijacking spurred others to try the same feat, but it does not follow that press reports of all terrorist attacks will lead to additional terrorism. The initial parachute hijacking in 1971 was unique. The same cannot be said about most bombings, kidnappings, and assassinations. An enormous amount of information already exists in books and articles on these topics, and any attempt to withhold news stories about such attacks will not prevent others from gaining an understanding of the issue.

Information does not necessarily cause terrorism. In fact, the media present a double-edged sword: the tremendous attention given to an attack can actually work to the disadvantage of terrorists. The supersaturation of news during the 847 hijacking and the *Achille Lauro* attack educated the public to the threat of terrorism and the need for strong government countermeasures. Had the media refrained from covering these episodes in an effort to prevent a contagious effect, it is doubtful the public would have supported the subsequent bombing of Libya.

Based on polls, it can be argued that the public have not been bamboozled by the excessive media attention given to acts of terrorism. If anything, they may be insufficiently informed about the danger it poses to Western democracies. In January 1980, following the Iran crisis, 21 percent of all Americans said the most important problem facing the country was Iran and terrorism.[61] This figure dropped to 9 percent the following month and by the end of the year to just 4 percent.[62] In October 1984 only 1 percent of all Americans believed terrorism was the most important issue.[63] After the TWA 847 incident and the *Achille Lauro* hijacking, concern rose to 6 percent but then fell to only 1 percent again in December.[64]

On the whole, Secretary Shultz believes the press have "done a good job" in their reporting on terrorism.[65] "I regard the general movement of opinion about terrorism and the importance of it and the importance of doing something about it as very healthy," he said.[66]

Shultz's comments do not absolve the media from any wrongdoing. To the contrary, journalists in print and electronic media regularly make mistakes and will undoubtedly continue to do so. But in all their coverage, it is highly doubtful whether the outcome of any incident would have been different had the media been less sympathetic to terrorists or had they reduced their coverage by 10, 20, or even 50 percent. Although the media have often overstepped the boundaries of professionalism, not one news story can be offered as evidence that caused the death of a hostage or delay in their release. News stories have been hyped or been in poor taste, but this is nothing new; it is the nature of news reporting. The public has been well served by the media performance in their coverage of terrorist events. The fact that Mohammed Abbas, the mastermind behind the *Achillo Lauro* attack, gained access to national television does not mean his threats and violent attacks will go unpunished or that he will be emulated. Knowing one's enemy can also harden the resolve of society to strike back. To deny the public knowledge of terrorist attacks is the worst of all possible actions. It keeps the public from knowing the full nature of the threat, thus preventing essential public support for strong government responses.

Notes

1. David Ignatius, "Terrorism by the Numbers," *Washington Post*, April 13, 1986.

2. John Dillin, "News Media Coverage of Hostage Story Raises Glaring Questions," *Christian Science Monitor*, July 2, 1985.

3. Edward Hallett Carr, *The Twenty Years' Crisis* (New York: Harper & Row, 1964), p. 108.

4. "Guerrillas Resume Violence in Chile," *Washington Post*, April 14, 1987.

5. Katharine Graham, "Safeguarding Our Freedoms As We Cover Terrorist Acts," *Washington Post*, April 20, 1986, p. C2.

6. Marshall McLuhan, *Understanding Media: The Extensions of Man* (New York: McGraw-Hill, 1964).

7. "The IRA'S Return to Terror," *Newsweek*, August 2, 1982, p. 31.

8. David Broder, "The Terror Next Time," *Washington Post*, June 30, 1985.

9. Laurence Zukerman, "The Dilemma of the 'Forgotten Hostages,' " *Columbia Journalism Review* (July–August 1986):34.

10. Ibid.

11. "Olympics May Draw Biggest Worldwide Audience Ever—and There'll Be Plenty to See," *Broadcasting*, August 21, 1972, p. 29.

12. "ABC's Grim TV 'First,' " *Newsweek*, September 18, 1972, p. 67.

13. "Olympics May Draw Biggest Worldwide Audience Ever," p. 29.

14. Shana Alexander, "Blood on the Playground," *Newsweek*, September 18, 1972, p. 35.

15. "Satellites Giving Networks Greater News Freedom," *Broadcasting*, July 14, 1986, p. 42.

16. Frazier Moore, "90 Minutes: On the Edge of the News with CNN," *Southern Magazine* (May 1987):51.

17. Kathy Sawyer, "U.S. Hostage Urges 'Action,' " *Washington Post*, January 29, 1985.

18. Nora Boustany, "U.S. Hostage in Beirut Ties Fate to Held Arabs," *Washington Post*, May 15, 1987.

19. *Washington Post Magazine*, January 6, 1985.

20. Bill Abrams, "NBC News Gains Clout under Chief Grossman, But Problems Remain," *Wall Street Journal*, September 16, 1985.

21. David Broder, "Surfeit of TV News," *Washington Post*, July 7, 1985.

22. Ibid.

23. Michael J. O'Neill, *Terrorist Spectaculars: Should TV Coverage Be Curbed* (New York: Priority Press Publications, 1986), p. 26.

24. Editorial, *Washington Post*, July 4, 1985.

25. Karen DeYoung, "Thatcher Tells Media: Starve the Terrorists of Publicity," *Washington Post*, July 16, 1985.

26. Jody Powell, "Ratings, Ratings, Ratings," *Washington Post*, June 30, 1985.

27. Sam Donaldson, "This Week with David Brinkley," ABC News, June 23, 1985.

28. Statement by Richard Kennedy, under secretary for management, before the Senate Foreign Relations Committee on June 10, 1981, in *Department of State Bulletin*, (September 1981):65.

29. Sarah Midgley and Virginia Rice, *Terrorism and the Media in the 1980's* (Washington, D.C.: Media Institute, 1984).

30. Ibid.

31. Frank Perez, acting director of the Office for Combatting Terrorism, Conference on Violence and Extremism: A Leadership Response, October 29, 1981, in *Department of State Bulletin* (January 1982):56.

32. Frank Perez, conference on terrorism sponsored by the Instituto de Cuestiones Internacionales, Madrid, Spain, June 10, 1982, in *Department of State Bulletin* (August 1982): 24.

33. *Public Report on the Vice President's Task Force on Combatting Terrorism* (Washington, D.C.: Government Printing Office, February 1986), p. 19.

34. Ibid.

35. Congressman Edward Feighan, Subcommittee on Europe and the Middle East of the Committee on Foreign Affairs, *The Media, Diplomacy, and Terrorism in The Middle East, Hearing*, July 30, 1985, p. 1.

36. Ibid., p. 100.

37. Ibid., p. 4.

38. Robert Oakley, Council for the United States and Italy Conference on Media and National Security, October 13–14, 1986, p. 25.

39. Ibid., p. 28.

40. Ibid.

41. Ibid., p. 29.

42. Ibid., p. 33.

43. Secretary of State George Shultz, "Terrorism and the Modern World" (speech before the Park Avenue Synagogue, October 25, 1984), in *Department of State Bulletin*, December 1984, p. 16.

44. Interview with Charles Redman, June 5, 1987.

45. John Goshko, "New Front in War on Terrorism: Cultivating Foreign Opinion," *Washington Post*, July 18, 1986, p. A17.

46. Ibid.

47. Ibid.

48. Eleanor Randolph, "Networks Turn Eye on Themselves," *Washington Post*, June 30, 1985.

49. Interview with Redman.

50. Zuckerman, "Dilemma of the 'Forgotten Hostages,' " p. 30.

51. Secretary of State George Shultz interviewed on "This Week with David Brinkley," ABC News, June 23, 1985.

52. Ibid., p. 34.

53. Interview with Redman.

54. "Press Gets Mixed Reviews on Coverage of Terrorism," press release by Times Mirror, based on national survey conducted by Gallup Organization, September 25, 1986, p. 12.

55. "King Henry of the Airwaves," *Newsweek*, July 1, 1985, p. 37.

56. DeYoung, "Thatcher Tells Media."

57. Ibid.

58. Interview with Redman.

59. Ibid.

60. For a list of the parachute hijackings, see Schmid and Di Graaf, "Insurgent Terrorism and the Western News Media."

61. CBS News/New York Times poll, January 1980.

62. Ibid., February and March 1980.

63. Ibid., October, 1984.

64. Ibid., November and December 1985.

65. John M. Goshko, "Shultz Warns on Terrorism Coverage," *Washington Post*, July 10, 1986.

66. Shultz, interviewed on "This Week with David Brinkley."

8

Low-Intensity Terrorism Against Technological Infrastructures

Robert K. Mullen

T he course of terrorism over the past few years has been relatively consistent. Hostage takings, aircraft hijackings, assassinations, car bombings, and so on continue and likely will continue to do so. Venues may change with circumstances, but such may be in degree rather than substance. This is not to say the character of terrorism will remain static. Indeed, there have been changes in the strategic nature of terrorism in some postindustrial nations and a developing sophistication in its applications.

Within the past few years, there have been organizational changes, mergers, and dissolutions of mergers among terrorist groups. There have been schisms in terrorist groups. Separatist terrorists and insurgent groups have sprouted up seemingly everywhere; North America is the only continent spared this phenomenon. Symbiotic relationships have developed between drug traffickers and terrorists; the state sponsorship of terrorism has elaborated and become more obvious as a result.

But with few exceptions, such developments have not had noticeable impacts on the course of terrorism. These activities have not signaled an evolution or new direction in terrorism. Moreover, these crude and callous activities have rarely been of national security significance.

This is not the case for a significant proportion of relatively unpublicized—if less spectacular—terrorist activities in some postindustrial nations. Although there are historical precedents for virtually all these activities, there is none for the scale of them. No less important has been a developing sophistication in target selection, as indicated by the roles such targets play in the systems they support. Sophistication is apparent also in the uses of an absolute minimum of resources to sabotage a target and to degrade the functioning of the system of which it is a part.

The economic costs of terrorist activities directed against these targets are high; the potential impacts on national security are as significant. Terrorist attacks on state infrastructures of energy, transportation, and telecommunications; on developing advanced technology in these areas; on centers associated with the development of biotechnology and information science; on centers associated with developing advanced technology for military applications; and on facilities that implement some of these newer technologies are increasing in scope and effectiveness. At present, the impacts of these terrorist activities on national security are tolerable. The potential impacts are much greater, whether in peacetime or during a period of national emergency.

Technological developments by terrorists that could influence the directions of terrorism in postindustrial states have been few. Among the more impressive, however, has been the terrorist development of sophsiticated ordnance and electronic equipment, in some instances now into the third generation. These developments reflect evolutionary changes in terrorist capabilities with national security implications.

Low-Intensity Terrorism

In industrialized nations, terrorists have undertaken to sabotage social and economic infrastructures in ways that have serious national security connotations. But for the most part, these activities remain unreported beyond the parochial news media. They do not receive analytical attention commensurate with the seriousness of the issues they raise. Airport assassins, aircraft hijackers, and the like receive far more attention from news media and analysts, but their acts rarely imperil a nation's national security. The activities of those who engage in low-intensity terrorism, on the other hand, possess clear potentials for becoming serious national security issues.

Low-intensity terrorism is not new. It is a concept appealing to diverse groups and individuals and is frequently as much antitechnology as it is antistate. One author has traced the origin of the concept in West Germany, where it is flourishing, to various radical and underground publications that appeared there in the 1970s.[1] As it was then envisioned, it would be a popular front of radicals across the spectrum of the political left. The front would resist the state through small, individually insignificant acts of destruction and by rioting and residential squatting. These levels of resistance to the state could be achieved almost spontaneously in response to such local or regional issues as fare increases in public transportation, highway construction, housing shortages, and nuclear power.[2]

Since the 1970s, the concept of a popular front of antistate radical leftists has matured. In the early 1980s, the radical booklet *Guerrilla Diffusa* repeated the popular front concept[3] and described the existence of so-called autonomous groups, those that engaged in low-intensity terrorism but did not identify themselves.[4]

From 1984 to the present, the rate of antitechnology sabotage in West Germany has increased dramatically, as have the economic costs of such activity. Low-intensity terrorism associated with the antitechnology movement in West Germany is the violent expression of a movement lacking a coherent ideology. Those involved in acts of sabotage against the technological infrastructure are so-called radical militants (anarchists, Marxists, and socialists), some of whom are revolutionaries and others not. The movement embraces activities directed at slowing or stopping the development or application of technology in general, at slowing or stopping the development or application of specific technologies, and at pursuing a broader political agenda in which antitechnology is but one expression.

One of the most visible aspects (in terms of media coverage) of the antitechnology movement in West Germany is that directed against the nuclear power industry. The antinuclear power movement there may be the most persistently violent of its kind anywhere else in the world. It also has facets not frequently seen elsewhere.

Although the sheer size of some antinuclear demonstrations in West Germany (scores of thousands) is impressive, there are parallels, including in the United States. What seems unique to West Germany is the intense campaign of sabotage against the infrastructure supporting the devleopment, construction, operation, and security of nuclear power. A number of facilities and institutions are affected by this ongoing campaign: primary distribution power lines from nuclear power stations; railroad systems; trucks transporting nuclear materials; offices of firms providing consulting services to the nuclear power industry; manufacturers of equipment and supplies for the nuclear power industry; assets of firms associated with the construction of nuclear facilities; architect and engineering firms associated with nuclear power projects; assets of firms providing security services to the nuclear industry; institutions that participate in financing nuclear power construction; and scientific and technical institutes involved in pure and applied research in nuclear power. The names and addresses of many firms in this nuclear power industry infrastructure have appeared on lists in various radical publications in West Germany.[5] Some of the firms on these lists experienced over thirty arson or bombing attacks each in 1985–1986.[6]

The antitechnology movement in West Germany embraces much more than antinuclear activists. During a two-year period beginning in 1985, those involved in the movement were responsible for heavily sabotaging electrical distribution systems; over 160 structures and facilities were sabotaged during this period.[7] Actual acts of sabotage or attempts at sabotage that failed affected or could have affected operation of five nuclear power reactors.

Because of sabotaging the primary distribution lines (the power lines from the power station switchyard to the first substation) of these power reactors, some were forced to reduce electrical output by one-third to one-half or to shut down completely. Quite aside from the consequences to consumers of electrical power, the value of electricity generated by a 1,000 megawatt station is roughly $1 million per day. To whatever extent and for however long a power station cannot generate electricity, that revenue is lost. In addition, the owners of an affected power station often must purchase power from other generators in the grid to make up for that lost during the sabotage-induced downtime. Repairing equipment directly damaged by the sabotage and any other equipment in the distribution system that may have been secondarily damaged is costly.

This effective form of economic sabotage is not limited to antinuclear activists, although these activists can frequently be differentiated from more general antitechnology saboteurs on the basis of target selection. Sabotage by antinuclear activists tends to be selective with respect to induced consequences; that of anti-technology saboteurs (some of whom simply oppose electricity) is for the most part nonselective in this regard. Electrical power targets are chosen by an-titechnology saboteurs less for their criticality in a grid than for their isolation, ease of access, and vulnerability. Further, antinuclear saboteurs tend to use ex-plosives to topple power pylons; antitechnology saboteurs may saw them down or employ cutting torches.

Such activity should not be viewed as quixotic. It is serious because it has the potential to compromise national security—not only for West Germany but for its NATO allies and, supranationally, NATO itself. Should antitechnology saboteurs begin to conduct their activities with an eye to causing consequences of national security concern, there is little reason to doubt they would be successful. For exam-ple, in 1984, West German anarchists cut the power supplies to the landing system at the U.S. military airfield at Wiesbaden-Erbenheim to protest the autumn NATO exercises.[8] And in 1985, power to the landing system at Luxembourg's Findel Air-port was cut with multiple explosive devices. For several months, the airport was forced to divert all foul weather and night traffic to airports in neighboring coun-tries.[9] The revenue loss, aside from the $1.5 million repair cost, was substantial. The implications for national security are equally substantial.

Railroad systems are the second most popular sabotage target of antitechnology extremists in West Germany. Low-intensity terrorist sabotage of rail system has in-cluded loosening of track frog plates, removal of track ballast, and damaging traffic control systems and signals. In general, these acts have been directed at the rail systems and certain technologies they support: nuclear power, technologies other than nuclear power that generate toxic wastes, and military weapons technology. The publicly stated motives for these sabotage activities are that violent acts perpetrated against antihuman technologies are justifiable and that there is a broad consensus of support for this activity.[10] Branded as antihuman technologies are electrical power systems, railroads, autobahns, any technology that has been "militarized," and the NATO technological infrastructure.

The saboteurs claim, however, that they have rejected sabotage that may en-danger innocent members of the public. But this is a little like saying that a bomb laid in a publicly accessible location does not endanger the public at large. An open switch is virtually as indiscriminate and proximate a public danger as is a bomb. In contrast, the saboteurs assert that killing security guards at nuclear power in-stallations is acceptable because such acts serve the greater good of deterring the construction of nuclear facilities or impair their operation.[11]

Perhaps more to the point, however, have been some of the recent acts of low-intensity terrorism directed against railroads by so-called autonomous groups in the antitechnology movement. In West Germany, and in particular in Bavaria, many of these ad hoc groups have participated in the explosive growth of antitechnology sabotage. It was inevitable that these activities—in which there is virtually no coordination of action—would lead to situations dangerous to the general public; protestations to the contrary.

For example, in October 1986, an attempt was made to topple a power pole onto the tracks of the Munich-Tutzing railway and into the path of an express train full of weekend travelers. Only the overhead wires prevented the pole from falling onto the tracks, the train passing just underneath it.[12] In December 1986, two 30-meter pine trees were cut down and laid across the tracks of the Nürnberg-Regensburg railway one-quarter mile apart. Both were struck by passenger trains reported to have been traveling at more than 100 kilometers per hour. No injuries were reported in these incidents, but the potential for causing many casualties among the traveling public was present.[13]

Aside from the potential for injury, there are national security aspects to consider. For example, rendering inoperable the first or second tier of switches (or both) of exit or entrance (or both) tracks at a classification yard could severely affect rail traffic over a wide region. The sheer numbers of sabotage acts in the recent past are indicative of what could be accomplished against rail systems generally. From January 1 to the end of April 1987, there were sixty-two incidents of electrical and railway system sabotage.[14]

The antitechnology movement in West Germany is broad based. The targets selected for sabotage cover a spectrum of technologies aside from electrical power and railway systems. Since January 1984, low-intensity terrorism has become increasingly directed at the cutting edges of technological developments in the fields of information sciences, biotechnology, telecommunications, and transportation.

The attorney general of West Germany has stated on several occasions that one particularly threatened area of technology is that of information science.[15] The January 1984 bombing of the regional computer center at Reutlingen is held to be the first indication of a new terrorist threat against state-automated data processing.[16] Other bombings directed against information-handling technology include those of a computer consulting firm, of the Hamburg facilities of a manufacturer of computer control systems, of computer facilities at a firm in Cologne, and of a computer plant manufacturing decoding devices.

Since August 1985, a number of biotechnology facilities have been bombed. The motivations of some of those professing to have done the bombings reflect a zealous antitechnology bias affected in significant degree by ignorance, naiveté, and paranoia. Representative incidents:

- The newly completed genetics building at the Max Planck Institute in Cologne was bombed in August 1985

- The bombing in September 1985 of a supplier of control systems used in biotechnology, in Hamburg

- The University of Cologne Botanical Institute was bombed in October 1985

- In August 1986, the Münster University Institute for Human Genetics was bombed

Reflective of the motives and states of mind of the terrorists who bombed the Max Planck Institute in Cologne is the following statement:

> Political plants are being cultivated here; the result of this work is worldwide control of agriculture by some multinational concerns and the securing of their profits.[17]

Those who bombed the Münster University Institute for Human Genetics in August 1986 said, "This Institute is a building block in the FRG's [Federal Republic of Germany's] projected system of comprehensive genetic and social control over human life and reproduction."[18] They went on to say that the work at Münster is a continuation of the "fascist selection and liquidation policy."[18]

In July 1986, the Fraunhofer Institute for Laser Technology at Aachen, which carries out telecommunications research, was heavily damaged by a bomb. The institute is engaged in telecommunications research. In an apparently unrelated incident, the house of the institute's director was bombed about three weeks later. The attacks were seemingly carried out by two separate, ephemeral, and ad hoc groups. The group, which identified itself as the Sheban Atlouf Combat Unit, stated its motive as opposition to a technology that establishes "networks connecting all central military and government offices, companies and research, and the apparatus for activities by the cops and the secret service."[19]

The attack against the institute director's house was claimed by the Militant Nuclear Power Plant Opponents. The stated motive was opposition to the institute's cooperation with the "nuclear mafia," a code phrase used by the left in referring to government and private institutions involved with the nuclear power industry.[20]

Perhaps one of the more curious and unambiguously antitechnology incidents was the bombing in April 1987 of a demonstration electromagnetic railway in Berlin/Kreuzberg. A group calling itself the Demolition Society for Potemkin Villages claimed the event. It objected to the railway, which was still undergoing tests in preparation for Berlin's 750th anniversary, in pure antitechnology terms: the project would emphasize West Berlin's position as a center for high technology.[21]

Since 1984, low-intensity terrorism involving sabotage of the West German technological infrastructure has markedly increased. It can be said to have been occurring on four levels. The most extreme forms have been the assassinations of industrialists and other equally heinous acts carried out by the Red Army Faction (RAF). Today such acts are viewed by many in the violent left as counterproductive. The criticisms of the RAF from those on the left have resulted in an apparent distancing from the activities of the RAF and an isolation of it.[22]

At the next level are the bombing and arson attacks against institutions and facilities associated with advanced technology, physical and biological. Some of these actions show evidence of a modest sophistication. Explosive or arson devices are appropriate for their intended purposes and are effectively placed; subsidiary targets at the same facility are sometimes simultaneously attacked; and research records or documentation of equal importance are stolen or destroyed.

The third level is represented by destructive acts against power lines, railways, construction firms, and other assets of or supportive of the existing technological infrastructure. Bombings are less common at this level; simple mechanical destruction or arson is more frequent. Typical of this level is the sawing down of power pylons, the mechanical destruction or sabotage of various elements of railway system, and the setting afire of cement trucks or construction equipment.

At the fourth level are acts of violence against property and persons by violent elements of antinuclear or antimilitary demonstrations. Terrorists may hurl Molotov cocktails, shoot at police and security personnel with ball bearings or stones propelled with slingshots, cut fences, set out caltrops on site access roads, place burning barricades on roadways, and the like.

Activities at each of these levels can impair national security. Those of the RAF and other terrorist groups are well known. They are of relevance here only insofar as the apparent increasing irrelevance of those elitist terrorists, as perceived by the radical left, stimulate them to evaluate their effectiveness. The RAF and its ilk cannot be dismissed as threats to national security, but given their modes of operation—at least of the covert elements of these groups—they are currently seen as less such a threat than is the violent radical left.

Sophisticated Low-Intensity Terrorism

Low-intensity terrorism in West Germany is for the most part executed in relatively unsophisticated fashion. Halfway around the world, it is another story. In Japan, since 1985, the Chukaku-ha (Middle Core Faction) has executed acts of low-intensity terrorism that are sophisticated in concept, development, and application. In addition, the Chukaku-ha supports an ordnance development capability that, given the circumstances under which it exists, is remarkable.

The Chukaku-ha is quite different in origin and structure from the autonomous groups of the violent radical left of West Germany. Its roots extend to the Japan Revolutionary Communist League, formed in 1957. Following several organizational schisms over the following five years or so, the Chukaku-ha developed. Aside from the usual anti-imperialist proclamations, it further identified itself as anti-Stalinist and adherent to the theories of Leon Trotsky. The Chukaku-ha advocates violent proletarian revolution and renounces parliamentary systems of democracy. Various of the other factions evolving from the old Japan Revolutionary Communist League were, and are, considered enemies. The Kokumaru-ha (Revolutionary Marxist

Faction), formed at about the same time as the Chukaku-ha, is considered a mortal enemy, with enmity in 1974 arising to a level of "internal battle of death," the objective of which is the complete elimination of the Kokumaru-ha.[23] This objective was still being pursued at least as late as September 1986.[24] Most estimates place the membership of the Chukaku-ha at about 3,000. Of this, 230 or so are thought to constitute its military wing, the People's Revolutionary Army (PRA), which consists of two divisions.[25] Most of the members are middle-aged blue-collar workers. A significant number of them are said to belong to the Chiba Railway Workers' Union.

In terms of sophistication, the Chukaku-ha is probably unique among terrorist groups worldwide regarding the ordnance its members have developed and the technology it employs. Members have developed and successfully deployed a flamethrower, for example. Its first apparent use was in January 1985; the target was the National Police Agency (NPA) Science Research Institute in Tokyo. The device was truck mounted, and reported to be constructed of six 50-kilogram propane cylinders. Two of these contained a compressed gas, and four contained a mixture of gasoline and kerosene. Through a mixing valve, the compressed gas carried the combustible liquid and discharged it out a nozzle. A heated nichrome wire on the nozzle ignited it. The NPA research facility was set afire. The NPA recovered the vehicle with flamethrower, its having been left at the scene.[26]

There has been since 1985 a rapid evolution in the design and capabilities of rockets and rocket launchers developed by the Chukaku-ha. Recent reports ascribe a range of 3.8 kilometers to these rockets. This compares to a range of 1.2 kilometers for the rockets used in the simultaneous attacks on Narita and Haneda Airports in 1985. Impact fuses, warhead explosives, rocket fuel, rocket configuration and stabilization devices (airframe), and ignition systems were designed, developed, produced, and tested by Chukaku-ha.

Design, development, and production of a family of rockets is impressive enough; actual testing of successive designs even more so. What Japanese authorities characterize as "large-scale firing tests" were carried out at least at one location in the Chichibu Mountains of Saitawa Prefecture. This testing was carried out by the PRA. According to reports, the Chichibu Mountains location was one of several test sites used by the Chukaku-ha in mountainous regions. There is also a report of the testing of a new Chukaku-ha rocket named Icarus somewhere on the shores of the Sea of Japan.[27] The rocket launchers themselves have been of sophisticated design. They are multiple launchers, most commonly for five rockets. The rockets are fired in sequence, and provisions are made for the entire assembly to be destroyed after the last rocket is launched. The launcher used in the Tokyo summit incident on May 4, 1986, provided for a device to open the sliding glass window in the apartment in which it was located, to discharge the five rockets in sequence, and to ignite an incendiary device that would set fire to the apartment and presumably destroy the launcher. The last failed.[28]

Another device the Chukaku-ha has developed is designed to cause signal loss in the automated train control (ATC) equipment of the Japanese National Railroad

(JNR). It has been used at least once on the Sanyo rail system, causing the control system to cease functioning. It is a simple device consisting of two nine-volt batteries, an integrated circuit, and enough wire to connect the two rails. It intercepts signals from the ATC equipment, and the system shuts down. The device is easily hid underneath track ballast. JNR technicians, when encountering the device, were said to be "astounded."[29]

It has been reported also that the Chukaku-ha has used transmitters to conduct extensive sabotage operations and to jam police frequencies during these operations.[30]

At 3:20 A.M., November 29, 1985, the telephone connecting the main JNR control room with the Chiba Railroad control center went dead, and the lights on the Tokyo Metro Area Program Route Control control board began to go out. The Chukaku-ha had sabotaged the JNR system near and in Tokyo and Osaka. Communications and control cables had been almost simultaneously cut at over thirty locations. Thirteen million rail passengers were stranded. Some 850 freight cars loaded with 30,000 tons of freight did not move. The overall cost of this low-intensity terrorism sabotage, including that for repairs to restore service, exceeded 2 billion yen.[31]

Early in the investigation of this incident, authorities estimated that three to four Chukaku-ha PRA members had been deployed to each cable sabotage site; several others set fire to the Asahusabashi Station on the Sohu line. This means the PRA deployed 100 to 130 people in a highly coordinated action. Even if these estimates are high by a factor of two, this action by a group of terrorists was unprecedented in Japan for the numbers of people deployed in a coordinated sabotage action. If it is assumed the Chukaku-ha PRA had the cooperation of some members of the Chiba Railway Workers' Union, if only in the planning stages of the operation, that would detract in no way from the sophisticated manner in which it was conducted.

Another lesson can be derived from this episode. At twenty-eight of the twenty-nine places where cables were cut in the Tokyo metropolitan area, the cable trough covers were left off by the saboteurs. This permitted repair crews to locate quickly where cables were cut and to have the rail system backup and operating at a useful level in half a day.[32] If the saboteurs had replaced the cable trough covers, the system would not have recovered so swiftly. Thus, this incident could be considered a warning by the Chukaku-ha. The group may have felt that demonstrating its capabilities was sufficient at that time.

It is clear the Chukaku-ha is capable of precipitating events of national security concern, for it already has. As noted previously, the PRA is generally held to consist of about 230 individuals. Its organization has been variously described. That which seems closely to approximate those descriptions, coupled with the evidence of its operations, is as follows:

- Intelligence unit (gathers information concerning potential and actual targets)
- Procurement unit (acquires supplies, transportation, safehouses, materials for constructing ordnance designed by the Design and Development unit, and so forth)

- Design and Development unit (designs, develops, constructs, and tests ordnance)
- Operations unit (the unit[s] put together just prior to an operation, and that conducts the operation)

The remarkable thing about the Chukaku-ha, and of whom others may come to imitate, is not only sophistication regarding ordnance development and deployment and development and use of electronics but its target selection, operations planning, coordination of multiple units in the field, and ability to field somewhere around 100 people in extraordinary sabotage operations. There would appear to be no other terrorist group in the world that has demonstrated such levels of sophistication and operational effectiveness.

Ecoterrorism

Terrorism undertaken in the name of environmental causes is recent but not new. As yet, it is not troublesome insofar as national security is concerned or very common. Its practitioners, however, have demonstrated capabilities to employ sophisticated technology, to target sensitive high-technology targets, and to turn technology on itself with the use of rudimentary resources. Ecoterrorists clearly have the potential for becoming threats to national security.

Not all ecoterrorists threaten national security. For example, the zealots who drive nails into trees to be logged in an effort to discourage logging are in this category. Unfortunately, they place sawmill employees at risk, at least one of whom has already received a life-threatening injury when a sawblade came into contact with such a spike.[33]

Those who attacked the French Super-Phenix fast breeder reactor in 1974 with rocket-propelled grenades while the facility was still under construction may be of concern.[34] The fact they went to such extremes to express their opposition to this facility argues for the proposition that they could be stimulated to similar activity during a period of national emergency if they were not in sympathy with the premise.

A rather high level of ecoterrorist sophistication was discovered in 1978 by the FBI. The Bureau uncovered a plot to bomb whaling ships off the coast of Chile. For this purpose, the perpetrators were reported to have acquired the necessary explosives and diving equipment. The latter included a two-man submersible.[35]

In 1982, an environmental group in Canada bombed the Dunsmuir substation on Vancouver Island. They were objecting to the utility's spraying herbicide at the site. The saboteurs gained entry to the 20-acre site by cutting through the fence. The bombing showed a considerable degree of sophistication. The saboteurs placed several kilograms of explosive underneath each of four $1 million shunt reactors. The subsequent simultaneous explosions destroyed all four of these pieces of equipment, in addition to a $400,000 oil pumping facility and a 22-ton capacity crane. The on-site manager estimated it would take sixteen months to replace the shunt reactors.[36]

Mass Destruction Terrorism

Any act of terrorism resulting in mass destruction by chemical, biological, or nuclear means is of national security concern.[37] Nuclear terrorism is the terrorist use of a nuclear explosive, sabotage of a power reactor with intent to release radiation, sabotage of spent nuclear fuel in transit, or dispersal of radioactive materials sufficient to threaten large numbers of people at the locus of contact. The prospect for such terrorism seems remote, however, because of the numerous ways in which a project to acquire such a capability can fail, the range of possible consequences of an act of nuclear sabotage, the alternatives to a nuclear means to achieve the same or similar end, and what could motivate or discourage a group to undertake an act of nuclear terrorism.[38]

Although the acquisition of chemical and biological agents (CB) is much easier than is the acquisition of a nuclear capability, nevertheless, the possibility for their use seems remote. Perhaps the most important reason is the opprobium that would certainly descend on any terrorist group that used such a weapon. If the RAF finds itself isolated for committing mundane acts of assassination, one would anticipate that at the least a group employing a CB agent would find itself in rather more restrictive straits.

There must be a link between a terrorist action and those the terrorists consider victims of what is being attacked. That is, for a terrorist group to be considered relevant by its constituency and its supporters, there must be some proportionality between what is done and why it is done. Because this was lacking in the murders of Karl-Heinz Bekurts and the U.S. soldier Pinmental by the RAF, those actions were considered "politically unwise" and "senseless," respectively, by the radical left in West Germany.[39]

To a considerable degree, this requisite of proportionality underlies the activities even of terrorist groups in the Middle East. In any case, much of what passes for subnational terrorism in the Middle East is actually war on the cheap pursued by some of the nations of that region. Nations directly and indirectly victimized by this war are gradually coming to grips with the problem. West Germany, France, and Switzerland exhibit increasing tendencies to follow the lead of the United States (the Iran–Contra aberration aside), and within their constitutional constraints are resolving to hold terrorists accountable. In the Western Europen community, furthermore, the sharing of intelligence among nations about terrorists is at unprecedented levels. In this climate, it seems even less likely than a few years ago that terrorists or state-sponsored terrorists would find it in theirs or their sponsor's interests to precipitate an act of mass destruction with a CB agent.

There are precedents for the attempted acquisition of CB capabilities by individuals and groups in the United States and elsewhere. There is also precedence for the use of chemical agents to contaminate patent medicines, food, and beverages. The actual contamination incidents were criminal in nature, and in any case, outside the scope of a discussion of mass destruction. Insofar as is known, the attempts at acquisition of a CB mass destruction capability all failed. In some cases, effective law enforcement was the proximate cause of failure; in others, the reasons are not clear. In some cases, the intended employment of a chemical or biological agent could not have resulted in mass destruction, or even in any casualties at all. Ignorance by the would-be perpetrators was the paramount factor in these cases. In yet other cases, there were no indications that appropriate dispersal devices had been acquired, or even conceived.

Thus, although the prospect of a terrorist CB mass destruction event is plausible, it is not likely. There is no indication, whatever terrorist hyperbole may exist to the contrary, that terrorists are moving in a direction that will in the next few years take them to undertake CB mass destruction.

Conclusions

There is a continuing residue of terrorist assassinations, car bombings, aircraft hijackings, and hostage taking from which there is little indication of respite. This is particularly true of hostage taking. It is a low-risk, high-payoff tactic that is intractable of solution by means acceptable to Western sensibilities. It in fact shows signs of becoming an institutionalized form of terrorism in the Middle East. As long as Westerners insist on providing an inventory of potential victims, the phenomenon of hostage taking will continue until there is a radical and lasting change in the relationships between Islamic fundamentalism, as practiced by Muslim revolutionaries, and the West.

Two observations may be made with respect to this residue of terrorism. First, the activities do not denote any changes in terrorist tactics, capabilities, or even goals and objectives. Second, the consequences of their activities do not constitute issues of national security importance except in rare instances. These exceptions have involved the kidnappings of individuals who by virtue of their vocations possess knowledge of national security importance.

By contrast, low-intensity terrorism has the potential for becoming a serious national security issue. Its practice can make nations more vulnerable to hostile interests in periods of apparent peace and can impair a nation's capabilities to respond to national emergencies induced by outside hostile interests. The groundwork has already been laid in two of the most advanced nations in the world, West Germany and Japan. Its exportability to the United States is only a matter of circumstance. Some would argue that the rudiments of it are already here.

Low-intensity terrorism is practiced differently in West Germany than in Japan. In West Germany, it is relatively unsophisticated and involves large numbers of people who lead otherwise overt, normal lives. In Japan, it is highly sophisticated and practiced by no more than 100 to 200 people. In both nations, it is a relatively low-risk pursuit. The potential payoffs are much greater than so far achieved. Notwithstanding that, the payoffs of some individual acts have already been significant indeed and should give pause regarding the potential for impairing national security.

In Japan, the adversary has contemptuously exhibited a capability to paralyze rail traffic for a significant period. The Chukaku-ha may seem vulnerable, if only because of its small numbers of active adversaries. Their high degree of sophistication in planning, coordinating complex operations, and equipment development, however, make them a group to be reckoned with, even if their numbers are reduced by half. In West Germany, the motive to impair national security among those active in low-intensity terrorism may not be there. In any case, the organization of the autonomous cells is such that they could not support a highly coordinated operation. On the other hand, the sheer numbers of adversaries in West Germany—which might expand greatly in a period of national emergency or controversy—provide the movement with a capability to impair national security even through a campaign of uncoordinated acts of sabotage.

Ecoterrorism can be considered another form of low-intensity terrorism that has been conductd at a low activity level for some years. By itself, it is not of national security concern.

The advent of mass destruction terrorism would be of national security concern; but however much it is talked about, there appear no indications of its imminence, even in the long term.

A major change in the direction of terrorism is perceived to have occurred within the past three years or so. The saltatory evolution of low-intensity terrorism has significant potential for affecting the national security of the United States, of some of its allies, and of NATO, more so than virtually any other form of terrorism.

Notes

1. David Th. Schiller, "Germany's Other Terrorist," *Terrorism* 9, no. 1 (1987).
2. Ibid.
3. Cited by ibid.
4. Ibid.
5. "Schwarze Liste," *Anti-WAA-Pfingstcamp/Programm/Sondernummer* (Infodienstes München/Nürnberg, n.d.); "Schwarze Liste," *Atom* (October–November 1985), "Schwarze Liste," *Aktion Anarchistisches Magazin*, March 22, 1986; "Schwarze Liste," *Radi Aktiv* 7 (April–May 1986); "Gelbe Seite Aktiv für die WAA," *Radi Aktiv* 8 (June–July 1986).
6. Robert K. Mullen, data base on energy asset sabotage, 1956–current (unpublished).
7. Ibid.
8. Ibid.
9. Ibid.

10. "Yes, We Also Engage in Sabotage," *Der Spiegel*, September 1, 1986.

11. Ibid.

12. "FRG Authorities Intensify Counterterrorist Efforts," *Frankfurther Allgemeine Zeitung*, December 1, 1986.

13. "Hungry Hearts," *Der Spiegel*, December 8, 1986.

14. "Is the RAF Hard Core Preparing New Terrorist Attacks?" *Die Welt*, May 13, 1987.

15. "Rebmann Expects Serious New Attacks—'Specific RAF Targets Cannot Be Predicted'—'Key Witness' Failure Regretted," *Süddeutsche Zeitung*, December 12, 1986.

16. "Deteriorating from Within," *Der Spiegel*, September 22, 1986.

17. "Political Plant," *Der Spiegel*, December 2, 1985.

18. Oliver Tolmein, " 'Red Zora" against Human Genetics Experts," *Die Tageszeitung*, August 7, 1986.

19. "Deteriorating from Within."

20. Foreign Broadcast Information Service, "Scientific Institute Director's Home Damaged," *Daily Report, West Europe*, November 24, 1986.

21. Foreign Broadcast Information Service, "Group Claims Responsibility for Berlin Attack," *Daily Report, West Europe*, April 21, 1987.

22. "Yes, We Also Engage;" Kurt Kister, "The RAF Believes Itself to Be at War with Washington—'Anti-Imperialist Resistance' throughout Europe Is the Objective of the Red Army Faction," *Süddeutsche Zeitung*, August 2, 3, 1986.

23. Tsuyoshi Osawa. "High Technology Observed in 'Chukaku-ha' Terrorist Activities," *Seikai Orai*, February, 1986.

24. "Radicals may Rise against JNR Division, Privitization," *Sentaku*, December, 1986.

25. "Chukaku-ha Army Members Said to Number 230," *Daily Yomiuri*, March 4, 1987.

26. Tsuyoshi Osawa, "High Technology Observed in 'Chukaku-ha' Terrorist Activities," *Seikai Orai* (February 1986).

27. "Testing of Mortar Shells by Chukaku-ha Reported," *Yomiuri Shimbun*, March 12, 1987.

28. "Launch Device Used in Tokyo Summit Incident Described," *Asahi Shimbun*, May 6, 1986.

29. Osawa, "High Technology Observed."

30. Associated Press, December 1, 1985.

31. Osawa, "High Technology Observed."

32. Ibid.

33. Larry B. Stammer, "Eco-Terrorist Focus of Mill Accident Probe," *Los Angeles Times*, May 15, 1987; Dale Champion. "Tree Sabotage Claims Its First Bloody Victim," *San Francisco Chronicle*, May 15, 1987.

34. "Reactor Attacked in France," *Washington Post*, January 20, 1982; "French Breeder Struck by Rockets: Damage Termed Not Serious," *Nucleonics Week*, January 21, 1982.

35. Bill Richards. "Whale War," *Washington Post*, September 5, 1978.

36. Public Utilities Committee, "Sabotage of Utility Substation," *Public Utilities Security Newsletter* #2 (1982).

37. Robert K. Mullen, "Mass Destruction and Terrorism," *Journal of International Affairs* 32, no. 1 (Spring–Summer 1978).

38. Robert K. Mullen, "Nuclear Violence," in *Preventing Nuclear Terrorism*, eds. Paul Leventhal and Yonah Alexander (Lexington, Mass.: Lexington Books, 1987).

39. "Yes, We also Engage. . . ," op. cit.

9
Managing the Crisis
of Hostage Families

Nancy Rodriguez Asencio

Terrorism, as a late twentieth-century explosion of violence, has been analyzed from many perspectives, but the least studied has been its impact on individuals. There are some who blame the Iran–Contra scandal on the failure of high government officials, hostage families, and the media to understand and cope effectively with the intense stresses created by a terrorist incident and the complex human responses that often are evoked by that kind of crisis.

There is merit in the charge. Throughout 1985 and 1986, families of hostages being held in Lebanon exerted heavy pressure on President Reagan to find some means to secure the release of these hostages. It is said that these pressures became so acute that the president uttered a perhaps fateful phrase: "Do something!" The impact of such pressures was reinforced by Lieutenant Colonel Oliver North's July 10, 1987, testimony to the Iran–Contra committees of Congress. Discussing the anguish he felt for the families of hostages, North said that this emotional turmoil may have affected his decisions or even those of the president. On July 23, 1987, Secretary of State George Shultz testified before the same committee that when the question of the legality of the arms sales to Iran was pointed out to him, President Reagan was so visibly frustrated that he said that the American people would never forgive him if he allowed a legal technicality to stand in the way of freedom for the American hostages.

Focusing on the Hostage Family

Evaluating the Situation

Hostage taking exerts perhaps a unique kind of stress on the people involved. When prisoners are taken during a war, it is a predictable situation. Such happenings are a feature of warfare, there are rules of war respecting the treatment of prisoners, and usually when the conflict ends the prisoners are repatriated to their respective countries. (There are, of course, war-related problems such as those concerning missing in action, that remain unresolved and ongoing family tragedies.)

Hostages taken in acts of terrorism find themselves in a different situation. Their involvement in the incident often is completely random and could not have been predicted, it often has no clear purpose, is not subject to international rules about the care of hostages, and the confinement is indefinite in duration. They are held under threat of death, pending the concession of demands that are often politically unacceptable. Such qualities tend to make each hostage situation unique. There is little in the way of group experience that is readily to be drawn upon. Crisis managers and families have a common problem, therefore, in that it is necessary to apply some consistent approaches to dealing with an event that is probably unique in the life of the victim.

Identifying the Victims

There seems to be a consensus among psychiatrists and psychologists that often families of victims suffer more psychologically than does the hostage. The hostage knows how he or she is, but the family suffers the sustained stress of not knowing whether the victim is dead or alive or being mistreated. Not knowing the welfare or condition of the hostage, members of the family do not know how they are supposed to feel. Their sense of loss and their grief must remain unresolved.

The victim is viewed in three distinct ways. The hostage is perceived by the captors as a symbol—a citizen of a given country or a member of an ethnic, religious, or political group. Government officials tend to view the victim of a terrorist kidnapping as an individual to be retrieved from a politically sensitive situation with as few side effects as possible. Most important, the hostage is a human being who is an intrinsic part of a family and a community.

It is of utmost importance for crisis managers to view the hostage as an individual, as part of a family unit, and as part of a community. The family unit encompasses not only spouses, children, and parents. The family could be children of a single parent or adult dependents. Children whose only parent is taken hostage present very special problems, as do adult dependents who are frail and elderly. In some cases, the family is a fiancé or significant other person.

In other words, the crisis manager needs to know the human context of the hostage as fully as the nature of the terrorist incident and the motives of the terrorists. Close contact with the family, or significant others, will facilitate understanding of the human qualities of the hostage. Crisis managers will become aware of preexisting stresses of victims. They will learn of stresses within hostage families, and they will be able to help the families cope with the incident instead of becoming part of the problem. Creating that sort of bond with the family produces an atmosphere of trust, promoting faith and hope during the crisis and acceptance in the aftermath.

Classes of Victims

The State Department has identified three types of victims: direct victims or those who are injured; indirect victims, such as friends, colleagues, and families of the direct victim; and hidden victims, the members of the crisis team or task force who must solve the problems created by the crisis while dealing with their own sometimes very intense reactions to the situation.[1]

The three types of victims are clearly identifiable in the 1980 incident in Bogotá, Colombia, where the chiefs and other senior officials of sixteen diplomatic missions were taken hostage by a Colombian terrorist group. One of the direct victims, and of special concern to me personally, was the U.S. ambassador to Colombia and my husband, Diego Asencio. My immediate family and I were indirect victims, but also among the indirect victims was Frank Crigler, deputy chief of mission of the U.S. embassy and therefore the senior deputy to Ambassador Asencio. Crigler was in the awkward position of having to take charge of the embassy, although since the ambassador had not "left the country," he was not officially chargé d'affaires. Moreover, this was a most unusual hostage situation in which the hostages were able to communicate by telephone with their embassies and families almost daily. My husband, as well as his ambassadorial colleagues in captivity, intruded himself into the negotiations with the terrorists, and he continued to direct the embassy using the telephone. One of the reasons he did that was that he felt his situation was unique: he was in constant touch with the kidnappers, able to communicate with them, understand their demands, and read their moods. Hostage negotiators usually do not have that kind of asset.

Crigler was faced with conflicting views and instructions from Washington and from his ambassador. He was responsible for running the embassy, for keeping in touch with the fifteen special foreign delegates sent to Bogotá by the countries whose ambassadors were captive, and for dealing with high Colombian government officials as the senior U.S. official able to conduct business with them. In addition, Crigler considered it his responsibility to keep me informed practically on a daily basis.

A month into the incident, the State Department sent a high-ranking official as the U.S. special delegate. However, the peculiar situation of an ambassador in captivity seeking to exert his influence on events outside remained a feature of the incident to its resolution.

There were also hidden victims in the Bogotá incident; some have not yet fully recovered from their trauma. In some cases conflicts with superiors that were brought to the surface in this crisis had negative career repercussions. Preexisting stress was a catalyst that caused one task force worker to experience severe and lasting emotional problems. Another worker could not accept working for a supervisor during the crisis and after the ambassador's release was instrumental in provoking a serious misunderstanding between the ambassador and that supervisor. Difficulties also arose in the relationship of workers and hostage family members. Some of these problems were due to displacement of anger.

Sometimes indirect victims suffer from psychosomatic illnesses. The mother of an ex-hostage from Tehran had gastrointestinal problems during her son's captivity. These problems worsened after his release, probably a delayed reaction, and she was diagnosed as having bleeding ulcers. She conjectures that possibly her condition was aggravated by the extreme emotional stress of reunion, a happy event that was nonetheless a crisis.

Supplying Information

Prompt and regular communication is the key to satisfactory relations between crisis managers and hostage families. Information is central to establishing that relationship. It begins with conveying the bad news. This information should be given as soon as possible, in the most complete manner, and if possible by a person who has some training and sensitivity in dealing with such situations. This person should be aware of the possible psychological reactions that such news may elicit.

Families I have interviewed feel that information should be shared with them as often as developments occur. Even when there are no developments, regular communications should be maintained. One crisis manager said that at a time when he knew a hostage family member was particularly low in spirits, he invited her to his office to show her the large volume of diplomatic correspondence he and others were conducting to get the hostage released.

The parents of an ex-hostage from Iran maintain a good feeling about the Department of State crisis managers. They were informed of their son's predicament directly by the Department of State, not the media, less than twelve hours after the incident began. They never felt that they were not receiving information. There was, however, one significant problem: they were told repeatedly to be prepared to find their son psychologically flawed as a result of his captivity. They refused to believe that this could happen, and it did not. Perhaps the choice of the word, *flawed,* was wrong. The intensity of the captive's ordeal would no doubt cause a change in him, but no one could predict whether it would be positive or negative.

Encouraging Counseling

Every hostage case is in some way different, but there are nonetheless predictable qualities of the human reaction to such events. These can be understood and possibly managed more effectively if they are understood early in the development of a crisis. Dr. Robert Blum recommends that family members consult with mental health professionals as soon as possible after the onset of a hostage crisis. Ideally, he says, they should follow through until the crisis is resolved, and preferably until the aftermath.[2]

The crisis manager can recommend such counseling and can facilitate consultation with a mental health professional. Often, however, family members fear that their behavior might be considered abnormal. Concerned that by seeing this professional they will be viewed by others as being mentally ill causes them to resist consultation with psychologists, psychiatrists, or other mental health professionals. An important part of the counseling is to emphasize that usually the behavior is normal but the circumstances abnormal.

Organizing Support Groups

To avoid the buildup of problems, as soon as possible after an incident begins, families need to know where to go for information and assistance. In case of a large incident involving a number of hostages, those affected by the crisis may find that both official and private support arrangements are helpful. Sheldon Krys, the executive director of the Bureau of Near Eastern Affairs during the Tehran hostage crisis, was the families' central liaison officer. Having access to high-level officials, he could convey their feelings, emotions, and thoughts. And because of the large number of families involved, a group of volunteers was formed to disseminate information, telephone the families at least once a week, and receive calls any time.

Based on his experience, Krys recommends that the central liaison officer not be a mental health professional, with whom some families might feel uneasy. He also suggests that an effort be made to expose the families to former hostages in order to keep alive the hope necessary to cope. For example, Richard Queen, a former Iran hostage, was released early when he became ill.[3] As soon as he arrived in the United States, he began meeting frequently with the families of the other hostages. He felt that he too was still a hostage until his friends were released. His warmth radiated to everyone, and the families were reassured by his presence.

Penne Laingen, organizer of FLAG (the Family Liaison Action Group created to support the Tehran hostage families) and wife of former Tehran hostage Bruce Laingen, writes that Queen was a "symbol of hope" to the family members.[4] She says that he was brought within close family circles not only because he could tell them about their loved ones but because he could empathize with them. Laingen believed that former prisoners of war and their spouses came closest to providing the empathy the hostage families needed. The women and their husbands provided a support system by helping with guidelines for setting up a family organization and by discussing their methods of coping with stress. Especially the fact that the POWs had returned reinforced hope in the hearts of the Tehran hostage families.

Political psychologist Leila Dane has done a study of long-term crisis coping with fourteen wives of the Tehran hostages.[5] One of the questions she asked was how support acted as a help to them. Four answered, "In every way;" four replied it "helped validate feelings;" two said it "helped share feelings." Others said they "never felt alone," "kept in touch with reality," or "gave emotional strength." Out of fourteen responses, there was only one negative answer: "No need for support." Support came to them from every direction; the whole country was sympathetic because the media kept the hostages before the public.

The sister of a hostage held in Lebanon since 1984 stressed to me how important it has been for her to have the support of the families of other hostages being held in the Middle East. Another great source of support has been a weekly telephone call from the Office of Citizens Services, Department of State.[6] This office was already functioning prior to the recommendations set forth by the vice-president in 1986 for the expansion of current support programs for hostage families.[7] The recommendations called for a broader outreach program, including visits, hot lines, information on private counseling services, and a personal contact for each family for communications even when there are no new developments.

British journalist hostage Alec Collett has an Amrican wife living in the United States. Because her husband is a British subject, she "falls through the cracks" when it comes to support from the U.S. government. Nevertheless, the other families have included Mrs. Collett in their group, exchanging information and giving support.

Church groups, individuals and some organizations have offered to help the families of hostages in Lebanon. The National Organization for Victims Assistance, which was created to aid victims of street crime, has been supportive of these families. This organization has been influential in obtaining inexpensive air travel for families visiting Washington. No Greater Love is another organization that has assisted the families, sometimes providing free lodging on visits to Washington.[8]

Although there is a general feeling of support for the hostages in Lebanon and most are regarded with sympathy, some have been criticized for having remained in the area after being warned of its danger to U.S. citizens. This criticism, perhaps in some cases warranted, has been distressing to the family members.

Psychological Responses and Preexisting Stresses of Victims

Anger, Guilt, and Idealization of Victims

Most psychologists use Elizabeth Kubler-Ross's stages of dying to explain the psychological responses of hostage family members.[9] Awareness of the life-threatening situation of their loved ones elicits shock, denial, anger, depression, bargaining, acceptance, and hope. Not all of these are experienced by everyone, or in the same degree. Responses are also manifested in many different ways depending on personalities.

In the Bogotá incident, upon learning of the takeover, with eyes closed and still holding the telephone to my ear, I slid down to sit on the floor in a fetal position. The next morning I had forgotten the absence of my husband until I looked at the emptiness on his side of the bed. The reaction was denial. Guilt was followed by depression: if I had accompanied my husband to the fateful party, I would be with him in his predicament. There was much bargaining in my prayers: "God, if you save him I promise . . . " The hardest part was having to accept the situation and hope that those in charge of negotiations would succeed. In one way, hope was kept alive by discussing the future. In our telephone conversations, my husband and I discussed writing a book about his experiences after his release.

Anger was displaced. Many hostage family members, I among them, directed anger at the White House, primarily at President Carter. The Bogotá incident occurred during the same time as the Tehran incident, and people concerned about those incidents objected to the idea that the government was using the same foreign policy for two distinct situations. Some parents and family members were particularly angry with President Carter after the rescue mission failed.

Running the gamut of emotions, frustration follows indignation. Families feel impotent not being able to direct their anger against the aggressors. Suppressed anger is often projected to the very people who are trying to solve the crisis, or an authority figure. This happens especially when the crisis managers do not pay attention to the family, and the family can become an adversary.[10] Usually, nothing is ever enough as far as the family is concerned until the victim is freed.

An example of devastating anger is the case of a wife who feels that her husband, a former hostage, never has received adequate public recognition for his ordeal and accomplishment. He was in captivity for a very long time, longer than the hostages in Tehran. But because he was not an employee of the government, there was no parade, no medals, no shaking hands with the president. In this kind of case, the family member, and sometimes the former hostage, feels that the rest of the world underrates the significance of the hostage experience. The former hostage and family members sometimes feel that merely surviving the incident is worthy of special recognition. Perhaps it is.

The wife of the hostage in this case was satisfied with the financial support her family received from the husband's employer during the crisis. Nevertheless, the sustained stress during the long captivity caused her to project her anger at the employer. When the husband was released, he resumed working for the same employer but later entered a new field. The passage of time and other changes have not enabled the wife to resolve her feelings of anger. She still feels that her husband was dealt with unfairly.

Elvira Johnson Elbrick, the widow of Ambassador C. Burke Elbrick, who was kidnapped by insurgents in Brazil in 1971 and held for six days, still feels hostility against former President Richard Nixon.[11] She said that she received no word or letter from President Nixon, who maintained that it was a "Brazilian matter." The Brazilian government, however, took pity on this ambassador, who had been there only fifty-seven days, and negotiated with the terrorists, giving in to their demands by allowing free conduct out of the country for fifteen leaders of their group. In the light of the type of negotiations revealed by the Iran scandal, one can speculate that Nixon's distant pose was a cover for covert pressure on Brazilian authorities to negotiate with the terrorists, and as a matter of established international practice, the problem was Brazil's to manage. Regardless of the position that might have been taken by Nixon, this is still another example of projecting the anger felt against the unavailable perpetrators onto the highest authority figure.

There have been numerous other cases in which, because of the danger it would pose to others, hostages and their families have had to keep secret their ordeals. These former hostages had no public recognition of their valor, nor were they able to write books about their experience. They and their families also have felt anger and guilt and have had little opportunity to vent their feelings. Among these are the scores of personnel of multinational corporations serving overseas who have been kidnapped, ransomed, and returned home in secrecy. Furthermore, although it might be the exception to the rule, there are some people who do not need public recognition. Some prefer to forget the incident and do not wish to discuss their experiences.

Many family members I interviewed discussed the idealization of victims. It is inconceivable to admit that a loved one who is in imminent danger of death could have any faults. One mother said that she kept thinking of her son as her little boy, although she knew he was a man. A wife had completely forgotten how authoritarian her husband was and was confused by his behavior when they were reunited.

Instant Fame

The late Andy Warhol originated the idea of the fleeting fifteen minutes of fame. Sometimes families of hostages are caught by an artificially magnified sense of importance that flows from the crisis. This is a human reaction to the attention being given to them by high government officials, the media, their neighbors, and friends. It is a delicate matter, which few people recognize in themselves and no one would ever admit.

According to Paul Eggersten, this publicity "high," which is felt upon becoming famous through identification with the victim, can be damaging not only to relations with crisis managers and others during the situation but after the release of the hostages, when deflation and accompanying depression are bound to occur.[12] For example, a family member who has been very involved with the media may suddenly feel left out of the picture. The wife of one hostage decided not to be involved with media until the hostage was released; by then, the media wanted only to interview the hostage. There followed very human reactions: she felt hurt that no one paid any attention to her; angry that her former hostage husband did not ask the media to notice her; and then guilty that she should feel anger against her husband, who had endured a life-threatening experience.

The Need to Act

Some people react to crisis with nervous energy due to the flow of adrenaline. They have an urgent need to get involved in some way. They call upon anyone they may perceive to have some influence in the matter. Often these people will neglect their other duties and spend all their time and energy trying to solve the critical situation. These persons are found among family members of a crisis victim and also among the crisis workers and interested third parties, such as members of Congress whose constituents are being held captive.

Kurt Carlson, victim of the TWA flight 847 hijacking, spent two weeks as a hostage in Beirut and relates in his book, *One American Must Die*, how his brother was involved in a plan for a rescue mission. The "Carlson commandos," as he called them, were in contact with persons inside Lebanon with whom they were discussing the rescue attempt.[13]

In the Dominican embassy incident in Bogotá, while family members of the hostages were frustrated by their inability to participate in helping resolve the situation, the daughter of the Israeli ambassador, who was one of the hostages, was fortunate in getting permission from the Colombian government to visit her father. The other family members clamored to be allowed the same privilege, without results. The Venezuelan ambassador's wife wanted to take a cake to her husband for his birthday. In such strained circumstances, even the absurd is considered. The most that families could do was to send food and clean laundry through the Red Cross twice a week. Cases of wine and many delicacies were also forwarded to loved ones. Hours were spent with friends cooking special dishes that would not need refrigeration. Some families sent food not only to the hostages but also to their captors, in hopes of moderating their behavior.

Families of hostages feel a need to band together to try to get things done, to pressure the government. The FLAG group met regularly for moral support and also as a political pressure group. Families of POWs and MIAs periodically have met with government officials. The MIAs have exerted so much pressure that in June 1987 the former chairman of the Joint Chiefs of Staff, General John Vessey, was sent to Hanoi to investigate the situation in hopes of appeasing the families. Family members of victims in hostage situations in Tehran and Beirut have traveled to those countries and talked with members of foreign governments. Although these efforts did not alter the victim's situation, it was something that these persons felt they had to do. They had to act to try to help.

Need for Decompression

When hostages are released, there is need for a period of decompression. During this period, the hostages must adjust to their freedom and relax the anxieties of captivity. At the same time, they must adjust to reentry into their social, work, and family life. Having been deprived of news, they must catch up on what has been going on. The feeling is comparable to emerging from a science-fiction time warp to learn that time and events have gone by without you. Often there is bad news, such as the deaths of relatives while hostages were being held captive.

The families of hostages also need a period of decompression. They must prepare for the stress of the happy reunion. A large dose of happiness can also be stressful. Both families and hostages have undergone changes.[14] Necessary time must be allowed for these changes to be absorbed by all for a successful adjustment. Recognizing that need, the mother of one of the hostages in Tehran declined an invitation by the U.S. government to meet her son in Germany. She felt that while he needed a period of decompression, she needed one as well.

Positive Results from Negative Situations

Studies have shown that families of hostages who manage to survive their ordeal admit to some beneficial consequences of the experience. Individuals become stronger. During the incarceration, hostages have time to reflect on their lives and often change their priorities. In some cases, former hostages prove to be better able to communicate with spouses and children, and children themselves seem matured by the experience.[15]

Gerard Vaders was a passenger on the train hijacked by Moluccan terrorists in the Netherlands in 1975. During the crisis, two hostages were executed. Vaders, thinking that he too was to be executed, asked to be permitted to leave a message for his family. He had marital problems and a foster child who did not get along with his wife. After his captors learned of his problems, they resolved not to kill him. The psychiatric explanation was that the Moluccans found it difficult to kill Vaders after he had exposed his humanness, his flaws, and was no longer a "faceless symbol." Although happy to be spared, Vaders nevertheless felt guilty when another hostage was executed, perhaps in his place.[16] In the aftermath, Vaders was able to resolve his domestic problems and improve his relationship with his wife.

Relationships can be changed in dramatic ways by the hostage experience. Anger may develop during the crisis and remain unresolved after the hostage's release. At times, the anger is directed at the former hostage. In one case, the hostage had always been a dominant figure in the household and had never consulted his wife on important financial decisions. During the long absence of the hostage, the wife faced problems that she had not been accustomed to dealing with. She was able to manage quite well but not without feeling anger toward her husband for having kept her so uninformed about business matters. She also said that she was angry with herself for having allowed him to keep her in ignorance. When this hostage was released, the couple, facing a role conflict, underwent a difficult readjustment. The wife no longer accepted the submissive role, and the husband was not inclined to accept the new situation. Moreover, the wife felt guilty about being angry with a man who had just undergone a life-threatening experience. Nevertheless, she decided that there had been a long-standing role conflict that needed resolution. The crisis situation served as a catalyst.

Situation Management and Orientation Guidelines

Government Employees Abroad

Between 1968 and 1983, there were 121 kidnappings, 136 barricade-hostage incidents, and 15 hijackings involving U.S. government employees.[17] Drawing on those experiences, the State Department publication, *Hostage Taking: Preparation, Avoidance and Survival*, cites guidelines for preventive measures and for behavior in the event of a kidnapping. Included are twenty-five suggestions relating to the role of the family. Describing the aftermath, possible psychological effects, and possible need of the former hostage for counseling, the book comments on the plight of the family members: "It must be remembered that the hostage's family has also been through an awfully stressful period and may require the same type of assistance."[18]

This type of publication reflects a growing concern within government about the problems of the families of hostages. In 1985, the Office of Citizens Services became more involved with family members of present hostages. The Department of State's Bureau of Diplomatic Security has developed a series of audiovisual materials, with the collaboration of the Overseas Briefing Center of the Foreign Service Institute, the Family Liaison Office, and the Medical Division. The purpose of these materials is to provide preventive psychological training for crisis situations and to do an "inoculation" for stress. The primary objective is to develop a sense of control, to maintain psychological balance in crisis situations. The most applicable materials to hostage family crises are *Living with the Threat of Terrorism, Managing before, during and after a Crisis, Crisis Work . . . Crisis Worker,* and *Managing Children during a Crisis.* This material is sent to posts abroad for use by personnel and their families, and it is also available to Washington-based personnel and their dependents. Guidelines suggest the most effective ways of dealing with the families of victims, and much of the training material is designed to help crisis workers manage their own stress.[19]

Through the Overseas Briefing Center of the Foreign Service Institute, training material is provided to assist families in anticipating as well as resolving human problems. The Family Liaison Office is expected to provide support to family members once a crisis arises. There are no specific programs established, but the workers of the Family Liaison Office use whatever resources are available to aid families. Services include referrals for assistance in financial, medical, and legal matters. The Association of American Foreign Service Women has formed a Crisis Committee, a group of volunteers ready to assist the Overseas Briefing Center and the Family Liaison Office in aiding families in crisis.

Military

Being a diplomat has become a high-risk profession only in our times. For the armed forces, however, the danger of dying in combat or being taken prisoner has been an intrinsic part of that risk-involved profession. Consequently each branch of military service has had an ongoing support system plan and an outreach program for families of their personnel during a crisis. Personnel officers have an established system to use the moment a crisis presents itself.

The army has developed a philosophy of life for its personnel and dependents. "A Family Action Plan" contains three critical elements: partnership, wellness, and sense of community.[20] "Partnership" is the relationship and commitment between army families and the army. The army cares for families, and families work to improve the army life. "Wellness" is a concept that emphasizes the positive aspects of army life and the standard of living instead of negative aspects. A "Sense of community" suggests that army families need to work together to form caring communities that can be active when events require and available to solve individual problems.

The army program uses both military and family member assets to help those in need. In case of an act of terrorism where soldiers are taken hostage, the plan works as follows. First, the wife and family of each hostage are notified; the commander personally chooses a trained individual to do so. That person probably will be accompanied by a chaplain and the commander's wife. After the wife is notified, the family is assisted by the wives of other soldiers in the unit. The personnel officer and staff are also able to offer financial or other types of administrative assistance.

There are several agencies and associations on which the army can draw for assistance, including the army community service, army emergency relief, Red Cross, and various wives' clubs. During the entire crisis, the unit commander's wife and other wives stay in close touch with the hostage's wife. They check with her daily, get her involved in activities, and keep her informed of developments. In case of death, a summary court officer usually is appointed to assist the widow in receiving benefits and taking care of household matters such as moving.

Business

According to the State Department's Bureau of Diplomatic Security, in 1985 there were more international terrorist attacks and more casualties than in any previous year since 1980. International terrorist incidents occurred in 72 countries during 1985, and attacks against the business sector rose to 227, up sharply from 165 in the previous year. Attacks against U.S. citizens and their property increased from 133 in 1984 to 170 in 1985. In 1985, 38 U.S. citizens were killed and 157 wounded. One hundred seventy attacks against U.S. citizens placed this country as the number two target of international terrorists. Number one was Israel, with 198 incidents. The next highest were: France, 46; Palestinians, 44; Spain, 37; United Kingdom, 29; West Germany, 27; Syria, 22; and Ivory Coast, 9. Tying for tenth place were Chile, Libya, and the NATO organization.[21]

Between 1970 and 1979, 567 Americans were reported kidnapped abroad; more than half the victims were businessmen.[22] This figure does not include unreported kidnappings and attacks on personnel of multinationals and their families. Many terrorist attacks remain unreported, especially in Latin America and Africa, because the companies often feel that the government and military establishments in these countries are in effect in combating terrorism. The companies are also afraid that publicity might produce more attacks and that their other employees will be alarmed.[23]

American businessmen abroad and their families have been the targets of terrorists for many years. They have been kidnapped and held for ransom. The companies have paid, and the former hostages have quietly been transferred out of the country where they were held. Many companies are heavily insured, with kidnap and ransom insurance premiums running as high as $500,000 a year.[24] During the last decade, Lloyds of London and other companies have insured hundreds, perhaps even thousands, of clients against the risk of terrorist kidnapping. Insurance companies try to keep this information from the public, and thus, they hope, from potential kidnappers. According to Richard Clutterbuck, in the first fifty cases handled by the British firm Control Risks, the kidnappers demanded $300 million. About $60 million was actually paid, and forty-seven victims were released.[25]

Given the unpredictability of acts of terrorism, business-sector preventive measures aim at strengthening the powers of threatened individuals and groups to cope with the unpredictable, when and if it occurs. Government and business have embarked upon a joint effort to confront such crisis. In 1986, for example, the secretary of state created the Overseas Security Advisory Council (OSAC) to link business and government, which is designed to strengthen ties in order to face crises. The primary purpose of the organization is to exchange information with the government as "a security information clearing house between U.S. public and private interests abroad."[26]

OSAC consists of twenty-five charter member companies and five federal agencies. The charter calls for six of the original member to be replaced periodically by six others. Members serve at least one year, and all representatives are required to have a secret clearance issued by the Department of State.[27]

The council has made three significant recommendations: (1) the establishment of a unit within the Bureau of Diplomatic Security as a base for security liaison between the Department of State and the business sector; (2) the creation and distribution of guidelines to help the private sector deal with crisis management; and (3) the creation of an electronic bulletin board. The first recommendation is being worked on. The second is embodied in a publication entitled, *Crisis Management Guidelines*, available free from the Bureau of Diplomatic Security. The electronic bulletin board might be operational in the fall of 1987.[28]

Crisis Management Guidelines, released in 1986, outlines valuable information for companies with respect to organizing an internal crisis management plan and crisis management team. The crisis teams are to work closely with the U.S. embassies or consulates. U.S. policy is clearly stated in the publication and, in a word, is "no deals with terrorists." However, communication with captors is permitted. Mentioned in the guidelines is the possibility of using humanitarian appeals to terrorists, who might be influenced by the fear of losing some supporters or receiving negative media coverage. Among the suggestions is for spouses and children of hostages to ask for the return of their family member.[29]

Companies must plan carefully for the event of a crisis situation. Clutterbuck advocates developing a contingency plan before there is a crisis and having the company security planner establish contacts with government officials, law enforcement agencies, and the media before a crisis arises.[30] He also suggests that the staff likely to be involved should be made aware of predetermined policies and contingency plans and that a confidential file should be kept on each high-risk employee, including schedules of family members, passport numbers, blood groups, special medications, up-to-date photographs, and names of the family doctor, lawyer, neighbors, and friends. Clutterbuck also suggests including samples of handwriting and voice recordings in the file. He adds that sometimes family members may also become targets, noting that when an employee is held hostage, family members run a higher risk of becoming direct victims.

If a contingency plan is to succeed, there needs to be close and complete cooperation among the company, the employee, and the family. Every family member of a high-risk employee is a target. This translates into tremendous stress for a family and may mean adjusting to a very rigid family life-style, involving controlling and curtailing many forms of normal social intercourse.

Living with the threat of terrorism often has two effects on the families of businessmen abroad. On the one hand, they may feel restricted in their social activities and pressure the employee to ask for a transfer. On the other, some family members develop a fatalistic attitude where they seem no longer afraid.

Academia

When teachers are recruited for overseas positions, usually no special guidelines are followed with respect to preparing them about potential threats to their security. There are American universities as well as American schools all over the world. Staff vacancies are advertised in the normal channels in the United States. Usually the president, dean of the university, or headmaster of the school travels once a year to the United States to recruit professors and teachers. Resumes are reviewed, interviews are scheduled, and contracts are signed. There is seldom any formal orientation to security conditions in the particular country. Moreover, academic habits on matters of this sort change very slowly. Indeed, traditional recruitment and orientation procedures were followed by the American University in Beirut (AUB) until about three years ago.[31]

American academicians have been the prey of kidnappers in Lebanon with some frequency since the abduction of AUB president David Dodge in 1982. In 1984, AUB librarian Peter Kilburn was seized and subsequently killed, and in 1985 AUB dean Thomas Sutherland was kidnapped. In 1986, Joseph James Cicippio and Edward Austin Tracy were taken hostage, and in 1987 Alann Steen, Jesse Jonathan Turner, and Robert Polhill were abducted along with Mithileshwar Singh, an Indian-born U.S. resident.

The kidnapping incidents in 1986–1987, as well as further deterioration in security conditions, led the Department of State to issue a travel advisory for Lebanon. That advisory recites possible revocation of an individual's passport or a fine of $5,000 in the event of a violation. However, there exist no guidelines and no orientation plan for prospective American teachers abroad. Nevertheless, some establishments do consult with Citizens Services at the Department of State. According to John Adams, formerly head of that office, there are many private requests for travel advisories, especially from missionaries and other religious groups.

Travel and Tourism

Notwithstanding the number of hijackings, airplane travel continues to be the most practical and thus most popular mode of transportation. Being hijacked is still statistically a low probability.

A Mediterranean cruise, moreover, used to be a form of rest and relaxation. For a time after the hijacking of the *Achille Lauro*, however, cruise bookings were poor, and especially by Americans. Although statistically the hijacking of another cruise ship is more improbable than the hijacking of an airplane, people have been afraid of sailing on ships that stop in countries bordering the Mediterranean. Only recently has there been a renewed interest in cruise tours.

In 1985 most victims of terrorism were caught by chance. They were random targets; some were tourists or persons who happened to walk by or be at a given airport or restaurant at the fatal moment. In April 1985 fifteen Americans were killed in a restaurant near Madrid when the place was bombed.[32]

Even given the widespread news coverage of terrorist incidents almost anywhere in the world, it is difficult to stay current on where the risk might be significant to travelers. To help deal with that problem, the Office of Citizen Services of the Department of State telexes travel advisories to over two hundred organizations, such as AAA and American Express, which disseminate the information. Private citizens contemplating travel or work overseas can solicit travel advisories directly from the Office of Citizens Services.

Among the members of OSAC are American Express, United Airlines, and Pan American World Airways. These companies have access to information that should be helpful in preventing their clients from being caught in a terrorist situation.

Conclusions

There are scores of books dealing with the problems of terrorism, motives for terrorism, dynamics of terrorism, policies concerning terrorism, outlook for terrorism, responses to terrorism, and the law and terrorism. However, in human terms what is important is what happens to three groups of people: victims of terrorism, the families of the victims, and the crisis managers and crisis workers. The victim of a kidnapping is perceived by his or her captors as a symbol. This symbol—employee, member of a political, religious, academic, or ethnic group—is also a human being, an intrinsic part of a family. In a hostage situation, the family can become an adversary to the crisis managers or in other ways can become part of the problem.

The family of a hostage needs information, a support system, and, ideally, counseling by a mental health professional. The family's main concern is the survival and return of the victim. The family probably will experience several psychological responses, mainly anger. This anger is often displaced; not being able to strike back at the perpetrators of the crime, family members may project their feelings of hostility against the crisis manager or an authority figure. Sometimes families may suffer more psychologically than does the hostage. The stresses families are exposed to take several forms, and they build through the crisis situation if unrelieved. The common stress sources include anxiety from not knowing how the victim is faring from one moment to the next, accentuation of preexisting stress in the relationship, guilt, and anger. There are other sources of problems, such as the idealization of the victim, depression when reunited, and adjustments to changes in personality and priority among people on all sides of the crisis. Neither victim nor family members, and sometimes crisis workers, are ever the same after the trauma. The pressures of the families are such that even the president of the United States seems unable to resist them completely.

An increasing number of crisis orientation programs are being developed aimed at creating an awareness of terrorism and its implications. These programs are designed for the benefit of high-risk personnel and their families. Business and government have developed joint programs for the exchange of security information. Orientation programs have been developed and are being improved for sensitizing potential victims, families, and crisis workers to the needs of such crisis situations. There is a growing focus on the needs of the families of hostage victims—not only military and government but also businessmen and other private citizens.

Recommendations

There is an urgent need for more studies of larger samples of former hostages and their families to test the hypotheses of behavior and psychological responses that have been identified but only partially tested. Comparative studies with families of MIAs and POWs and diverse types of hostages could be useful in identifying similarities and differences in human behavior in a crisis. Taken one step further, samples of families of hostages from other countries could be studied to isolate differences as well as common denominators in human responses. Meanwhile, if the accepted theories are to be followed, psychological counseling should be recommended and if possible made available to all families of hostages. Ideally this counseling should start at the onset of the crisis and follow through to the aftermath.

Founding the OSAC was a giant step toward using intelligence information as a preventive measure against terrorists attacks against Americans overseas; however, it remains to be seen how the members of the council disseminate this information and how classified information is handled. Council member William F. Beane, of United Airlines Corporation, suggests developing a system "to characterize the sources of information upon which analyses of terrorists' activity are based."[33] He means in part that readings on the seriousness and credibility of threats should be part of the information that is provided to OSAC members and through them to the business community.

It is of utmost importance for high government officials, heads of multinationals, religious leaders, and others to be aware of the potentially powerful pressure that families of hostages can exert. It is important to understand the psychological reasons for this behavior. At the same time, these leaders must stand firm behind policies that will discourge further kidnappings and hostage takings.

The terrorist blackmail attempt and the human tragedy a terrorist kidnapping initiates must be managed as parts of the crisis. To be sure, giving in to terrorist demands encourages more terrorism, but as the Iran scandal proved all too vividly, failing to deal effectively with the immensely stressful experience that hostage family members and crisis managers go through is a recipe for both personal and political disaster.

Notes

1. *Crisis Work . . . Crisis Worker* (Washington, D.C.: Department of State, September 1986), pp. 1–8. Also available on videotape.

2. Robert Blum is a psychiatrist, terrorism specialist, and a consultant to the Department of State. His comments were made during a personal interview on June 19, 1987.

3. Richard Queen, *Inside and Out* (Toronto: Academic Press Canada Limited, 1979), pp. 231, 246–256. Queen's illness was diagnosed as multiple sclerosis by the medical team at Rhein-Main Air Base in Germany.

4. Penne Laingen, *Living in a Stressful World: Part I, Learning to Live with Terrorism* (Arlington, Va.: Overseas Briefing Center, Foreign Service Institute, 1985), pp. 16–17.

5. Leila Dane, *The Iran Hostage Wives: Long Term Crisis Coping* (Ann Arbor, Mich.: University Microfilms International, 1984), pp. 35–41.

6. The Office of Citizens Services is an arm of consular services that deals with the problems of Americans all over the world. It has dealt with crisis situations in many countries. Following the terrorist attacks on the U.S. embassy in Beirut and subsequent hijackings and bombings affecting Americans, this office evolved as the central point of contact in the Department of State for families concerned about a hostage situation.

7. *Public Report of the Vice President's Task Force on Combatting Terrorism* (Washington, D.C.: Superintendent of Documents, U.S. Government Printing Office, February 1986).

8. "Consoling Hostage Relatives," *New York Times*, June 30, 1987, p. A14. Distributed in mimeograph form by the U.S. Department of State.

9. Elizabeth Kubler-Ross, *On Death and Dying* (New York: Macmillan, 1969), pp. 262–265.

10. Interview with Blum.

11. Elivira Johnson Elbrick, tape from *Foreign Service Family Oral History Project* (Washington, D.C., 1986).

12. Paul Eggersten, psychiatrist and terrorism specialist. Comments made during an interview on June 18, 1987.

13. Kurt Carlson, *One American Must Die* (New York: Congdon and Weed, New York, 1986).

14. Edna J. Hunter, "Captivity: The Family in Waiting," in *Stress in the Family* (New York: Figley & McCubbin, Brunner/Navel, 1983), 2: 166–184.

15. Ibid.

16. Frank M. Ochberg, *Victims of Terrorism*, Westview Special Studies in National and International Terrorism (Boulder, Colo.: Westview, 1982), pp. 17–29.

17. *Hostage Taking: Preparation, Avoidance, and Survival*, Office of Security, Department and Foreign Service Series 390 Department of State Publication 9400 (October 1984).

18. Ibid.

19. *Managing before, during and after a Crisis* (U.S. Department of State, February 1986), pp. IV-1 through IV-4, V-1, V-2. Also available as a videotape.

20. *The Family Action Plan III* pamphlet 608-41 (Department of the Army, May 1986).

21. *Patterns of Global Terrorism 1985* (Department of State, October 1986).

22. Neil C. Livingstone, *The War against Terrorism* (Lexington, Mass.: Lexington Books, 1982), pp. 149–150.

23. Ibid.

24. *Terrorist Attacks on U.S. Businesses Abroad* (Department of State, March 1986).

25. Richard Clutterbuck, *Terrorism* (New York: Crane Russak, 1982), pp. 125–137.

26. David R. Heinly, "When Business Needs Protection Overseas," *Security* (June 1987).

27. Ibid.

28. Ibid.

29. *Crisis Management Guidelines*, Overseas Security Advisory Council, Department of State Publication 9516, Bureau of Diplomatic Security (December 1986).

30. Clutterbuck, *Terrorism*.

31. Robert Stoddard, coordinator of American University, Beirut, telephone conversation of July 23, 1987.

32. *Patterns of Global Terrorism 1985*.

33. Heinly, "When Business Needs Protection Overseas."

10

The Iran–Contra Crisis and Its Impact on U.S.–Israeli Counterterrorism Cooperation

Yagil Weinberg

Israeli involvement in the Iran–Contra affair came, some say, at the worst possible time. In the months immediately prior to public disclosures regarding Israel's role in the Iran initiative, the relationship between the two countries had suffered major setbacks as a result of the Pollard spy case and criticism regarding Israeli cooperation with South Africa. With the advent of the Iran–Contra affair, some in Congress went so far as to blame Israel for dragging the United States into one of the worst policy crises in recent history. However, despite short-lived tension between the two nations, it is safe to assert that the basic need to collaborate and cooperate for the sake of each country's national interest remains intact. Most policymakers in the United States continue to regard Israel as a strategic asset rather than a liability.

The Iran–Contra affair is not a unique episode in U.S.–Israeli relations. Indeed it is only another manifestation of two long-standing trends in American-Israeli interaction and collaboration: Israel's role as a U.S. proxy and the continuous threat of international terrorism to both nations. The two trends, though seemingly unrelated, are instead closely related and provide an important foundation for what is regarded as the special relationship between the United States and Israel.

The mutual need for cooperation in the counterterrorism arena has not diminished as a result of the recent events. The alliance between the two countries in combating international terrorism is and can be expected to remain strong.

Israeli Involvement in the Iran Initiative

The relationship between the United States and Israel has matured through four decades of continuous interaction. Since President Truman first supported the establishment of the Jewish state, the two countries have enjoyed close and friendly relations. Despite the considerable gap in power resources between the two nations and Israel's obvious dependence on the United States for a substantial portion of its economic and military requirements—to the extent that its survival would be in question without such aid—this is no simple patron-client relationship. Rather it has emerged as a unique bilateral relationship between partners, notwithstanding frequent disagreements and confrontations over major policy questions.

Although U.S.–Israeli relations are rooted in four decades of history and shared moral values, the emerging alliance between the two nations is today based on shared strategic concerns.

Israel's enlarged role in U.S. strategic planning has produced an even greater interdependence between the nations. The advent of the conservative Reagan administration witnessed an expanded U.S. interest in strategic coordination and cooperation with Israel. Central elements in the new U.S. global strategy were the revival of the idea of countering the Soviets within geographical regions and a stress on informal, as well as formal, alliances in the containment process. The more aggressive U.S. stance toward the Soviets strengthened Israel's role in the formation of U.S. strategic considerations in the Middle East. Israel assumed a more important role since Iran was no longer a U.S. ally and due to the growing threat of international terrorism. These trends resulted in the signing of the U.S.–Israel Memorandum of Understanding on Strategic Cooperation in 1981. The memo remains in force, but the United States shelved it later in 1981 when Israel annexed the Golan Heights.

Israel as a U.S. Proxy

Israeli involvement in the Iran initiative, although seemingly unique on the surface, is merely another chapter in a long history of cooperation between the two countries. This cooperation involves other countries and is the least disclosed and most secret by-product of the U.S.–Israeli pursuit of mutual strategic interests. Through the years, Israel and the United States have created a number of triangular networks, with Israel and the United States as two sides of the triangle, together with a third party. In this connection, Israel has frequently provided political, military, and intelligence support to third parties as a means of advancing the policy goals of both Washington and Jerusalem. It can clearly be said that whereas the U.S.–Israeli objectives closely coincide, each has its own separate objectives when collaborating in such triangular relationships.

The use of Israel to advance U.S. interests can be traced back to 1970 and is indirectly related to the rise of international terrorism. Israel responded to a U.S. request to support its initiative to save the monarchy of King Hussein of Jordan in September 1970. The king, who had launched an attack on the Palestinian "occupiers" of Jordan, was threatened with Syrian intervention. A victory in Jordan for the Palestinians and Syria, who were backed both politically and financially by the Soviet Union, and the defeat of King Hussein, a long-time U.S. ally in the Middle East, would have been a major setback to U.S. interests in the region and amounted to an unprecedented foothold for the Soviets.

Nevertheless, while appearing to act as a U.S. proxy, Israel clearly has pursued its own national interests as well. Not only did it succeed in preventing Syrian occupation of its entire eastern border while at the same time striking a blow against the Palestinian ability to conduct future terrorist attacks, but it also proved its strategic value as a U.S. ally.

Israel also has become increasingly involved in arms sales to governments and opposition groups in third world countries and today is a major arms exporter. In many cases, Israel was either responding to a U.S. request to provide arms when Washington was prevented from doing so or accepting the role with tacit U.S. approval.

Israel has enjoyed direct benefits from such involvement. Arms sales provide a boost to its precarious economy and its military-industrial complex. For the most part, Israeli arms sales have been confined to U.S.-backed nations or opposition groups. Israel, in a sense, earns its special status and relationship with the United States by giving aid and arms to regimes that Washington supports but cannot overtly assist because of concerns about its international image, U.S. public opinion, or congressional prohibitions. Thus, Israeli aid to South Africa, Taiwan, El Salvador, Guatemala, Costa Rica, and Honduras benefited all the concerned parties. A State Department official was quoted as saying, "We have indicated we are not unhappy they are helping out."[1]

Israel came to play an important role in the U.S.–Sandinista conflict long before the Iran–Contra affair. In its support of Nicaragua's neighbors, Israel has played a major role in U.S. efforts to isolate the Sandinista regime. In October 1982, for example, Israeli foreign minister Itzhak Shamir visited Costa Rica and agreed to assist in establishing a settlement in northern Costa Rica, near the Nicaraguan border, which, "combined with the military buildup in Honduras, would create giant strategic pincers, physically isolating Nicaragua by land."[2]

The Reagan administration was actively involved in efforts to bring down the Sandinista regime. The centerpiece of this effort was aid to the Contras. Due to international criticism and congressional restrictions, the Reagan administration sought a third country to play a more visible role in the region and to launder U.S. money to the rebel groups.

After the Falkland Islands war in 1982, Argentina refused to continue its role of U.S. surrogate, providing military and financial support to the Contras. The responsibility then shifted to Israel, which has long-established ties to Central America, including aid to the deposed Somoza regime, and its support for the Contras could be explained as an effort to counter the Palestinian Liberation Organization (PLO), with which the Sandinistas had already established close links. Despite repeated denials by Jerusalem, it is evident that the Israelis took an active role in supporting the Contras at Washington's request.

The Senate Intelligence Committee's report on the Iran scandal argues that Israel helped the United States supply the Contras with captured Soviet-made weapons, an operation arranged by the Israelis and the National Security Council (NSC). As an Israeli official observed, "[Lieutenant Colonel Oliver] North drove us crazy with requests to supply weapons to the Nicaraguan rebels. . . . Israel did not transfer arms directly, but rather dealt with Americans involved with North. However, Israel knew the arms were destined for the Contras."[3]

The Iran Initiative

What is unique, in retrospect, about the Iran initiative is not the divergence of interests between the United States and Israel with respect to dealing with Iran. Rather, the exceptional factors in the initiative were the subsequent shape of events, the actions taken, the choice of intermediaries and representatives that played a role in the collaborative effort, the diversion of funds from the Iran arms deal, and, finally, the public scrutiny involved.

Striking a deal with Iran was expected to yield profound benefits for both the United States and Israel. From the Israeli perspective, it was perceived as a way to keep the war in the Persian Gulf going, a major strategic objective of Jerusalem. Outright victory by either side could shift the focus of contention in the Middle East back again to the Arab–Israeli conflict. Military support for Iran, by contrast, could advance Israeli contacts with the Iranian military and possibly create grounds for a future positive dialogue with the revolutionary regime. Israel was also concerned about the fate of an estimated 25,000 Iranian Jews. The United States, for its part, was interested in approaching so-called moderate elements in Iran in an attempt to gain a future "foot in the door" and hoped also to win the release of the U.S. hostages held in Lebanon. (Initially the chief U.S. impetus was the desire to secure the release of hostage Central Intelligence Agency station chief in Beirut, William Buckley.)

Paradoxically, though both the United States and Israel departed from their stated policies of no negotiation with terrorists in opening direct talks with Iran, a state heavily involved in support of terrorists, they nonetheless continued to pursue active counterterrorist measures against the state sponsors of terrorism and their proxies as the negotiations progressed. The Israeli–NSC operation resulted in a significant decrease of active Iranian support for terrorism. Although incidents in the Middle East increased by 60 percent in 1985, only thirty were linked to groups with ties to Iran.[4]

Further, the United States and Israel were reportedly engaged in planning various joint counterterrorism operations, including the rescue by commandos of the hostages in Lebanon, as well as using the so-called residuals from the arms sold to Iran to support other counterterrorism activities by Israel.

A great deal of debate has centered around where the Iran initiative actually originated. The Iranians could not deal directly with the United States but needed its support in the war against Iraq. They may have approached Israel to intervene, and Israel then convinced the United States to get involved in the complex operation. Israel has supplied arms to Iran since the early 1980s with, at the very least, the quiet knowledge and consent of U.S. officials. There can be little doubt that Israeli discussions, first with the unofficial U.S. representative, former terrorism consultant to the NSC Michael Ledeen, and then with the NSC staff, were initiated to ensure the replenishment of arms delivered from Israeli stockpiles. The strategic elements and the hostage issue were used as bait. However, as argued by Lieutenant Colonel Oliver North in his testimony before the special congressional committee, the United States and the actors on its side were well aware of the implications of their actions. The president, upon the advice of his NSC staff and CIA director William Casey, decided to pursue this plan for the sake of broad and significant U.S. interests.

Israel played a unique but unintended role in the Iran–Contra affair. White House officials used Israel to sidestep those U.S. agencies that are central to the execution of U.S. foreign policy: the CIA, the Pentagon, and the State Department, not to mention the Congress. In this sense, Israel functioned virtually as part of the U.S. government, albeit unintentionally; but this is not to lose sight of the fact that Israel always had its own national objectives in mind in facilitating the initiative.

Israel was also used as a U.S. instrument to carry out various anti-terrorist operations. The failure of the CIA to conduct extensive counterterrorist operations and the inability of the State and Defense departments to reach a consensus on the subject prompted CIA director Casey and the NSC staff to bypass the federal bureaucracy and to collaborate with Israel in an effort to act swiftly and consistently against terrorists and their state sponsors.

Terrorism as a Mutual Threat

The mutual need for continued cooperation between the United States and Israel regarding counterterrorism and the mechanics of that cooperation have not changed in the aftermath of the Iran initiative. In this connection, the United States and Israel remain two of the chief targets of international terrorism.

Palestinian terrorism took on a new meaning for U.S. policymakers in the aftermath of the 1967 Middle East war, for Palestinian violence was suddenly no longer limited to the eastern Mediterranean; it became a global phenomenon. For the Palestinians, all actions were justified, in all places, and against all people.

On July 23, 1968, a Palestinian organization, the Popular Front for the Liberation of Palestine (PFLP), launched its first international terrorist operation by hijacking an Israeli El Al jetliner and forcing it to land in Algeria. This attack was followed by the targeting of U.S. property. First came the bombing of the Tapline (oil pipeline) in May 1969. On August 29, 1969, a TWA aircraft was hijacked to Jordan and blown up after the passengers were evacuated. Secretary of State William Rogers described the act as "air piracy," adding a new term to the lexicon of international relations.[5]

Since that time, Palestinian violence has escalated at an ever increasing pace, and a growing number of victims have been citizens of the United States. The long-term U.S. commitment to Israel and its persistent refusal to bend to Palestinian demands continue to place its representatives and citizens throughout the world in constant danger. The link between the United States and Israel as targets is demonstrated by the Palestinian tactic of using terrorism against U.S. citizens to put pressure on Israel. In the majority of recent kidnappings of Americans, for example, the abductors have threatened to harm their captives unless Israel and other nations released large numbers of "anti-Zionist" terrorist prisoners.

In retrospect, the advent of Palestinian terrorism against the United States and Israel could have severely weakened or even destroyed the flourishing relationship between the two nations. Indeed, the U.S. might have distanced itself from Israel to remove its citizens, property, and interests from the line of fire. However, in addition to the strong U.S. commitment to Israel's survival, other considerations, including the dissolution of détente, the 1973 Yom Kippur war, the Arab oil embargo, and the absence of other methods to advance U.S. interests in the Middle East, ensured that the relationship would endure.

The United States as a Target

One important reason for the increased terrorist activity against the United States is the ongoing superpower competition, especially in the Middle East. The persistent attempts by the Soviet Union to advance its interests and minimize the U.S. role in the region have become an integral part of the Arab/Palestinian–Israeli conflict. By supporting the various Palestinian movements and their violent methods, the Soviet Union not only followed its long-standing political strategy—that assistance to nationalist movements is a stage in the eventual penetration by communist ideology—but also helped keep anti-U.S. sentiment alive. The origins of state-sponsored terrorism can be found in the Soviet perception that support of terrorist groups and terrorist regimes is an economical way to disrupt U.S. policy in the Middle East while avoiding direct confrontation with the United States.

The same method was adopted by Arab governments as part of an anti-Western, anti-U.S. policy that became even more intense following the Islamic revolution in Iran. Support of terrorist groups and their activities allows sponsoring governments to avoid unwanted escalation while contributing to the realization of their overall policy objectives.

Today in Iran, for example, the United States is regarded as the leading symbol of Western ideology and way of life, which Iran wants to eliminate in its quest to establish a radical Islamic society throughout the region. As the chief supporter to the late shah, the United States is identified with his methods, his corruption, and the economic plight that characterized a majority of the Iranian people.

U.S. Constraints in the War against Terrorism

Increasing attacks on U.S. interests presented policymakers with a major problem: how to counter the growing terrorist threat despite self-imposed legal and constitutional considerations. Following the Vietnam War, a number of laws were passed restricting the president's power to conduct covert, diplomatic, and military actions overseas. Public Law 93-558, passed in 1974, required the president to notify Congress in a timely fashion about the activities of the CIA and other intelligence agencies. It also mandated that the president give his personal approval to each covert operation by signing a finding, stating its justifications and general goals. The law was revised under President Jimmy Carter to require notification only of the House and Senate Intelligence committees. Another example is executive order number 12333, promulgated by President Reagan in 1981, which prohibits the United States from engaging in assassination.

Another problem in conducting an active counterterrorism policy was the lack of policy consensus within the Reagan administration. This was a result of continuing disagreements among various executive agencies coupled with animosity among high-ranking government officials on the matter. Consequently the emerging policy was one of indecision. Secretary of State George Shultz, for example, supported a tough active defense policy, whereas Defense Secretary Caspar Weinberger, among others, opposed such a policy. The objection stemmed from Secretary Weinberger's fear that the pursuance of an active anti-terrorist campaign could harm U.S. relations with Arab countries and in the long run affect U.S. commitment to other defense programs, such as the Strategic Defense Initiative (SDI).

Lack of International Cooperation

Because terrorism is an international problem, any effective policy to combat and contain terrorism requires cooperation among the victimized nations. Unfortunately, the United States has found it difficult to forge effective cooperative links with its allies in Western Europe. Until recently, the exchange of intelligence, a logical first step in combating terrorism, was in many respects inadequate. Although the affected nations agree that terrorism is increasingly intolerable, they cannot reach a consensus as to the basic definition of what constitutes a terrorist act, who is a terrorist, and what combined actions should be taken. The issue is made even more difficult because of conflicting interests among the Western allies involving their relations with states that sponsor terrorism.

Even when the United States and Great Britain have accumulated conclusive evidence against states that sponsor terrorism, they have generally not been able to convince other Western nations to act in concert against the offenders. France, for example, has an unfortunate history of making deals with terrorists, even permitting them to operate on French territory in exchange for assurances of safety for French citizens. Although presented with compelling evidence of Libyan complicity in terrorist acts against U.S. citizens, France apparently denied U.S. aircraft overflight permission during the April 1986 raid on Libya. Despite persuasive evidence that Syria had planned the in-flight destruction of an El Al aircraft with a bomb carried, unwittingly, aboard the plane by the pregnant girlfriend of an Arab terrorist, Great Britain was unable to win West European support for sanctions against Syria.

As another example, the United States failed to convince Egypt, Italy, or Yugoslavia to hold Mohammed Abbas, the mastermind of the seizure of the *Achille Lauro* cruise ship, or to gain the extradition from West Germany of Mohammed Hamadei, who was involved in the hijacking of TWA flight 847 and the murder of one of the passengers. Having made significant inroads against domestic terrorism, including successful action by the elite counterterrorism unit GSG-9 against the hijackers of a West German Lufthansa aircraft in Mogadishu, Somalia, in 1977, the West German government has refused an extradition request by the United States, fearing retaliation after two West German businessmen were abducted in Beirut.

U.S. allies in Western Europe have often rejected anti-terrorist collaboration with the United States on the basis that it could trigger terrorist retaliation. The West Europeans seem to have forgotten that terrorism is a worldwide threat that is carefully coordinated and sponsored by hostile regimes to destabilize Western democracies.

The United Nations was founded to protect the rights of all nations, but it has been unable to make any significant headway against international terrorism. Confronted with a majority of third world nations that resist any attempt to act against, or even condemn, the sponsors of terrorism, Western nations, and especially the United States, are stalemated. International organizations, even when they are able to achieve consensus on issues such as aircraft hijacking and violence against diplomats, have been able to implement few significant measures against terrorists and their state sponsors. U.N. condemnation of Israel after the Entebbe rescue operation in 1976 was harsher than its criticism of the terrorists or the Ugandan government, which aided them. Nor did the U.N. flinch from adopting a Libyan resolution condemning the April 1986 U.S. air strike against Libya, while refusing to act on the matter of Libya's pervasive support of terrorist activities.

The combined opposition of most third world nations, the Arab countries, and the Soviet East bloc satellites ensures that Western initiatives against terrorism are unlikely to succeed in international forums. This opposition has a practical explanation: countries that finance, train, and support terrorist operations could be compromised by multilateral international action. As a result, nations victimized by state-sponsored terrorism, including the United States, often are faced with only two alternatives: do nothing or strike back at the terrorists and their state sponsors unilaterally.

Basis for Israeli Cooperation

Israel has emerged as perhaps the only other country through which an active campaign against terrorism could be mounted. Long the primary target of the terrorists, Israel does not face the same kinds of institutional and constitutional constraints that the United States does.

Surrounded by hostile neighbors pledged to its destruction, Israel has always been guided by two assumptions: that the conflict with the Arab states is a given, not likely to be resolved in the near future, and that Israel's military vulnerability must be recognized. Thus Israel's security strategy has been based on avoiding unnecessary risks and adopting an active defensive policy to counter any threat.

A major element in Israel's strategy has been a basic consensus regarding its security needs. This consensus has some key characteristics, foremost of which is the need to be self-reliant; memories of the persecution of Jews throughout the centuries and the Holocaust under Nazi Germany serve as the cornerstone of Israel's justification for its actions. Israel perceives itself as a nation standing alone that must rely on its own strength and resources.[6] Anti-Israeli terrorism is seen as an ongoing and serious threat. By the same token, Israeli policymakers recognize the need for outside support. Thus Israel sought a partner that would be responsive to its needs but would not compromise its security; the United States has emerged as that partner.

In its active defense policy, Israel has, for all practical purposes, been the only other country consistently and without debate to oppose terrorists and their state sponsors. Indeed it was Israel's effective domestic anti-terrorist measures that first caused terrorism to become international, as terrorists sought targets beyond Israel's borders. In its invasion of Lebanon in 1982, Israel fought a full-scale war with Syria and the Palestinian organizations. It has repeatedly attacked Palestinian targets in Lebanon and elsewhere and was willing even to strike at the PLO headquarters in Tunisia in October 1985 despite the negative impact the Tunisian air raid had on U.S. interests in the region.

Israel can operate in ways the United States cannot. Where Israel is willing to take military action against governments that support terrorists, the United States has to consider the international implications of its actions and the possibility of escalation into a crisis between the two superpowers. Although it had enough evidence to implicate Syria in the suicide attack on the marine compound in Lebanon in October 1982, the United States preferred to avoid a direct confrontation with the Syrians over the issue. There was concern that because Syria is a major Soviet client, any military action against Syria would result in direct Soviet intervention.

Basic differences between the two societies provide another reason for the Israeli ability to act, in contrast to frequent U.S. restraint and indecision. The American public does not appreciate the immediacy of the terrorist threat, whereas it is a pervasive part of life for Israelis. The problem is not immediate for most Americans, whose first real exposure to terrorism came during the September 1972 Olympic Games at Munich, when Israeli athletes were massacred by members of the Black September Palestinian terrorist group. Americans initially were outraged; however, their anger quickly subsided.

It was not until a decade later, after the hijacking of TWA 847 to Beirut and the *Achille Lauro* affair, that the American public began calling for decisive U.S. government action against terrorism. Nevertheless, because such outrages do not directly threaten everyday life in the United States, most Americans still do not regard the problem with the same sense of urgency as do their Israeli counterparts.

As a consequence, Israeli action against terrorism has been perceived by some in the United States as a legitimate way to wage the war that the United States cannot fight directly and overtly, except in rare circumstances. Even if Israel does not always receive a green light from Washington to act, generally it enjoys U.S. support in the aftermath of its actions. The United States, moreover, has supported Israel in international forums on this issue and has vetoed anti-Israeli resolutions in the U.N. Washington initially even hailed the Israeli attack on the PLO headquarters in Tunisia, despite the fact that Tunisia is a close U.S. friend and the effect of the Israeli attack was to damage U.S. relations with moderate elements in the Arab world.

Richard Armitage, assistant secretary of defense for international security affairs, touched on this matter in an interview when he refused to condemn Israeli actions, saying that "as a world power there are very strict limits on us. We do not have the freedom of action that other countries enjoy. . . . It is necessary for the U.S. . . . to be absolutely correct and above board, morally, legally and in all ways, before we engage in retaliatory or pre-emptive action."[7]

Formal Cooperation in the War against Terrorism

Facing the mutual threat of terrorism, the United States and Israel have emphasized the need to collaborate in the fight against terrorism as a centerpiece of their growing strategic alliance. "The single most effective thing that the military or any government activity can do to combat terrrorism . . . is to gain firsthand, solid intelligence concerning the intentions of terrorists," according to Armitage.[8] Further, a U.S. military response to terrorism, although possible, must be based on a foundation of solid intelligence information.[9] It is generally accepted within the Western intelligence communities that Israel possesses the most comprehensive intelligence capability in the Middle East and therefore has the best information concerning hostile terrorist activity.

U.S. intelligence operational abilities were severely undermined by the Senate Select Investigating Committee headed by Senator Frank Church (D–Idaho) in 1975 and 1976. The so-called Church committee conducted an inquiry into alleged intelligence abuses such as CIA assassination plots and ultimately recommended rigorous congressional oversight of the CIA and other intelligence agencies, including the establishment of new procedures for supervising and monitoring intelligence operations.[10] The Carter administration subsequently issued its own restrictions on covert intelligence operations. During the Carter presidency, regularized scrutiny of intelligence affairs by the legislature became commonplace.[11]

Since that time, the capture, interrogation under torture, and execution of the CIA station chief in Beirut further reduced U.S. marginal operational capabilities in the Middle East. As a result, valuable information on CIA operations in the Middle East and the identities of its officers and agents reportedly were disclosed to the terrorists.[12] Since Saudi Arabia and Jordan, U.S. allies in the region, continue to support the PLO, they provide only selective intelligence assistance to the United States regarding Palestinian terrorist activities. Iraq, for its part, has a long affiliation with terrorism, having been on the U.S. list of terrorist sponsors until recently. The most solid information about terrorist plans and operations, then, can and must be supplied by Israel.

The United States and Israel have developed an extensive system for exchanging intelligence information. Israel provides data on the entire scope of Arab and Soviet military and political affairs, as well as information regarding terrorism, which has expanded dramatically with the increase of anti-American violence by Palestinian terrorist groups in recent years. While the U.S. contribution to the two countries' intelligence collection effort on terrorism comes primarily from technological intelligence gathering (such as electronic eavesdropping, satellite reconnaissance, and photography), Israel has generally provided information gathered through more traditional human methods. For example, Jerusalem was the one consistent source of warning to the United States of the turmoil in Iran during the shah's last months in 1978–1979. Israel continued to maintain close contacts with the Iranian military throughout the 1980s and became a major source of information on Iranian internal affairs, the Iran–Iraq war, and Iranian terrorist connections. Although not always successful, the Israelis have penetrated some Palestinian terrorist organizations and have helped the West preempt various terrorist operations and identify organizations and individuals responsible for past terrorist atrocities.

On an operational level, Israel offered the United States various suggestions designed to win the release of hostages after the seizure of the U.S. embassy in Tehran in 1979. It also warned Italy in 1985 that one of its cruise ships might be hijacked and provided the United States with proof that Mohammed Abbas was the operational chief behind the *Achille Lauro* hijacking. During that incident, Israel supplied the information that enabled the United States to intercept the Egyptian jetliner bearing the terrorists to a safe haven.

A joint U.S.–Israeli counterterrorism operation was devised in September 1985 to locate and rescue American hostages in Beirut. Although the mission was frustrated because the location of all the hostages could not be pinpointed, it illustrates the high level of cooperation that evolved during the Reagan administration prior to the Iran–Contra scandal.

Israel, with a sophisticated intelligence network in place in Lebanon, reportedly even has scale-model mock-ups of large areas of Beirut in anticipation of the time when they might be useful for anti-terrorist operations. The April 1973 raid on Beirut by special Israeli commando forces, when prominent leaders of the PLO were assassinated in their homes, and the systematic hunting and assassination of terrrorist leaders in the aftermath of the 1972 Munich massacre of Israeli Olympic athletes are two examples in a long list of secret Israeli counterterrorist operations.

The various U.S. and Israeli intelligence organizations have established formal liaison offices to exchange intelligence and facilitate cooperation. These include the military branches of the intelligence communities of both countries (the U.S. Defense Intelligence Agency [DIA] and the Israeli military intelligence); the civilian branches (the U.S. CIA and the Israeli Mossad); and the internal security services (the U.S. Federal Bureau of Investigation [FBI] and the Israeli Shin Bet). For the most part, the exchange of intelligence relating to terrorism is highly institutionalized and independent of the formal political relations between the two countries. It has become routine practice for high-ranking Israeli defense and intelligence officials to have briefings with the director of the CIA when in Washington. During the tenure of the late CIA director, William Casey, Israel frequently received raw intelligence material for assessment and had access to sensitive information. Beyond routine meetings between officials of the various agencies, there is extensive collaboration in the development of sophisticated electronic intelligence systems.

Israeli military intelligence has teamed with DIA to improve the capabilities of both agencies. Technical and operational teams and members of the research staffs of each country's intelligence agencies meet regularly to discuss collaboration with respect to future intelligence programs, to plan the development of new intelligence-gathering techniques, and to examine each other's methods of operation.

A critical element of this close cooperation is the evolution of close personal relationships between individuals who are members of the relevant agencies in both countries. A retired Israeli chief of military intelligence, Major General Yehoshua Sagi, was quoted as saying, "Casey now says 'yes' all the time."[13] Indeed, it would not have been possible for the United States to intercept the airliner carrying the *Achille Lauro* pirates without the close relationship that had developed between Lieutenant Colonel Oliver North and Amiram Nir, the former special adviser to the Israeli prime minister on counterterrorism. The prompt and immediate response of Nir, who mobilized the necessary Israeli resources and personnel to fulfill North's urgent request for intelligence information on the location and identification of the aircraft, carrying the terrorists, was fundamental to the successful interception of the Egyptian jetliner.

Even during times of misunderstanding and conflict, these long-established channels continue to be productive. Neither country is likely to want to abandon them, regardless of the political climate. One need only recall that while the United States publicly condemned Israel's 1981 attack on the Iraqi nuclear reactor, the U.S. intelligence services were effusive in their behind-the-scenes praise of the Israeli action.

Future Cooperation: The Implications of the Iran-Contra Affair

The Iran–Contra affair contains important implications with respect to U.S. anti-terrorist policies and capabilities, and it may also have a significant impact on the ability of the United States and Israel to collaborate on future anti-terrorist actions. The Iran–Contra affair is likely to create a political climate in the United States in which covert operations will find little public or congressional support.

The Reagan administration has pursued an aggressive counterterrorism policy in recent years. In 1986 an interagency committee (Operations Sub-Group), headed by Lieutenant Colonel Oliver North, was created to oversee U.S. anti-terrorist policy. President Reagan authorized the kidnapping of terrorists, and a new counterterrorism center was established in the CIA, which was responsible for the preparation of counterterrorist operations, many of which involved the Israelis.[14] The growing suspicion by the public and Congress regarding the U.S. intelligence community may now circumscribe such activities.

Secretary of State George Shultz, former CIA director William Casey, and former national security adviser Robert C. McFarlane and his aide, Lieutenant Colonel Oliver North, were among the key proponents of an active U.S. anti-terrorist policy. In the aftermath of the Iran–Contra affair, Casey was dead, North fired from his position at the NSC, and the Reagan administration in disarray. Casey's replacement, William H. Webster, has been one of the main opponents of an activist anti-terrorism policy.[15] As a former federal judge, he was very sensitive to the possible violation of international law if operations such as kidnapping terrorists abroad were conducted. Webster's new position as CIA director ensures that his views will carry great weight in the formation of future U.S. counterterrorism policies.

Recent events have also created constraints on the Israelis in conducting covert operations. The Pollard case and the Iran initiative prompted an inquiry by the Israeli Knesset into the involvement of Israeli government officials and intelligence agencies in these affairs. The Pollard case and the Iran initiative were clearly mishandled by the Israelis involved. Moreover, there have been recent revelations about improper procedures used in the interrogation of suspected terrorists by the Israeli secret services. The allegation regarding the abuse of power by the Shin Bet stemmed from the unexplained death of two Arab kidnappers of an Israeli bus and the false accusation of an Israeli military Druze soldier on trial for treason. These have prompted a cry for legislative restrictions on Israel's intelligence agencies and for a review of Israel's covert activities. Public opinion in Israel now demands better supervision of the secret agencies. Moreover, the political damage from the Knesset's inquiry may make Israeli political leaders more hesitant to approve covert activity.

Despite such considerations, the security problem Israel faces has not changed, and the public as well as the Knesset can be expected to remain essentially supportive of covert operations. The Israeli public simply wants to be assured that covert operations are conducted legally and properly.

Cooperation regarding anti-terrorism strategies and operations between the United States and Israel has seemingly been damaged by the departure of Casey, North, and Nir. Their successors may be excessively cautious and unwilling to take action or provide their counterparts with the means to operate effectively. Yet the need for cooperation still exists, the liaison arrangement for the continued exchange of intelligence is still in place, both sides are aware of their abilities and constraints, and the new officials responsible for this cooperation are likely to develop similar working relationships as those that existed in the past between, for example, Amiram Nir and Oliver North. The established channels of cooperation between the United States and Israel are likely to limit the negative implications of the Iran–Contra affair for U.S.–Israeli collaboration. It is likely to prevent any significant change in the relationship between the two countries. Further, it is unlikely that the United States will reduce the extent of its strategic help to Israel in the war against terrorism, from which the United States directly benefits.

The U.S. intelligence community has suffered a major setback in the aftermath of the Iran–Contra affair. Its intelligence collection abilities are likely to be further limited by more intensive oversight requirements, which will cripple its already weakened abilities in the Middle East in general and in Lebanon and Beirut in particular. It comes at a time when U.S. intelligence gathering in Lebanon is reported to be at its worst.[16] In this part of the world, U.S. intelligence agencies are likely to be less responsive to the growing need for human intelligence, crucial to preventing and combating terrorism. Israel, as a result, will of necessity continue to be called upon to play an expanded role in fulfilling U.S. needs in this region.

Congress and Israel: Ensuring Close Cooperation

In the post-Iran–Contra affair era, U.S. counterterrorism operations will be conducted with closer congressional and media scrutiny than in the past. Nevertheless, the need for tough action remains. Congress is leading the clamor for legislative changes in the institutions and procedures involved in the conduct of covert activities. Therefore, one can predict that in Congress there will be greater tendency to impose limits on U.S.–Israeli counterterrorism cooperation.

On the other hand, this political mood will come into conflict with past legislation and strategic realities. In 1984, Congress demonstrated the need for an active policy by passing an important law expanding U.S. criminal jurisdiction to cover terrorist acts overseas. Even if it wants to ensure close supervision of U.S. activities,

Congress is likely to allow, if not encourage, support for Israel's active pursuit of a productive counterterrorism policy. This will happen despite the temporary impression that there is a breach in the relations between the United States and Israel.

The strength of the relationship between the United States and Israel is partly the result of domestic factors, including the successful penetration of the U.S. political system by the so-called Israeli lobby. The strong support for Israel in all sections of U.S. political life ensures the continuation of a favorable public attitude toward Israel. This support is evident throughout American society: in the media, labor unions, large segments of the Christian community, conservatives, many influential think-tank groups, and an extraordinarily active and often influential Jewish community. Each has its own reasons to support Israel. The consistent votes in Congress to support Israel, to appropriate large amounts of funds, and to pressure the different administrations to maintain the same lines of support for Israel clearly suggest that constituents and their representatives are consistent in their pro-Israeli stance.

Congress has never attempted to apply the same standards to Israel as it has to other countries. Most observers expected criticism of Israel when it figured prominently in an administration report to Congress on countries supporting and collaborating with South Africa, but Congress largely ignored the report. The congressional resolution to stop U.S. aid to countries that did not sign the nuclear nonproliferation treaty specifically excluded Israel. Throughout the Pollard affair, moreover, Congress made no effort to punish Israel for its role. And during the hearings on the Iran initiative, it was clear that the Israeli role would not be made a central issue. Senator James McClure (R–Idaho), for example, came under pressure from his colleagues for expressing his dissenting opinion that Israel's actions served its own interests rather than those of the United States. In each case, the confluence of strategic reality, domestic politics, and political sentiment served to mute excessive criticism of Israel.

Congress is well aware of Israel's ability to advance the U.S. anti-terrorist campaign and can be expected to continue providing aid to Israel in order to further that effort. Despite some strains in relations between the two countries, the United States has found no better partner to take an active role in the war against terrorism. Neither Egypt nor Jordan nor Saudi Arabia is an obvious or likely candidate to serve as an alternative to Israel, for four reasons: (1) they do not enjoy the same kind of political sentiment in the United States as does Israel, (2) they are historically not considered reliable allies to the same extent as Israel, (3) they do not possess Israel's intelligence-gathering capabilities, and (4) the United States seeks to avoid the compromise of intelligence methods and information.

In each Arab state, the United States confronts numerous problems concerning the coordination of anti-terrorist policy. Each of these states has relations with the Palestinian terrorist organizations and is unlikely to cooperate with the United States in a way that may complicate inter-Arab relations. These problems surfaced, for example, in Egypt's handling of the *Achille Lauro* affair and in Saudi Arabia's condemnation of the U.S. raid on Libya. The Congress, then, is likely to encourage further Israeli involvement in the fight against terrorism while simultaneously placing new constraints on the government's ability to join the fight.

Conclusion

In the summer of 1979, President Reagan said, "The fall of Iran has increased Israel's value as perhaps the only remaining strategic asset in the region on which the U.S. can truly rely."[17] As the end of the Reagan presidency approaches, the statement still applies, and the issue of terrorism has become one major factor in that strategic reliance.

Israel and the United States will continue to fight this battle as allies because both face a mutual threat. Since the United States faces psychological, congressional, and international constraints on its own ability to act decisively against terrorists, it will continue to look to various partners. Israel clearly emerges as the only logical partner now available and will thus remain on the front line fighting this war for the entire West. It will do this with the recognition and blessing of the United States.

The Iran initiative was only one episode in a continuous drama of U.S.–Israeli cooperation. Israel has acted as a U.S. proxy in the past and will continue to do so in the future. Both countries will continue to benefit from this relationship. As long as terrorism remains a serious problem, the ongoing cooperation between the United States and Israel will be reinforced. The recent setbacks in relations will prove to be temporary incidents in a strategic cooperation that remains firmly structured and politically intact.

Notes

1. *New York Times*, December 17, 1982.
2. *Washington Post*, February 14, 1983.
3. Maariv (Tel Aviv, Israel), February 1, 1987.
4. Neil C. Livingstone, "1985 'Banner Year' of Terror Despite Altered Role of Iran," *Washington Times*, November 19, 1986.
5. *U.S. Department of State Bulletin*, September 15, 1969, p. 46.
6. Menachem Begin in his book *The Revolt* (in Hebrew) (Tel Aviv: Ahiasaf, 1950), p. 50, expresses these views when he writes: "The world does not pity the victims; it respects the warriors."
7. Interview with Richard Armitage in *American–Arab Affairs*, no. 20 (Spring 1987): 30–37.
8. Ibid.
9. Ibid.
10. U.S. Senate, Select Committee to Study Governmental Operations with Respect to Intelligence Activities, *Alleged Assassination Plots Involving Foreign Leaders: An Interim Report*, Report No. 94-465, 94th Cong., 1st sess., November 20, 1975.

11. John M. Oseth, *Regulating U.S. Intelligence Operations: A Study in Definition of the National Interest* (Lexington, Ky.: University Press of Kentucky, 1975), pp. 169–170.

12. Thomas David, "Buckley Warned CIA against Posting Him to Beirut," *New York City Tribune,* January 30, 1987.

13. Wolf Blitzer, *Between Washington and Jerusalem: A Reporter's Notebook* (New York: Oxford University Press, 1985), p. 88.

14. John Walcott and Andy Pasztor, "Covert Action: Reagan Ruling to Let CIA Kidnap Terrorists Overseas Is Disclosed," *Wall Street Journal,* February 20, 1987.

15. Ibid.

16. Conversations with staff members of the congressional Select Committee on Secret Military Assistance to Iran and the Nicaraguan Opposition, 1987.

17. Steven L. Spiegel, "U.S. Relations with Israel: The Military Benefits," *Orbis* (Fall 1986):475–497.

11

Counterterrorism as Enterprise: The Iran–Contra Investigations Spotlight the New Private Sector

Peter J. Brown
Terrell E. Arnold

In the past two decades, a new private sector has evolved in response to the challenge of terrorism. Fairly quickly it became a sophisticated and diversified copartner and competitor with governments in the Western countries in the provision of counterterrorism and security services and equipment. New firms emerged to meet part of the new demand for terrorism-related security, but established private security companies and consulting firms, many of which had offered similar specialized services for years, provided the nucleus of this new industry.

By the mid-1980s, the new private sector was well established. It had achieved enough experience and credibility so that members of the National Security Council (NSC) staff, who were looking for a way to get work done without raising an official profile, felt they could contract with private firms and individuals for delicate elements of a covert operation. The NSC staff sought someone to act as go-between in the transfer of arms to Iran in an effort to obtain release of U.S. hostages held in Lebanon. As a separate enterprise, in the early phases at least, members of the NSC staff were looking for ways to assist the Nicaraguan Democratic Resistance, the Contras, without attracting too much attention and debate from critics of the program.

Why the Private Sector?

The idea was hardly new. Cover has been an essential element of covert operations by governments for centuries. Achieving that cover through "cutouts," perhaps properly called unlabeled intermediaries, was probably invented about simultaneously with recognition of the needs for stealth and secrecy that go with covert operations. What perhaps was new in the situation was the existence of a well-developed private infrastructure for doing the types of work NSC staff members were seeking. The origin of that phenomenon was a changing world security environment not only at the level of subnational conflict, but also in the potentially lucrative fields of individual and corporate safety.

Neither the market nor the new private sector blossomed overnight. During the past decade, however, two factors have shaped and expanded the field for this new industry: the increase in the number and violence of terrorist attacks through the early 1980s and a sharp increase in corporate demand for security services, especially executive and facility protection.

The Look of a New Industry

The new industry's pioneers and present luminaries mirror the image of the wealthy clients, government agencies, and corporate board rooms they serve. Far from being opportunistic fear merchants, knuckle-dragging goons, or high-strung purveyors of paramilitary force, the new entrants mainly are skilled, experienced, and articulate experts and consultants. They shun publicity and seek to assist their clients with minimum visible profile. Moreover, they have sought to respond effectively to a market that has been episodic, often lean and without employment, but sometimes frantic in the wake of sensational terrorist incidents.

The firms in this dynamic new field represent a wide range of size, capability, experience, and revenue. Some experts call the smallest firms cottage industries because they operate out of homes or small offices and provide a limited range of services or products. Many of these firms have few employees, and their operations are barely profitable. By contrast, the leading firms do a nationwide business, employ thousands of people, and enjoy annual revenues of several hundred million dollars. These firms provide security services to government and major private firms throughout the United States and operate abroad in many countries.

The Market

The market of the counterterrorism industry represents a scattershot sampling of the whole society. There is no standard definition of terrorism in the industry; therefore everybody's definition applies. The product, broadly defined, is avoiding, discouraging, preempting, or defending one's self or client against terrorist activity. The industry responds often to events and threat conditions as perceived by the client rather than as defined by some objective authority. In any case, the product takes the form of preventive measures, countermeasures, facilities or personnel protective measures, or defensive actions. The supply of the services and equipment necessary to support such measures is the business of the new private sector.

Each act of terrorism is a political statement made through a criminal act. Thus everyone in the private security industry is also in the front line of the counterterrorism industry because they are associated significantly with efforts to avoid, deflect, or prevent crime. Every alarm or closed circuit television monitor is a device positioned to prevent crime first and to deter terrorists second. Counterterrorism therefore represents a subset of the security business, which some experts say will reach $50–60 billion by the turn of the next century. It represents part of an equipment market that has reached $5 billion or more per year.

As it has evolved to date, the counterterrorism industry hardly presents a neat and orderly profile for examination. To understand what the industry is, what it is capable of doing at the present time, and which elements of it looked both attractive and useful to government in the development of covert operations, it is worthwhile to look briefly at the leading firms; information and intelligence activities; the terrorism information business; training and related activities; and operations.

The Leading Firms

The new private sector is part of an estimated $35 billion annual private sector security business in the United States. American Brands and Borg Warner dominate the field with ownership of three companies: Pinkerton's, Wells Fargo Guard Services, and Burns International Security Services. These are the big three. Not far behind and perhaps catching up in annual sales are two companies that provide security guard and facility protection services: Wackenhut and California Plant Protection. In addition, Wackenhut, based in Coral Gables, Florida, offers comprehensive community support services, including emergency medical response and fire protection.

The big three are not treated here as part of the new private sector because they developed their businesses long before terrorism became a significant threat. These firms offer investigative, facility and personnel protection, technical systems, and related services, all developed over a period of many decades to deal with theft, kidnapping, industrial espionage, embezzlement, and other crimes against their corporate clients.

In many respects, the new private sector and the established security firms inceasingly overlap. None of the old firms is stagnating with respect to the range of services, the technologies, or the consultant skills it provides. Moreover, the kinds of security services and systems the old firms customarily provided can easily be turned to the task of thwarting terrorists.

Rapid and significant changes in state of the art hardware, software, training and techniques have caused the old firms and the new to move in the same directions. High tech devices for access control, perimeter and area surveillance, motion detection, intrusion alarm, or other crisis event monitoring and reporting devices are now manufactured by several hundred firms in the United States and abroad. Both the established and new private sector security firms tend to be takers and users of these systems rather than originators, although there is intensive interaction between customers and manufacturers in these fields, particularly respecting the design of computer software.

Some of the established security system manufacturing firms have moved into lines that enhance their traditional businesses as well as provide support to the new private sector. For example, Diebold, headquartered in Canton, Ohio, has produced vault doors and smaller secure enclosures for more than 120 years. Its current product lines include modular vaults, a computer-based security network monitoring and information management system, localized security monitoring terminals, sensing and alarm systems, video surveillance, and other high tech systems using computers and microprocessors. Diebold management reportedly has given some thought to providing the security services that go with its diversified security product lines, but it has not yet entered the new private sector to that extent.

Another illustration of this adaptive process is the Everett I. Brown Company of Indianapolis. Brown is a third-generation family-owned architect and engineering (A&E) firm whose president, the grandson of the founder, decided a decade ago to computerize the firm's design-related activities. Brown now is one of the most advanced A&E firms in the country with computer-aided design capabilities to create, store, retrieve, analyze, and revise designs quickly on the basis of specific threat information. Such capabilities can be used, for example, to show a client vulnerabilities of a facility to specific types of terrorist attack, to advise a client on likely resistance of a given structure to bomb blast effects, to suggest security changes in response to a known type of threat, or to design a new facility with security systems completely integrated in building design and function.

Such adaptive processes indicate that the boundary between the new private sector and the established security business, or business that never saw their activities as security related, is not clear-cut, and it is likely to become less so. The relation of the terrorist threat to other types of security risk is a major reason for this trend.

No one interviewed for this chapter suggested that the risk of being attacked by a terrorist was any greater than the possibility of being struck by lightning. Thus in actuarial or insurance terms, the threat of terrorism is lower than the threats that usually flow from ordinary violent crime, avarice, or negligence. Taken with the fact that the systems and services needed to deal with terrorism are broadly the same as those needed for coping with other types of security threat, the new private sector is only in limited respects a stand-alone business. In the long run, the direction the security systems and services arrow will point is a function of information perception and attitude toward specific threats.

Information and Intelligence Activities

A big piece of the business of the new private sector centers on identifying high threat situations. The counterterrorist information- and intelligence-gathering activities of new private sector security firms, much like governments, are aimed at predicting, preventing or deterring terrorist incidents. A primary goal is to overcome the advantages of stealth and surprise typically enjoyed by the terrorists. With good information and intelligence, the private firms hope to carry out counteroperations that will cause the terrorists to rethink their plans, to reevaluate their chances of success, and possibly to abort an operation.

Terrorist Profiling

Part of this effort consists of developing good profiles on the terrorists who threaten a specific client or who operate in countries of interest to the firm. As a result of using information to develop such profiles, leading security firms have concluded, for example, that terrorists make rational choices; they tend to shy away from operations where the costs outweigh the potential benefits. This means, in part, that suicide attacks are an aberration, not the norm. It also means that the terrorists are conservative and almost conventional in their conduct. They try to plan their activities on the basis of sound intelligence, and they seek to use surprise and careful timing to increase their chances of success. Their aim is to stay alive.

Risk Analysis

Much of the new private sector information-intelligence-gathering effort is focused on so-called risk analysis directed at advising a client on the risks in an environment where the client already must operate and at assessing the risks of a potential new business location. This kind of analysis requires the new private sector firm to gather information and interpret political conditions, assess the stability and vulnerability of leadership, estimate the capabilities and tendencies of volatile elements in a country, and identify the sources of potential instability. This sort of information can provide a client with an appreciation of political risks involved in any new or established venture. Only one of the sources of risk in these assessments is the prospect of terrorism. The other sources include natural disasters, vandalism, theft, violent crimes, insurrection, hostile corporate, and government activity.

Risk analysis gets the new private sector firm into areas of intelligence collection and assessment that traditionally represent the domain of governments. Several aspects of the firm's need for information, however—the client's particular problem—caused the firm to develop its own ways to get information. First, only recently have U.S. authorities been actively concerned about the threat posed to Americans by criminal activities abroad, and even now the information that is usually available is quite general in nature. It usually would not meet the needs of a client for specific information about given areas of a city or specific categories of threat. Second, terrorism caught the U.S. intelligence community in a very awkward posture of having little or no contact with law enforcement agencies in other governments; therefore the U.S. government was inhibited in its ability to tap police-level investigative activities to find out what the terrorists were doing or plotting and where.

The United States and other Western governments are attempting to rectify this situation. Third, out of concern for the protection of sources and methods, government intelligence agencies as a rule were not prepared to share sensitive information with private firms.

The effort to overcome such obstacles led the new private sector to create its own intelligence networks. As Jim Hougan explained in his book, *Spooks*,[1] the private networks have become proficient in surveillance, surreptitious entry, and electronic eavesdropping—traditional elements of intelligence operations—and in putting together assessments of the information obtained to help a client make judgments. To the extent that Hougan's assessment is correct, the activities of these firms mirror the functions of the directorates of operations and of intelligence in the Central Intelligence Agency (CIA). Hougan suggests that one firm, Intertel, a company that has recently advertised in the *Wall Street Journal* and elsewhere, would make its services available for operational purposes. Indeed, Intertel advertises itself as "Your Solution to Terrorism." That is a bold claim, but Hougan implies that such companies are perhaps more skilled than governments in high tech intelligence gathering.

Threat Mapping

In order to serve the needs of a wide variety of clients, the new private sector firm must get deeply into the "threat" map of a country. Overall or country-wide information is not likely to be specific enough. Cities must be profiled, and incidents must be tracked not only on the basis of the identity of terrorists but also on the basis of areas or neighborhoods or particular types of targets that may be threatened. That information must be collated with other sources of risk, such as ordinary crimes of assault, mugging, robbery, and murder.

Assembling this data base in complex, and very few potential client companies have the resources to do the intelligence work or the analysis. Many firms operating abroad thus find it most convenient to buy such services, and they seem to consider that the cost of the information and advice they get is incidental, given the possible consequences of failing to be forewarned and forearmed.

Uses of Computers

A problem of the new private sector is information acquisition, storage, and analysis, or, broadly stated, information management. The computer proves to be the central vehicle for all of these functions.

The first part of the information management problem centers on getting a data stream in accessible form. The magnitude of the task is enormous. In 1986, for example, there were over 700 international terrorist incidents and close to ten times that many domestic ones (incidents that occur entirely within a country and are carried out by and against people of that country). International attacks occurred in eighty or more countries, and domestic incidents were even more widely distributed. Among the specific attacks were kidnappings, hijackings, assassinations, bombings, arson, aircraft sabotage, letter bombs, and paramilitary operations.

New private sector firms of any substance must have all of this information, not just the international elements of it. The search for means to achieve that has led to extensive experimentation with data base management systems, expert systems, artificial intelligence (AI), and on-line data services provided by a number of firms.

The Expert Systems

Terrorism, or more accurately terrorist logic, has attracted the interest of computer programmers as well as behaviorists because there seem to be fairly predictable patterns to the types of incidents carried out and the tactics adopted by terrorists. Much of that apparent pattern may be mere imitation, but the fact that terrorist groups appear to have such signatures has attracted a number of universities, think tanks, and corporate laboratories into the fields of computer software design and experimentation with various analytical systems, particularly the development of logic and algorithms for expert system and AI approaches for several purposes including: to understand what the data mean, to predict what might happen next, and to design a suitable response.

At Yale University until 1985, the frontiers of AI were being probed by a computer that knew nothing except terrorism. Its knowledge on this subject was astounding. The computer was called IPP (integrated partial processing), and it thrived on a diet of terrorism data fed directly to it from the United Press International wire. The data came in bursts called script demons, and IPP took in each event and broke it down into its component elements. IPP then extracted from the data a comprehensible pattern of tendencies and outcomes.[2]

Long before IPP began feeding so richly on script demons, the Rand Corporation's RITA (rule-directed interactive transaction agent) was put to work on applying so-called heuristic modeling techniques to the analysis of terrorism information. RITA's models provided a framework for analysis that was limited mainly by the ability of the programmer to write the rules. With such inputs from experts on terrorism and terrorist incidents, however, RITA could break incidents down into subepisodes and flag areas of difference or novelty. Similar work is being done at other sites, including the National Center for the Analysis of Violent Crimes of the FBI Academy at Quantico, Virginia.

Perhaps at the pinnacle of this line of effort lies the multi-expert knowledge-based system (MKBS). The U.S. Navy and other government agencies and private firms interested in crisis management are working to apply expert systems to process analysis, especially to assessments of phenomena involving large numbers and varied types of events. Once a terminal has been loaded with the knowledge of the experts, suitably broken down into processes or algorithms, the MKBS reviews the cases presented to it, lists the elements, and suggests the best solutions in its bank of expert options.

The new private sector is vitally interested in such lines of work because the political violence they study is a forest of an almost infinite number of trees. Since many of the professionals in the new private sector are the experts who work with the systems, however, progress is heavily dependent on what these people already know or can guess. Nevertheless, the computer programs are helpful even in that situation because they offer immense storage capacity, reliable memory, and high processing speeds though they are not yet able to reason. Thus the expert systems and other computer aids can help the security consultant understand and classify a situation and derive from it profiles with some predictive value.

Risk of Abuse

The accumulation of many in-depth profiles on individuals, groups and organizations within a country poses obvious risks. The data could be inaccurate, and the information banks could be subject to abuse. In this respect, the new private sector is as vulnerable as its clients to errors of fact or to the activities of computer hackers, renegade employees, and hostile organizations. Law enforcement organizations have faced this problem for some time and have sought means to audit and update their data bases and to defend their files against tampering. The National Law Enforcement Telecommunications Systems, Inc., a state-government-funded organization that oversees interstate flow of law enforcement communications, goes to great lengths to ensure the integrity of the system. Means have been devised to restrict access to authorized personnel.

Competition with the Public Sector

The creation of information and intelligence networks and uses of psychological and behavioral profiling by the new private sector make it increasingly competitive with public sector activities in these fields. For years, governments set the standards and provided much of the innovative thinking because governments have vast human and material resources to devote to security problems.

An example of the kind of work government does in these fields is the profiling of potential aircraft hijackers by the Federal Aviation Administration (FAA). These profiles, based on criteria that the FAA is careful to keep to itself, have been used to detect numerous potential hijackers before they boarded an aircraft.

The key asset dominated by government has been skilled and experienced people, but the vast majority of government personnel in security-related fields have been brought up in the traditions of small-scale warfare, police work, or the conventional security business. Most of them have not been trained by and large to apply their skills against the terrorism target, but many of them have basic training that is readily adapted to work in counterterrorism fields.

Human Resource Pool

Many of those people, who now are retiring at relatively young ages, make up the experienced resource pool of the new private sector. They come with information and intelligence backgrounds, technical systems skills, crisis management experience, special operations, or police investigative and other law enforcement credentials. Like the pilots who in the past few decades have been trained in the military services and later entered commercial aviation, former government counterterrorism and security experts are setting the personnel standard for the new private sector.

To trained individuals leaving government, the new private sector appears to offer some advantages the established security business does not, mainly chances for quick advancement, high income, and interesting work. Indeed those appealing qualities have led to a glut of job seekers, so that firms can be highly selective.

It became obvious during the Iran–Contra hearings that the new private sector and government have many natural points of contact. They exist both through the pattern of established contracts between new private sector firms and government for specified services and through the personal relations between government officials and new private sector consultants, company officials, and technicians.

Areas of cooperation between government and many sectors of private activity are themselves a growth industry. Among them is a growing cooperation between private business and government on assessing and responding to threat conditions abroad. The vehicle, developed by the Department of State in 1985, is the Overseas Security Advisory Council (OSAC). The aims of this new collaboration are to provide reliable institutional channels for communication between business and government on security matters, to share information of significance on security conditions or specific threat situations abroad, and to share ideas on how to deal with crises.

OSAC is made up of some twenty major company representatives and officials from the five federal agencies concerned with terrorism and security abroad. Business sector representation on the council changes from time to time and all members must have at least a secret clearance to participate. Interestingly, the membership of OSAC tends to come from firms that usually are clients of the new private sector rather than members of it.

Lieutenant Colonel Oliver North provides an excellent example of the way firms or families first encounter the new private sector. The search for the sector can begin quickly, especially when provoked by a near panic situation. In testimony given on July 8, 1987, during the congressional Iran–Contra hearings, North indicated that he began his search upon learning that he and his family were being targeted by Abu Nidal's Revolutionary Council, a group that has killed and wounded more than 400 people worldwide. North searched via telephone for competent assistance but was unsuccessful. He was told, for example, that he would have to wait because there was a heavy demand for residential security systems. Frustrated and concerned about his family's safety, North turned to General Richard Secord for help. Secord brought in the firm of Glenn Robinette, which set up the North residence with an enormous pole on the front lawn bristling with video cameras. A heavy gate was installed at the entrance, and a direct wire was established to the Fairfax County police headquarters. Those were probably sensible moves of some deterrent value, as well as sources of psychological comfort.

North's case raises a number of questions: how does one evaluate or verify the reputation or credentials of the security consultant in question, however, let alone determine that the recommended course of action is the best answer to the problem at hand? Should North have even remained in his home given the circumstances? Was the hardware necessary, or did it draw attention to the home? If the family hardened the home, did they also alter their habits, routines, and schedules, especially with respect to daily commuting?

North sought help in the new private sector because he apparently saw no way to get it at the time from official sources. Those sources later responded, and U.S. Navy security forces began to provide protection to North and his family, but before that occurred, he was reduced to going into the market for help or to go without, a choice he apparently was not prepared to accept.

The new private sector takes as one of its givens the kind of risk exposure experienced by North and his family. It is a reflection of the growing vulnerability of Western society. The second given illustrated by North's experience is that the normal protections provided by law enforcement agencies are frequently not available or are not adequate to special threat situations. The older security businesses saw this need for security services tailored to individual situations long ago and made a business of fulfilling it. The new private sector is responding to the fact that the threat of terrorism has exposed a new gap in conventional protective services, whether provided by law enforcement agencies or by the private sector. Some time ago, people largely accepted the idea that private security arrangements may be necessary to supplement or even to take over specific protective tasks from law enforcement agencies. It has taken a while for public perception to see terrorism among the commonplace types of threats.

The Trade in Information

The new private sector has been led, fed, entertained, and advertised by a voluminous literature on every aspect of their activity. Terrorism and counterterrorism have been the subjects of volumes of reports, studies, and books over the last two decades. Scholarly journals have entered the field. Other periodicals have found a terrorism theme that fits their usual content and readership. *Harper's*, the *New Yorker*, the weekly news magazines, airline magazines, and numerous institutional publications occasionally deal with terrorism. A lot of the coverage is in the high-adventure *Soldier of Fortune* genre, the stock in trade of old-time pulp magazines.

Print and electronic media have pursued intensive coverage of the major terrorist incidents. The depth and editorial perspective of a great deal of coverage has excited considerable debate over whether the media actually end up helping the terrorists.

Pulling the majority of these sources together is a periodical of the Defense Department, *Terrorism*, a special edition of the series of media compilations called *Current News*. That service spreads its net widely, and it can be counted upon to capture practically everything of interest that happens in the field.

Information services, mostly computerized, heavily support the new private sector. Firms such as Mead Data Central (NEXIS), News Net, and Compuserv's Executive News Service are available to customers at home on a personal computer. Various services will build and maintain specific libraries for the user on subjects such as terrorism.

Newsletters are available in both electronic and printed form. News Net features wire service bulletins as well as Frost & Sullivan's Political Risk Letter and the International Travel Warning Service. Specific information provided in such newsletters includes travel advisory notices published by the U.S. Department of State on countries with significant threat conditions. Risk International, Inc., of Arlington, Virginia, provides newsletters sent out weekly, monthly, and quarterly. The firm offers access to a data base with 25,000 incidents on file and can give brief updates to clients. Interests Inc., of Bethesda, Maryland, publishes *Counterterrorism: Intelligence Report on Terrorism Defense* on a weekly basis.

Two trade magazines, *Security Management*, put out by the American Society of Industrial Security (ASIS), and *Security World*, are published monthly, essentially by and for the new private sector.

Conferences to share the immense pool of information that is generated and to find out what the experts think about it are a regular feature of the new private sector's life cycle. For the past five years, ASIS has sponsored an annual two-day "Government/Industry Conference on Terrorism." One security consultant estimated that there are now at least one hundred such conferences held each year nationwide, in addition to law enforcement briefings.

Videotapes are a natural and successful entry into the terrorism and security information field. Brief, portable, usually dealing with a single topic, and comparatively inexpensive, they are an increasingly useful training tool. Some are fairly ambitious. For example, *Terrorism: A Corporate Concern*, produced by Varied Directions, Inc., of Camden, Maine, is a two-tape set that features a short travel security briefing for executives along with a longer tape addressing possible ways a company can approach security and security planning.

It is worth asking whether the terrorists themselves, and their various state sponsors, do not find this immense flow of information as useful to them as it may be to their enemies. It may not be easy to picture a group of terrorists poring over books and journals to find out what their targets and their enemies might be doing, but several experts suggest that one disregards the thought at his or her own peril.

Training and Related Activities

On looking at its training and human resource development activities, one discovers quickly that the new private sector features a diverse set of products, activities, and talents. At one extreme, members of the sector who produce various kinds of hardware and software view the security threat situation as a market. They do not get involved except through equipment and related services sales. In the middle, consultants, vendors of support services, instructors, commentators, and writers view the threat situation as the primary source of their activity. They respond to the threat through activities that include contingency planning, crisis management, facility and personnel protection, and the whole roster of conventional security services. They are seldom aggressive or combative in the measures they undertake. At the other extreme, a number of individuals and organizations specialize in providing police-like or special forces-like skills. They tend to present themselves as action or response teams, able to deal with the problem head on. Where one fits in this spectrum determines the kind of training that is likely to be provided.

Training that is specifically associated with the new private sector does not emerge as such until one approaches the third category. Hardware- and software-related training generally takes place in academic, industrial, and other institutional channels. Facilities and personal protective training have a base in established law enforcement and private security programs, but terrorism has added new dimensions that now are offered by firms in the new private sector. Examples are defensive driving, surveillance detection and avoidance, and other personal protective measures the individual can take to reduce exposure to attack.

Several facilities provide parts of the activist-defensive category of training: the Protection Institute, founded in Berryville, Virginia in the 1970s; the Pan Am Institute of Public Service in Gainesville, Georgia; Executive Security International in Aspen, Colorado; and J. Mattman Security in Fullerton, California. Training by these firms ranges from conventional executive or personal protective measures to what to do in the event of an attack.

The services offered by firms in the training sector usually combine classroom training with field experience. The founder of the Executive Protection Institute, Richard W. Kobetz, for example, travels continuously, offering seminars on such subjects as contemporary terrorism, aircraft security, hostage negotiations, and physical security. One of his goals is to achieve nationwide acceptance of a set of standards and levels of certification for the private security profession as a whole. Kobetz lectures throughout the country and several times a year conducts training sessions at his North Mountain Pines Training Center in Virginia. His courses attract candidates from industry and state, local, and federal governments, notably personnel assigned to protect key personnel overseas. For his week-long intensive course, "Providing Protective Services," Kobetz charges a fee of roughly $2,000, and only a few dozen attendees graduate each year.

In the basic security training field, the influence of the FBI, the U.S. Secret Service, the Customs Service, and the Bureau of Alcohol, Tobacco and Firearms (BATF) is substantial. This mainly is exerted by former agents who, with former military personnel, comprise the mainstays of security instruction in the new private sector. The training they offer tends to hew more closely to established police investigative and response methods than to paramilitary ones. Those training methods and their objectives are perhaps best treated under the heading of operations.

Operations

In the new private sector, *operations* has several distinct meanings. First, operations is the daily business of running physical facility security programs for client organizations. Second, it is the conduct of personnel protective activities. Third, it is private-eye kinds of activity related to surveilling or otherwise gathering information about situations, people, and facilities of interest to a client. Fourth, it is proactive, suggesting activities to preempt, break up, or destroy a would-be terrorist group or to retaliate for a past attack. Finally, it is special operations, military or paramilitary activities, designed to achieve a client's goal (for example, a change in policy or leadership).

Controversy quite rightly centers on the last two concepts because proactive measures and special operations place the firm or group undertaking the activity in the position of carrying out functions normally reserved to governments. Even governments reserve such activities for the extreme cases.

The Perot Doctrine

H. Ross Perot helped to create the activist, paramilitary image of the new private sector with his bold approach to getting his employees out of Iran. He undertook a private rescue mission when it appeared to him that no meaningful response was likely from the U.S. government. As he told the media, Perot felt that corporations had a moral obligation to take action when their employees were harmed or threatened with harm. If Perot's mission had failed, or if several personnel had been killed in the process, he would have been caught in an awkward position. In succeeding, however, Perot's team amplified the difference between the new private sector's uninhibited activist stance and the government's usually cautious, constrained, and sometimes apparently disinterested response to terrorist challenge.

Perot's achievement was good for American morale, but it was not unique; the Canadian ambassador to Tehran, who worked a covert operation to get five Americans out of Iran, demonstrated that official boldness also works when the conditions are right. However, with his exploit, Perot captured the imagination of many people, and his willingness to use his own money in bargaining with terrorists who had taken Americans hostage placed him in a position of supplementing official efforts to obtain the release of hostages. Critics may argue that Perot's unwillingness to accept the status quo was not unique, nor was his rescue effort a milestone, but with or without intending to, he defined a role and a style for the new private sector.

Perot's activism probably also reinforced the natural tendency of corporate management to rely on its own devices rather than turn to government. Given the future prospect, as seen by a number of terrorism experts, that terrorists will concentrate on private citizens (businessmen, other professionals, and tourists) as their primary victims, Perot's doctrine represents an important inducement to business executives who seek out the new private sector.

Mike Weinstein, chairman of the Committee on Terrorist Activities of the American Society for Industrial Security (ASIS), drives this point home by noting that U.S. corporations have always been attractive targets. They are usually softer than any government facility, and they have a reputation for being willing to negotiate when their employees are kidnapped. Weinstein is also making a point underscored by U.S. government officials concerned with terrorism: kidnappers continue to take hostages because the business is profitable. Thus, businessmen should be on notice that the efforts of government to harden official targets, as well as business habits of paying ransom, make it probable that they will become even more enticing targets.

G. Gordon Liddy

The activities of (or, perhaps more precisely, the image presented by) G. Gordon Liddy fuel the activist and romantic notion of new private sector operations. Along with his movable security academy, a three-week $2,700 course in all facets of security work, and his own Gemstone Security firm, Liddy created the so-called Hurricane Force, a strike team for hire. In June 1987 for NBC and other network television cameras, he orchestrated dazzling demonstrations during which his Hurricane Force engaged in mock hostage rescues. In these demonstrations, Liddy did something governments very rarely do: publicize the highly specialized skills, modes of operation, and organization of a strike force. Such public displays have created an environment in which, according to Kobetz, "The gap between the realities and the myths in this business are immense."[3] Liddy has fed the public's imagination, making people believe that such teams are numerous and that they are used with some frequency. For example, Liddy reportedly told NBC News that he had dispatched the Hurricane Force three times by mid-1987.

The Liddy type of operation is not widely supported in the industry. One former associate of his called this approach a grossly distorted concept saying that Liddy's methods had evolved from a focus on training, not on operations. The associate was suggesting that the Hurricane Force was put together as a training tool, not as an actual strike force. It was not, this associate suggested, for the sort of operations that the public image of Liddy suggests he is actively promoting.

But a number people embrace Liddy and others of the activist school because some part of them want to see action. For others, the Liddy approach is theatrical and entertaining. High-speed evasive driving, rescues, shootouts, footage of British commandos storming the Iranian embassy in London as they did in May 1980, and similar episodes interest the public. This perspective put Liddy's activities in the same class as television activist heroes.

In this area, the boundaries between fact and fiction are fragile. Contributing to that fragility is the fact that for media, the new private sector training facilities and the operational training facilities of governments, the weapons, clothing, tactics, and scenarios for responses and terrorist incidents all tend to be much alike. There is a pervasive paramilitary quality about all of them. Thus one cannot distinguish by appearances among a terrorist attack, a Hurricane Force rescue drill, a British rescue at the Iranian embassy, a practice simulation at a special forces shooting house in North Carolina, or a strike operation that terminated the villain in the movie *The Fourth Protocol*.

Irangate and the New Private Sector

That background set a natural trap for the U.S. Congress when it began the Iran–Contra hearings. Through its normal television viewing, the public was already prepared to accept the idea that governments run covert operations and that governments may use people and organizations in the private sector to deal with crooks, dissidents, foreign agents, or cutouts. Telling the public, through the medium of the hearings, therefore, that Oliver North was carrying out an operation could be expected to arouse little public excitement and no animosity.

How and to what degree did the new private sector get involved in Oliver North's NSC-run operations? The answer is that private individuals and firms were used extensively, but new private sector involvement was very limited. The people who figured most prominently in the scandal are only marginally in the new private sector. First, the key American figures in the scandal, former general Richard Secord for the Iran side and former general John Singlaub for the Contra side, tended to play traditional intermediary roles in weapons acquisitions and transfers for which they were fitted by their military backgrounds. Southern Air Transport and other private firms engaged or created by North to handle Contra logistics support fit an older pattern, echoing Air America ventures initially run decades ago by the CIA in the Congo and in Vietnam. Thus, while much was made during the Iran–Contra hearings of the so-called privatization of covert operations, the promoters of that theory revealed a poor grasp of facts and little sense of history.

On balance, the profiles of the individuals and firms involved in the Iran–Contra operation fall outside the norms of new private sector security activities, although they overlap with the legendary images of activism promoted by Ross Perot and G. Gordon Liddy. As a general matter, however, such operations are peripheral to the main activities of the industry and remote from the concerns of most firms in this sector.

Where Does the New Private Sector Fit?

Where does the new private sector fit? What kind of regulatory regime is needed, if any, to deal with the evolving pattern of quasi-law enforcement activities being conducted by some firms in the new private sector? When private sector firms enter public institutional fields normally reserved to governments, should the public be comfortable with the growth of numerous, largely autonomous police-like organizations, or should society demand licensing, guidelines, ground rules, minimum training, and regulatory oversight?

The answers to those questions depend on what the new private sector firm does. A firm engaged in producing, installing, and monitoring high tech physical and electronic security systems does not seem to warrant special supervision beyond that normally exercised within industry respecting the characteristics and performance standards of equipment. Firms engaged in providing security services within banks, industrial compounds, and other facilities are not engaged in activities that duplicate or interfere with the work of law enforcement agencies. They also perform security services that as a rule public law enforcement officers do not undertake, except possibly as a retirement job or as a second source of income. By and large, the public interest in such security activities would seem adequately served so long as the contract between the firm and the security organization is consistent with the public interest, and local licensing requirements are observed.

The training of individuals in these types of new private sector activities appears to pose no areas of public concern. Providing site security or producing, selling, installing, and supporting high tech security systems are not controversial. The issues become more complex, however, as a firm moves into the areas of paramilitary or so-called survival training and operations now conducted by a few firms. A firm effectively has gone outside the normal landscape of the new private sector when it provides a potential paramilitary strike force to bail out a client in some remote place.

Consider, for example, a training camp run by a group such as the Aryan Nations to train a band of rebels against the laws and leadership of the United States or the kinds of training provided by Frank Camper's RECONDO Mercenary School in Dolomite, Alabama, before that school was closed down? In 1985, a number of Sikh separatists trained in Camper's school in preparation to attempt the assassination of India's prime minister. Following discovery of that plot, Attorney General Edwin Meese assured Prime Minister Rajiv Gandhi that such training would be brought under control. Meese clearly concluded that training such as that offered to the Sikhs is contrary to the public interest.

Given such possibilities as this case suggests, the questions are how, what kind, and how much control the public should expect government to exercise over training facilities of this type. Whether we decide to go so far as to declare such training activities contrary to the public interest, the indication of the case is that this category of training may pose a threat to constituted governments. The need for government oversight seems clear.

Under the Arms Export Control Act, when foreign citizens are involved in training or when U.S. instructors go abroad, the U.S. Customs Service is responsible for monitoring such activities. Enforcement of this act, which is the basis for International Traffic in Arms Regulations (ITAR), was upgraded in early 1985 with a view, among other things, of seeing whether training and support of terrorist activities abroad could be prohibited. That represented an immediate effort of the Reagan administration to acquire authority proposed in the Prohibition against Training or Support of Terrorist Organizations Act of 1984, which died in committee at the end of that legislative session.

The impact of federal law on the offer of so-called counterterrorism training remains quite limited. More than a dozen camps similar to Camper's were known to be operating at the end of 1985. They tended to exist alongside the new private sector, however, rather than as part of it, and their activities largely are immaterial to the new private sector except for the ongoing contribution of such camps to sustaining the Hurricane Force type of mythology.

Federal authorities control certain firearms permits, but individual states retain control of the private security industry through issuing licenses and registering personnel. There are no uniform standards, however, and the states do not have authority to intervene in interstate commerce. California and perhaps a half-dozen other states impose fairly stringent regulations, but the majority exercise limited oversight.

Awareness of the regulatory issues raised by the growth of the private security industry is increasing. In 1986, Maine experienced a strike that boiled over into a violent clash between strikers and an out-of-state private security force. A similar confrontation arose in Ashland, Kentucky when a security firm sent trained strikebreakers to intervene in a coal strike on behalf of management. Such experience convinced some officials in Maine and Kentucky that stricter regulation of the security sector was needed, though little seems to have been done since the incidents to stiffen regulation.

Some leading members of the new private sector itself are looking at the problems and seeking self-regulatory actions. ASIS is engaged in a continual process of self-examination, and the results appear every month in *Security Management* magazine. How much movement ASIS-type activities may have generated toward adoption of industry standards is difficult to tell. It appears doubtful that any significant movement has occurred toward regulating the operational end of the business.

Conclusions

The new private sector has been moving quickly in many directions of immense interest to the public and to government. The image of the lone plant guard, who walked constantly by preset checkpoints and punched a clock to prove it, is not entirely gone, but in its place are increasingly elaborate systems of electronic identification checkers, door controls, monitors, sensors, automated logging devices, automatic telephone call systems, and computerized programs that help the user make decisions in a crisis. In the same vein, the hefty, tough-looking, and barely literate bodyguards are being replaced by smooth, well-educated, physically and mentally fit experts who use a panoply of communication, transportation, defensive, and sensory support devices to help them protect their client. Both the physical and personal protective service organizations rely increasingly on a flow of current information and analysis about potential threats and political sources of risk that would have delighted the Byzantine soul of any European monarch less than a century ago.

Little of that, however, is of pressing public policy concern. At the most, the capabilities suggest that governments no longer have a virtual monopoly on access to current information on sensitive and important events or situations. In public policy terms, the main purpose of this development is that official reaction times have been shrinking, a trend that media uses of remote sensing satellites and other information systems already had made completely apparent.

Public policy concern about activities of the new private sector must center on certain categories of training and on operations. The Reagan administration sought in 1984 to deal with training in terrorism-related fields by obtaining congressional passage of the Prohibition against Training or Support for Terrorism Act of 1984. The objective of that legislation was to keep Americans from providing assistance to terrorist groups or to their sponsoring states. That legislation failed due mainly to the concern of civil libertarians about the right of free political association. Perhaps the draft legislation was flawed in that respect, but the lack of such legislation leaves open the issue of what should be done about the Campertype of training operation in which would-be assassins might get the skills they lack or merely brush up on their marksmanship. Is there a public need for this kind of training activity that indicates it should be allowed to continue? If it continues, should it be closely watched and regulated? If so, how and by whom? Finally, where do private military and paramilitary operations fit in the long-term American scheme of things? If the United States really needs the Hurricane Force, should it not be in the public sector, as are other U.S. special forces, suitably funded, with adequate oversight, and with necessary protection from exposure?

The answers to these questions do not lie in assessing what the new private sector is capable of doing. Clearly it can mount complex and elaborate security operations, including a paramilitary strike, if that is what the client wants. Problems lie almost entirely with policy control, accountability, and the ability to explain or justify actions to other governments or peoples. On the issue of policy control, for example, government policies and corporate business policies on payment of ransom in hostage cases are normally 180 degrees apart. In this area, as the new private sector represents a growing number of business clients, it can only have the effect of undermining stated official policy on the issue. On the issue of paramilitary or strike force operations, to what degree can the U.S. government handle the presence within society of multiple, independently targetable, private strike forces whose actions can wreak havoc with a given country relationship? That tolerance is limited because the ability to explain either the activities or the presence of such groups abroad is quite limited.

The operational capabilities of the new private sector have not grown in a vacuum. They have grown out of a combination of felt needs in the private sector for facility, personnel, asset, and business opportunity protection. They have grown also out of particular views of individuals about the most desirable responses to acts of political violence abroad. Consequently the emergence of paramilitary and strike force operational capabilities in the new private sector is an indication of needs that are not being met through official action. The evolution of operational capabilities in the new private sector thus leaves government with two problems: how to control this potential monster if it is decided to let it live, and how to persuade its promoters and developers that solutions to the problems they seek to solve exist in more appropriate form. The choice does not get easier with passage of time.

Notes

1. James Hougan, *Spooks* (New York: William Morrow, 1978).

2. Jeffrey Rothfeder, *Minds Over Matter: A New Look at Artificial Intelligence* (New York: Simon and Schuster, 1985), pp. 114–49.

3. Comment made to author Peter Brown during an interview with Richard W. Kobetz in July 1987.

12

New Directions in Using the Law to Combat Terrorism

Terrell E. Arnold

F ollowing attacks on the U.S. embassy and the U.S. Marine barracks in Lebanon in 1983, the Reagan administration began to reexamine the national policy approach to combating international terrorism. The vehicle for this review was a draft national security decision directive, NSDD 138, which was finally issued in June 1984. NSDD 138 had been preceded by earlier directives of the Reagan administration, but their principal aim was to organize the U.S. government to deal with terrorist incidents, as well as to clarify and formalize the lead roles of government agencies in managing such incidents. The lead roles followed closely the legally assigned responsibilities of the agencies concerned:

Department of State: Terrorist incidents outside U.S. jurisdiction.

Federal Bureau of Investigation: Any incident within U.S. jurisdiction.

Federal Aviation Administration: Incidents involving aircraft in flight anywhere within U.S.-controlled air space.

Department of Energy: Incidents involving nuclear materials.

NSDD 138 was designed to force an interagency review of U.S. policies and programs to combat international terrorism; its focus was on available means and the resources to implement them.

Debate over Means

The objective of at least certain senior officials in two agencies involved in the drafting—Defense and the CIA—centered on wresting lead agency responsibility away from the State Department. The debate was not over lead responsibility per se. Rather it centered on determining the most appropriate and most likely to be successful means to use in combating terrorism. The choices discussed ranged from conventional diplomatic approaches to unilateral and covert uses of force. A debate of that nature and intensity practically ensured that NSDD 138, issued as a top secret document, would be made public practically before the ink was dry.

The brief public discussion of published contents of NSDD 138 focused on the heart of the internal debate. NSDD 138 had been leaked by hawks for whom the leading issue was whether the Reagan administration would move toward adoption of proactive measures against terrorists. "Proactive" in the minds of the most suspicious critics of the administration, as well as in the minds of the most hawkish anti-terrorists within the administration, meant assassination.

The debate about the language of NSDD 138 was part of a continuing discussion of how to deal with terrorists who could not be brought within the jurisdiction of legal authorities. This was an important issue. How to ensure that terrorists operating against the United States in a foreign country will be deterred, detained, tried, and punished raises the central challenge posed by international terrorism, and achieving those results legally is the issue for countries that adhere to the rule of law.

The debate therefore did not divide over who favored legal means and who favored extralegal ones. The split was between people who did not see any legal means to ensure that the terrorists would be brought to book and those who insisted that legal means either had to be found in existing laws or must be created to achieve that result. In the end, the considered view of the agencies most concerned was that the terrorist who managed to escape or to avoid U.S. legal jurisdiction was one the United States could not do much about under existing laws.

NSDD 138 as issued specified that the U.S. government would combat terrorism by "all legal means." There was no hidden agenda in that language, but the need to extend the reach of U.S. law enforcement to meet the challenge of terrorism was clearly identified.

Simultaneously with the debate over NSDD 138, the administration put together a legislative package of four bills to extend the legal basis for combating terrorism.[1] Three of these bills, implementing the U.N. Convention against aircraft sabotage, the U.N. Convention against hostage taking, and authorizing payments of rewards by the secretary of state in terrorism cases, were noncontroversial, and they were passed by the Congress with minor changes as parts of the 1984 Act to Combat International Terrorism. Enabling legislation to carry out the treaty obligations involved in ratifying the two U.N. conventions was provided in the Comprehensive Crime Control Act of 1984. The fourth bill sent to Capitol Hill by the administration, the Prohibition against Training or Support for Terrorism Act of 1984, did not make it out of committee, although elements of it appeared by interpretation to be included in the Crime Control Act[2] and in International Traffic in Arms Regulations.

Although the first three bills excited little public attention, they were responsible for the initiation of basic changes in the way federal authorities approach the uses of law to combat international terrorism. In fact, their enactment proved to be a watershed that went largely unnoticed except in fairly narrow legal circles. Specifically they began to improve the chances of apprehending terrorists for prosecution.

Vice-President's Task Force

Following a series of terrorist attacks in late 1984 and 1985, including the murder of two U.S. citizens on board a hijacked Kuwait airliner and the hijacking of TWA flight 847, President Reagan asked Vice-President George Bush to take another look at U.S. policy and organization to deal with terrorism. The task force working group Bush created held interviews with dozens of private experts and conducted intensive review of policies and programs with the leadership of U.S. agencies concerned with terrorism. At the end of this process, the task force produced a report confirming that the "interagency system and the Lead Agency concept for dealing with incidents" was "soundly conceived."[3]

The published report of the task force listed more than twenty recommendations, and reportedly a much longer list of suggested actions appeared in the classified report. Among the leading recommendations were building up the National Security Council (NSC) staff to discharge the interagency coordinating role; designating an official spokesperson so that the government would speak with one voice; improving international cooperation, especially on matters of extradition; improving collection, assessment, and sharing of terrorism-related intelligence; seeking legislation making murder of a U.S. citizen abroad a crime; and providing for a death penalty in terrorism cases.[4]

Members of the vice-president's task force working group had struggled once again with the issue of proactive measures. Mostly young, middle-grade military officers, the task force working group members were frustrated by the apparent inability of the United States to fight back against the terrorists. In making recommendations such as creation of a "national program document" they were following a will-o-wisp that tugs at the imagination of many activists in Washington: they hoped to find an organizational structure and a statement of policy designed to make the management of complex challenges like terrorism easy, straightforward, and reliable. However, they could not get the major agencies concerned (State, Defense, CIA, Justice and the FBI, FAA, and Treasury) to agree on any significant organizational changes, because those agencies were not convinced that the problems they faced during terrorist incidents were organizational in origin. The working group was unable to articulate the overarching policy that would bring together the interests, concerns, and responsibilities of the more than thirty federal agencies dealing with some aspect of terrorism. The solution they did achieve—to expand the one-man show then being run in the NSC staff by Lieutenant Colonel Oliver North and give him a staff to exercise interagency coordination responsibility over counterterrorism policies and programs—was a precursor of the Iran scandal.

The task force generally, however, was on a sound tack. Virtually half of its public recommendations had to do with changes or amendments to laws and treaties or applications of them. The issue of proactive measures once again had waxed and waned, but little change had been wrought on that front. Changes indeed were coming, but they had more to do with uses of law than with uses of force.

Move toward Legal Procedures

Spurred by the issue of NSDD 138 and the policy studies it triggered and reinforced by the recommendations in the vice-president's task force report, the focus
of U.S. government efforts to deal with international terrorism moved increasingly
toward applying the basic practices of criminal prosecution: the careful marshaling of evidence, witnesses, and arguments on the issues for presentation in court.

Equipping law enforcement agencies to pursue that course effectively was a
collaborative effort of the executive branch with the leadership of House and Senate
committees on Foreign Affairs, Foreign Relations, and the Judiciary. One of the
first efforts was to extend the authority of U.S. law enforcement officers and prosecutors abroad through changes in jurisdiction over specific terrorist crimes.
Another was to position Justice and the FBI more effectively to gather, preserve,
and use evidence against accused terrorists in international terrorism cases. A third
was to expand international cooperation on applications of law through bilateral
and multilateral understandings and agreements, particularly respecting such matters as extradition.

Basic to this approach is a belief of Justice, the FBI, and many state and local
law enforcement agencies that terrorism can and should be dealt with through reliance
on criminal laws and procedures. At the federal level, the criminal statutes are contained in the U.S. Code, but these laws do not deal with terrorism as such. Rather,
they deal with specific crimes, many of them the kinds of acts terrorists commit.

Nonetheless, by mid-1987 the body of U.S. legal documents dealing explicitly
with terrorism issues had become impressive. In early 1987, at the request of the
chairman of the House Foreign Affairs Committee, Dante B. Fascell (D–Florida),
the House Foreign Affairs Committee staff and the Congressional Research Service produced a compilation of laws, treaties, resolutions, executive orders, and
other documents reflecting U.S. treatment of terrorism in law. The result, which
covers actions over a period of more than twenty-five years, is nearly a thousand-
page collection of several hundred documents showing a continuing effort to find
applications of law and to fill gaps in law where those appear significant. Key examples of the 1980s, including the laws already mentioned, are:

1984 Act to Combat International Terrorism: Permitting the secretary of state
to pay rewards in terrorism cases, approving ratification of the U.N. Convention against Aircraft Sabotage, and approving ratification of the *International
Convention against the Taking of Hostages*.

Comprehensive Crime Control Act of 1984: Enabling legislation to support
U.S. ratification of the U.N. Convention against Aircraft Sabotage, enabling
legislation to support U.S. ratification of the U.N. Convention against the Taking of Hostages, and specifying extraterritorial jurisdiction in case an American
is taken hostage and in cases of sabotage to aircraft.[5]

U.S.-U.K. Supplementary Extradition Treaty of June 25, 1985: Removing violent crimes from the coverage of the Political Offense Exception in the U.S.-U.K. extradition treaty.[6]

Omnibus Diplomatic Security and Terrorism Act of 1986: Providing broadly defined extraterritorial jurisdiction over terrorist acts against U.S. nationals abroad.[7]

Importance of Jurisdiction

Traditionally U.S. lawmakers have proceeded from an assumption that U.S. laws would apply within U.S. territory and that the accused normally would be available or could be brought legally within U.S. jurisdiction for trial. But terrorist attacks and other criminal activities abroad, including drug traffic, increasingly have exposed the limitations of that philosophy. In a rising number of cases, crimes of assassination, kidnapping, aircraft hijacking, and bombings in which Americans were casualties or victims have occurred entirely outside U.S. jurisdiction, and the culprits generally remained outside the reach of U.S. law enforcement officers. Amendments to the U.S. Code such as those just outlined were designed to cover such cases by extending U.S. law enforcement jurisdiction beyond the boundaries of U.S. territory.

The watershed noted earlier can be summed up as congressional legislation to assert the extraterritorial jurisdiction of U.S. law enforcement and prosecutory authorities over terrorist crimes against Americans anywhere in the world. Thus, to the degree that changes of domestic law can project the legal authority of one government into the territory of another, U.S. laws have been upgraded significantly toward enabling U.S. authorities to combat international terrorism through uses of law.

Internationally Cooperative Steps

Paralleling those domestic activities in the legal arena are internationally cooperative efforts to gather information and share it, which would permit apprehension and prosecution of suspected terrorists, and the development of definitions and procedures that would inhibit abuses of international treaty obligations relating to the status of diplomats and diplomatic missions. These changes or clarifications of what constitutes appropriate diplomatic conduct are likely to have impact over time on the ability of governments to extradite people who ordinarily would be protected by diplomatic immunity. These activities, pursued mainly in the context of the economic summit meetings of the seven major Western economic powers, also have enhanced the legal environment for combating terrorism.

The issues addressed in these meetings and in related summit declarations are vital to the legal battle against terrorism. The Declaration of the May 1986 Tokyo summit, for example, provided for:

Limits on the size of diplomatic missions for countries suspected of using terrorism and closure of such missions in certain instances.

Denial of entry to persons excluded or expelled by another country on grounds of suspicion or conviction for involvement in terrorism.

Improvements in extradition procedures.

Stricter immigration and naturalization controls over nationals of terrorism-sponsoring states.

Closer bilateral and multilateral cooperation among law enforcement and security organizations and other relevant authorities.

The declaration of the June 1987 Venice summit focused more sharply on the uses of law to combat terrorism. That declaration states in part:

Each of us pledges increased cooperation in the relevant fora and within the framework of domestic and international law on the investigation, apprehension and prosecution of terrorists. *In particular we reaffirm the principle established by relevant international conventions of trying or extraditing,* according to national laws and those international conventions, those who perpetrated acts of terrorism. (Italics added)

New Approaches by Justice and the FBI

The Venice summit language highlights the growing focus of U.S. and other Western efforts on gaining jurisdiction of a suspected terrorist and then applying evidence toward prosecution and conviction. The changes of law made by Congress between 1984 and 1986 improved Justice and FBI capacity to achieve those results, and those changes initiated basic revisions in the U.S. presence abroad where the law is concerned.

For many years the United States has maintained legal attachés in a number of important capitals. Legal attachés as a rule were senior middle-grade officials of the FBI on assignment abroad to carry out legal representation and liaison activities respecting criminal and civil cases of interest to the United States: pursuing requests for the extradition of persons accused of crimes, taking depositions from witnesses, and processing legal documents. Legal attachés usually were stationed in major foreign cities. Their role in general had more to do with law enforcement functions than with the functions of the prosecutor.

The Kuwait Airline hijacking of December 4, 1984, in which two U.S. government employees were killed, revealed a shift in the emphasis of U.S. legal activities abroad more toward support for prosecution.[8] When Iranian authorities took over the airliner and ended the hijacking in Tehran, they took custody of the hijackers and announced intent to put them on trial, but that never happened. Meanwhile, applying the principle of the Comprehensive Crime Control Act of 1984,[9] which became law shortly after the incident occurred, the Justice Department sought ways to gain jurisdiction over the hijackers in order to bring them to trial in the United States. That effort was not successful. The hijackers of that flight are still at liberty. Even so, the effort spurred considerable thought on how to obtain and preserve evidence in terrorism cases that occur abroad, effectively outside immediate U.S. law enforcement jurisdictions.

Gathering the Evidence

The procedural changes that occurred fairly quickly after passage of the Comprehensive Crime Control Act were substantial, particularly respecting hostage debriefings. In February 1985, when Jeremy Levin made his escape from his radical Shiite captors, Hesbollah, a team of experts went to Wiesbaden, Germany, to debrief him before his appreciation of the conditions of his captivity and information he might have about the kidnappers or other hostages had grown too cold. The debriefing team was essentially an intelligence team, including a State Department Office of Security (now the Bureau of Diplomatic Security) specialist on the hostage cases and CIA and Defense Intelligence Agency officers. By the time other Hesbollah captives were released in 1986, however, new procedures had been adopted under which Justice and FBI officials led the teams that went abroad for the first debriefings of returning hostages. In the meantime, Justice had begun to send out teams to gather evidence in such cases as the hijacking of TWA flight 847, which would assist U.S. authorities in identifying suspects in that case and would ensure that relevant evidence was gathered and preserved for later use in court.

The TWA flight 847 case is an excellent one for examination of the issues involved in the effort to apply legal prosecutory approaches to combating international terrorism. Although the crime was committed in the air over the Mediterranean and on the ground in Algeria and Lebanon, Justice authorities decided they would follow normal procedures to put together a case against the hijackers. To that end, Justice sent a team to Wiesbaden to question the returning hostages about the elements of the crime and the identities of the hijackers. Justice also sent investigators to Beirut and, with the cooperation of TWA, was able to do forensic work on the aircraft itself before it returned to the United States. There were limits to what might have been discovered in that instance, because, as flight 847 Captain John Testrake reported, the hijackers "completely trashed the plane's cabin."[10] Nonetheless, based on information gathered through these investigations, Justice was able to obtain indictments and issue warrants for the arrest of the four original hijackers. The problem was that all four of the hijackers were outside the United

States, at the time apparently at large in Lebanon. In the circumstances, even with extraterritorial jurisdiction, the culprits themselves were not readily to be had.

Hamadei Case

Prospects brightened in January 1987 with apprehension in Frankfurt, Germany, of Mohammed Ali Hamadei. Based on the information provided by witnesses, Hamadei had been identified as one of the four original hijackers of flight 847, a warrant for his arrest was in hand, and U.S. authorities had been on the lookout for him through police and intelligence channels. Information obtained from witnesses also placed Hamadei behind a curtain in the forward area of the aircraft at the time one or more hijackers had beaten and killed U.S. Navy diver Robert Dean Stethem.

On the basis of such information, U.S. authorities formally requested extradition of Hamadei to stand trial in the United States for murder. German authorities were made aware of the case developed by Justice and the FBI against Hamadei, and witnesses who were victims of the attack on TWA flight 847 were sent to Germany with an official U.S. delegation to see if they could identify Hamadei.[11] In fact, the existence of a constructive case against Hamadei was never disputed by German authorities. Before they had had much time to ponder the request, however, members of Islamic Jihad—possibly Hesbollah, although that is not clear—went on the streets of Beirut and added two German businessmen to the list of hostages, which already numbered close to twenty. This was an obvious effort to blackmail German authorities into refusing to extradite Hamadei, and it succeeded. Although German official reaction to that pressure was not immediate, in June 1987 German authorities announced that they would not extradite Hamadei but would try him in Germany.

The crime at issue—the murder of Robert Dean Stethem—was a crime against a U.S. citizen, and it had occurred during the commission of multiple crimes (hijacking a U.S. aircraft and keeping thirty-nine Americans hostage for seventeen days). Nevertheless, under the terms of its extradition treaty with the Federal Republic of Germany, the United States could not object to a decision by German authorities to try Hamadei rather than to extradite him. As reaffirmed in the Venice Declaration of June 1987, either remedy is appropriate under the terms of the treaty. The problem with Germany's decision not to extradite was that it had been made in response to terrorist blackmail.

The matter does not end there, however, because although the initial identification of Hamadei was made by German authorities, the basic case against him is a U.S. one. In historical maritime terms, the scene of the crime was U.S. territory. In evidentiary terms, the body of evidence necessary to be presented against Hamadei was gathered by U.S. authorities. Most of the witnesses who could place Hamadei at the scene of the crime and establish his culpability are Americans.

Thus, not surprisingly, U.S. officials expressed concern as to whether, in the absence of the American evidence and American witnesses, German authorities would have a case. It was not clear when German authorities decided not to extradite that the evidence against Hamadei, little of which had been gathered by German authorities inside Germany, could be introduced in court under German trial procedures and found admissible under German rules of evidence.

Nevertheless, U.S. authorities made it clear to Germany that the U.S. evidence in the case would be provided and that U.S. witnesses would be urged to present themselves in court in Germany when that proved necessary to hearing the case. Since the case will be heard in a court outside the United States, however, the appearance of American witnesses is a voluntary act on their part. There is no subpoena-like means by which the Germans can compel an American witness to appear.

Prospect of Frustration

Given that combination of factors, the prospect exists that the best test case to date of the uses of law to deal with an international terrorist crime against an American will be frustrated. The case has not yet come to trial in Germany. Until it does, U.S. authorities will not know whether the evidence they can provide can be used, whether U.S. witnesses will appear, or whether German authorities will prove willing to proceed in the face of continuing terrorist pressure.

International terrorism cases are more than likely to pose such issues. Take the case, for example, of the November 1985 hijacking of an Egyptair flight to Malta by members of the Abu Nidal terrorist group.[12] After some hours of waiting and watching, Egyptian troops stormed the plane, killing sixty of the people on board. Before that occurred, the terrorists murdered several people, including an American woman, and wounded other American passengers. After the shootout, a remaining hijacker was detained by Maltese authorities, who now seem inclined to let him leave the country rather than put him on trial.

Malta has not responded to a U.S. request for extradition of the Egyptair hijacker, but if the suspect were to leave Malta, U.S. authorities might have a chance to take him into custody. In that event, the chances for a successful prosecution by Justice would depend almost entirely on evidence now in Egyptian hands. Whether Egyptian authorities would be prepared to make it available is impossible to say until a compelling reason, such as U.S. custody of the hijacker, requires them to make a decision.

Importance of Jurisdiction

The ability to use the law in dealing with international terrorism cases depends on the ability of authorities to apprehend suspects and deliver them to court for trial.

If that cannot be achieved, the criminal justice system cannot function as a tool to combat terrorist crimes. As recent cases have demonstrated, jurisdiction is not easily obtained when the site of the crime and the criminal can move freely across international boundaries and where states that sponsor the terrorists or are sympathetic to them refuse to cooperate. Only after months of planning and surveillance were U.S. authorities able to capture Fawaz Younis, one of the hijackers of an Air Jordan flight in June 1985, and bring him to the United States to stand trial. He was arrested in September 1987 on a yacht off the Coast of Cyprus after he was lured to the yacht by an FBI informant.

Even when a friendly government is known to have custody of a suspect, the going is far from smooth. The spectacular detention of the hijackers of the Italian cruise ship *Achille Lauro* by U.S. aircraft over the Mediterranean and subsequent delivery of the hijackers into Italian custody showed that obtaining jurisdiction even when the terrorists are apprehended is hardly guaranteed. In that case, Italian authorities allowed the ringleader of the *Achille Lauro* hijackers, Abul Abbas, to leave Italy despite a U.S. request for his extradition in connection with the crime.[13] Yugoslav authorities also refused extradition.

Two other cases illustrate this point. After the series of Hesbollah kidnappings began in Lebanon, U.S. authorities learned that one of the ringleaders, Moughniyeh, was in France.[14] When the United States asked informally for custody, however, French authorities apparently warned Moughniyeh, and he was able to slip away. In 1983, U.S. and British intelligence officers exposed a plot by a terrorist, who probably was a member of the Abu Ibrahim (15 May) group, to place a suitcase bomb on a flight out of Athens destined to link up with PanAm out of Rome.[15] With U.S. and British information, Greek authorities were able to take the individual into custody. Instead of putting him on trial for attempted aircraft sabotage, however, they allowed him to leave on a flight for Algeria before the United States or other governments could formalize a request for extradition.

The reasons for those decisions were more political than procedural. In each case, the extradition of the individuals in question would have been entirely consistent with the terms of the extradition agreements in force between the United States and those countries. In any of these cases, extradition could be reasonably refused—for example, if there were significant doubts about the evidence against the suspects. That, however, was never the issue. Rather, Italian authorities appear to have been moved by sympathy for the Palestinian cause; the French obviously had cause for concern about French hostages being held in Lebanon by Hesbollah; and the Greek reaction was characteristic of the Papandreou government, which generally has been uncooperative with other governments on counterterrorism matters. In the Hamadei case, German authorities could not be seen to bend to U.S. pressures in a situation where the lives of German citizens were at issue.

Jurisdictional Options

There is no easy way to brush such considerations aside. The question is how the criminal justice system can operate around those types of official responses to requests for custody of suspected terrorists. If the formal procedures of extradition, under the terms of treaties that now exist with many countries, cannot be counted upon to deliver in these cases, justice would seem doomed to frustration unless other governments are willing to take on the task of trying and punishing individuals for crimes committed against Americans abroad.

One approach has been to develop informal alternatives to formal extradition procedures in terrorism cases. The solution appears to lie with low-level understandings between police organizations in different countries as to when something less than formal extradition proceedings is appropriate for a given case. A Justice Department attorney commented to me, "If I were to discover that I was standing next to Moughniyeh in Paris, since I have in hand a valid warrant for his arrest on a charge of kidnapping, I would be perfectly comfortable with slapping handcuffs on him, putting him aboard a plane, and bringing him to the United States." The attorney suggested that this could be done without anything in the way of a formal agreement from local authorities. It would require their knowledge and acquiescence, however, at least through approving the prisoner's passage through customs and immigration on departure from France.

The key legitimating authority is a valid arrest warrant issued on the basis of significant evidence of the involvement of the individual in question in a crime. Without that warrant, even detaining a well-identified terrorist like Moughniyeh in a foreign country could be perceived to be a kidnapping.

Such informal procedures might be expected to work in cases that are clear-cut and where there is little or no publicity. Local official receptivity to this procedure could vary widely, depending on the nature of the crime and on whether the individual sought was a national of their country or of some third country. It is doubtful that informal procedures could be counted on in any of the highly publicized instances.

Importance of International Action

Seen in this light, the limitations on the jurisdiction of constituted authorities of various governments to obtain custody of terrorists suspected of crimes against their citizens outside their countries pose substantial barriers to the uses of law as an instrument for combating international terrorism. Those barriers can be partially overcome by resort to formal extradition proceedings. They can be further overcome in some degree by informal understandings with respect to taking suspected criminals into custody by authorities from jurisdictions with an interest in the crime. These processes clearly can be frustrated, however, by political considerations, which may prompt a government to spirit a suspect away to avoid facing formal requests for extradition, to avoid argument with another government over informally extraditing one of its nationals to a third country, or, as in the German case, to placate a terrorist group seeking to blackmail them. Such decisions can make a weak reed of the criminal justice system as a means to combat terrorism.

Future Tasks

These considerations raise real prospects that many terrorists who can get out of range of constituted authority will live to terrorize another day and that many governments whose leaders would not admit that they are in any way sympathetic to or supportive of terrorist activities end up helping the terrorists.

Extradition and the closely related issues of jurisdiction and criminal procedure have become central matters for governments in the West to refine in their efforts to deal with international terrorism. In the present regime of traveling terrorists, many of whom go abroad specifically to engage in terrorist activity, a failure to deal with the extradition and jurisdiction issues will more than likely perpetuate the export of terrorist violence.

The solutions to this problem lie mainly with the way we perceive and handle political crimes. In Western nations generally, the great majority of terrorist acts are crimes regardless of the motives of the perpetrator. Unless a similar philosophy can be adopted in international terrorism cases, ensuring that the terrorists are delivered into appropriate jurisdictions for trial would seem to face insuperable obstacles.

Governments must treat terrorism as crime and ensure trial and punishment. They must put aside the political content of terrorist motives and deal with cases of international terrorism in the same way they would domestic criminal cases. In that light, the provisions of the Omnibus Diplomatic Security and Antiterrorism Act of 1986 may not be helpful because they specify in effect that U.S. extraterritorial jurisdiction in terrorism cases is limited to acts that on their face are political. In short, the ordinary crimes of murder or kidnapping would not be covered. Such language forces us to treat international terrorism as politics, a distinction that to date has given the traveling terrorists and their sponsors great latitude.

A better move, made through Senate approval and U.S. ratification of the Supplementary Extradition Treaty with the United Kingdom, is to exclude violent crimes from the category of political offenses. The language of that treaty remains to be tested in court, but its basic concept should be adopted in extradition treaties with all countries maintaining legal systems compatible with those of the United States. Moreover, building on the improvements in jurisdiction embodied in U.S. domestic laws since 1984, the United States should work closely with other governments to define and extend jurisdiction in terrorism and other criminal cases so that neither terrorists nor other international criminals can hide in the spaces between national legal systems. With such steps we can extend the boundaries of law and make the law the primary instrument for combating international terrorism.

Notes

1. Two of these bills sought authority to ratify U.N. conventions, one against aircraft sabotage and the other against the taking of hostages. One sought authority for the secretary of state and the attorney general to pay rewards in terrorism cases. The fourth bill sought to prohibit Americans from providing training and support for terrorism.

2. The act prohibited so-called murder for hire arrangements one example of which was a plot uncovered in Florida to assassinate the President of Honduras.

3. *Public Report of the Vice President's Task Force on Combatting Terrorism* (Washington, D.C.: Government Printing Office, February 1986).

4. Ibid., pp. 22–27.

5. Section 2002 (a) Chapter 55 of Title 18, U.S. Penal Code—the Act for the Prevention and Punishment of the Crime of Hostage Taking—provided that it would be a crime under U.S. law if in a hostage taking "(A) The offender or the person seized or detained is a national of the United States; (B) the offender is found in the United States; or (C) the governmental organization sought to be compelled is the Government of the United States." Section 2011, cited as the Aircraft Sabotage Act, effectively made acts of aircraft sabotage a crime under U.S. law no matter where in the world the acts occurred.

6. Article I of the revised treaty starts by saying that acts covered by the major international treaties and conventions (respecting aircraft sabotage, hijacking, crimes against protected persons, or hostage taking) "shall not be regarded as an offense of a political character." The treaty then goes on to exclude murder, manslaughter, assault, kidnapping and related crimes, and several offenses related to explosives, firearms, and ammunition.

7. This section of the legislation is aimed specifically at jurisdiction over terrorism cases because it specifies that no prosecution for any of the crimes described in this section shall be undertaken by the United States except on a written certification by the attorney general or his highest-ranking subordinate that the offense in question "was intended to coerce, intimidate or retaliate against a government or a civilian population."

8. The Kuwait Airline flight was en route to Karachi, Pakistan, when it was hijacked and taken to Tehran. The hijackers demanded release of prisoners being held in Kuwait for six bombings in December 1983, including attacks on the U.S. and French embassies.

9. Chapter XX of the act states in part: "Whoever, whether inside or outside the United States, seizes or detains and threatens to kill, to injure, or to continue to detain another person in order to compel a third person or a government organization to do or abstain from doing any act as an explicit or implicit condition for the release of the person detained, or attempts to do so, shall be punishable by imprisonment for any term of years or for life." The term "whether inside or outside of the United States" establishes the basis for exercise of extraterritorial jurisdiction.

10. John Testrake, *Triumph over Terror on Flight 847* (Old Tappan, N.J.: Fleming H. Revell Co., 1987); Dave Ferman, "A Hostage Who Had Faith," *Dallas Morning News*, April 6, 1987, p. C1.

11. "TWA Crew in Germany to Identify Hijacker," *Washington Times*, June 16, 1987, p. 6.

12. According to the State Department report, "Patterns of Global Terrorism: 1985," "The Arab Revolutionary Brigades—a covername used by the Abu Nidal Group—claimed responsibility for the hijacking jointly with the Egyptian Revolution." See p. 40.

13. Abul Abbas is the leader of the Palestine Liberation Front, a small group affiliated with the Palestine Liberation Organization. The *Achille Lauro* hijackers are members of this group, and there is communications evidence that they were in constant touch with Abbas during the hijacking. Abbas was permitted by Egyptian authorities to accompany the hijackers on an Egyptair aircraft—ironically the same one that was involved in the Malta hijacking. After the Egyptair plane was forced to land in Sigonella, Sicily, Abbas and the hijackers were handled over to Italian authorities.

14. There are factions within Hesbollah, and it is difficult to tell precisely who is in charge of specific kidnappings. Lebanese Shiite Mohammed Hussein Fadlallah is the Beirut-based spiritual leader of Hesbollah, but he claims he is not responsible for any of the kidnappings. Moughniyeh is one of his lieutenants who has figured in several intelligence reports as one of the guiding hands in the hostage takings. The Musawi brothers, who lead a hardline Hesbollah faction based in the Bekaa valley, appear to have been responsible for several kidnappings of Americans, including Jeremy Levin, William Buckley, Benjamin Weir, Lawrence Martin Jenco, and David Jacobsen.

15. The 15 May group has specialized in aircraft sabotage. They are the suspected culprits in the bomb destruction of a Gulfair flight over the Arabian desert in 1983, as well as in the early 1986 explosion aboard TWA flight 840 on its approach to Greece. All passengers and crew were killed in the Gulfair bombing. Four Americans were killed in the flight 840 explosion.

13

Extraterritorial Apprehension as a Proactive Counterterrorism Measure

E. Anthony Fessler

Developing a Counterterrorism Strategy

The Challenge

In February 1986, in response to an unrelenting onslaught of savage terrorist attacks against the citizens and institutions of the United States and its Western allies, a vice-presidential task force published an important report on combating terrorism. The task force of senior government officials reported that Americans view terrorism as one of the most serious problems facing the government today. It cited the growing threat from increased terrorist activities against U.S. citizens and interests abroad, noting that in 1985 alone, there were 812 international terrorist incidents, with a loss of 926 lives, including 23 Americans, a decidedly upward trend from the preceding year.[1]

Among the many specific recommendations developed to improve U.S. counterterrorism policy was one calling for the more effective application of law as an instrument in the war against terrorism:

> International and domestic legal systems are adequate to deal with conventional war and crime. However, on occasion, questions of jurisdiction and authority arise when it comes to terrorism. For example, there are ambiguities concerning the circumstances under which military force is appropriate in dealing with terrorism. The lack of clarity about international law enforcement relationships and legal systems could limit government's power to act quickly and forcefully. The Departments of State and Justice should encourage private and academic study to determine how international law might be used to hasten—rather than hamper—efforts to respond to an act of terrorism.[2]

The views expressed in this chapter are exclusively those of the author and in no way represent those of the Department of Defense or any other agency or officer of the U.S. government. Although the chapter was submitted by the author while he was a participant in the Advanced Research Program for the Naval War College, publication in no way constitutes an endorsement by that institution or any other agency or department of the U.S. government.

What the task force did not address is how better to apply domestic and international law to win the war against terrorism. One of the most fundamental of American institutions, the legal system, has been little used as a counterterrorism measure. Instead the United States and its Western allies have relied heavily on political, diplomatic, economic, and, as of April 1986, military sanctions. Unfortunately, even the increased commitment to the cooperative application of such sanctions is unlikely to turn the tide in favor of those combating terrorism.

The historical case in support of winning a war through the use of such sanctions is not particularly persuasive. Karl von Clausewitz teaches in his incomparable treatise on the policy and strategic implications of armed conflict, *On War,* that victory can be achieved only through decisive and offensive measures directed at what he·refers to as the enemy's "center of gravity."[3] If von Clausewitz is correct and indeed the United States and the allied Western democracies are engaged in a true war against terrorism, then victory will be achieved only by undertaking clear decisive and offensive measures against the center of gravity of this international menace.

The first step is to identify that center of gravity that was so important to von Clausewitz in building a strategy of warfare. In the case of international terrorism in the 1980s, there are two critical elements to that center of gravity. The first is the mutually supportive network of states that covertly sponsor, and in some cases even direct, international terrorism in its war against the democratic states. The second critical element is the leadership and operational elites within the terrorist organizations that mastermind the attacks, recruit the disaffected, and maintain the discipline of individual units. These two elements form the center of gravity that the United States and its allies must destroy if the war against terrorism is to be won.

The sanctions now being applied are largely directed against the state sponsorship element of the enemy's center of gravity. Even if the sanctions can be effectively applied, there is little reason to believe that they will have a direct or lasting impact on the committed, radicalized terrorist networks themselves. Counterterrorism measures must be found that effectively address both elements of the center of gravity. It is necessary to reach the leadership and operational elites responsible for the lethal functioning of the terrorist networks themselves. One of the instruments available that has the potential for attacking both elements of the enemy's center of gravity is domestic and international law enforcement.

To the extent it has been used, law enforcement has proved effective as a counterterrorism measure. When terrorists have been located within the jurisdiction of the United States or another nation committed to holding terrorists accountable for their acts, criminal prosecution has been used to punish the offenders. However, the application of the criminal justice system has been frustrated by voids in the law used to prosecute the terrorists and by the inability of responsible states to gain physical custody over the terrorist offenders. The application of that domestic criminal law developed to address terrorism has often been prevented by the fact that terrorists tend to operate and stage their attacks from areas well beyond the effective reach of those states committed to criminal prosecution. The essential challenge is to develop domestic criminal law to the fullest extent so that it applies to terrorists operating beyond state borders and then to find a permissible means of securing jurisdiction over such terrorists so that they can be effectively prosecuted under that law.

Jurisdictional Base for Building an Effective Criminal Law

Internal law has historically favored two bases of jurisdiction for nation-states seeking to apply their domestic or so-called municipal criminal law. The most traditional jurisdictional principle is that of territoriality. Under this principle, a state is authorized to regulate and proscribe conduct within its territorial borders applicable to all persons found therein. A slight modification of this principle is the principle of quasi-territorial jurisdiction under which a state may selectively proscribe or regulate criminal conduct beyond its territorial borders but only under circumstances that are arguably extensions of its territory, as in the case of vessels and aircraft registered to the state that bear its national character. Also widely accepted is the jurisdictional principle of nationality by which a nation-state is entitled to regulate and proscribe the conduct of its nationals without regard to the situs of such conduct.

In the case of many acts of international terrorism, these accepted jurisdictional principles have often been of little use. Terrorist acts committed beyond territorial borders by foreign nationals cannot be prosecuted through criminal law based on either the territoriality or nationality principle of state jurisdiction. To cope with this circumstance, states victimized by international terrorism have sought to extend the reach of their criminal justice systems through the application of alternative bases of jurisdiction recognized in varying degrees by international law. One of three major alternative bases of providing for extraterritorial jurisdiction is the passive personality principle. Under this principle, a nation applies its criminal law beyond its borders in circumstances where its nationals, their property, or institutions having a national character have been the subject or victim of the offense, particularly one of a violent nature. This basis of extraterritorial jurisdiction has not been greatly favored in the international legal and political community, which fears the potential for state interference with the legitimate and perhaps greater interests of other states. Nevertheless, the principle has been gaining favor as a means of justifying the enactment of criminal laws that can be used to prosecute acts committed beyond state borders by foreign nationals. Israeli criminal law made an assertion of extraterritorial criminal jurisdiction based upon this principle in 1972.[4] The French adopted a similar provision in 1975 but found it did not apply retroactively against the notorious Palestinian terrorist Abu Daoud, who had to be subsequently released from custody notwithstanding his violation of a law founded on the principle of passive personality.[5]

The United States has generally not favored the passive personality principle as a basis for justifying the extraterritorial application of its criminal law; however, section 402 of the authoritative American Law Institute, Restatement of the Law Second, may signal a reversal in this traditional perspective. A Restatement provision recognizes a state's right to prescribe law with respect to "conduct outside its territory which has or is intended to have substantial effect within its territory."[6] Moreover, recent U.S. congressional legislation seems to have relied, at least to some extent, on the passive personality basis of extraterritorial jurisdiction.

A second alternative jurisdictional principle that recognizes a state's right to extend its municipal law to foreign nationals found beyond its borders is based on the necessity to defend or protect key national interests. Referred to as the protective principle, this basis allows a state to extend its municipal criminal law to offenders who commit acts that undermine the integrity of the state itself, its vital institutions, and, in particular, its national security interests. To be applied credibly, this principle requires a reasonable nexus between the criminal conduct and fundamental national interests, particularly those related to national security or the existence of the nation-state. The U.S. Congress has favored this principle as a basis for extending U.S. criminal jurisdiction to proscribe the conduct of foreign nationals in overseas areas. The protective principle appears to be the primary jurisdictional basis for the Comprehensive Crime Control Act of 1984, which implements several international conventions designed to suppress a range of terrorist acts.[7]

The principle of universal jurisdiction constitutes the third major basis recognized in international law for states extending their municipal law beyond territorial boundaries to foreign nationals. Universal jurisdiction is predicated on the theory that certain types of conduct are so reprehensible and destructive of the civilized world order that they are proscribed without regard to where they are committed or the nationality of the offender. This jurisdictional principle is most typically associated with piracy on or over the high seas and war crimes. Some legal theorists have recently made persuasive arguments that international terrorism, international narcotics trafficking, and certain other kinds of conduct should be brought within the penumbra of universal criminal jurisdiction. If their argument prevails, terrorism may one day be subject to prosecution by any nation having personal jurisdiction over the offender without regard to his or her nationality, the location of the offense, or the nationality of the victim.

The recent development of several major anti-terrorism conventions demonstrates a growing commitment by responsible nations to apply municipal criminal law to counteract international terrorism. Typical of these conventions are the International Convention against the Taking of Hostages,[8] adopted December 1979, and the Convention on Offenses and Certain Other Acts Committed on Board Aircraft,[9] adopted in September 1963. Despite the mutual commitments made in these conventions to prosecute or extradite international terrorists, most recognized authorities on international law still maintain that no customary or conventional law standard has arisen that would justify the application of municipal law based on the principle of universal jurisdiction. Unfortunately, there still appears an inadequate international consensus as to when particular acts constitute prosecutable acts of terrorism. Recent actions within the United Nations coupled with the increased interest of states in the multilateral anti-terrorism conventions may soon provide the basis for asserting that at least the more violent acts of terrorism are crimes against humanity and subject to the application of universal extraterritorial jurisdiction.

Although they must be applied with discretion, these principles of extraterritorial jurisdiction are providing a foundation upon which the United States and it allies are extending the reach of their substantive criminal law. By invoking one or more of these extraterritorial bases of jurisdiction, national legislators are broadening the municipal criminal law so as to make it applicable to foreign national terrorists who commit their acts beyond the territorial limits of the state. The problem that remains is how to secure physical custody over the terrorist offender. The preferred method has been by means of regional or bilateral extradition treaties. Alternatively, less formal methods can be employed to transfer criminal offenders from the state in which they are found to the prosecuting jurisdiction. The transfers may be done with the express or tacit consent of the state in which the criminal offender is found, often referred to as the asylum or sanctuary state. In some instances, the transfers have been accomplished covertly and in the absence of even tacit consent from the asylum state.

Villanova University law professor John F. Murphy in *Punishing International Terrorists* provides a comprehensive legal analysis of the various methods of "rendition," which he defines as the "generic term" for the return of alleged offenders to the "requesting country" or prosecuting state.[10] Murphy concludes in his analysis of rendition, prosecution, and punishment of terrorists that the application of criminal law is ultimately dependent upon at least some form of consent by the state in which the terrorist is found. In Murphy's view, forcible removal of an alleged terrorist offender in the absence of some form of consent or acquiescence from the asylum state would be unlawful as a matter of international, if not domestic, law. The term he applies to forcible seizures conducted in the absence of asylum state consent is *irregular rendition*. In referring to forcible seizures accomplished without asylum state consent, this study will also employ the term *irregular rendition*.

Murphy and others who share his perspective conclude that the principle of the inviolability of state territorial integrity, coupled with the important individual rights guaranteed in the expanding international law of human rights, legally preclude most, if not all, irregular renditions. As an alternative, these publicists advocate the increased development and use of bilateral and multilateral extradition treaties under which states commit themselves either to prosecute or formally transfer terrorists to other states with an interest in doing so. Extradition is accomplished with the consent of states parties to the treaties and typically involves no question of excessive or unreasonable force being applied to the offender being transferred.

Current U.S. counterterrorism policy supports the concept of increased use of this formal mechanism for extending the application of municipal criminal law. The U.S. government has actively participated in developing the multilateral anti-terrorism conventions that require states to prosecute or extradite terrorists. It strongly encourages nonsignatory states to accede to these conventions. Moreover, the Reagan administration has repeatedly expressed its commitment to developing extradition treaties that substantially curb the availability of the troublesome "political offense exception." Under this exception, some terrorists have been successful in preventing their extradition from the asylum state based on claims that their activities were not criminal but political in nature. Courts in the United States and elsewhere have all too frequently honored these claims and allowed the political offense exception as an effective bar to extradition. Some of the most notorious of these cases have occurred within the United States itself, where courts have honored the claims of members of the Irish Republican Army opposing their extradition to the United Kingdom on serious criminal charges.

The United States, its Western allies, and other responsible states have made substantial progress in improving the level of international cooperation for the purpose of extending criminal sanctions to acts of terrorism committed beyond state borders. There is cause for much optimism that the trend toward greater cooperation will continue and that more and more states will see it in their interest to join the anti-terrorism conventions. However, even with the favorable prospects for better international cooperation, serious barriers to achieving effective, comprehensive international law enforcement will persist. One of the most serious of these barriers is the all too common problem of the terrorist group that operates out of an area where there is little or no effective government control—what this study will refer to as an *uncontrolled area.* Perhaps even more troublesome is the terrorist organization that enjoys the overt or covert protection and support of a sanctuary state regime. In either case, increased international cooperation offers little prospect of reaching terrorist offenders with municipal criminal law in these areas.

Secretary of State George P. Shultz in a major policy address in New York City in October 1984 referred to the problem in these terms:

> The heart of the challenge lies in those cases where international rules and traditional practices do not apply. Terrorists will strike from areas where no governmental authority exists, or they will base themselves behind what they expect will be the sanctuary of an international border. And they will design their attacks to take place in precisely those "gray areas" where the full facts cannot be known, where the challenge will not bring with it an obvious or clear-cut choice or response.[11]

All the efforts to extend the coverage and jurisdictional reach of U.S. and allied criminal law, all the diplomatic initiatives to improve the level of international cooperation through the development of better extradition vehicles, and all the political, economic, and even military sanctions offer little prospect of coping with the problem Secretary Shultz identified. If the problem of sanctuary states and gray areas is to be resolved, it will be necessary to find a means by which terrorists can be reached in these sanctuaries. These areas and the terrorist leadership and operational elites operating freely within them must be reached by effective counterterrorism measures if the West is to destroy the enemy's center of gravity.

Fortunately, the national and international political and legal systems that are under unrelenting attack possess the means to respond. Although various proactive counterterrorism measures, including the use of preemptive military force, are now being applied, not all appear to have the potential to destroy the enemy's true center of gravity. This study proposes that serious consideration be given to a measure that has been largely ignored in the rapid development of alternative counterterrorism strategy options. Misunderstandings and even false assumptions as to both law and policy have precluded a close examination of a measure that offers genuine potential for undermining the sanctuary states and stateless areas while simultaneously striking at the leadership and operational elites of international terrorism staging from within the borders of such states and areas.

What is proposed and will be examined in this chapter is the forcible apprehension of international terrorists in the stateless or so-called gray areas and sanctuary states from which they now operate. Seizures would be directed by the United States or another responsible state wishing to acquire criminal jurisdiction over the alleged terrorist offender and would be conducted without the consent or acquiescence of the asylum or sanctuary state regime if one exists. I refer to this proposed proactive counterterrorism measure as *extraterritorial apprehension* in order to distinguish it from the broader range of seizures that Murphy calls irregular renditions. What will be examined is a highly selective type of rendition action designed for use against international terrorists who project their violence from a limited number of stateless areas and sanctuary states.

The proactive counterterrorism measure proposed must be reviewed in terms of both its domestic or municipal law as well as international law implications. Since no worthwhile political or military strategy can be sensibly developed outside its factual and operational context, close attention must also be given to the practical aspects of such an approach to combating the terrorist threat. A counterterrorism measure that appears politically acceptable and legally defensible may be of little value when examined in the context of the real world in which it must achieve a stated objective. The study will consider this measure in terms of its costs and benefits, as well as its advantages and disadvantages, when compared with alternative counterterrorism measures.

This study proposes a counterterrorism measure that would identify, locate, apprehend, and criminally prosecute members of the international terrorist leadership and operational elites previously protected by stateless gray areas and sanctuary states. As a point of departure for considering such an option, it is necessary to discover whether an adequate legal foundation exists upon which such a counterterrorism measure can be built.

Permissibility and Application of Extraterritorial Apprehension under Municipal Law

The permissibility of extraterritorial apprehension under municipal law will generally be determined in the context of the court considering the issue of jurisdiction. If the court determines that an accused terrorist brought before it by means of a government-authorized extraterritorial apprehension is not subject to the law that the prosecution is attempting to apply or that the government's action violated fundamental rights of the defendant, it may well act to divest itself of jurisdiction. The matter of establishing and maintaining proper jurisdiction is the foundation upon which extraterritorial apprehension as a counterterrorism measure will rest. For this reason, it is important to examine the issue of subject matter jurisdiction over the offense and the propriety of the trial court's personal or in personam jurisdiction over the accused terrorist brought before it by means of extraterritorial apprehension.

Establishing Subject Matter Jurisdiction over the Offense

Antiterrorist Offenses in the U.S. Code. With the increased public alarm in recent years over the rise of terrorism, the United States and its allies have acted to extend the reach of their substantive criminal law. It is beyond the scope of this study to provide a comprehensive analysis of the substantive criminal law that the United States and its allies might use as the basis for prosecuting terrorists secured through extraterritorial apprehension. Nevertheless, several of the more recent congressional enactments, as well as legislative initiatives under consideration, provide a good indication of what terrorist actions are most likely to give rise to the actual application of extraterritorial apprehension as a proactive measure.

The 1984 Act for the Prevention and Punishment of the Crime of Hostage Taking specifically implemented the International Convention against the Taking of Hostages adopted by the United Nations in December 1979.[12] The act amended the federal kidnapping statute to provide for federal jurisdiction over any kidnapping in which a threat is made to kill, injure, or continue to detain a victim in order to compel a third person or governmental organization to take some action. The United States has jurisdiction over the taking of hostages outside the country under this legislation if the perpetrator or a hostage is a U.S. national, if the perpetrator is found in the United States, regardless of nationality, or if the United States is the government coerced by the hostage taker.

This legislation implements the Hostage Taking Convention's recognition that a state party may assert jurisdiction over hostage takers (including accomplices) on the basis of its national being taken hostage. The 1984 implementing legislation appears to be a clear assertion of extraterritorial criminal jurisdiction based upon the passive personality principle.[13] Had the United States been able to acquire in personam jurisdiction over the Palestinians involved in the October 1985

Achille Lauro hijacking, it is clear the U.S. attorney responsible for prosecuting would have based the government's case in large part upon a violation of this 1984 statutory provision.[14]

The Congress also adopted a series of amendments to 18 U.S.C. 32 during 1984 designed to expand U.S. jurisdiction over aircraft sabotage. This legislation provides for implementation of the Convention for the Suppression of Unlawful Acts against the Safety of Civil Aviation adopted at Montreal in September 1971, the so-called Montreal Convention.[15] Under the Montreal Convention, nation-states are required to establish jurisdiction over certain offenses affecting the safety of civil aviation. Under the newly adopted statutory implementation of the Montreal Convention, it is a federal offense to destroy any aircraft in the special aircraft jurisdiction of the United States, whether it is military, stateowned, or civilian. The statute also makes it an offense to commit an act of violence against any person on the aircraft, not simply its crew members, if the act is likely to endanger the safety of the aircraft. The statute and convention also provide the basis, and indeed obligation, for the United States to prosecute any person who destroys a foreign civil aircraft outside the United States if the offender is later found in the United States.

The Congress further acted in 1984 to authorize the prosecution of an offender who murders, kidnaps, or assaults an immediate family member of certain federal officials where such crimes are committed with the intent to interfere with those officials in the performance of their duties or where the offenses are committed to retaliate against them for the performance of their duties. Under 18 U.S.C. 1114, enacted prior to 1984, the Congress had declared it a felony to kill certain federal officials, not including U.S. military personnel, acting in the performance of their duties. The 1984 enactment contained in 18 U.S.C. 115 now extends protection to immediate family members of the president, vice-president, members of Congress, all federal judges, the heads of executive agencies, the director of the CIA, and federal law enforcement officials.

In addition to these extensions in the U.S. substantive criminal law, the Congress acted to broaden the already existing special maritime and territorial jurisdiction of the United States contained in 18 U.S.C. 7. This well-established provision in the U.S. code recognizes a limited federal extraterritorial jurisdiction for certain serious crimes committed in areas specified to be within the special maritime and territorial jurisdiction. The 1984 amendment served to expand greatly the definition of that jurisdiction so that it now encompasses any place outside the jurisdiction of any nation where the offense is committed against a national of the United States. This legislative action again appears to be a congressional expression of the passive personality principle of extraterritorial jurisdiction as recognized in international law.

Among the offenses that may be prosecuted when committed within the special maritime and territorial jurisdiction of the United States and that often characterize terroristic conduct are arson, maiming, murder, manslaughter, attempts to commit murder and manslaughter, and malicious mischief.[16] Under 18 U.S.C. 3231, U.S. federal district courts have jurisdiction over all offenses against the United States. Pursuant to 18 U.S.C. 3238, the trial of all offenses begun or committed upon the high seas, or elsewhere out of the jurisdiction of any particular state or district, shall be in the district where the offender is arrested or first brought. Neither this section nor any other within the U.S. Code limits the manner or means by which the offender is brought before the court to stand trial for a charged violation of federal criminal law.

One further 1984 enactment now makes murder for hire a federal crime. Under 18 U.S.C. 1952A, the United States may prosecute anyone, without regard to nationality, who travels or uses facilities in foreign commerce with the intent to murder for pecuniary compensation. Although the elements of this offense may be difficult for a prosecutor to establish in the case of an international terrorist, it may nevertheless be useful in some cases.

These and other provisions of the U.S. federal criminal law offer prosecutors a range of offenses that may be applied against international terrorists without regard to their nationality. However, unless the statute expressly provides for its application in foreign states, U.S. courts wil presume jurisdictional application is limited to no more than the special maritime and territorial jurisdiction of the United States. Except for those laws where the Congress specified extraterritorial application to include offenses committed within a foreign state, U.S. prosecutors have no substantive law with which to prosecute acts of terrorism or other crimes actually committed in a foreign country against a U.S. national.

Legislative Remedies. In general, the Congress has been cautious in extending U.S. criminal jurisdiction on an extraterritorial basis. It has preferred to extend U.S. criminal jurisdiction only where there is a discernible and direct U.S. interest.[17] To date, probably the furthest extension of U.S. substantive criminal law with regard to terrorism has been the hostage-taking provisions in the 1984 Comprehensive Crime Control Act. The Congress has not enacted legislation to proscribe the murder, attempted murder, or perpetration of a serious assault upon a nonofficial U.S. national outside U.S. borders except to the extent such offense can be tried under the newly expanded special maritime and territorial jurisdiction of the United States. State Department legal adviser Abraham D. Sofaer revealed that this void in the U.S. federal criminal law frustrated efforts to bring indictments against those thought to have been responsible for the slaying of two American businessmen in El Salvador in 1985.[18]

One of the most significant legislative proposals under consideration in the Congress is the Terrorist Prosecution Act. The act is designed to amend title 18 of the U.S. Code to authorize prosecution of terrorists who attack U.S. nationals abroad without regard to where the offense occurs or the nationality of the offender. The legislation received consideration as Senate bill 1429 during July 1985 in hearings conducted by the Senate Judiciary Committee's Subcommittee on Security and Terrorism. The clear purpose of the legislation is to provide relatively comprehensive subject matter jurisdiction to federal prosecutors for use against international terrorists who perpetrate the most serious acts of violence against U.S. nationals abroad.

Unlike the extraterritorial jurisdictional provisions in the 1984 Comprehensive Crime Control Act, which are primarily based upon the passive personality principle, the Terrorist Prosecution Act would be based upon the more widely accepted protective principle. Section 2331 of the bill contains a statement of findings and purpose for the proposed legislation:

> (b) it is an accepted principle of international law that a country may prosecute crimes committed outside its boundaries that are directed against its own security or the operation of its governmental functions;
>
> (c) terrorist attacks on Americans abroad threaten a fundamental function of our Government: that of protecting its citizens;
>
> (d) such attacks also threaten the ability of the United States to implement and maintain an effective foreign policy;
>
> (e) terrorist attacks further interfere with interstate and foreign commerce, threatening business travel and tourism as well as trade relations.[19]

It is particularly interesting that the legislative histories for Senate bill 1429, as well as a number of other recent bills receiving active consideration in the Congress as means of dealing with the threat of terrorism, contain numerous approving references to abduction or forcible seizure as a way of gaining jurisdiction over offenders.[20] In the final floor debate on Senate bill 1429, Senator Arlen Specter (R–Pennsylvania), the bill's chief sponsor and a former prosecutor, argues:

> In many cases, the terrorist murderer will be extradicted or seized with the cooperation of the government in whose jurisdiction he or she is found. Yet, if the terrorist is hiding in a country like Lebanon, where the government, such as it is is powerless to aid in his removal, or in Libya, where the government is unwilling, we must be willing to apprehend these criminals ourselves and bring them back to trial. . . .
>
> Forcible seizure and arrest is a strong step, but the threat of terrorism requires strong measures, and this is clearly preferable to the alternatives of sending in combat troops or bombing a few neighborhoods.[21]

Senator Specter's views concerning how the Terrorist Prosecution Act might be implemented are by no means unique. During the same floor debate, Senator Patrick Leahy (D–Vermont) remarked:

> The United States needs a comprehensive counterterrorist strategy. Part of the strategy must be to improve our intelligence so that discriminate use of force against terrorists who have committed or are about to commit violent acts becomes feasible and legitimate.

Our strategy must also include laws which provide for the criminal prosecution in the United States of terrorists over whom we can obtain jurisdiction through extradition and *other means*. (Emphasis added)[22]

After considerable floor debate replete with similar endorsements of forcible seizure and abduction or what this chapter refers to as extraterritorial apprehension, the Senate unanimously adopted Senate bill 1429 on February 19, 1986, and transmitted it to the House of Representatives, where it awaits consideration.

Senate bill 1429 and other legislation addressing international terrorism is under consideration in the Judiciary Committee of the U.S. House of Representatives. With public concern about international terrorism running high, it is likely the Congress will enact some form of the Terrorist Prosecution Act and, by so doing, provide a powerful new law for federal prosecutors to use in the war against terrorism.[23]

A review of recent congressional enactments and pending legislation confirms that some basis for subject matter jurisdiction already exists and the prospects for this basis being expanded in the near term are excellent. Of even greater importance, there appears to be a significant political constituency prepared to support extending U.S. criminal jurisdiction to the maximum extent possible for purposes of reaching international terrorists located in stateless areas and sanctuary states. If the legislative history for Senate bill 1429 and related bills as it has developed to date is any indication, this constituency is also prepared to support efforts by the United States and its allies to secure in personam jurisdiction over terrorist offenders by means of extraterritorial apprehension. In sum, there is a positive mood in the Congress in support of such a proactive counterterrorism measure.

Securing in Personam Jurisdiction by Irregular Rendition

Ker-Frisbie Doctrine. Once it has been established that the terrorist's conduct has violated municipal criminal law and there exists an appropriate nexus between the United States or some other prosecuting forum state and the crime based upon one of the jurisdictional principles recognized in international law, it is necessary to consider the legality of the means of securing jurisdiction over the person of the alleged offender. Extradition agreements and other forms of rendition using informal or irregular means often serve as the vehicles for physically acquiring jurisdiction over the defendant. In the United States and other Western judicial systems, the accused has the right to challenge the jurisdictional authority of the court based on the means used to acquire custody over his or her person. A considerable amount of case law has been developed interpreting the legality under municipal law of various means of rendition, irregular or otherwise. For purposes of this study, the central objective will be to understand what this case law, particularly that of the United States, holds with regard to irregular renditions.[24]

The foundation for the existing U.S. doctrine on irregular rendition was established by the U.S. Supreme Court in an 1886 landmark decision in *Ker v.*

Illinois.[25] Defendant Ker, then residing in Peru, was indicted in Illinois for larceny and embezzlement. Pursuant to a bilateral extradition treaty, the president of the United States issued a warrant authorizing a private investigator to secure custody of Ker from Peruvian authorities. However, the warrant could not be served due to a state of hostilities between Chile and Peru; at the time, Chilean forces had occupied the Peruvian capital of Lima. Despite these conditions, the investigator forcibly apprehended Ker and delivered him to U.S. authorities.

Ker contended that his Peruvian residence afforded him a right to asylum and that the fact an extradition treaty remained in force between the United States and Peru precluded his return other than under the terms of the agreement. He further argued that the seizure violated his due process rights under the U.S. Constitution. The Supreme Court rejected Ker's contention, holding that the existence of the bilateral extradition treaty did not necessitate the conclusion that obtaining physical custody over the offender, by means other than through the agreement, violated its provisions. In affirming Ker's conviction in the lower court, the Court held:

> "Due process of law" . . . is complied with when the party is regularly indicted by the proper grand jury in the state court, has a trial according to the forms and modes prescribed for such trials, and when, in that trial and proceedings he is deprived of no rights to which he is lawfully entitled.[26]

As is the case with most of the other decisions rendered by the courts over the past century bearing on the legal propriety of irregular renditions, the *Ker* holding is subject to more than one interpretation. Legal analysts displeased with the apparent willingness of U.S. courts to condone most forms of irregular rendition argue that in *Ker*, government authorities intended to comply with the extradition process but were precluded from doing so by reason of the exigent hostilities. Such analysts read the *Ker* decision narrowly, concluding that, at most, *Ker* stands for the proposition that U.S. courts are prepared to ratify forcible seizures by private agents under extraordinary circumstances and where the prosecuting state has no direct role.

An alternative interpretation of *Ker*, which better conforms to subsequent judicial reading of the case, is that it establishes a rule under which U.S. courts may ratify irregular renditions where extradition is unavailable or precluded by exigencies in the asylum state. What is incontestable about the *Ker* holding is that it establishes a rule that due process of law is not jeopardized by "mere irregularities in the manner in which [a defendant] may be brought into the custody of the law."[27]

In 1952, the U.S. Supreme Court specifically upheld its ruling in *Ker* in a companion landmark decision involving irregular rendition within the United States. In *Frisbie v. Collins,*[28] the Court ruled that due process was not violated when defendant Collins was forcibly apprehended in Chicago by Michigan police, handcuffed, blackjacked, and returned to Michigan to stand trial for murder. Writing for a unanimous Supreme Court, Justice Hugo Black overturned a Sixth Circuit holding that the Federal Kidnapping Act had invalidated the *Ker* rule. Justice Black also rejected the defendant's contention that his due process rights had been violated:

> This Court has never departed from the rule announced in *Ker v. Illinois* . . . that the power of a court to try a person for crime is not impaired by the fact that he had been brought within the court's jurisdiction by reason of a "forcible abduction." [Footnote omitted.] No persuasive reasons are now presented to justify overruling this line of cases. They rest on the sound basis that due process of law is satisfied when one present in court is convicted of crime after having been fairly apprised of the charges against him and after a fair trial in accordance with constitutional procedural safeguards.[29]

The *Frisbie* decision articulated by Black, often considered one of the Court's staunchest defenders of civil liberties, made clear that the Court's emphasis remained on issues of fair trial and constitutional safeguards, which it did not consider contravened by "forcible abduction," even when undertaken by government agents acting in the absence of asylum state consent.

Together these two historic Supreme Court decisions formulate what has come to be known as the *Ker-Frisbie* doctrine, which, with one notable exception, U.S. courts have consistently relied upon to retain jurisdiction over defendants apprehended by various irregular means. The facts and circumstances surrounding a series of recent cases involving forcible seizure of criminal defendants found in foreign countries vary considerably. None precisely describes the unique circumstances under which members of the leadership and operational elite of terrorist organizations would be seized under a counterterrorism measure of extraterritorial apprehension. However, several of these cases do offer important principles upon which such a proactive counterterrorism measure can be built to ensure compliance with U.S. constitutional and municipal law requirements.

Toscanino Caveat. The sole exception to the continuing line of cases reaffirming the *Ker-Frisbie* doctrine arises from the Second Circuit Court of Appeals 1974 decision in *United States v. Toscanino.*[30] Toscanino, an Italian national charged with conspiracy to import narcotics into the United States, alleged in an affidavit that he and his pregnant wife were lured from their Montevideo home on January 6, 1973, by a telephone call from a Uruguayan police officer acting as a paid agent of the U.S. government. He claimed he was then knocked unconscious with a gun, bound, blindfolded, and driven without the knowledge or consent of the Uruguayan government to the Brazilian border, where he was surrendered to Brazilian authorities. Toscanino further alleged that Brazilian authorities held him incommunicado and interrogated him over several days, denying him food, water, and sleep. He claimed that during this period he was subjected to acts of torture, including being kicked, beaten, having electrodes attached to his extremities, and the flushing of alcohol and other fluids into his eyes, nose, and anal passage. Of particular note, he alleged that on at least one occasion, he believed a U.S. government agent was physically present in the vicinity of the violent interrogation being performed by the Brazilian authorities. At the conclusion of the interrogation, Toscanino claimed he was taken to Rio de Janeiro, drugged by Brazilian and U.S. government agents, and placed on a Pan American flight destined for the United States and the arms of arresting federal agents.

The Second Circuit used Toscanino's allegations of outrageous government conduct to fashion an exception to the *Ker-Frisbie* doctrine. The court appeared to limit the *Ker-Frisbie* doctrine by applying the expanded interpretation of due process protections recognized in *Rochin v. California*[31] and *Mapp v. Ohio*[32] to cases where in personam jurisdiction is acquired by irregular rendition. The *Toscanino* court recalled that in *Rochin v. California,* the Supreme Court relied upon the due process clause of the Fourteenth Amendment to invalidate a state court conviction won through evidence obtained by police brutality.[33] The Second Circuit reasoned that *Rochin* established the rule that convictions obtained by "conduct that shocks the conscience" violate the defendant's due process rights. The *Toscanino* court then chose to apply the exclusionary rule fashioned in *Mapp v. Ohio*[34] as "a judicially-created device designed to deter disregard for constitutional prohibitions."[35] The court concluded that *Rochin* and *Mapp* represented an expansion of the due process clause that could not be reconciled with the *Ker-Frisbie* doctrine.[36]

At least in the Second Circuit, it now appeared that courts were required to divest themselves of in personam jurisdiction over the accused where such jurisdiction was acquired by deliberate, unnecessary, and unreasonable invasion of the defendant's constitutional rights. Noting the gravity of the defendant's allegations and that if true they would constitute a violation of his due process rights, the court ordered an evidentiary hearing in which Toscanino was to be given an opportunity to prove those statements made in his affidavit.[37]

An important foundation for the *Toscanino* decision was the court's recognition that to require the *Ker-Frisbie* doctrine to yield to due process considerations, it would be necessary to extend the U.S. constitutional protections to foreign nationals not within the United States at the time of the alleged violation. The court held foreign nationals are entitled to invoke Fourth Amendment protection against the U.S. government's conduct abroad.[38] Judge Mulligan reasoned that this extension of U.S. constitutional rights to aliens not even present in the United States was justified on the notion that the Fourth Amendment protects "people" rather than "areas" or "citizens."[39] The judge further reasoned that the Constitution is in force whenever the sovereign power of the government is exercised.[40]

This part of the *Toscanino* decision is relevant to the development and planning of extraterritorial apprehension as a counterterrorism measure. The court's broad interpretation of the scope of protection afforded by the U.S. Constitution is consistent with the trend in rulings of the U.S. Supreme Court and other federal circuit courts that uniformly hold that basic human rights protections should be accorded to all individuals, whether citizens or not, and without regard to whether a person is present within the United States.[41] The significant point is that the apprehended international terrorist is entitled to the full force and protection of the U.S. Constitution from the point he or she is subjected to effective U.S. government control. The actions of U.S. government personnel, possibly even including surrogate agents, engaged in an act of extraterritorial apprehension would have to be in substantial compliance with due process and other constitutional guarantees afforded citizens within the United States.

In addition to basing its decision on Toscanino's constitutional rights, the Second Circuit took note of an apparent violation of the territorial sovereignty of Uruguay as guaranteed under two international agreements to which the United States was a party. The issue of state sovereignty and whether another state has a right to breach the territorial integrity of the asylum state seems to have been raised as a basis for the court's action in *Toscanino*. In terms of analysis of the municipal law implications of *Toscanino*, it is significant that at least the Second Circuit was prepared to examine the issue of irregular rendition, or what it referred to simply as abduction, in terms of U.S. obligations to the asylum state under international law. The *Toscanino* decision has undergone substantial refinement and, at best, represents that law in only one federal circuit. Nevertheless, the court did focus on what it perceived as relevant international obligations of the United States and considered their apparent violation a basis for ruling against the government.

Ker-Frisbie: Reaffirmed But Refined. While *Toscanino* appeared to strike a blow, at least in one federal circuit, to the *Ker-Frisbie* doctrine, a significant body of subsequent case law has done much to ameliorate its effects. Within six months of the *Toscanino* decision, the Second Circuit published its opinion in *United States ex rel. Lujan v. Gengler*[42] in which the court's prior holdings were substantially narrowed, reinterpreted, and clarified. Lujan, a resident of Argentina, was the subject of an outstanding U.S. federal warrant related to his role in a conspiracy to import to and distribute a large quantity of heroin in the United States. U.S. Drug Enforcement Administration (DEA) agents employed a foreign national agent who engaged defendant Lujan, a pilot, to fly to Bolivia. Once lured out of Argentina to Bolivia on the promise of attractive employment, Lujan was taken into custody by Bolivian police acting not on behalf of their own government but as agents for the DEA. Lujan was held in Bolivia and subsequently placed on a plane bound for New York, where he was arrested by waiting federal agents.

Chief Judge Kaufman, speaking for the Second Circuit, noted that the court's prior decision in *Toscanino* could scarcely "have meant to eviscerate the *Ker-Frisbie* rule." Judge Kaufman observed that in the *Toscanino* decision, the court "did not intend to suggest that any irregularity in the circumstances of a defendant's arrival in the jurisdiction would vitiate the proceedings of the criminal court."[43] *Lujan* clearly narrowed the holding in *Toscanino*. The rule under *Lujan*, which still applies in the Second Circuit, is that absent outrageous or shocking government conduct, irregular rendition is not in and of itself a violation of due process rights.[44]

As in *Toscanino*, the Second Circuit in *Lujan v. Gengler* addressed alleged violations of international law predicated on an apparent absence of consent or acquiesence to the seizure from the asylum state. On this issue, the *Lujan* court appeared to narrow further the holding in *Toscanino*, noting that the defendant did not have a private right to raise the issue of sovereignty. Specifically distinguishing *Lujan* from *Toscanino* on this issue, Judge Kaufman wrote:

> But unlike Toscanino, Lujan fails to allege that either Argentina or Bolivia in any way protested or even objected to his abduction. This omission is fatal to his reliance upon the [United Nations and Organization of American States] charters. The provisions in question are designed to protect the sovereignty of states, and it is plainly the offended states which must in the first instance determine whether a violation of sovereignty occurred, or requires redress.[45]

The court in this statement seemed to imply that abduction may violate international law, but the asylum state may cure any real or apparent violation by its acquiescence. Moreover, the court seemed to be saying that if there is no protest from the asylum state, the court may imply consent or acquiescence. In any case, the defendant may not raise the issue of sovereignty under traditional international law since it is a question for the sovereigns themselves to resolve.

The Second Circuit further retreated from the *Toscanino* holding in its 1975 decision in *United States v. Lira*.[46] In *Lira*, the defendant, a Chilean national, was arrested by Chilean police at the request of the U.S. DEA. He alleged that thereafter he was brutally tortured at a Chilean naval base over a period of several weeks. Lira claimed that following a period of interrogation, he was taken to the airport, drugged, and put on a plane for the United States, escorted by both Chilean police officers and agents of the DEA. Judge Mansfield, author of the *Toscanino* decisions, ruled that because the defendant could not prove overt U.S. government participation in his alleged ordeal, the district court was not required to divest itself of jurisdiction over the accused.[47] The court recalled its holding in *Lujan* and determined that Lira could not allege a violation of Chilean law if Chile as the asylum state was itself aware of an apparent violation of its sovereignty yet failed to protest to the government of the United States.[48] Based on the allegations of police brutality in this case and some suggestion of DEA involvement, it is very difficult to distinguish this set of facts from those in *Toscanino*. the only mildly distinguishing factor seems to be the court's position that there is no evidence to support the defendant's allegations of possible U.S. DEA involvement in the abduction and torture.

Unfortunately, none of the *Ker-Frisbie* doctrine line of cases specifically fits all the operative circumstances likely to arise during a U.S. government or allied nation apprehension of a terrorist in a stateless area or sanctuary state. It is virtually certain that such extraordinary apprehensions would be conducted without the consent or acquiescence of any regime in the stateless area or sanctuary state. Sanctuary states providing overt or covert support for international terrorists operating within their borders can be expected to voice outrage and alarm at an extraterritorial apprehension being conducted within their territory.

Another circumstance that might be expected in the apprehension of international terrorists in stateless areas or sanctuary states would be the direct and substantial use of U.S. government forces or agents. Depending upon the security threat posed by the terrorists themselves or the security forces of the local area, it may prove necessary and prudent to use military, paramilitary, or specialized intelligence agency operatives. None of the *Ker-Frisbie* line of cases deals with facts even remotely resembling this sort of scenario in which there could be substantial involvement of U.S. government personnel during the extraterritorial apprehension operation itself.

Two decisions in the *Ker-Frisbie* line of decisions do provide at least some indication of how U.S. courts might view a case of extraterritorial apprehension with regard to the almost certain protest that can be expected from the sanctuary state. In *Ex parte Lopez*,[49] the petitioner was seized while in Mexico and forcibly returned to the United States for trial upon narcotics charges. The government of Mexico intervened at trial asking that the court surrender custody of the petitioner. In support of its request, the Mexican government cited existing treaties between the United States and Mexico, which it alleged had been violated by the seizure of its territory. Notwithstanding, the Texas court stated that the Mexican government's claim would not affect its jurisdiction. The court speculated that the Mexican government may wish to present the matter to the executive department of the U.S. government. As in the *Lira* case, the Texas court viewed the matter of sovereignty as essentially a political question to be resolved by the executive branches of the governments involved.

A more recent case involves two American bounty hunters who kidnapped Sidney Jaffe, a U.S. national, from Toronto in May 1981. Jaffe had fled the United States to avoid prosecution by Florida state authorities for fraudulent land sales. Florida authorities instituted extradition proceedings, which were ineffective due to the state's failure to follow proper procedures.[50] The bounty hunters were engaged by the bail bondsman, who in turn was encouraged by Florida prosecutors to return the defendant to allow continuation of the criminal trial. The government of Canada vigorously protested Jaffe's seizure as a violation of its sovereignty and cited the existing U.S.–Canadian extradition treaty as a basis for its objections.[51]

The Florida state court rebuffed the Canadian protest, refused to release Jaffe, and convicted him of land sale violations. The court cited a Florida state rule permitting bounty hunters to pursue and return bail jumpers to the jurisdiction of the court. The Florida court virtually ignored the Canadian protest. The Canadian government sought the intervention of the U.S. Department of State and demanded that the two bounty hunters be extradited to Canada to stand trial for a violation of the Canadian kidnapping statute. The two bounty hunters were subsequently extradited to stand trial in Canada.[52] In this instance, the U.S. federal authorities appeared genuinely concerned about the apparent violation of Canadian sovereignty and the state of Florida's failure to exercise the extradition treaty to the fullest extent.

Ex parte Lopez, Jaffe, and other cases where there have been affirmative protests from the asylum state have invariably resulted in the courts retaining jurisdiction. In *Lopez,* the court viewed the issue as a political matter to be resolved between the executive branches of the respective national governments. In *Jaffe,* the state court largely ignored the issue, perhaps based on the assumption that the bounty hunters were acting indepedently of any state action. What these and other cases involving a state protest seem to indicate is that courts have been reluctant to divest themselves of in personam jurisdiction once acquired. Courts have even retained jurisdiction when foreign asylum states have protested the irregular rendition as a violation of their sovereignty. Such in personam jurisdiction has been retained even in cases involving asylum states that have cordial relations with the United States and are closely linked to it by treaties pledging mutual respect for sovereignty or committing the countries to the use of extradition.

United States v. Reed[53] provides still further indication as to how U.S. courts might view extraterritorial apprehension. Reed and two accomplices had been charged with mail fraud and conspiracy to commit securities and mail fraud. Prior to the selection of a federal jury in the Eastern District of New York, Reed jumped bail and was tried in absentia while a fugitive. He was subsequently located in the Bimini Islands in the Bahamas, where covert CIA agents lured him on board a small private plane they claimed was bound for Nassau. Once on board the aircraft, Reed alleged that one of the agents pulled a gun and made him lie on the floor. He alleged the agent held a cocked revolver to his head and threatened to "blow [his] brains out." Upon arriving in Fort Lauderdale, Reed alleged that one of the CIA agents twisted his arm badly while he was deplaning and in the process of being surrendered to waiting FBI agents. Although an extradition treaty existed between the United States and the Bahamas, there is no indication that any attempt was made to invoke it to gain Reed's return.

The court held that luring Reed onto the plane under false pretenses, the use of a revolver pointed to his head, and the threatening language was not conduct that involved gross mistreatment in contravention of *Toscanino*'s due process standard.[54] The court further held that the fact the United States has an extradition treaty with the Bahamas, from which the defendant has been "abducted by CIA agents," had no bearing on the legality of the arrest where the Bahamian government had not sought the defendant's return or made any protest. The court concluded that in the absence of any such protest, the defendant had no standing to raise a violation of international law as justifiable issue.

Reed also asserted that his fundamental constitutional rights were violated on the theory that any "abduction" from another country with which the United States has an extradition treaty under the coerced circumstances alleged constituted an unreasonable seizure within the meaning of the Fourth Amendment.[55] The court found Reed's seizure pursuant to an arrest warrant issued with probable cause was reasonable for purposes of the Fourth Amendment. The court specifically held:

The existence of an extradition treaty provides an individual with certain procedural protections only when he is extradited. And abduction is no more or less objectionable simply because of the existence of an extradition treaty. As for the manner of the seizure, custody obtained by executing an arrest warrant is not invalidated because of the use of excessive force, even though the defendant might have a suit for damages against the government agents involved.[56]

The Second Circuit might have chosen to limit the application of the *Ker-Frisbie* doctrine in a manner similar to its interpretation in *Toscanino* but basing its analysis on Reed's argument that his Fourth Amendment rights had been violated by a forcible seizure in a country with which the United States had an extradition treaty. Not only did this 1981 decision reject this analysis, but it once again made clear that an extradition treaty does not preclude the use of forcible seizure, at least in the absence of a protest from the asylum state.

In yet another argument made to the court, Reed maintained that divestiture of jurisdiction was required under its judicial supervisory powers to curb abuses by government agents. The defendant argued that his "abduction" at the hands of government agents "breeds contempt for the law, mocks our stated concern for human rights, and jeopardizes our standing in the international community."[57] The Second Circuit responded to this argument by noting:

> We see no pattern of repeated abductions necessitating exercise of our supervisory power here in the interests of the great good of preserving respect for the law. Appellant, [Reed] a fugitive from justice with no respect for the law whatsoever, is hardly in a position to urge otherwise.[58]

In this statement, the court does seem to imply that it would have reservations if it saw a pattern of repeated abductions. However, it nevertheless approved the government's actions and refused to divest itself of jurisdiction over the defendant. Of even greater interest, the court was quick to note the defendant's apparent lack of respect for the judicial system and seemed to balance this against the extraordinary law enforcement actions of the government. This may signal that future courts, sitting in judgment of international terrorists who assert violations of their constitutional and human rights, may view such claims in the context of the defendants' contempt for the rights and civil liberties of their victims.

Application of the *Ker-Frisbie* Doctrine to Extraterritorial Apprehension. The *Ker-Frisbie* doctrine remains a dynamic area of the law; it will continue to evolve and be refined. The line of cases interpreting and clarifying the doctrine fundamentally supports irregular rendition, albeit with important qualifications bearing on the constitutional rights of the apprehended person and the impact such actions may have on the sovereign rights of the asylum states. What is important for purposes of this analysis is that the doctrine provides a basis in U.S. municipal law for developing extraterritorial apprehension as a counterterrorism measure. The evolving doctrine offers important standards and criteria that must be folded into any detailed operational plan designed to carry out a proactive counterterrorism measure involving extraterritorial apprehension.

The *Toscanino* decision and its successors establish attainable standards of conduct for those U.S. government or allied nation personnel and surrogate agents who may be directly involved in the apprehension operation. These decisions establish that brutality, torture, or grossly excessive and unreasonable force under given circumstances may cause a U.S. court to divest itself of jurisdiction. It is equally clear that the use of ruse, trickery, paid foreign agents, and perhaps even the administration of tranquilizing drugs to facilitate transfer of the apprehended person will not offend the sensibilities of most courts. Nor will courts necessarily examine the precise amount of force applied to effect the apprehension so long as there is some reasonable justification for the manner and extent to which it is applied under the circumstances.

The line of *Ker-Frisbie* decisions includes cases where the apprehension was accomplished directly by U.S. government personnel, others where foreign agents appeared in charge, and still others where there was some vague combination of foreign and U.S. agents operating in concert. If there is any lesson to be discerned from the courts' consideration of the governmental identification or agency relationships in these various cases, it is that the more directly the apprehending persons are associated with the U.S. government, the higher is the standard of conduct to which they will be held. There is no question that when U.S. government personnel are directly involved in an extraterritorial apprehension, they must conduct themselves so as not to disregard the constitutional rights of the person being apprehended. It is also likely that foreign or private surrogate agents operating pursuant to a detailed U.S. government plan or under the close direction of the U.S. government will be held to an equally high standard of conduct.

The *Ker-Frisbie* line of decisions, starting with *Ker* itself, makes clear that extradition is not an exclusive remedy. The existence of an extradition treaty will not bar the court from proceeding in the case of a defendant brought before it by irregular rendition. However, the courts have recognized that irregular renditions carried out in lieu of such extradition treaties may give rise to a diplomatic protest from the asylum state at the national executive level of the government. Although the authority in this area is not well developed, there is no reason to believe that such a protest will necessarily cause the court to divest itself of in personam jurisdiction over the apprehended defendant. Divestiture seems a particularly unlikely possibility if the protest is made by a regime of questionable authority purporting to be the government in a stateless area or, alternatively, when the objections originate from a sanctuary state widely recognized as engaged in the state sponsorship of international terrorism.

Two issues among those considered in the *Ker-Frisbie* decisions remain significant points of contention. The first is the question of whether irregular rendition is permissible when the violation of the asylum state's sovereignty is accomplished through the fully authorized and intentional efforts of the apprehending state. The second issue that remains largely open is whether under the expanding international law of human rights, the apprehended defendant now has a personal right to protest his seizure, notwithstanding the acquiescence, consent, or silence of the asylum state. Answers to these remaining issues must be derived from international law. Nevertheless, their resolution will be developed in the context of, and incorporated within, the evolving *Ker-Frisbie* doctrine. The answers to these issues are fundamental to the overall question of the permissibility of extraterritorial apprehension as a counterterrorism measure.

The Right of Extraterritorial Apprehension under International Law

Import of International Law on Strategy Development

The foundation of contemporary international law is the concept of a minimum world public order system designed to maintain peace and security through the development of friendly relations and cooperation among nations. Implicit in the maintenance of international peace and security is the concept of equality, justice, and respect for fundamental human rights of nations and their citizenry— without regard to political, economic, and social system or level of development.[59] Sophisticated terrorist leadership elites do not subscribe to this minimum world public order system under international law. In fact, a principal objective of international terrorism is to undermine this fundamental system by whatever means possible.

Despite their contempt for the minimum world public order system, international terrorist elites and their sanctuary state sponsors have learned to exploit the rights and protections afforded under international law. Ironically these rights were established to preclude war, violence, and suffering and are now used by international criminal elements to prevent responsible states from holding them accountable for their acts against innocent persons and peaceful institutions. Any reasonable analysis and application of international law must have as its point of departure this fundamental understanding of the minium world public order system and its underlying interest in the maintenance of peace and security among nations along with a guarantee of human rights for all people.

The principle of state sovereignty and concepts of human rights are two facets of international law that thus far have precluded a more intense and effective proactive counterterrorism response. At issue is whether a state's right to territorial integrity or political independence as guaranteed under Article 2(4) of the United Nations Charter[60] applies without qualification. Does a state that enjoys Article 2(4) protection have corresponding obligations of its own, and, if so, what are those obligations and to whom are they owed? Also at issue is whether the human rights guarantees that have been recognized by the United Nations itself and many regional groups of nations speaking through multilateral conventions shield the international terrorist from effective law enforcement or other counterterrorism measures. Whether or not terrorists enjoy a state status or international personality, can they assert that proactive counterterrorism measures violate their fundamental human rights?

Toscanino and some of the other *Ker-Frisbie* decisions have raised these types of questions without satisfactorily resolving them. Resolution will be required if the United States adopts extraterritorial apprehension as a counterterrorism measure. Both the U.S. Constitution and Supreme Court decisions make clear that the U.S. courts are absolutely bound by international law. In its historic decision in *Paquete Habana*,[61] the U.S. Supreme Court stated:

> International Law is part of our law, and must be ascertained and administered by the courts of justice of appropriate jurisdiction, as often as questions of right depending upon it are duly presented for their determination. For this purpose, where there is no treaty, and no controlling executive or legislative act or judicial decision, resort must be had to the customs and usages of civilized nations.[62]

Paquete Habana confirmed the incorporation of international law within U.S. municipal law. It also established that unless provided to the contrary by federal statute, customary international law governs.[63]

The courts are mandated under U.S. common law to presume conformity between international law and U.S. congressional enactments unless it is unmistakably apparent that an act was intended to be in disregard of a principle of international comity.[64] Since there is no U.S. statute that either explicitly authorizes or prohibits extraterritorial apprehension, it is clear that U.S. courts will be obligated to examine closely international law as well as their own constitutional and municipal law-based decisions in determining the permissibility of extraterritorial apprehension as a counterterrorism measure. If extraterritorial apprehension does not comport with international law with regard to fundamental nation-state rights or those human rights now being guaranteed to all persons, a U.S. municipal law court may divest itself of jurisdiction.

Right of Extraterritorial Apprehension

Sanctuary State Sovereignty. The predominant claim by the critics of irregular rendition is that forcible seizures by one state in the territory of another violate the latter's sovereignty unless it has given its consent, explicit or implied, to the action. As a general principle of international law, it is understood that sovereignty involves the supreme, absolute, and uncontrolled power of a nation-state to control that which occurs within its territorial boundaries.[65] All persons found within the state's boundaries are subject to the exclusive power of the state. Absent such state's consent, no other state is entitled to exert jurisdiction over matters arising within its territory.[66] Under traditional international law, only the asylum state could exercise in personam jurisdiction regarding the status of the person within that state.[67] The forcible removal of a person without the consent of the asylum state violated this principle of international law.

The sovereign rights of states create corresponding obligations for other states to limit the extension and application of their municipal law beyond national boundaries. In effect, the various principles of extraterritorial jurisdiction recognized in international law and discussed at the outset of this study reflect the mutual obligations of nations to respect one another's sovereignty in the application of municipal law. Most interpretations of the principle of sovereignty provide that under customary international law, states are forbidden to send agents into the territory of another state to capture criminals.[68] Even the right to hot pursuit of criminals is limited by customary law interpretation of state sovereignty so that pursuing police are typically precluded from crossing territorial boundaries of foreign states in the absence of at least implied consent.[69] Many international law authorities also maintain that the principle of sovereignty protects states against violations of their territorial integrity caused by other states "allowing" their nationals to engage in bounty hunting and other private actions intent on apprehending fugitives within the asylum state.[70]

National rights to sovereignty and territorial integrity as historically developed in the customary international law are now incorporated in Article 2, paragraph 4, of the U.N. Charter, which provides: "All members shall refrain in their international relations from the threat or use of force against the territorial integrity or political independence of any state, or in any other manner inconsistent with the Purposes of the United Nations."[71] The court in *United States v. Toscanino*[72] specifically referred to this paragraph as well as a similar provision contained in Article 17 of the Charter of the Organization of American States (OAS)[73] in its determination that the abduction of the defendant from Uruguay constituted a violation by the United States of its treaty obligations. Publicists have frequently cited Article 2(4) of the U.N. Charter and other treaty obligations, as well as customary international law, guaranteeing state sovereignty as an absolute bar to irregular rendition.

In the much celebrated 1960 seizure of World War II SS officer and Nazi Adolf Eichmann, the U.N. Security Council specifically addressed an act of state-sponsored irregular rendition in terms of the rights afforded under Article 2(4) of the organization's charter. Eichmann had been hiding in Argentina under the name Richard Klementz and was discovered by Israeli agents following a relentless hunt that began almost immediately after the surrender of Nazi Germany.[74] On May 11, 1960, Israeli agents kidnapped Eichmann in Buenos Aires, interrogated him for a period of time, and caused him to sign a statement that he was "voluntarily" leaving Argentina. Without the knowledge or consent of the Argentine government, Eichmann was removed to Israel aboard an El Al airliner. Once in Israel, authorities charged Eichmann under an Israeli law that retroactively outlawed Nazi war crimes and acts of collaboration.

Following Prime Minister Ben Gurion's May 23, 1960, announcement that Eichmann had been apprehended, Israel and Argentina engaged in an intensive exchange of diplomatic notes. The Ben Gurion government apologized for what it admitted was a violation of Argentine sovereignty, but noted "the special significance" of bringing to trial the man responsible for the murder of millions of Jewish people.[75] As the dialogue continued, the Frondizi government in Buenos Aires insisted that Israel make reparations in the form of the return of Eichmann and the extradition of those responsible for the kidnapping. When Israel refused, the Argentines requested an "urgent meeting" of the U.N. Security Council to consider "the violation of the sovereign rights of the Argentine Republic resulting from the illicit and clandestine transfer of Adolf Eichmann from Argentine territory to the territory of the State of Israel."[76]

During the course of the Security Council debate, Argentina argued that all states had an interest in condemning the Israeli action "because of the dangers which this act and its possible repetition engender for the maintenance of peace and international security."[77] The Argentines raised the possibility that the Eichmann seizure, if not condemned by the Security Council, might be used as a precedent to justify future "violations of the sovereignty of other states."[78] Golda Meir answered for Israel, arguing that the true threat to international peace and security lay not in Eichmann's seizure but in allowing Eichmann the war criminal to remain at large. Articulating the Israeli case, Meir asked rhetorically of the council: "Is this a threat to peace—Eichmann brought to trial by the very people to whose total physical annihilation he dedicated all his energies?"[79]

After considerable diplomatic effort by several of the permanent members of the council to reach a consensus, a resolution was adopted declaring that Eichmann's seizure had violated Argentine sovereignty and was incompatible with the U.N. Charter. With the Soviet Union and Poland abstaining, the council requested the "Government of Israel to make appropriate reparation" in accordance with the U.N. Charter and rules of international law.[80] Following the adoption of the Security Council resolution, Argentina and Israel negotiated a compromise under which the two governments agreed to an exchange of new ambassadors. The governments issued a joint communiqué in which they announced their decision "to regard as closed the incident that arose out of the action taken by Israeli nationals which infringed upon fundamental rights of the State of Argentina."[81]

The Israeli seizure is a case bearing many similarities to the proposed counterterrorism measure of extraterritorial apprehension. Eichmann was forcibly seized by state agents and without the consent or acquiescence of the asylum state. It is less certain whether Eichmann represented a genuine threat to international peace and security or to the Israeli state. In all probability, Eichmann's seizure and trial were more acts of retribution for his outrages against the Jewish people and less acts in the interest of crime prevention or deterrence. Noting the Security Council condemnation of the Israeli action as a violation of Argentine sovereignty and as incompatible with the U.N. Charter, it may seem there is little possibility that extraterritorial apprehension would be viewed otherwise.

Although the Security Council action in the Eichmann case represents an authoritative interpretation of Article 2(4) of the charter, it is not in and of itself international law. Even more important, the Security Council debate did not in any significant way address the existence of possible exceptions to the sovereign rights and protections recognized under Article 2(4). Although Meir implied Eichmann could be viewed as a general threat to world peace, there was no specific demonstration that he posed a continuing, imminent, and serious threat to international peace and security or, alternatively, to the national security of the state of Israel. Finally, it may be significant that the Security Council resolution, although unanimous, was declaratory in nature and made no attempt to impose sanctions upon Israel. The ultimate facts are that Eichmann was tried by the apprehending state, found guilty under its municipal law, and executed for his universal criminal conduct, notwithstanding any diplomatic apologies or U.N. Security Council resolution.

One other aspect of the Eichmann case must be carefully weighed when considering its impact on the permissibility of extraterritorial apprehension. At the root of a violation of state sovereignty brought about by irregular rendition is the deep embarrassment caused to the asylum state. The seizure constitutes an exposure of the asylum state's inability to maintain credible control of actions occurring within its borders. In the Eichmann case, as well as in the case of the vast majority of irregular renditions, the state performing the seizure has no desire or intent to embarrass the asylum state. In most instances, the state benefiting from seizure would prefer to distance itself from the act of apprehension and to deny any state support for it. In the Eichmann case, the official Israeli position was that the abduction was not state supported. Israeli relations with the Argentines had been cordial. In fact, the two governments were in the process of entering into a bilateral extradition treaty when the seizure occurred.

The circumstances that will tend to surround the application of extraterritorial apprehension are quite different. As a counterterrorism measure, it is designed and intended to embarrass the sanctuary state or stateless area. One of the desired outcomes of such an apprehension would be to undermine the credibility of the regime through the limited and temporary violation of its territorial integrity. Rather than denying the action was state supported, the apprehending state would publicly acknowledge the seizure and explain the reasons for it.

Rights of Other States and the Minimum World Public Order System. Many of the analyses of irregular rendition under international law have tended to focus on the rights and interests of the sanctuary state or even the individual subjected to the seizure. The interest of the sanctuary state in the maintenance of its sovereignty and territorial integrity is of such gravity that extradordinary protection is provided under international law. It is to be expected that international law is extremely protective of the nation-state unit, which continues to form the basic component in the minimum world public order system.

While sovereign state rights to territorial integrity and political independence are important, international law encompasses other vital interests in the minimum world public order system. Unfortunately many analyses of irregular rendition have tended to ignore these other interests, instead excluding them from the formation of applicable international law. Viable and enforceable international law is not founded upon the interests or rights of any single state, group of states, or isolated juridically recognized entity. Instead it is based upon a comprehensive analysis and balance of the interests and rights of all participants in the minimum world public order system.

A reliable international law analysis of extraterritorial apprehension must consider the interests and rights of other key participants: the apprehending state, other states affected by the terrorists to be seized, and the minimum world public order system as a whole. At issue is whether there are interests protected by the conventional or customary international law so substantial that, on balance, the right of the sovereign state to territorial integrity and political independence may be forced to yield. The case law interpreting the *Ker-Frisbie* doctrine has not yet produced a careful analysis of interests beyond those of the sanctuary state or "abducted defendant." Accordingly, it is necessary to look beyond these decisions to identify these other key interests and any law that may serve to protect them.

While the sanctuary states are entitled to the protection of Article 2(4) of the U.N. Charter, such protection is also available to the apprehending state and other members of the world community of nations. In the case of international terrorists who may be supported by the sanctuary state, their attacks perpetrated on the nationals and institutions, public or private, of other members of the international community are clearly in contravention of their obligation to "refrain . . . from the threat or use of force against the territorial integrity or political independence of any state, in any other manner inconsistent with the Purposes of the United Nations."[82] Moreover, the "Purposes of the United Nations" as articulated in Article 1 of the charter[83] are certainly not consistent with the state sponsorship of, or even acquiescence in, international terrorism directed at other members of the world community from within a state's borders.

Sanctuary State Responsibility for Terrorism
Emanating from within its Territory

Categories of State Liability. Sovereign states are held responsible or liable to other states for their actions or omissions that violate the legitimate rights of other states in the minimum world public order system. The principle of external responsibility derived from the fundamental concepts of the rights and obligations of sovereign states provides that one state's violation of another's external political or territorial sovereignty is a delinquency that imposes liability on the offending state.[84] This same principle extends to state agents as well as nationals of a state acting independent of any state direction.

Under international law, the sovereign state bears direct liability for acts of organs of its government. The U.S. government clearly hoped to mount sufficient evidence against the Qaddafi regime in Libya to establish a credible case based on this theory of direct liability in undertaking the April 14, 1986, military air strikes against the terrorist infrastructure in Tripoli and Benghazi.[85] In support of its actions, U.S. government spokesmen repeatedly claimed they had "incontrovertible proof" that the Libyan government had been directly implicated in the April 5, 1986, bombing of La Belle Disco in West Berlin, which resulted in the deaths of a U.S. serviceman and a Turkish woman and the injuring of some 230 other persons.[86]

Alternatively, a sovereign state may be held to be liable vicariously where it knowingly allows private persons to perpetrate activities from within its territory that injure other states. The theory of vicarious liability under international law provides that a state has a recognized duty to exercise reasonable care to prevent "illegal acts" that may originate in its territory. In the event such acts occur, the sanctuary state has a responsibility to the injured state to punish the wrongdoers or to compel them to make reparation.[87]

The principle of vicarious liability was made applicable to states sponsoring or acquiescing in terrorist activity within their borders through the 1970s Declaration of Principles of International Law adopted by the U.N. General Assembly.[88] Among its other provisions, the declaration prohibits state acquiescence to activity within its territory that aims at fomenting civil war or committing terrorist acts in another state. The declaration may not constitute a firm codification of customary international law; however, it does represent an authoritative interpretation of the obligations undertaken by sovereign states under the U.N. Charter as understood by a sizable majority of the General Assembly.

Theories of Vicarious State Liability. Under international law, vicarious liability may be imputed to the state for its failure to control terrorists operating within its territory under one of three theories: fault liability, acts on behalf of a state, or absolute liability.[89] Under the theory of fault liability, a sanctuary state incurs responsibility for hostile acts emanating from its territory unless it was unaware of such activity or knew but was unable to prevent it.[90] The fault liability theory is the most widely recognized of the three theories of liability by the international community. The International Court of Justice appeared to invoke the fault theory in its adjudication of the historic 1949 *Corfu Cannel* case in which it noted that a state is liable if it knowingly permits its territory "to be used for acts contrary to the rights of other States."[91] Although this theory allows an injured party to hold states liable when they are aware of the terrorist activity within their borders, it does not serve as a basis for establishing state responsibility in cases where the state is unaware of such activity. Nor can it be used to establish liability in the stateless gray areas where there may be awareness of the terrorist activity but no responsible and capable sovereign authority in existence to take remedial action.

A state may also be held vicariously liable under international law for the conduct of persons who act on its behalf. Under this theory, if a state accepts the benefits derived from the actions of an individual or group, it is deemed to have consented to and ratified the actions.[92] In the case of international terrorism, unless it can be firmly established that the acts are committed at the direction of or in direct support of a state (as at the West Berlin La Belle Disco bombing), it may be difficult to evidence a sanctuary state's acceptance or ratification of the "benefits" of the terrorists' acts.

The third basis for imputing liability to states holds them strictly accountable for terrorist acts that originate from within their territory.[93] Under this theory, a state is strictly liable if it tolerates the use of its territory for staging an intervention into a foreign territory. Sanctuary states and stateless areas remain accountable for all acts of terrorism staged from within their borders regardless of whether they were aware of such acts or were able to prevent them.[94]

Of the three theories of vicarious liability applicable to states, strict liability is clearly the broadest. It would even provide a basis for imputing liability in stateless areas to the extent there is any vestige of a sovereign regime in existence. However, since an imprudent application of the absolute liability theory may work even as against a nonaccomplice or "innocent" state, the principle has not received wide acceptance in the international community. For this reason, it would have to be applied selectively, if at all, as a basis for justifying proactive counterterrorism measures against a sanctuary state that sponsors or condones a terrorist presence within its borders.

International law recognizes that sovereign states are entitled to substantial protection against the infringement of their rights to political independence and territorial integrity as recognized in Article 2(4) of the U.N. Charter. However, international law also recognizes that implicit in the universal respect for such rights is the corresponding obligation of states to refrain from interfering with the political independence and territorial integrity of other states. The contemporary world public order system is substantially one in which nation-states form the paramount authority over politically designated geographic areas. These states are charged under the principle of state responsibility and its supporting liability doctrine with maintaining control over activities within their borders that could interfere with the sovereignty of other states. A state's intentional or negligent failure to meet its obligations undermines its own sovereign status under international law and gives rise to self-help remedies by other states injured as a result.

Remedies under International Law

Doctrine of Self-Defense. Both customary and conventional international law have long recognized that even the rights to political independence and territorial integrity inherent in the fundamental principle of national sovereignty must yield in the interest of maintaining international peace and security. A right to individual national, or more recently, collective, self-defense arises in a state or states faced with the imminent threat of armed attack.

The violent acts of international terrorists tend to be directed against targeted state institutions, public or private, and the nationals of such states. When individuals become the targets of terrorist attacks, those individuals are placed in that position because of their relationship with the actual target of the terrorist, an identified state, or a political system. In other words, terrorist acts may be perpetrated against an immediate and often very innocent victim with the real intent of causing some response from, or injury to, the actual target, a sovereign state or political system. When such violent acts emanate from a sanctuary state and liability for them can be imputed to that state, an act of aggression has been committed. The state or states that the terrorists sought to influence by their actions acquire under international law a right to engage in self-help against the responsible sanctuary state aggressor. In the case of a stateless area, the very existence of sovereign rights themselves may be in question. However, to the extent such rights do exist and have any application to an area, the same priniciple applies.

A right of individual or collective self-defense arises authorizing the victims of the aggression to respond with necessary and proportional measures to preclude an imminent attack or to stop an attack already underway. It is this fundamental right of the nation-state and groups of nations to engage in self-help, usually as a matter of last resort when other remedies prove ineffective or unavailable, that provides the basis for lawful intervention into the sanctuary state or stateless area implicit in the right of extraterritorial apprehension.

Customary International Law of Self-Defense. The customary international law right of self-defense not only authorizes a state to respond to an actual attack but also to engage in preemptive actions in anticipation of an imminent attack.[95] A state may undertake such preemptive action, referred to as anticipatory self-defense, whether the aggression directed against it is conventional or unconventional in nature.[96] International law authorizes the use of force in individual national self-defense where a state reasonably apprehends that it will be the object of an attack by some external force or entity. Customary international law recognizes four prerequisites to exercising the right of self-defense: (1) the existence of an imminent threat; (2) a compelling necessity to act in response to an imminent or ongoing threat; (3) the exhaustion of all practical peaceful procedures to avoid the use of force; and (4) that the force employed to counter the threat is proportionate to the threat and does not exceed that which is necessary to repel the aggression.

The principal international law authority cited for the doctrine of self-defense and, in particular, the right to anticipatory self-defense, is the celebrated *Caroline* case.[97] When viewed in a contempoary counterterrorism context, the circumstances in the *Caroline* case seem particularly timely and relevant. The steamer *Caroline* was employed in 1837 to transport personnel and equipment from U.S. territory across the Niagara River to Canadian rebels on "Navy Island" and from there to the mainland of Canada. The U.S. government had not prevented this assistance to the Canadian rebels, who were presumably engaged in various dissident and violent acts directed against the British administration in Canada.

In the contemporary context, it would not be difficult to understand how British authorities might come to view the crew of the *Caroline* as engaging in terrorist activity with the acquiescence, if not support, of the United States. Not only was the United States the flag state for the *Caroline*, but it was also providing sanctuary for the crew and a source of supply for the rebels. There is no indication that the Canadian rebels were engaged in the sort of violence that typifies contemporary terrorism, and to this extent there is no exact analogy to current events. Nevertheless, the case dealt with the issue of state responsibility for the private acts of those under its control in an instance when those acts were directed against another state.

Canadian government troops crossed the Niagara River and entered the territory of the United States. After killing two U.S. nationals, the troops set the *Caroline* adrift, and it was destroyed on Niagara Falls. In the ensuring diplomatic exchange, Great Britain maintained it acted as a matter of justifiable self-defense. The United States did not deny that circumstances might exist that would authorize force in self-defense; however, it denied the facts in this situation justified the resort to force. The diplomatic exchange terminated with the British issuing an apology but without any assumption of legal responsibility for the death of the two U.S. nationals. The absence of any reclama from the U.S. government is broadly interpreted as its tacit acceptance of the permissibility of the British action in self-defense.[98]

Examined in the contemporary counterterrorism context, the British undertook action against private interests freely operating from the United States as a sanctuary state. British action violated U.S. territorial integrity to the extent the Canadian forces entered the state of New York, actively engaged U.S. nationals, and destroyed a U.S. flag vessel. The British action was directed against the privately owned and crewed *Caroline* and not the U.S. government. However, the U.S. government had done nothing to restrain the *Caroline* crew from actions that derogated the British rights to the territorial integrity and political independence of its Canadian colony. International law provided that under these circumstances, the United States had compromised its right to sovereignty, which temporarily yielded to the British right of self-help in the form of individual self-defense.

Self-Defense under the U.N. Charter. The concept that national sovereignty is not absolute in international law and is qualified by an individual and, more recently, a collective, right if self-defense is specifically recognized in the U.N. Charter. Article 51 of the charter provides:

> Nothing in the present Charter shall impair the inherent right of individual or collective self-defense if an armed attack occurs against a Member of the United Nations, until the Secretary Council has taken the measures necessary to maintain international peace and security.[99]

The doctrine of self-defense as recognized in Article 51 qualifies the sovereign rights of nation-states guaranteed in Article 2 of the charter. Article 51 authorizes a nation or group of nations to use force against an aggressor state or states in accordance with the customary international law of self-defense. Implicit in Article 51 is that the use of force in individual or collective self-defense may well affect the aggressor nation's territorial integrity or political independence.

Unfortunately, Article 51 does not eliminate all the ambiguities surrounding the exercise of individual or collective self-defense. It is not clear from this provision whether anticipatory measures are authorized or what may constitute an armed attack justifying a response. A number of publicists, and at times the Security Council itself, have preferred a restrictive reading of Article 51. Advocates of the restrictive view argue that Article 51 is clear and unambiguous on its face and that it does not apply to any form of aggression other than an "armed attack."[100] One such proponent, Kunz, has argued:

> This term means something that *has* taken place. Art. 51 prohibits "preventive war." The "threat of aggression" does not justify self-defense under Art. 51. Now in municipal law self-defense is justified against an actual danger, but it is sufficient that the danger is imminent. The "imminent" armed attack does not suffice under Art. 51.[101]

Advocates of the restrictive view also argue that a single isolated incident may not be sufficient to justify a self-defense response and that it is necessary to look to the totality of a series of armed attacks to confirm that a systematic campaign of aggression exists.[102] Under this restrictive view, sanctuary states engaged in the support of terrorist activities may be able to argue that selective acts originating from their borders do not constitute armed attacks within the meaning of Article 51. These sanctuary states may maintain that they have not committed the requisite armed attack against other states, justifying a defensive response against them.

The advocates of a restrictive interpretation of the right of self-defense might have a persuasive argument but for the repeated failure of the United Nations as an organization to maintain international peace and security through the institutional mechanisms provided for in the charter. With few exceptions, the Security Council as the organ responsible for maintaining peace and security has failed to meet its institutional responsibilities. During the course of Security Council meetings designed to address cases of rising tension or even open warfare between U.N. members, more often than not the body is paralyzed by political disagreement among the five permanent members. If these permanent members fail to reach a consensus, the council is unable to order sanctions or other peacekeeping measures against the aggressor state.

The more persuasive interpretation of self-defense under Article 51 and the one supported by contemporary custom and usage retains the concept of reasonable anticipatory measures and permits action without meeting specific institutional preconditions of the United Nations itself. International law authorities McDougal,

Feliciano, and Mallison, in examining the preparatory work or legislative history of the U.N. Charter the "*travaux preparatoires,*" indicate that the general purposes and demands projected by the parties drafting the agreement strongly favor a broad interpretation of Article 51.[103] Mallison notes:

> The formulation of Article 51 cannot be rationally construed as both preserving the "inherent" right of self-defense and simultaneously eliminating those central elements of it involving anticipatory self-defense. Since the basic community policy in maintaining at least minimum world public order is made possible by including reasonable anticipatory defense within the "inherent" right, this seems the better interpretation on policy grounds as well as consistency with the preparatory work.[104]

Consistent with this analysis, it is axiomatic in international law that treaties and other international agreements limit the rights of parties only to the extent that the parties have explicitly agreed. Since the U.N. Charter nowhere expressly prohibits anticipatory self-defense but instead provides in Article 51 that it shall not impair the inherent right of self-defense, a broad interpretation of the language is by far the more persuasive.

Under this broad interpretation, a state is fully entitled to undertake counterterrorism measures against a state that bears responsibility for the acts of terrorism staged within or from its borders. The state subject to the armed terrorist attacks is not obligated first to seek peaceful resolution if it reasonably apprehends that preemptive measures are necessary.[105] However, consistent with the customary law of self-defense, if alternative means are reasonably available to address the threat and circumstances permit pursuing such means, the threatened state is required to invoke the less coercive measures. Whether preemptive measures are authorized is a question of necessity, the imminent nature of the threat, and the means available and required to address it.

Self-Defense as a Basis for Intervention. In the actual application of extraterritorial apprehension, prosecutors would first obtain a sealed indictment from a federal grand jury or a warrant of arrest from a U.S. magistrate. Prosecutors would introduce sufficient evidence to establish probable cause that a crime had been committed and that the identified defendant terrorist or terrorists had committed the crime. Having met these threshold requirements, actual in personam jurisdiction over the indicted terrorist would have to be achieved through some lawful means of intervening in the stateless area or sanctuary state.

The sanctuary state would have to be shown to be directly or vicariously liable for the past actions of the terrorist or the terrorist's organization. In the case of a stateless area, where the existence of sovereign rights may be in question, the entire issue of establishing a right to intervene may be less important. Having established the direct or vicarious liability for terrorist activities of the sanctuary state and possibly that of whatever regime may purport to be the constituted legal government for the stateless area, the right of self-defense may be exercised as against the sanctuary state or stateless area itself. The threatening terrorist activities within the sanctuary state or stateless area give rise to the right of self-help and the right to intervene through the exercise of self-defense under international law.

Extraterritorial apprehension founded upon a right of individual or collective self-defense should satisfy the four customary international law requirements for application of the doctrine. Evidence of past terrorist conduct and present capability to strike will normally satisfy the first two requirements to demonstrate that the apprehending state has a compelling need to act and in response to an imminent or ongoing threat. However, an apprehending state may not be able to satisfy these requirements if the indicted terrorist has clearly ceased his or her activities for a sustained period of time or redirected actions against other states.

In fulfilling the third customary law requirement that the endangered state exhaust all practical peaceful procedures, the apprehending state will have to be able to demonstrate that extradition or other less formal means of rendition are unavailable or useless under the circumstances. Actively meeting this requirement will serve as a useful check against misapplication of extraterritorial apprehension to states that are actively cooperating in either bilateral or multilateral extradition treaties or conventions.

The fourth and all-important requirement of self-defense is that the endangered state demonstrate that its response is proportional to the threat. Just as legal scholars have debated the scope of Article 51 with regard to anticipatory self-defense, they disagree over whether proportionality should be based upon only the immediate threat facing the endangered state or whether such state may consider an "aggregation" of past illegal acts or events.[106] As noted by Gregory F. Intoccia in his evaluation of U.S. counterterrorism strategy, "Disagreement exists over whether the legality of a response is to be determined by reference to the prior illegal act which brought it about, or whether the legality of the response is to be determined by reference to the whole context of the relationship between involved parties."[107] Intoccia notes that the Security Council has formally condemned as an illegal reprisal any attempt to justify the totality of violence based upon an accumulation of events.[108]

Experience and recent statements by senior U.S. government officials indicate that individual self-defense as recognized in Article 51 of the charter will generally serve as the basis for U.S. counterterrorism measures involving the use of force.[109] The requirement that such force meets the criterion of proportionality is particularly important if the United States is to avoid strident criticism from the international community. What makes extraterritorial apprehension a particularly attractive option when compared with other proactive measures is the relative ease with which the proportionality criterion is met.

Extraterritorial apprehension generally need not turn on an aggregation of past illegal acts or events. Instead it will often result from and be based upon one or more specific acts of terrorism. These acts will form the basis for the indictment or warrant of arrest. Whether preemptive self-defense is justified will be related to the continuing proclivities and capabilities of the terrorist or terrorist elite element to be apprehended.

Recent U.S. proactive counterterrorism measures have been based upon the right of self-defense. In his April 14, 1986, address to the nation announcing that "air and naval forces of the United States launched a series of strikes against the headquarters, terrorist facilities and military assets that support Muammar Qaddafi's subversive activities,"[110] President Reagan explicitly cited the right of self-defense in justifying U.S. actions:

> When our citizens are abused or attacked anywhere in the world on the direct orders of a hostile regime, we will respond so long as I'm in this Oval Office. Self-defense is not only our right, it is our duty. It is the purpose behind the mission undertaken tonight, a mission fully consistent with Article 51 of the United Nations Charter. We believe that this preemptive action against his terrorist installations will not only diminish Col. Khadafy's capacity to export terror, it will provide him incentives and reasons to alter his criminal behavior.[111]

In the aftermath of the air strikes, the Qaddafi regime and its supporters charged that the U.S. military action was indiscriminate, resulted in unnecessary loss of civilian lives and property, and was itself an "act of state terrorism." The U.S. case in support of its action was generally considered persuasive by Western allied leaders who were made privy to classified intelligence reports linking the Qaddafi regime to the La Belle Disco bombing as well as planned future attacks. Nevertheless, following the relatively precise air strikes in Libya, adversaries of the United States argued that various preconditions for the exercise of the right of self-defense had not been met and that therefore the action violated international law.

Extraterritorial apprehension would certainly have far more focused objectives than direct military strikes of the type conducted in April 1986. Its application would invariably be more selective. Presumably there would be little debate as to whether the apprehension was proportional to the threat, assuming the use of minimum military force in conjunction with the apprehension. The self-defense doctrinal requirement of proportionality would permit the use of sufficient force in conjunction with the apprehension to suppress terrorist and sanctuary state or stateless area forces that interfere with the operation.

Depending upon the location of the targeted terrorist leadership or operational elite and prevailing circumstances in the sanctuary state or stateless area, occasions may arise that require overt military action to suppress such resistance using naval, air, or ground forces. However, in the majority of cases, the initial phases of the extraordinary apprehension will be best achieved by the covert insertion by specially trained forces that conduct the seizure without the knowledge of either the sanctuary state or local terrorist elements. A well-planned extraterritorial apprehension mission should be able to meet the proportionality requirement of the customary international law of self-defense. Moreover, although not part of the proportionality requirement of self-defense, extraterritorial apprehension is far more likley than other proactive coercive measures to be selective, minimizing collateral injury and damages sustained by innocent persons.

Application of the International Law of Human Rights

Expanding International Law of Human Rights. *United States v. Reed*[112] touched on the issue of human rights with the defendant arguing that his "abduction" by CIA agents breached the U.S. commitment to the expanding body of international law. The court deflected the argument by noting it saw no repeated pattern of abuse by the government. The *Reed* decision leaves open the issue of whether irregular renditions of any sort might be impermissible under this branch of international law and, by its incorporation into U.S. municipal law, a basis for divestiture of criminal court jurisdiction.

A number of commentators have argued that notwithstanding the *Ker-Frisbie* doctrine's perspective that constitutional due process is not violated by such seizures and that only states have standing to complain of violations of their sovereignty, the defendant's fundamental human rights as now recognized by international law are violated. Since international law is incorporated into the U.S. municipal law, these commentators maintain that any violation of the apprehended defendant's human rights resulting from irregular rendition is absolute grounds for a U.S. municipal court's divesting itself of jurisdicton.[113]

The expanding international law of human rights has received the full public support of the U.S. government and its principal Western allies. Although this body of law has historical antecedents predating the nineteenth century, its nucleus emerged with the adoption of the U.N. Charter in 1945[114] and the Universal Declaration of Human Rights adopted in 1948.[115] The charter declares that one of its purposes is to promote and encourage respect for human rights and fundamental freedoms for all.[116] Article 55(c) states that "the United Nations shall promote . . . universal respect for, and observance of, human rights and fundamental freedoms for all without distinction as to race, sex, language or religion." Article 56 mandates "all Members [to] pledge themselves to take joint and separate action in cooperation with the Organization for the achievement of the purposes set forth in Article 55."[117]

Over more than forty years, these provisions have been enshrined, reinforced, and expanded upon in a variety of international human rights conventions (including the International Covenant on Civil and Political Rights[118] and the American Declaration on the Rights and Duties of Man),[119] as well as General Assembly resolutions. These conventions and resolutions have increasingly given juridical content to the charter and the 1948 declaration commitment to the more fundamental of these rights.[120] The International Court of Justice expressly established the existence of human rights as universally recognized legal obligations in its 1971 Advisory Opinion on Namibia (Southwest Africa).[121] Judge Fuad Ammoun of the International Court of Justice in his separate opinion on the case observed that although the affirmations of the Declaration (Universal Declaration of Human Rights) are not binding *qua* international convention . . . they can bind States on the basis of custom . . . , whether because they constituted a codification of customary law . . . , or because they have acquired the force of custom through a general practice accepted as law.[122]

Under President Carter's administration, international human rights became a centerpiece of U.S. foreign policy.[123] One of many congressional declarations in support of this increasingly more important element in U.S. foreign policy was adopted in section 502B as a 1976 amendment to the Foreign Assistance Act of 1961 and provides:

(a) (1) It is the policy of the United States, in accordance with its international obligations as set forth in the Charter of the United Nations and in keeping with the constitutional heritage and traditions of the United States, to promote and encourage increased respect for human rights and fundamental freedoms for all without distinction as to race, sex, language, or religion. To this end, a principal goal of the foreign policy of the United States is to promote the increased observance of internationally recognized human rights by all countries.[124]

Although the Reagan administration redirected the focus of U.S. foreign policy to the problem of international terrorism, it did so without disavowing the U.S. commitment to human rights. In fact, many early Reagan administration statements concerning the redirected focus of U.S. foreign policy in the 1980s addressed international terrorism as fundamentally inconsistent with the expanding commitment to universally recognized human rights.

Application of Human Rights to Extraterritorial Apprehension

Unlike the more traditional international law, the new international law of human rights creates enforceable rights in the individual and not the sovereign. Whether these rights are derived from customary international law or through multilateral convention, advocates argue with increasing authority that the rights apply to all persons, irrespective of their nationality.[125] Under the developing doctrine, the state can no longer waive fundamental human rights without in most instances disregarding its international obligations. Some states have been slow to sign or ratify the conventions. Other states may refuse the concept of human rights altogether as provided for in the conventions and even refuse to acknowledge the existence of a growing customary international law of human rights as essentially codified in the U.N. Charter and 1948 Declaration of Human Rights. Nevertheless, the relatively aggressive U.S. affirmation of human rights in its legislation and through its executive branch declarations over the past ten years virtually precludes it from seriously denying their application within U.S. municipal law.

Publicists maintaining that the new human rights doctrine is a challenge to irregular rendition note that *Ker* and a number of subsequent decisions denied the defendant the right to raise violations of sovereign treaty obligations. Several of the *Ker-Frisbie* line of decisions reasoned that only states may object to apparent violations of their sovereignty brought about by unauthorized foreign state seizures within their borders. In the absence of a protest from the asylum state, the courts have been prepared to assume acquiescence or implied consent to the seizure. But today, under the new international law of human rights, this line of reasoning may no longer be available to the well-informed court.[126]

U.S. courts considering cases of extraterritorial apprehension will be asked whether the government action comports with human rights guarantees under both the U.S. Constitution and international law. Judicial review of the international human rights issue in irregular rendition cases is probably overdue. However, just as it will be necessary for courts hearing a terrorist prosecution case brought by extraterritorial apprehension to balance the rights of all interested state participants in interpreting the international law as it applies to sovereign rights and issues of self-help, so also will it be crucial to balance the human rights of all interested persons. The application of international human rights to the issue of extraterritorial apprehension will result in an excessively narrow and erroneous interpretation of international law if it examines the rights of only the international terrorist defendant without also considering the rights of the nations, institutions, and, in particular, persons victimized by the acts of terror.

The apprehended international terrorist will see it in his or her interest to assert various human rights that appear to have received essentially universal recognition under international law. Using the Universal Declaration of Human Rights[127] as persuasive authority for, if not an actual codification of, customary international law, the apprehended terrorist may allege the seizure constitutes a violation of several provisions. The terrorist may assert that the seizure violates Article 3, which provides that "everyone has the right to life, liberty and the security of person."[128] There may be a claim that the irregular rendition violates the Article 9 guarantee: "No one shall be subjected to arbitrary arrest, detention or exile."[129] He or she might maintain a derogation of rights under Article 12, which states: "No one shall be subjected to arbitrary interference with his privacy, family, home or correspondence, nor to attacks upon his honor and reputation. Everyone has the right to the protection of the law against such interference or attacks."[130]

In taking note of the availability of these rights for the benefit of apprehended terrorists, it is important to understand that by definition, human rights have a universal application. They are not limited to any one class or category or individual. Whether based upon the Universal Declaration of Human Rights as a codification or authoritative statement of customary international law or some specific multilateral convention, these rights apply to all persons, regardless of nationality and status. Moreover, in applying these rights, it must be understood that they do not exist in the absence of corresponding obligations imposed on states and other persons. The rights and obligations of the state and the persons within society must be balanced through judicial and administrative processes. Human rights cannot exist in a lawless, violence-ridden environment of the type promoted by international terrorism.

As important as the doctrine of human rights may be to the political-legal system and society as a whole, it provides particularly important guarantees to the direct victims of terrorist violence. Article 3 of the Universal Declaration of Human Rights specifically states that "everyone has the right to life, liberty and the security of person."[131] Article 8 of the declaration provides that "everyone has the right to an effective remedy by the competent national tribunals for acts violating the fundamental rights granted him by the constitution or by law."[132] Article 5 further provides, "No one shall be subjected to torture or to cruel, inhuman or degrading treatment or punishment."[133] Any professionally competent and reasonable court of law addressing issues of fundamental human rights during the prosecution of an apprehended terrorist would be constrained to balance the defendant's rights against those of the community at large and the individual victims in particular.

Extraterritorial apprehension initiated by a probable cause finding by either a U.S. grand jury or federal magistrate and justified upon reliable facts as an appropriate self-help measure of self-defense is not ipso facto illegal or arbitrary. Conducted pursuant to reasonable guidelines with the objective of providing the terrorist defendant a fair trial before a court of competent jurisdiction, extraterritorial apprehension may do much to serve the international community's interest in the advancement of human rights. A counterterrorism measure of this type affirmatively addresses the continuing derogation of human rights perpetrated by the terrorists on their innocent victims. Moreover, it does so at less human cost than might otherwise result from the application of more coercive proactive enforcement measures.

Considerations Prior to Apprehension

The decision as to whether to adopt extraterritorial apprehension as a counterterrorism measure will also depend on an understanding of a number of key issues arising before and after the actual apprehension occurs. In this and the following section, a set of political, operational, and ancillary legal issues will be examined for their possible impact on this counterterrorism measure and its implementation. This section examines issues that would have their principal impact prior to the actual apprehension of the terrorist. Accordingly, these are considerations that would have to be taken into account early in the process of deciding whether to adopt such a counterterrorism measure. If the measure is to be adopted, these considerations would also have to be weighed closely throughout the planning process.

Case Formulation

Should the president adopt extraterritorial apprehension as a proactive counterterrorism measure, it will be essential that planning and development proceed on a broad interagency basis. Whereas counterterrorism strategies and measures developed to date may have involved more than one department or agency of the U.S. government, few have encompassed the range of functions, expertise, and support that will be required to achieve a program of aggressive criminal prosecution through the exercise of the right of extraterritorial apprehension.

Early planning and implementation of extraterritorial apprehension will require the cooperative efforts of the Department of Justice and various agencies within the U.S. intelligence community and the Department of State, which is the lead agency on international terrorism policy and international law. Although the Department of Justice has criminal and counterintelligence collection capabilities in direct support of its normal law enforcement mission, information on international terrorist elites is more likely to originate from sources and methods not under the direction of the department and the FBI. Criminal prosecutors working directly for the Department of Justice or the various U.S. attorneys' offices throughout the country are charged with the immediate responsibility of applying available intelligence and investigatory evidence to construct criminal cases against terrorists suspected of having violated federal criminal law.[134]

The Department of Justice has had considerable experience in prosecuting cases of so-called domestic terrorism occurring within the United States. With the adoption of the 1984 Comprehensive Crime Control Act[135] and the increased interest in applying other federal criminal law with extraterritorial reach to terrorists located beyond U.S. borders, the Department of Justice has begun to use its law enforcement capability aggressively against international terrorism. A number of the department's U.S. attorneys are engaged in a concerted effort to reach and prosecute international terrorists located beyond U.S. borders, particularly where the acts of terrorism have been directed against the United States and its nationals. The procedures applied in criminal cases recently developed against in criminal cases recently developed against international terrorists could well be employed in connection with extraterritorial apprehension. The appropriate U.S. attorney's office in conjunction with the Department of Justice reviews available intelligence and investigatory evidence to ascertain whether sufficient admissible, relevant, and credible evidence exists on every element of one or more criminal counts. If prosecutors determine that the evidence is sufficient to support a minimally sufficient legal case, the prima facie case, the U.S. attorney or his or her designated assistant seeks a criminal indictment or arrest warrant against the suspect international terrorist.

The Fifth Amendment to the U.S. Constitution provides that "no person shall be held to answer for a capital or other infamous crime unless on a presentment or indictment of a Grand Jury."[136] The actual exercise of this right is accomplished in the federal criminal justice system by an assistant U.S. attorney presenting evidence regarding one or more crimes to a grand jury of from twelve to twenty-three persons. Grand juries are empaneled, supervised, and instructed by a U.S. district court judge. They can, and frequently do, operate in secret and may be instructed by the supervising district court to maintain strict confidence regarding all proceedings, witnesses, and actions taken. If twelve or more members find that the evidence presented by the federal prosecutor constitutes probable cause to believe that a crime has been committed and that the named suspect committed the crime, they vote to indict. If the grand jury believes the evidence does not support a single count, they vote a "no true bill."

If the offense to be charged is a misdemeanor, the federal prosecutor may seek to have a U.S. magistrate issue an information. U.S. magistrates are also authorized to issue warrants of arrest for misdemeanors and felonies. In either case, the U.S. magistrate, like the grand jury, is required to find probable cause as a basis for his or her actions. Some or all of these procedural actions may be held in confidence by the district court or its magistrates, ordering proceedings and documents sealed under court order.

These standard preliminary procedures have been applied in various combinations in several efforts to prosecute international terrorists under U.S. federal law. In most, if not all, of these cases, U.S. prosecutors have sought sealed indictments or arrest warrants to avoid alerting terrorist suspects in advance and to preclude release of sensitive information. In response to the October 1985 hijacking of the Italian flag cruise ship *Achille Lauro* and murder of Leon Klinghoffer, the U.S. attorney for the District of Columbia acted with extraordinary speed to formulate a case sufficient to support a request to Italian authorities for the provisional arrest of alleged mastermind Mohammed Abul Abbas Zaiden and his Palestine Liberation Front (PLF) accomplices.[137]

On October 11, 1985, an assistant U.S. attorney for the District of Columbia presented a U.S. magistrate with sufficient evidence to establish probable cause that a warrant should be issued for the arrest of Abbas and charging him with a violation of 18 U.S.C. 1203, hostage taking, as well as piracy and conspiracy to commit both offenses.[138] Unfortunately, the Italian government took the position that the U.S. evidence concerning Abbas and a second PLF representative was insufficient to support a request for provisional arrest pending their extradition under the International Convention against the Taking of Hostages.[139]

Most significant about the *Achille Lauro* case is the manner in which the terrorists were actually apprehended and the extraordinarily effective interagency coordination achieved within the U.S. government in a matter of hours. Overall coordination and direction of the U.S. reaction was the responsibility of the National Security Council (NSC) staff. However, individual departments not accustomed to routinely working with one another were suddenly thrust into executing a complex counterterrorism law enforcement action. The Department of Justice and the U.S. attorney for the District of Columbia formulated at least a preliminary theory of prosecution and marshaled sufficient evidence to make a showing of probable cause to a U.S. magistrate. Political and diplomatic considerations, particularly those involving the Italian government, were addressed by the Department of State. Necessary intelligence collection and the actions to intercept, divert, and escort the Egyptair Boeing 737 with the six PLF terrorists embarked to Sigonella Naval Base in Sicily using U.S. Navy F-14s were clearly the responsibility of the Department of Defense, the Joint Chiefs of Staff, and subordinate operational commanders.[140]

As the opportunity arose to apprehend the hijackers, cognizant officials from each of these principal departments coordinated personally with members of the NSC staff and one another to ensure that all necessary technical experience and expertise were brought to bear on the problem. Although it was Italian authorities who ultimately secured in personam jurisdiction over the four hijackers, the U.S. government demonstrated an impressive capacity to plan and execute a complex counterterrorism law enforcement operation with little or no prior warning. It is particularly worth noting that notwithstanding the coerced diversion of the Egyptair 737 over international waters, the Italian court has shown no inclination to divest itself of jurisdiction due to concerns with "irregular rendition."[141]

The Department of Justice has also sought and obtained arrest warrants for three men believed to have originally hijacked TWA flight 847 in June 1985.[142] Other cases reportedly under investigation and development by the Department of Justice relate to the abduction of six Americans missing in Beirut, the infamous Abu Nidal terrorists allegedly responsible for the December 1985 Rome and Vienna airport massacres, and terrorists suspected of perpetrating the bombings in 1983 of the U.S. embassies in Beirut and Kuwait, as well as of the marine garrison at Beirut International Airport.[143] The details of Department of Justice efforts on these and other cases remain classified; any indictments or warrants are sealed. But it appears that the process of case formulation, investigation, location of the criminal defendants, and an evelution of extradition opportunities is well underway. What remains is to find a means of securing jurisdiction over a named defendant in those instances where extradition is not available.

Congressional Role

The separation of powers provided for in the U.S. Constitution encourages competition and even conflict among the branches of government. The potential for competition and conflict is often the greatest in twilight zones where the Constitution is vague or even silent as to which branch has primary responsibility for a particular function. The problems associated with developing an effective counterterrorism policy and strategy often arise within such twilight zones. What must be remembered in analyzing counterterrorism policy and strategy in general, and perhaps extraterritorial apprehension as a measure in particular, is that substantial interests as well as authority exist in all branches of government. The better the interests, responsibilities, and authority of the branches are understood, the better will be the policy and strategy produced and administered by them.

Congressional interests, responsibilities, and authority as related to counterterrorism are largely a function of the powers provided in Article 1, Section 8 of the Constitution. Among the other enumerated powers, the Congress is charged:

10. To define and punish piracies and felonies committed on the high seas, and offenses against the law of nations.

11. To declare war, grant letters of marque and reprisal, and make rules concerning captures on land and water.

12. To raise and support armies. . . .

13. To provide and maintain a navy.

14. To make rules for the government and regulation of the land and naval forces. . . .

18. To make all laws which shall be necessary and proper for carrying into execution the foregoing powers and all other powers vested by this constitution in the Government of the United States, or any department or officer thereof.[144]

These and other powers of the Congress provide it an important role in the development, if not planning and execution, of extraterritorial apprehension as a counterterrorism measure. It is the Congress that possesses the power to declare crimes under its clause 10 mandate to define the specified offenses. The enumerated provisions related to the raising and regulation of the U.S. armed forces also require a level of congressional oversight. Its power to declare war and "make rules concerning captures on land and water" may be a curiously relevant, if obtuse, reference to concepts such as extraterritorial apprehension. Powers such as these coupled with the exclusive congressional powers of authorization and appropriation of revenue make it a key participant in counterterrorism policy and strategy development.

To understand the precise role of the Congress in the immediate case, it is necessary to inquire as to the means the legislative branch has used to regulate and monitor the actions of the executive branch. Strategy planners must ask whether it is necessary to seek congressional authorization to engage in extraterritorial apprehension. Does a requirement exist to consult with or notify the Congress if military forces are to be used in an extraterritorial apprehension? Even if military forces are not employed, are there other requirements imposing a duty to consult or notify the Congress either before or after the apprehension? If so, with whom and when should the notification or consultation occur? What are the political and operational costs and benefits to various methods of communication or other relationships between the branches? These and other issues must be addressed in developing any counterterrorism strategy option and may be particularly important in the case of extraterritorial apprehension.

War Powers Resolution

In the event that an extraterritorial apprehension is conducted using U.S. military forces, whether in a direct or major supporting role, the operation may be subject to the War Powers Resolution.[145] The War Powers Resolution (WPR), adopted over the vigorous opposition and veto of President Nixon, became law in 1973 with the expressed purpose "to fulfill the intent of the framers of the Constitution of the United States and insure that the collective judgment of both Congress and the President will apply to the introduction of United States Armed Forces into hostilities."[146] Key provisions of the WPR that may apply to extraterritorial apprehension are contained in sections 2 through 4 of the resolution.

Section 2 ("Purpose and Policy") provides that the president can "introduce the United States Armed Forces into hostilities or into situations where imminent involvement in hostilities is clearly indicated by the circumstances:" [147] (1) following a declaration of war; (2) pursuant to specific statutory authorization; or (3) in a national emergency caused by an attack on American territory or armed forces. While this section provides a congressional definition of the limits of executive war powers effectively advising the president of the political risks of ignoring the resolution, it is probably little more than what Senator Thomas Eagleton (D–Missouri) once described as a "pious pronouncement of nothing."[148]

Section 3 ("Consultation") and section 4 ("Reporting") establish the procedures the president must follow whenever U.S. armed forces engage in nonroutine activties, ranging from involvement in hostilities to a significant buildup of forces in a foreign country. Section 3 provides that the president "in every possible instance consult with Congress before introducing United States Armed Forces into hostilities or into situations where imminent involvement in hostilities is clearly indicated by the circumstances."[149] Section 4 requires the president to report to Congress whenever the armed forces are introduced into hostilities, introduced into the territory of a foreign nation while equipped for combat, or significantly built up in a foreign nation.[150] Under this provision, the president is to report on the circumstances that require the action, the estimated scope and duration of the action, and his authority for ordering the action (for example, statute, resolution, the president's inherent authority as commander in chief under the Constitution, or some other authority).

Legal interpretations of each of these sections vary widely. Proponents of limiting the president's war-making powers argue that the executive may introduce U.S. armed forces only pursuant to congressional action or a national emergency narrowly defined as a direct attack upon the United States, its territories, possessions, or armed forces. These proponents further tend to emphasize the president's obligation to consult in every possible instance before the introduction of armed forces.

Advocates of broad executive power in foreign and military affairs maintain that the president retains substantial constitutional authority as commander in chief. These advocates disagree with the proponents of limited executive power on the issue of the constitutionality of the resolution and precisely what sorts of military actions should give rise to its being invoked. There is also disagreement over what constitutes "consultation"—merely informing or something more akin to seeking consent. Still further controversy arises over the issue of when, in the military planning and execution process, consultation should occur. Moreover, since the resolution is silent on the details of the consultation, no one is certain as to precisely who in the Congress is to be consulted.

At first glance, sections 2 through 4 might appear to have automatic application to any introduction of U.S. armed forces into situations where imminent involvement in hostilities is indicated. This might often be the case if military forces were to be used in conducting an extraterritorial apprehension in a sanctuary state or even a stateless area like Lebanon where heavily armed militias are present. However, proponents of broad executive discretion argue that "in every possible instance" implies that there may be instances in which it is not possible to consult before ordering the introduction of forces.[151]

Section 4 requiring the president to report whenever he introduces U.S. forces "into hostilities" or "into situations where imminent involvement in hostilities is clearly indicated by the circumstances; into the territory, airspace or waters of a foreign nation, while equipped for combat" was not drafted with counterterrorism operations in mind. The legislative history of this and other provisions of the WPR indicates the resolution was intended to address the problem of conventional or even substantial nonconventional intervention, which has characterized the post–World War II and Vietnam experiences. The concept of a precise use of military forces to facilitate a counterterrorism law enforcement objective was not contemplated by Congress when it adopted the WPR.

Since the legislative history does not contemplate proactive counterterrorist actions, a strong argument exists that the WPR has little, if any, application in instances where military forces may be used to conduct or support an extraterritorial apprehension of international terrorists. It may be argued that the major objective of extraterritorial apprehension would be to avoid broader-scale hostilities between the United States and the sanctuary state that could result if the targeted leadership or operational elites of the terrorist organizations were not apprehended. In other words, such preemptive action by the executive would actually work toward the reduction of tensions and serve to reduce the possibility of having to introduce U.S. armed forces in a conventional or major unconventional warfare role. As for the requirement that the president consult before forces are introduced, the executive could maintain, as has occurred in other military operations, that the constraints of time and secrecy coupled with difficulties in arranging extensive consultations with enough key members of Congress militate against anything but the most limited dialogue.[152]

In practice, the resolution has been invoked and applied in a number of different manners depending upon the circumstances and prevailing attitude within the particular administration toward the Congress. President Ford reported that he had ordered U.S. military forces to rescue the crew and retake the *Mayaguez* after it had been seized in the Gulf of Thailand by Cambodians in 1975. His report cited section 4(a)(1) of the resolution covering the introduction of forces into hostilities but gave as authority for his actions the power of the executive and the authority of the president as commander in chief.[153] President Carter reported on the Iranian hostage rescue operation on April 26, 1980, two days after the unsuccessful attempt had been mounted. Carter's action could clearly be construed as a counterterrorism measure aimed at Iranian state-supported terror. The president stated in his report to the Congress that the operation was ordered and conducted under the president's constitutional powers as chief executive and commander in chief of the U.S armed forces, expressly recognized in section 8(d)(1) of the WPR.[154]

More recently, at about 4 P.M. on the afternoon of April 14, 1986, within approximately three hours of U.S. warplanes reaching their targets, President Reagan consulted with key congressional leaders regarding his planned preemptive action against terrorist infrastructure and supporting military installations in Libya.[155] On this occasion, the White House indicated that while there was little time between the consultation and the initiation of the strikes, the warplanes could have been called back if strenuous opposition had been voiced by those members he consulted.[156] The pattern that seems to have evolved since 1973 suggests an executive branch policy of avoiding confrontation with the Congress but making no specific concession as to the applicability or even the overall constitutionality of the resolution.[157] It seems likely that this general policy will continue and may very well have an impact on whether and how there is to be WPR consultation in the case of an extraterritorial apprehension that employs U.S. armed forces.

In the event U.S. armed forces are used to conduct or otherwise support extraterritorial apprehension, there may be strong congressional pressure to apply the resolution. Although the resolution is silent on who is to be consulted within the Congress and when, past practice seems to suggest that the executive is not required to consult well in advance or with more than a limited number of members. If the Iranian hostage rescue mission is an appropriate precedent for highly sensitive proactive counterterrorism measures, it may be acceptable to consult after the fact. But to avoid consultation altogether where U.S. armed forces are engaged in even a limited armed intervention of a sanctuary state or stateless area where resistance may be expected will raise serious political, if not legal, challenges to the executive's action.

It may well be that the executive could prevail in a legal challenge as to the constitutionality or intentional nonapplication of the WPR. Nothing in the legislative history or on the face of the resolution itself requires consultation when deploying the U.S armed forces in support of a proactive counterterrorism measure, particularly one in which enforcement is the principal objective. However, the broader issue at stake is developing and maintaining an essential spirit of mutual support and cooperation between the legislative and executive branches of government.

Despite the difficulties related to its application, the experience since 1973 demonstrates that the executive benefits from widespread congressional support that usually results from legislative involvement either before or concurrent with the commitment of the U.S. armed forces. Although the argument may be made that the resolution need not apply to the use of U.S. armed forces in the case of limited counterterrorism measures, the executive should carefully weigh the overall consitutional, if not political, interests, responsibilities, and authority of the Congress before choosing to ignore it. Overall it would seem the political benefits that would stem from a partnership between the branches in this area strongly militate in favor of a dialogue of some type, whether by means of the WPR or some other vehicle.

Intelligence Oversight

With respect to covert actions by the U.S. government, the Congress has sought to legislate its relationship with the executive through the adoption of the Intelligence Oversight Act of 1980[158] and various related provisions in the intelligence authorization acts adopted for particular fiscal years.[159] The Intelligence Oversight Act of 1980 was adopted as part of the Intelligence Authorization Act for Fiscal Year 1981 and was codified as Title V of the National Security Act of 1947.[160] The 1980 act requires that the director of central intelligence (DCI), as well as heads of departments, agencies, and other entities in the U.S. government involved in intelligence activities, keep the Select Committee on Intelligence of the Senate and Permanent Select Committee on Intelligence of the House of Representatives "fully and currently informed of all intelligence activities," including "any significant anticipated intelligence activity." The latter term is specifically defined by way of an amendment to the Hughes-Ryan amendment[161] to include all CIA covert action operations. Prior to 1980, the law required that eight separate committees of the Congress be notified of such operations.[162]

Section 412(a)(1) of the act provides that the provision to inform of all intelligence activities shall not require the president to seek approval of the committees prior to initiation of any anticipated intelligence activity, if the president determines it is essential to limit prior notice to meet extraordinary circumstances affecting vital interests of the United States. When such a presidential determination is made, notice of the significant anticipated intelligence activity is to be limited to the chairman and ranking minority members of the intelligence committees, the Speaker and the minority leader of the House of Representatives, and the majority and minority leaders of the Senate.[163]

The 1980 act also contains provisions that protect the executive's discretion with regard to intelligence operations. The initial proviso to section 413(a) provides that the reporting obligations in this subsection exist only

> to the extent consistent with all applicable authorities and duties, including those conferred by the Constitution upon the executive and legislative branches of the Government, and to the extent consistent with due regard for the protection from unauthorized disclosure of classified information related to intelligence sources and methods.[164]

Under this provision, the executive has some basis for withholding information from the Congress entirely, when to do so is within his constitutional powers or disclosure to the Congress would unacceptably increase the risks of unauthorized disclosure. But there are definite limits on the executive's discretion to withhold information. Section 413(e) of the act contains a clear limitation in its proviso on legislative construction:

> Nothing in this chapter shall be construed as authority to withhold information from the intelligence committees on the grounds that providing the information to the intelligence committees would constitute the unauthorized disclosure of classified information or information relating to intelligence sources or methods.[165]

Notwithstanding this limitation on executive discretion, the preambular language of section 413(a) is still regarded as a solid basis for the executive to withhold prior notice of a covert action from the Congress. This interpretation is supported by section 413(b) of the act, which expressly authorizes the president to inform the intelligence committees in a timely fashion of covert actions for which prior notice was not given. In such instance, section 413(b) requires the president to provide a statement of the reasons for not providing such notice.[166]

Even with the Intelligence Oversight Act and other provisions of the law contained in the annual intelligence authorization acts, various ambiguities continue to exist regarding the relative responsibilities of the legislative and executive branches in the area of covert operations. The president's substantial national security and foreign affairs powers arise from his Article II constitutional grant of authority as national commander in chief and as the executive officer charged with making of treaties and providing for the appointment of ambassadors. The Supreme Court in *United States v. Nixon*[167] and *United States v. Reynolds*[168] specifically recognized that the president's substantial constitutional authority was broad enough to permit withholding certain limited categories of sensitive information from the Congress.

The Congress can just as legitimately cite its various Article I powers as a basis for its maintaining a reasonable level of oversight over the covert activities of the intelligence agencies. While the executive may resist or attempt to constrain congressional efforts to force consultation or some form of notification of significant covert actions, the realities of shared government power and legislative control over appropriations argue strongly for the development of a partnership between the branches if policy and strategy are to be effectively developed and carried out.

A number of potential issues arise in attempting to apply the Intelligence Oversight Act of 1980 to extraterritorial apprehension. If the CIA is designated to participate actively in an extraterritorial apprehension, the Hughes-Ryan amendment[169] will require that the president find that such an operation is important to the national security of the United States.[170] Once the president so determines and authorizes CIA involvement beyond a mere intelligence-gathering role, he is mandated under Hughes-Ryan to treat the involvement as a "significant anticipated intelligence activity" for purposes of section 413 or Title 50. The activity must then be reported under the Intelligence Oversight Act, unless the executive maintains his constitutional prerogative to withhold notice from the Congress. In the event the executive elects to withhold notice, he will have to provide the required statement describing the authority under which he does so or be prepared to face political and legal challenges if the activity is discovered by the Congress. It is likely that CIA involvement in an extraterritorial apprehension would eventually become public.

It is doubtful the congressional intelligence committees would long accept an executive plan in which they receive notice of extraterritorial apprehension after the fact. If troublesome political controversy arises over the extraterritorial apprehension as a result of congressional irritation with ex post facto reporting, an unnecessary constraint would be placed on the future application of the measure by executive branch decision makers wishing to avoid unnecessary conflict with the Congress.[171]

Considerable disagreement may also arise regarding what constitutes reportable "intelligence activities" or "intelligence operations in foreign countries" under the act. Is an extraterritorial apprehension in a stateless area or a sanctuary state an intelligence activity? Is it an intelligence activity in a foreign country when the apprehension is conducted in a stateless area? Could the executive argue that if no intelligence operatives are involved and if the mission is clearly in support of the law enforcement functions of the government, it does not fall under the Intelligence Oversight Act reporting requirements? There is no indication in the legislative history that the Congress contemplated proactive counterterrorism measures in establishing the intelligence oversight system. Certainly extraterritorial apprehension was not considered when Congress established the oversight procedures for the intelligence agencies. Neither the act itself not its legislative history provides clear answers to the many questions surrounding application of the Intelligence Oversight Act to counterterrorism measures like extraterritorial apprehension.

There is also the issue of whether, and under what circumstances, special warfare or other unique unconventional military operations become reportable under the Intelligence Oversight Act. Although Hughes-Ryan appears to require automatic notification of most operations in which the CIA has an active role, no such requirement is legislatively imposed on other departments or agencies. An important consideration in developing and planning a counterterrorism measure that could be construed as an intelligence activity or intelligence operation and may be carried out by a department or agency other than the CIA is whether the Congress may elect to expand its oversight authority to activities not previously subject to its review.[172] Congressional action to legislate oversight over departments and activities not previously subject to legislative monitoring could represent a significant political cost for the executive branch. The mere possibility of incurring such a cost militates in favor of the executive's developing at least an informal understanding with the Congress with regard to the areas of ambiguity in intelligence oversight reporting of extraterritorial apprehension missions.

Reconciling Executive and Legislative Roles

As is clear from even a cursory review of the WPR and the Intelligence Oversight Act of 1980, there remains substantial ambiguity regarding the authority and responsibilities of the two branches in the area of proactive counterterrorism measures. This ambiguity has the clear potential for giving rise to divisive political and legal disputes between the two branches. Such disputes, should they occur, will serve only to undermine the chances of developing an effective, broad-based counterterrorism policy and strategy.

Citing the danger inherent in the Congress and executive not working cooperatively with regard to war powers and intelligence oversight, Senator David Durenberger (R–Minnesota) made these remarks to the Johns Hopkins School of Advanced International Studies:

> My problem with the War Powers and Intelligence Oversight frameworks is that they will more often operate to inhibit rather than encourage . . . consultation, because of the intricate legal [gamesmanship] that inevitably results.
>
> The executive branch spends its time figuring out whether and how a particular activity fits into either framework, when we might be conducting a more *meaningful* exchange of ideas on the wisdom of underlying basic policy, or even the advisability of a particular operation as a whole.
>
> This is not a theoretical problem. It exists today. In the view of the Administration, notification of Congress is tantamount to public disclosure. Therefore, in shaping the options available to counter a terrorist threat, planners in the executive department limit their consideration to actions which do *not* fall under the War Powers Act. What may be the most effective course of action from the military or political point of view may be rejected because of the current requirements for notification.
>
> In short, the Administration may prefer to do the wrong thing in secret, rather than doing the right thing with congressional knowledge.
>
> The system has truly been stood on its head—and the effect could be disastrous.[173]

In developing a counterterrorism option of extraterritorial apprehension, the benefits to be derived from a meaningful partnership with the Congress far outweigh the costs. The implementation of the partnership may be based on the nonspecific WPR system in which the executive typically elects to consult with key members of the congressional leadership. Alternatively, such a partnership could be based upon the existing intelligence oversight system, which offers the substantial advantages of being permanently in place, tested, and able to maintain operational security. The recipients of the information for the Congress are limited in number and may be granted appropriate security clearances.

In April 1986, Senate majority leader Robert Dole (R–Kansas) joined other senators in introducing legislation that would grant the president expanded powers to respond to terrorist acts. The legislative proposal exempts counterterrorist actions conducted by military forces from the constraints of the WPR.[174] Extraterritorial apprehension as a counterterrorism action would fall squarely within the purview of this proposed legislation. The bill eliminates any requirement for advance consultation with the Congress and authorizes both pre-emptive and punitive strikes in response to terrorist threats from abroad. Other provisions in the proposed legislation require the president to report the results of actions taken under this congressional "authorization."[175] If this legislative proposal is adopted, it will serve as the foundation for the executive's partnership with the Congress in implementing a counterterrorism measure of extraterritorial apprehension.

Specific Limitations on Planning and Execution

Apart from the constraints imposed by the War Powers reporting and intelligence oversight requirements, a number of specific organizational and functional limitations could affect the development of extraterritorial apprehension as a counterterrorism measure. No exhaustive list of such limitations can be provided in the absence of highly specific apprehension scenarios. Nevertheless, a number of limitations can be identified that are likely to have a general impact on a range of possible scenarios. Since such limitations may influence the preparation of operational plans and organizational structures, it is useful to include them among the considerations to be reviewed.

Executive Order 12333. Executive order (EO) 12333 of December 4, 1981, establishes an executive branch intelligence oversight and accountability structure. The order specifies the jurisdictional responsibilities of the intelligence agencies as well as certain substantive rules and limitations governing the conduct of their activities. The substantive rules are of general applicability, with detailed implementation left to regulations ("procedures") promulgated by the head of each intelligence agency. Such regulations are subject to review by the U.S. attorney general.

The involvement of the Department of Justice in the elaboration of these rules was so extensive during the Ford and Carter administrations, that under the latter, it was necessary to create a separate office within the Justice Department known as the Office of Intelligence Policy and Review.[176] This office reviews agency regulations and procedures and approves applications submitted by the agencies made to the Foreign Intelligence Surveillance Court established under the Foreign Intelligence Surveillance Act.[177].

Executive branch oversight is further developed under executive order 12334 signed December 4, 1981.[178] This order reestablishes the president's Intelligence Oversight Board (PIOB). The PIOB consists of three members charged with safeguarding the lawfulness of activities of the various intelligence agencies. Board members are to be distinguished citizens from outside the government. They are required to inform the president of intelligence activities that any member believes are in violation of the Constitution or laws of the United States. The PIOB is also required to perform a variety of oversight functions, including reviewing practices and procedures of the inspectors general and general counsels of the intelligence community to ensure that the intelligence system maintains a check on its own actions. It may be appropriate for the PIOB to review the legality of extraterritorial apprehension in support of any NSC study of this counterterrorism strategy option.

Additional executive branch oversight results from review procedures within the departments and agencies themselves. One of the principal purposes of these internal agency procedures is to ensure sensitive activities are reviewed and approved by senior agency officials. The general counsel for each of the agencies, or, in the case of the military departments, their respective judge advocates general, are given substantial responsibilities along with senior deputies to ensure oversight and proper implementation of EO 12333.[179] Depending upon which departments and agencies may be charged with conducting an extraterritorial apprehension, these internal procedures will be brought to bear to review not only the lawfulness of the proposed operational plan but also its overall value from a policy and operational perspective.

Under EO 12333, covert actions are euphemistically designated as "special activities" and are defined as

> activities conducted in support of national foreign policy objectives abroad which are planned and executed so that the role of the United States Government is not apparent or acknowledged publicly, and functions in support of such activities, but which are not intended to influence United States political processes, public opinion, policies, or media and do not include diplomatic activities or the collection and production of intelligence or related support functions.[180]

If a proposed special activity fits within this definition, it is subjected to the EO 12333 executive review procedures by the proposing agency that forwards it to the NSC staff for presentation to the NSC principals themselves. It is not at all clear that extraterritorial apprehension would constitute a special activity as defined in the order. Although planning for a specific extraterritorial apprehension would be highly classified to ensure the success of the operation and safety of the apprehending force, it would not be actively "planned and executed so that the role of the United States Government is not apparent or acknowledged publicly." Moreover, the very operation itself could be viewed as intended, at least in part, "to influence the political processes, public opinion, policies, and media" within the United States.

Once again it is not completely clear whether an existing management and oversight system applies to the proposed counterterrorism measure of extraterritorial apprehension. In any case, operations mounted in support of a publicly acknowledged apprehension may have to remain covert and unacknowledged. At a minimum, such supporting operations would be subject to the EO 12333 and internal agency review and determination processes.

Best known of the substantive rules contained in EO 12333 is the prohibition on engaging in assassination or participating in or requesting others to do so. This provision could be publicly or secretly canceled or selectively suspended as has been openly proposed in the media and even in pending legislation.[181] However, most extraterritorial apprehension scenarios would not include such direct action as an objective. Measures to apply on-scene force during the apprehension phase would be mounted for the express purpose of providing for the self-defense of those conducting the seizure and would appear to fall well outside the purview of the order's prohibition on assassination.

Limitations on Performing Law Enforcement Functions. The CIA is precluded by the National Security Act of 1947 from exercising any "police, subpoena, [or] law enforcement powers."[182] However, EO 12333 does authorize intelligence agencies to provide assistance to law enforcement authorities:

> Para. 2.6. *Assistance to Law Enforcement Authorities.* Agencies within the Intelligence Community are authorized to: . . .
> (b) Unless otherwise precluded by law or this Order, participate in law enforcement activities to investigate or prevent intelligence activities by foreign powers, or international terrorists or narcotics; . . .
> (d) Render any other assistance and cooperation to law enforcement authorities not precluded by applicable law.[183]

This paragraph appears to authorize the CIA to assist the Department of Justice in the apprehension of suspected terrorists on foreign soil. There may be some question as to whether CIA involvement in an extraterritorial apprehension would constitute a direct exercise of law enforcement powers prohibited under the National Security Act of 1947 itself. There may also be a question as to whether the agency would be acting pursuant to a valid request for assistance and delegation of authority from the Department of Justice. A defense counsel representing an apprehended terrorist will almost certainly argue that any role the CIA plays in the apprehension represents more than mere assistance and is instead a direct assertion of law enforcement authority prohibited under the 1947 act.

In *United States v. Reed,*[184] CIA agents operated in the Bahamas in apparent support of the FBI. The issue of the agency's authority to provide such support was not seriously challenged or litigated on appeal. It appears likely that if planners ensure that the apprehension is documented as pursuant to the express request of the U.S. attorney general and at the direction of the president, any defense challenge asserting a bar to the CIA's authority is bound to fail. It is likely that U.S. courts would view the 1947 National Security Act prohibition as one designed to preclude the CIA from acting on its own initiative and as an independent law enforcement arm of the government. They are unlikely to rule that CIA involvement is a violation of the act when it is performed on a case-specific basis, at the express request of the chief U.S. law enforcement officer, and subject to the close direction of the president.

The Posse Comitatus Act prohibits military departments from participating in law enforcement activities except as specifically authorized by the Constitution and the laws of the United States.[185] The act does not have general application outside the United States, and, moreover, exceptions can be granted by the U.S. attorney general. Amendments adopted by the Congress in 1981 were designed to authorize the use of the military in support of the U.S. Coast Guard and other civilian law enforcement agencies engaged in the interdiction of both international and domestic drug smuggling.[186] The Posse Comitatus Act does not preclude the use of the U.S. armed forces in extraterritorial apprehension. There is no indication that the act in any way inhibited U.S. Navy participation in the interception and diversion of the Egyptair 737 in the *Achille Lauro* case, a clear instance of direct support for a law enforcement function.

In *United States v. Cotten*,[187] the defendants were seized and forcibly removed from South Vietnam to Hawaii at the direction of U.S. government personnel. In addition to charging their constitutional rights were violated, the defendants objected to the use of U.S. Air Force aircraft and personnel to return them forcibly to the United States, asserting a violation of 18 U.S.C. 1385. This code provision provides that whoever willfully uses any part of the army or air force as a posse comitatus or otherwise to execute the laws violates federal law. The court dismissed the defendants' claim, noting that the remedy for the conduct complained of, if any remedy even existed, was not divestiture of jurisdiction by the court.

To ensure the Posse Comitatus Act is not an issue either overseas or upon return to U.S. territory, planners should ensure that military units act at the express request of and under the authorization of the U.S. attorney general. Legal challenges that have resulted from the U.S. Navy's support of the U.S. Coast Guard in its drug interdiction operations demonstrate the extreme importance of having such requests and authorizations well documented in advance. Operational orders should reflect any waivers to the act so that on-scene commanders understand they are acting with proper authority and in support of a law enforcement function. Applicable Department of Defense and military department instructions that regulate the provision of assistance to civilian law enforcement agencies should be carefully followed to assist U.S. federal prosecutors in easily defeating defense objections based on alleged violation of the Posse Comitatus Act.

International Reaction to Extraterritorial Apprehension

Presenting the U.S. Position. A major consideration for the U.S. government in evaluating extraterritorial apprehension as a counterterrorism strategy is the reaction of the international community at large and the Western allies in particular. U.S. economic military actions taken against Libya in 1985 and 1986 clearly demonstrate a willingness to undertake unilateral action and, when necessary, to take the lead in combating terrorism. Nevertheless, there is a clear recognition of the need for international cooperation in addressing the problem. While the Western Summit Conference in Tokyo in May 1986 recognized the right of nations to take unilateral actions, the meeting as a whole emphasized the need for greater international cooperation.[188]

Western leaders at the Tokyo summit meeting reportedly discussed a range of counterterrorism options, including improved international law enforcement through greater use of extradition.[189] There was no indication that extraterritorial apprehension or any form of irregular rendition was discussed. Consistent with the U.S. commitment to improved cooperation with the allies in combating terrorism, it would seem advisable to inform them quietly but firmly of any U.S. intention to exercise extraterritorial apprehension as a counterterrorism measure. During the course of consulting with the allies on this subject, the legal and policy reasoning in support of extraterritorial apprehension should be thoroughly explained. U.S. representatives should note that the municipal courts in many nations, including the United Kingdom, Belgium, Canada, France, and Israel, have ruled to retain jurisdiction of offenders notwithstanding their irregular rendition.[190]

The United States should emphasize that it is exercising jurisdiction on a very selective basis in an application of the protective principle of jurisdiction and basing its limited intervention on what it considers to be a serious, continuing, and imminent threat to its vital or major national interests. During these consultations, the point should be made that extraterritorial apprehension will be directed against the international terrorist leadership and operational elites operating in stateless areas and sanctuary states where there appears to be little or no hope of gaining good-faith prosecution or extradition. The purpose of these allied consultations would be to gain multilateral support in the aftermath of an actual extraterritorial apprehension or, at a minimum, quiet acquiescence to unilateral U.S. action.

U.S. spokespersons should be prepared to make substantially the same legal and policy case to the world community following the first actual apprehension. Because the official reaction from nonaligned states and the socialist bloc countries will probably be negative, the United States must make its case with clarity and conviction, emphasizing that it is acting as a matter of self-help out of its right to individual self-defense, that its action is directed against only those states and stateless areas that harbor or support terrorists and frustrate accepted procedures for prosecuting or extraditing those who threaten international peace and security, and that the action is undertaken with the objective of avoiding more forceful measures, which would also have been justified under the circumstances. The last point may prove the most persuasive when making the political and legal case to both the nonaligned and socialist bloc states. In general, these states might be expected to prefer the least coercive counterterrorism response and may see it in their interest to accept this option reluctantly as the lesser of the evils under the circumstances.

U.N. Resolutions as Source of Support. Recent U.N. resolutions in the Security Council and General Assembly provide added impetus to the political, if not legal, case in support of proactive counterterrorism measures. Although these resolutions do not constitute international law, they provide evidence of a growing political consensus among the 159 U.N. members that state-sponsored terrorism is contrary to the principles and objectives of the world organization. On December 19, 1983, the General Assembly denounced terrorism and called on all states "to fulfill their obligations under international law to refrain from organizing, instigating, assisting or participating in acts of civil strife or terrorist acts in another State, or acquiescing in organized activities within their territory directly toward the commission of such acts."[191] On December 9, 1985, the General Assembly approved an even stronger condemnation of terrorism in resolution 40/61, which declares that it

> *further urges* all States to co-operate with one another more closely, especially through the exchange of relevant information concerning the prevention and combatting of terrorism, apprehension and prosecution or extradition of the perpetrators of such acts, the conclusion of special treaties and/or the incorporation into appropriate bilateral treaties of special clauses, in particular regarding the extradition or prosecution of terrorists.[192]

Nine days later, on December 18, the Security Council adopted a resolution sponsored by the United States, Britain, France, Australia, Denmark, Egypt, and Peru that focused on incidents of hostage taking and terrorist abduction. In addition to "condemning all acts of terrorism, including hostage-taking" and recalling the General Assembly Resolution 40/61 adopted earlier in the month, Resolution 579 provides that the Security Council:

> 4. *Appeals* to all States that have not yet done so to consider the possibility of becoming parties to the International Convention against the Taking of Hostages adopted on 17 December 1979, the Convention on the Prevention and Punishment of Crimes against Internationally Protected Persons Including Diplomatic Agents adopted on 14 December 1973, the Convention for the Suppression of Unlawful Acts against the Safety of Civil Aviation adopted on 23 September 1971, the Convention for the Suppression of Unlawful Seizure of Aircraft adopted on 16 December 1970, and other relevant conventions;
>
> 5. *Urges* the further development of international co-operation among states in devising and adopting effective measures which are in accordance with the rules of international law to facilitate the prevention, prosecution and punishment of all acts of hostage-taking and abduction as manifestations of international terrorism.[193]

Resolution 579 with these provisions was adopted by all fifteen members of the Security Council without debate. Although the effective measures called for are certainly not intended to include extraterritorial apprehension, the resolution on its face can be read to encourage devising measures apart from those contained in the anti-terrorist conventions. The case may be made that extraterritorial apprehension is justifiable as a measure of self-help in international law and is an effective measure within the scope of this resolution.

These recent declarations of both the General Assembly and Security Council are strong condemnations of international terrorism. The unanimous Security Council action represents a major political setback for international terrorists and their state sponsors. Although nothing in these resolutions can be read as specifically authorizing extraterritorial apprehension, the U.S. political case must take note that its actions are fully consistent with the political emphasis the United Nations has placed upon the prosecution of terrorists and the encouragement of nations to cooperate actively in extradition measures.[194]

Advanced Coordination of Allied Support. Apart from the United States engaging in advanced consultation with its Western allies and making the general case to the world community in support of extraterritorial apprehension, direct negotiations may be necessary with one or more allied or friendly nations for the purpose of securing specific logistical or intelligence support. In some instances, the apprehension may involve units or agents of an allied or friendly foreign country. In other instances, it may be useful to agree in advance as to which of several countries will apply its municipal criminal law and assume in personam jurisdiction over the apprehended terrorist offender(s). These and other matters should be the subject of advanced international coordination and agreement with interested states. In the *Achille Lauro* case, there was insufficient time to negotiate the details of the apprehension in advance. However, if extraterritorial apprehension is adopted as a counterterrorism measure, most operational plans could be designed to facilitate the necessary advanced coordination with countries that would be asked to participate or provide support.

One matter that should not be overlooked in planning advanced coordination with allied or friendly nations is the possibility of inadvertently exposing an apprehended terrorist to third country foreign criminal jurisdiction. Once the apprehension is completed, it will be necessary to transport the terrorist or group of terrorists to the United States or some other preselected forum state for arraignment and prosecution. The transportation can best be facilitated through the use of a naval vessel or military aircraft. Depending upon the proximity of U.S. naval vessels to the apprehension site, the apprehending units or force may be able to transfer the terrorist part or all the way back to the United States aboard a fleet unit. Alternatively, the terrorist may be put aboard a U.S. military aircraft equipped for inflight refueling.

In the event neither of these techniques can be used, it may be necessary to make in-transit stops in allied friendly foreign countries. Once an apprehended terrorist is landed in a foreign country, he or she will become subject to its civil and criminal law unless that country has affirmatively waived jurisdiction. For this reason, unless the United States is prepared to allow a foreign country to assume jurisdiction over the apprehended terrorist, he or she should be transferred directly back to the United States, or a waiver of foreign criminal and civil jurisdiction must be arranged in advance for any non-U.S. area where an in-transit stop is contemplated.

As an alternative, the United States may be able to assert sovereign immunity over the vehicle transporting the terrorist. In the case of warships, the doctrine of sovereign immunity is widely recognized under international law. So long as the terrorist remains on board the warship and in the absence of consent by the commanding officer, no foreign authority would be permitted to come aboard even in a foreign port for the purpose of assuming jurisdiction or custody over the apprehended terrorist.

A number of countries, including some U.S. allies, have not been prepared to acknowledge the application of the principle of sovereign immunity to military or other state-owned aircraft. If the principle is applied, a military or state-owned aircraft may land in an in-transit status and not be subject to search or inspection. Cargo and passengers remaining on board would also be free of any assertion of jurisdiction by the host nation. However, should an apprehended terrorist be landed in a state that does not recognize this principle as applicable to military or state-owned aircraft, serious difficulties could arise. The best solution for this problem is advanced coordination with those states in which it may be necessary to make in-transit stops or to avoid such stops altogether through a nonstop transfer to the United States or other prosecuting forum state.

Considerations following Apprehension

The ability to plan, execute, and justify a strategy of extraterritorial apprehension would be of no consequence if prosecutors are unable to secure a conviction. The very purpose of extraterritorial apprehension is to subject international terrorist elites to a fair trial under the constitutional guarantees afforded to defendants under the U.S. or some other Western system of justice. In trying international terrorists dedicated to the destruction of the very system that seeks to hold them accountable, the government will be forced to respond to an array of political and legal tactics designed to undermine its prosecutorial efforts. These tactics may be ethical by legal standards, or they may be quite unethical. Prosecutors, the courts, and the public at large will have to be prepared to cope with an onslaught of such tactics.

Use and Protection of Intelligence Information,
Sources, and Methods

Fair Trial Rights vs. Protection of National Security Interest. If there is one thing upon which the intelligence community and criminal prosecutors agree, it is that the protection of sensitive intelligence information, sources, and methods in a criminal proceeding can be a challenging task. Of the issues to be considered in evaluating a strategy option of extraterritorial apprehension, none is more troublesome, or important, than ensuring effective prosecution, protection of sensitive intelligence information, and a fair trial for the defendant. Although each case will have its own unique set of national security issues, it is important to recognize the legitimate interests of both the defendant and the government along with available measures that may serve to reconcile these interests where they are in conflict with one another.

It is difficult to imagine a trial of an international terrorist brought before the court by means of extraterritorial apprehension where classified information, sources, and methods would not become an issue. It is likely that as the Department of Justice constructs its criminal case against such terrorists, it will do so on the basis of highly classified information relating to the identification of particular terrorists, their location at various points in time, the acts they are alleged to have committed, their future plans, their associations with other terrorists or sponsoring governments, their source of financial or arms support, and the methods they employ. Such information will be essential in the planning and execution of the extraterritorial apprehension of the terrorist or terrorists.

At least some of this information will also be important in establishing the proof that a terrorist committed an offense under the laws of the prosecuting state. Not all such intelligence-derived information will be relevant or admissible during the course of the criminal trial; however, constitutionally based fair trial rights require that the accused know the evidence to be introduced against him or her and be able to examine and, if appropriate, rebut it. In terms of the procedures used in the arrest, the securing of evidence, and other investigative matters, he or she also has substantial rights to know how the government developed its case. Such information assists in confirming that the evidence presented at the trial has been obtained consistent with constitutional limitations and is not subject to exclusion under the so-called exclusionary rule. In other words, even the terrorist defendant has a right to confirm that the evidence against him or her is not tainted or improperly secured in violation of those constitutional rights afforded to him or her, even as a foreign national apprehended beyond U.S. borders. At issue is whether sufficient evidence can be presented adequately and fairly to try the case for both prosecution and defense and at the same time protect sensitive classified information from disclosure, which would be damaging to national security.

Classified Information Procedures Act. Prior to 1980, the conflict between introducing sufficient evidence into a criminal proceeding and protection of sensitive national security interests might well have precluded serious consideration of extraterritorial apprehension as a counterterrorism strategy. However, during the 1970s, U.S. prosecutors confronted several serious cases in which classified national security information played a critical role in trial proceedings. Known as the graymail cases, these trials involved former intelligence agents and others who had

had access to classified information and threatened to expose or demand the government expose such information during criminal proceedings. The defendants in these trials attempted to force the government to dismiss the cases by claiming that they could not receive a fair trial unless the government disclosed, or they were allowed to disclose, highly classified information. The government faced the dilemma of trying the case and exposing the classified information or, alternatively, dismissing the charges against the defendants as the price for protecting highly classified information.

Congress responded by adopting the Classified Information Procedures Act of 1980 (CIPA)[195] in an effort to put an end to the graymail dilemma. The Congress wished to find a procedural means by which to afford the criminal defendant fair trial rights but at the same time preclude the defense from using classified information to maneuver the government into a forced dismissal of the proceedings.[196]

Section 1 of CIPA provides a definition of terms, including *classified information* and *national security*. Under subsection a, *classified information* is defined as

> any information or material that has been determined by the United States Government pursuant to an Executive order, statute, or regulation, to require protection against unauthorized disclosure for reasons of national security and any restricted data, as defined in paragraph r. of section 11 of the Atomic Energy Act of 1954 [42 U.S.C. Sec. 2014(y)].[197]

Subsection b defines *national security* to mean the "national defense and foreign relations of the United States." The courts have consistently ruled that both of these key terms are sufficiently clear to inform the accused of the nature of classified information and national security.

Under section 2 of the act, at any time after the filing of a criminal indictment or information, any party may move for a pretrial conference to consider matters relating to classified information that may arise in connection with the prosecution. The federal district court must then conduct a pretrial conference to establish the timing of requests for discovery. This conference also serves to initiate a procedure established by section 6 of CIPA to determine the use, relevance, or admissibility of classified information. Section 2 further provides that during the course of this conference, "the court may consider any matter which may promote a fair and expeditious trial." Substantive issues concerning the use of classified information are to be decided at a separate hearing required under section 6.

Section 3 provides for court protective orders that may direct the defendant not to disclose classified information already known to him or her which is made available by the government during the course of the prosecution. This provision may have little application in the prosecution of an apprehended terrorist. Unlike many of the graymail cases where defendants had had prior legitimate access to classified information as former agents or government employees, any classified information disclosed to terrorists during an extraterritorial apprehension operation will be considered effectively compromised and presumably no longer subject to protection. Section 3 of CIPA has been interpreted to provide the government the right to request the issuance of protective orders ex parte and in camera, that is, before the court in the absence of other parties (such as, the defendant) and in confidence or secret. A part of section 3 that may prove useful in terrorist prosecutions are provisions allowing the court to establish controlled handling of classified information throughout the course of proceedings, including on appeal. Violation of court orders issued pursuant to section 3 is punishable by contempt of court.

Section 4 of CIPA provides that upon its request, the government may be authorized to avoid disclosure of classified information through the use of alternative forms of evidence. Specifically, in responding to the defendant's discovery requests and upon a sufficient showing by the government, the court may authorize the prosecutor to delete certain items of classified information. In lieu of the information being deleted, the government may be permitted to substitute a summary of the information or a statement admitting the relevant facts that the classified information would tend to prove. Closely resembling procedures contained in Rule 16(d)(1) of the Federal Rules of Criminal Procedure, [198] this provision authorizes prosecutors to demonstrate in an ex parte, in camera submission to the court that the use of such alternative forms of evidence is warranted.

The legislative history of section 4 establishes that the court may take national security interests into account when considering the prosecution's request to allow deletions, substitutions, or summarizations of classified information.[199] The importance of national security interests in these judicial evaluations has been recently underscored by the decision of the First Circuit Court of Appeals in *United States v. Pringle.*[200] In *Pringle,* the defendants sought discovery of classified materials relating to the surveillance, boarding, and seizure of a ship that they had used to smuggle narcotics. The federal district court, applying principles enunciated by the Supreme Court in *Roviaro v. United States*[201] and determining that the classified information sought was not properly a matter for discovery under Rule 16 of the Federal Rules of Criminal Procedures and *Brady v. Maryland,* [202] held that the defendant's interest in gaining the information was outweighed by the concomitant prejudice to the national security. In affirming the lower court decision, the circuit court held:

> We also reject defendants' contention that the protective orders issued by the district court violated their due process rights. We have reviewed the classified information and agree with the district court that "it was not relevant to the determination of the guilt or innocence of the defendants, was not helpful to the defense and was not essential to a fair determination of the case."[203]

The First Circuit holding interpreted the Supreme Court ruling in *Roviaro* as requiring the district court to "balanc[e] the public interest in protecting the flow of information against the individual's right to prepare his defense."[204] Section 4 of CIPA establishes the mechanism for the court to perform this crucial task of balancing this critical public interest against the defendant's fundamental fair trial rights.

The actual procedures for trying cases involving classified information are contained in section 6 of CIPA. Under this section, adversarial hearings may be conducted in camera to determine the use, relevance, and admissibility of the classified information concerned.[205] Prosecutors may notify the defendant at a hearing provided for under section 6 of classified information that will be at issue during the trial. However, with the court's approval, it may provide a generic description of the classified material in lieu of disclosing the actual information itself, particularly parts that may tend to disclose sources and methods.[206]

If the court determines that the classified information at issue is not relevant or admissible, the trial proceeds without the information. However, if it determines that it is relevant and admissible, then the government is afforded the right under section 6(c)(1) to request the court to order the defendant to accept as a substitute a statement "admitting relevant facts that the specific classified information would tend to prove" (a stipulation of facts) or "a summary of the specific classified information." Section 6(c)(1) further requires the court to grant such motion if it finds that the statement of the summary will provide the defendant with substantially the same ability to make his or her defense as would disclosure of the specific classified information.

The court may allow a summary or stipulation in lieu of disclosure only if "the defendant's right to a fair trial will not be prejudiced."[207] The concept of the legislation is that the defendant should not stand in a worse position as a result of the alternative forms of evidence. The statutory standard is "substantially equivalent disclosure" by which the Congress did not intend precise, concrete equivalence.[208] Section 6(c)(2) of CIPA allows the government to submit to the court an affidavit of the U.S. attorney general "certifying that disclosure of classified information would cause identifiable damage to the national security of the United States and explaining the basis for the classification of such information." If requested by the government, section 6(c)(2) requires the court to examine the affidavit ex parte, in camera.

Other provisions in section 6 authorize the court to impose a sliding scale of sanctions against the government as a means of compensation for the defendant's inability to present proof regarding specific items of classified information. Sanctions may include dismissal of the indictment, dismissal of specific criminal counts of an indictment, finding against the government on issues to which classified material relates, or striking or precluding all or part of the testimony of witnesses.[209]

Section 7 of the act provides for an interlocutory appeal by the government from any decision or order of the trial judge "authorizing the disclosure of classified information, imposing sanctions for nondisclosure of classified information, imposing sanctions for nondisclosure of classified information, or refusing a protective order sought by the United States to prevent the disclosures of classified information."[210] This provision, which also provides for expedited consideration at the appellate court level, is intended to alleviate the graymail dilemma of disclose or dismiss, which previously had to be addressed by prosecutors during the course of district court proceedings.

Section 8(a) specifically recognizes that the classification of writings, recordings, and photographs containing classified information remains an executive, not judicial, function. Concomitant section 8(b) clarifies the so-called rule of completeness found in Rule 106 of the Federal Rules of Evidence, which provides:

> When a writing or recorded statement or part thereof is introduced by a party, an adverse party may require him at the time to introduce any other part of any other writing or recorded statement which ought in fairness to be considered contemporaneously with it.[211]

To preclude "unnecessary disclosure" of classified information, section 8(b) of CIPA permits the court to order admission into evidence of only part of a writing, recording, or photograph. Alternatively, the court may order into evidence the whole writing, recording, or photograph with excision of all or part of the classified information contained in it. The provision does not provide grounds for excluding or excising part of a written or recorded statement "which ought in fairness to be considered contemporaneously with it." Accordingly, the court may admit into evidence part of a writing, recording, or photograph only when fairness does not require the whole document to be considered.[212]

Finally, section 8(c) affords the prosecutor a means of precluding a witness from disclosing classified information in response to defense counsel's questions posed at either pretrial or trial proceedings. Under CIPA, if the defendant's counsel knew that a question or line of questions would result in disclosure of classified information, notice should have been provided the government under separate section 5 of the act and the matter resolved during a section 6 hearing. Section 8(c) is designed to supplement these procedures by allowing prosecutors to object to any question or line of inquiry requiring a witness to disclose classified information. The court then requires the government and defense to proffer information in support of their respective positions.

Application of CIPA during Prosecution. The mechanism afforded by CIPA must be understood in the context of congressional purpose and the judiciary's constitutional mandate to afford the criminal defendant a fair trial. The screening mechanisms provided by the act are largely designed to protect the government against defense threats to disclose information already in the defendant's possession, that is, to address the graymail disclose-or-dismiss dilemma. It does, however, also protect information not known to the defendant but potentially involved in developing the government's case. The prinicpal function of CIPA, as crafted by the Congress, is to provide uniform procedures under which the government is made aware, prior to or even during trial, of whether classified information will have to be disclosed in open proceedings. Should that appear necessary, the act affords prosecutors the opportunity to make an informed and reasoned decision on whether the interests in prosecuting outweigh the damage to national security that may occur as a result of disclosure.

CIPA does not change existing standards for determining the use, relevance, and admissibility of evidence in a criminal trial. *United States v. Smith,*[213] decided by the Fourth Circuit in 1984, held that a district court conducting a section 6(a) hearing is not empowered to exclude classified evidence relevant to the accused's defense on the grounds that the prevention of harm to the national security outweighs the defendant's need. *United States v. Collins*[214] rules that CIPA does not undertake to create new substantive law governing admissibility. The act does not reduce the government's burden to produce sufficient evidence at trial to prove the defendant guilty beyond a reasonable doubt of each and every element of each count in its indictment. Nor is the act a vehicle to prevent a defendant from marshaling sufficient relevant evidence to present a reasonable defense and to be able to challenge that evidence presented against him or her.

Appreciating that CIPA affords no panacea for difficult cases involving classified evidence, it nevertheless arms the prosecution with an important instrument with which to approach a very thorny problem. Where classified information available only to the government in a terrorist prosecution is critical to the defendant's fair trial rights, it may be possible to apply the act's mechanism for ex parte, in camera review of proposed substitutes or alternatives to the actual evidence. It may be possible to develop summaries or admissions that the court would review to ascertain whether the defendant is left in a position of having substantially the same ability to make his or her defense as if the classified information itself were disclosed at trial.

Ultimately the success or failure of prosecution of an apprehended terrorist will depend upon three factors. First is the absolute necessity of a high level of cooperation between members of the intelligence community and the prosecution team. Such cooperation must occur at the very earliest stages of prosecution case formulation and apprehension planning. A prosecution team with appropriate security clearances must ascertain as specifically as possible what evidence it will need at pretrial proceedings, as well as at the trial itself. Prosecutors must have an understanding of what information, sources, and methods require absolute protection even at the risk of having a case dismissed or sanctions applied for failure to disclose. The prosecutors will have to appreciate fully that the overriding objective of the intelligence community is the preservation of reliable sources and methods. Without these sources and methods, there would be no intelligence. Equally important, the intelligence community will need to understand that intelligence information that is never applied in the interest of overriding national policy and strategy serves no useful purpose.[215]

The second factor crucial to the effective prosecution of a terrorist case is the existence of an energetic, dedicated, and innovative prosecution team. Prosecutors must be aggressive in using the provisions of CIPA, the Federal Rules of Criminal Procedure, the Federal Rules of Evidence, and existing federal case law to preclude unnecessary defense discovery and to protect classified information against disclosure. They must do so while allowing sufficient evidence to be introduced in support of the prosecution and the defense cases.

Early coordination between the intelligence community and the prosecution will greatly facilitate the development of independent lines of evidence that in no way rely upon classified sources or methods. When it is determined that a particular evidentiary showing is essential on the merits or for procedural reasons but the available evidence cannot be disclosed, innovative prosecutors and intelligence officers may be able to identify other ways and means of obtaining essentially the same information through wholly independent and unclassified sources and methods.[216] The key in every case will be advanced planning, aggressive interdepartmental or interagency communication, close coordination, and innovative thinking.

Finally, successful prosecution will depend upon courts, both trial and appellate, that are prepared to exercise their judicial discretion in the interest of trying cases in which substantial interests of the adversarial parties must be carefully balanced. Thomas Kennelly, an attorney experienced in both the prosecution and defense of cases involving national security issues, described this factor in connection with *United States v. Felt-Miller:*

> I think our case demonstrates that where there is a will, there is a way. If the government and the court want to try a case, they'll find a way to do it. At least at the trial level. They'll find a way to do it whether or not you've got the Classified Information Procedures Act. What I would suggest, however . . . is that the legislation does not solve all the problems, any more than passing a constitutional amendment to balance the budget balances the budget.
>
> I think you've got to exercise a great deal of judicial discretion, and I would hope that in the future there might be a greater amount of executive discretion exercised before a case of this type is brought.[217]

The willingness of the court in *Felt-Miller* to exercise this discretion, in conjunction with the prosecution's innovative use of various protective mechanisms under the Federal Rules and CIPA, facilitated the presentation of the government's case using summaries and other alternatives to the actual disclosure of highly classified information. Although the case was protracted, costly, and entailed the laborious handling and review of tens of thousands of classified documents, it was tried.[218]

The court's willingness to exercise its inherent judicial powers will play a critical role in addressing issues that are not resolved in either the CIPA or the Federal Rules. For example, the introduction and management of classified information in grand jury or magistrate's proceedings will have to be governed by the district court's judicial powers. These powers may also be required in instances where the defense counsel requires access to classified information but will not or cannot qualify for a security clearance. Court options include arranging for alternative counsel who can qualify for a clearance or imposing extraordinary protective orders on the use of the evidence.[219]

Ultimately it will be the court that balances the governmental interest in protecting classified information against the defendant's constitutionally guaranteed rights to a fair trial. Recent experience in *Felt-Miller* and other cases seems to suggest that the courts are prepared to take on this heavy responsibility at least where the government selects its prosecution cases carefully. But as Kennelly noted in his remarks, "Where there is a will, there is a way." If it is the national will to prosecute terrorists in municipal courts, concerns for the protection of classified information, sources, and methods should not stand in the way. With innovation, patience, and hard work, the problem can be resolved.

Defense Issues at Trial

An active, and possibly dissident, defense team can be expected to challenge the government's intended prosecution prior to and throughout the criminal proceedings. In addition to using graymail tactics and challenging the jurisdiction of the court, it seems likely the defense will raise a number of other defenses in an effort to defeat prosecution.

Act of State Doctrine. The act of state doctrine under international law provides that the court of one state will not judge the legality of an act committed by a government official of another state. During the Eichmann trial, Dr. Servatius, the defense counsel, argued on behalf of his client:

> One sovereign state does not dominate or sit in judgment on another sovereign state. . . . A person who operates on behalf of a state, who carries out, in other words, an "act of state," cannot be tried for such an act, if it be criminal, by another state without the concurrence of the former. . . . Not the individual but the state on whose behalf he acts is responsible for any violation of international law.[220]

An international terrorist may argue that he or she is acting as a government agent of either a sanctuary state or even an organization that claims an internationally recognized status like the Palestinian Liberation Organization (PLO).

The act of state doctrine is not likely to prove an effective defense for an international terrorist in U.S. and most Western allied courts, no matter how strong the connection with the sanctuary state or parent organization. In the Eichmann trial, the district court rejected the defense, noting that a state that plans and implements genocide cannot be treated as *par in parem* but only as a "gang of criminals."[221] The court noted that the doctrine had been repudiated with respect to international crimes in the judgment of the Nuremberg Tribunal and that this position had been adopted by the United Nations and by the Convention for the Prevention and Punishment of Genocide.[222] The Israeli Supreme Court held that acts contrary to the law of nations are "completely outside the 'sovereign' jurisdiction of the State that ordered or ratified their commission, and therefore those who participated in such acts must personally account for them."[223]

It is likely any U.S. or other responsible criminal court will respond in a similar manner to any act of state defense that a terrorist defendant puts forward. There seems virtually no way in which terrorism can be justified as legitimate when it has been so widely condemned by responsible nations and by the United Nations in the recent series of General Assembly and Security Council resolutions.

Superior Orders. A second possible terrorist defense, also employed in the Eichmann trial, is that the accused acted pursuant to superior orders. Arguing for Eichmann, defense counsel Servatius asserted:

> Everything he did was inspired by the highest authorities, who enforced obedience by holding him to his oath. Had Eichmann refused to obey, at great personal cost, others would have carried out the task in any case, and his sacrifice would have been in vain.[224]

The Jerusalem District Court ruled that "all civilized countries" had rejected the superior orders defense as an exemption from criminal responsibility.[225] The court further noted that its position was acknowledged by the United Nations and that even jurists of the Third Reich "did not dare set down on paper that obedience to orders is above all else."[226] Finally, the court noted there is "no principle recognizing such a defense crystallized in international law."[227] The Nuremberg Tribunal considered an accused's acting pursuant to superior orders to be a matter of mitigation of punishment, not as an absolute defense.

It is unlikely Western courts will grant any more favorable recognition to this generally discredited defense. Since extraterritorial apprehension as a counterterrorism measure is most likely to be reserved for leadership and operational elites, it may prove difficult for defendants to establish that they were acting under orders other than of their own design. Even if defendants are acting under the orders of others, they would be required to establish duress. U.S. law would impose a heavy burden on the defendant to show that he or she had no opportunity to escape from the control of superiors prior to the commission of the criminal conduct. In the unlikely event such duress could be established, like the Israeli court, U.S. courts will treat such fact as a matter of extenuation and mitigation in assessing punishment and not as an absolute criminal defense, particularly in cases where deadly force or serious bodily injury is the object of the offense.

Inability to Receive a Fair Trial. The most difficult defense for the government to overcome will be claims that the accused terrorist cannot receive a fair and impartial trial in the prosecuting forum state. The defense will point to pre-trial publicity, suggestions that the true gravamen of the indictment is an offense against the prosecuting nation-state itself, and the fact that an alien defendant is being judged not by a tribunal or jury of peers but instead by persons of a totally different national and cultural background. If the defendant is not fluent in English or the language employed by the prosecuting forum state's courts, objections will be raised as to his or her capacity even to understand the nature of the proceedings themselves, much less the concept of the judicial system. Finally, the defense can be expected to allege that the defendant, as an alien, could not have been on notice as to his or her obligations under the forum state's laws.

Each of these arguments is of sufficient import to merit a careful and detailed prosecution response. However, examining the line of cases in support of the *Ker-Frisbie* doctrine, several of which involved the prosecution of foreign nationals in U.S. courts, there is no reason to believe that a fair and impartial trial cannot be afforded alien defendants. *United States ex rel. Lujan v. Gengler,*[228] *United States v. Quesada,*[229] and *United States v. Herrera*[230] all involved acts of irregular rendition to bring foreign nationals before U.S. courts. Each of the cases resulted in a conviction that was affirmed on appeal. No case in the *Ker-Frisbie* line of decisions has over-turned a conviction of an alien by reason of the defendant's inability to receive a fair trial in a U.S. court.

To be sure, extraordinary measures will have to be undertaken to ensure fair trial rights for an apprehended international terrorist. Media coverage of the trial should remain under strict judicial scrutiny. In the event the victims of the alleged terrorist's acts reside in the district to which the terrorist is first brought, a change of venue may be appropriate. Prosecutors and the court will have to ensure that defendants not fluent in the national language are provided a competent interpreter at all points prior to and during investigatory and trial proceedings. The court may wish to per-mit foreign national legal counsel to join the defense team. Jury selection through the voir dire process will have to be handled expertly by the prosecution, which will be under a particularly heavy burden in the face of an uncooperative defense to ensure the selection of impartial fact finders. Publicity surrounding the trial itself may well require the jury to be sequestered during the course of proceedings.

These and other extraordinary measures must be considered to ensure that ac-cused terrorists are afforded, and are perceived by the world community to be receiv-ing, a fair and impartial trial. But assuming U.S. or other forum state authorities will prepare carefully and bear the considerable expense of such proceeding, there is every reason to believe the trial can comport with constitutional and court-established fair trial guarantees.

Countervailing Actions by Terrorists and Sanctuary States

Once the fact of an extraterritorial apprehension becomes public knowledge, the United States or other prosecuting forum state, including any state known to have provided direct support to the mission, will be under a substantially increased threat of countervailing action. Such action may be perpetrated by sympathetic terrorists or by the sanctuary state in which the defendant was apprehended. Experience demonstrates that terrorists are likely to respond to proactive counterterrorist actions with escalated violence and reprisal. In the aftermath of the April 14, 1986, U.S. air strikes in Tripoli and Benghazi, reprisals were conducted against targets associated with both the United States and Great Britain.[231]

Countervailing action may come in the form of random acts of violence against prosecuting state installations or nationals located in vulnerable overseas areas. One particularly likely scenario would be the kidnapping of prosecuting forum state nationals in retaliation for the extraterritorial apprehension. Kidnap victims would undoubtedly be held ransom for the unconditional release of the apprehended terrorist. Since it is stated U.S. national policy not to negotiate with or make concessions to terrorists, the U.S. government would have to be prepared to hold firm, even in the face of a significant number of American nationals being held ransom for a limited number of terrorist defendants in a proposed prisoner exchange. Alternatively, allied nationals could be kidnapped in the hopes of bringing political and diplomatic pressure to bear or for the purpose of driving a wedge between the prosecuting forum state and its allies. Either countervailing action would be designed to bring political pressure to bear while simultaneously demonstrating the impotence of the prosecuting forum state to respond under the circumstances.

Another potential countervailing action would be a direct attack upon the court proceedings themselves. One federal prosecutor involved in counterterrorist investigations indicated that the trial of an apprehended terrorist will all but result in "drawing concentric circles around the U.S. courthouse where the proceedings will be conducted."[232] Extraordinary physical security measures will be required to protect government facilities, including the courthouse, the prosecutor's offices, and lockup. Even more important, measures will have to be in place to provide credible protection for all personnel involved in any way with the proceedings: the judge and staff, jury, prosecutors, witnesses, and possibly members of their families. The personal inconvenience of such security measures to those being protected and the substantial expense to the government are two additional costs to be considered in evaluating the merits of bringing an international terrorist to the United States or any friendly forum state for prosecution.

Another factor to be considered is the possibility that other states will assert their right of extraterritorial apprehension against the United States and its allies. Under the principle of reciprocity recognized in international law, if the United States or another state asserts its right to extraterritorial apprehension, there must be a willingness to acknowledge that such right is available to other states as well. How would the United States respond, for example, if the Soviet Union or Nicaragua engaged in the extraterritorial apprehension of a Contra guerrilla leader present in the United States? In the light of the principle of reciprocity, it is essential the United States define extraterritorial apprehension narrowly and make clear its application is limited to stateless areas and sanctuary states that support or actively condone international terrorism and refuse to prosecute or extradite those responsible. The threat posed by the international terrorists to U.S. or allied interests must also be demonstrated in unmistakable terms in explaining the action.

These and other countervailing responses are significant costs that may be experienced following an extraterritorial apprehension. Since they are significant, the threat they represent to the United States and its allies must be weighed carefully in deciding whether to adopt such a counterterrorism measure. In the event the proposed measure is adopted, these costs would generally militate in favor of applying this option only when the terrorists to be apprehended represent significant elements in the structure of international terrorism. In considering countervailing costs, decision makers and planners must compare the costs of this measure with other counterterrorism options, including the option to do nothing at all. On balance, extraterritorial apprehension may well prove less costly as compared with options entailing greater force or the decision to do nothing and endure the terrorist violence.

Liability of the Apprehending State and Its Agents

Foreign Criminal Liability of Apprehending Agents. Certain forms of legal liability may arise in the aftermath of an extraterritorial apprehension and must be weighed along with other considerations. In the event the apprehending personnel experience resistance in the sanctuary state or stateless area and any of their number are captured, they could be subjected to local criminal prosecution. Assuming such captured personnel are not summarily killed by local forces, they may be charged by the sanctuary state or authorities in the stateless area with violations of municipal criminal law. Such charges might be expected to include kidnapping, spying, criminal trespass, criminal assault, and attempted murder. In the light of the circumstances, it is clear the United States or any other apprehending state would have neither political nor legal leverage to effect the release of these personnel. The captured personnel would in all probability be exploited in a propaganda campaign not unlike some of the displays endured by the United States when its pilots were captured by the North Vietnamese during the Vietnam War.

Little can be done about this contingency other than to recognize that steps must be taken during the planning process to minimize the possibility of capture. Ways and means of ensuring that such personnel can be fully supported by necessary force and "exfiltrated" under all foreseeable circumstances must be incorporated into any apprehension plan.

Claims and Civil Action against the Apprehending State. Another possible area of legal liability is civil liability in the form of an administrative claim or suit for damages brought against the apprehending state. Any administrative claim or civil action brought against the U.S. government will have to overcome the doctrine of sovereign immunity, which generally bars civil actions against the government except where it has expressly granted its consent to be sued.[233] The Congress has adopted a number of claims acts that waive U.S. sovereign immunity under specified circumstances. Claims acts that may have some potential for use by apprehended terrorists against the U.S. government include the Federal Tort Claims Act (FTCA),[234] the Foreign Claims Act (FCA),[235] and the Military Claims Act (MCA).[236] While the chances for a terrorist prevailing under any of these acts is remote, the potential for such action against the U.S. government must still be evaluated.

Adopted in 1946, the FTCA provides a broad waiver of sovereign immunity that makes the United States liable for injuries caused by

> the negligent or wrongful act or omission of any employee of the Government while acting within the scope of his office or employment under circumstances where the United States, if a private person, would be liable to the claimant in accordance with the law of the place where the act or omission occurred.[237]

At the outset, the apprehended terrorist seeking to file a claim or bring a civil action upon denial of a claim will have to meet the burden of establishing that he or she was injured, his or her property was damaged, or his or her constitutional rights were in some manner violated by the actions of the U.S. government personnel. To do this, the terrorist claimant would have to establish both the government's duty to him or her and a causal connection between the government's failure to perform that duty and his or her injuries. In the case of an alleged violation of constitutional rights, the terrorist would have to establish clearly that due process rights or some other constitutionally protected interest were violated by the acts or omissions of the apprehending personnel. The *Ker-Frisbie* line of decisions suggests this burden may be almost impossible for the apprehended defendant to meet.

The FTCA enumerates a series of claims that are not within the scope of liability under the act, one or more of which will probably always apply in cases of extraterritorial apprehension.[238] First, the act precludes payment for any claim based upon an act or omission of an employee of the government exercising due care in the execution of a statute or regulation, whether such statute or regulation is valid. Under a reasonable application of this provision, even if a court determined extraterritorial apprehension improper as a matter of law, if the employee exercised due care in carrying out assigned duties, no liability would arise.

The act also precludes any claim arising out of assault, battery, false imprisonment, false arrest, malicious prosecution, and various other intentional torts, except where such wrongs arise from the acts or omissions of investigative or law enforcement officers.[239] For the purpose of this provision, "investigative or law enforcement officer" means any officer of the United States empowered by law to execute searches, seize evidence, or make arrests for violations of federal law. In the event military or even CIA personnel are used in the actual apprehension, they may or may not fall within this definition. If they are not so defined, their actions, even if otherwise tortious, come under this enumerated category of claims not payable under the FTCA.

The FTCA also excludes "any claim arising out of the combatant activities of the military or naval forces, or the Coast Guard, during time of war." There is at least some potential that a court could construe the circumstances surrounding an armed intervention into a sanctuary state or stateless area as tantamount to an act of war and therefore subject to this exception. Notwithstanding all else, the FTCA provision that precludes payment of any claim arising in a foreign country will normally serve to protect the government. Since it is likely that the basis of the terrorists' allegations will be acts or omissions arising in a foreign sanctuary state or stateless area, this provision will almost invariably preclude recovery under the FTCA even if the tort can be established.

The Foreign Claims Act (FCA)[240] constitutes an alternative mechanism under which the apprehended terrorist may attempt to gain recovery against the U.S. government for alleged wrongs arising out of his or her seizure. The FCA allows claims for personal injury to, or death of, any inhabitant of a foreign country or damage to, or loss of, real or personal property of a foreign country occurring outside the United States and caused by its (U.S.) military forces or individual members or otherwise incident to noncombat activities of such forces. The purpose of the FCA would seem to exclude the terrorist or even those sustaining collateral injury or damage in the sanctuary state of stateless area from the category of eligible claimants. The stated purpose of the act is "to promote and maintain friendly relations" in foreign countries "through the prompt settlement of meritorious claims."[241] Certainly a presidentially authorized extraterritorial apprehension in a stateless area or sanctuary state identified with supporting or actively condoning international terrorism is well beyond this waiver of immunity intended by the Congress in enacting the FCA.

Nevertheless, the FCA provides some specific provisions, which may well serve absolutely to preclude recovery. Claims for damage to, or loss or destruction of property, or for personal injury or death resulting from action by the enemy, or resulting directly or indirectly from any act by armed forces engaged in combat are not payable under the FCA. In general, claims that are payable are those related to noncombat activities. If U.S. armed forces are involved in an extraterritorial apprehension in a stateless area or sanctuary state, it would be most difficult to categorize the operation as noncombatant and the terrorists or sanctuary state forces as anything but the enemy.[242]

The Military Claims Act (MCA)[243] provides statutory authorization to pay claims against the U.S. armed forces for damage to or loss or destruction of real or personal property, or for personal injury or death, caused by either military personnel or civilian employees while acting within the scope of their employment or otherwise incident to noncombat activities. Unlike the FTCA, there are no geographical limits on claims under this act; however, the act provides no right to sue, and claimants are limited to filing administrative claims for adjudication.

The MCA does not authorize the payment of claims resulting from action by the enemy or resulting directly or indirectly from any act by armed forces engaged in combat. It also excludes claims from any inhabitant of a foreign country who is a national of a country at war with the United States or of any ally of such an enemy country unless it is determined that the claimant is friendly to the United States. The first of these bars to recovery, if not the second, would appear to preclude any international terrorist from gaining successful adjudication on any claim against the U.S. armed forces involved in an extraterritorial apprehension.

Civil Action against Individual Government Personnel. In most cases, government personnel whose conduct gives rise to a civil action against the United States are immune from suit brought against them personally. In the case of the FTCA, immunity arises from case law, and the immunity must be pleaded and proved.[244] But in instances where the doctrine of sovereign immunity effectively bars action against the government, the apprehended terrorist may attempt to bring a personal action against one or more government personnel who directed, planned, or executed the seizure. As in the case of a claim or action against the government, an action against an individual employee of the government will have to allege an appropriate legal cause of action, most likely one based on an intentional tort theory or a violation of the terrorist defendant's constitutional rights.

Assuming that the extraterritorial apprehension is executed with particular attention to the standards established in *Toscanino* and subsequent cases under the evolving *Ker-Frisbie* doctrine, it is highly unlikely that an apprehended terrorist would prevail in such harassing litigation against U.S. government agents or personnel in their own individual capacity. Nevertheless, civil action against those directing, planning, and executing the apprehension remains a possibility and must be considered in assessing the overall merits of this counterterrorism measure.

The court in *United States v. Reed*,[245] in determining that the defendant's seizure pursuant to an arrest issued with probable cause was reasonable for purposes of the Fourth Amendment, commented:

> As for the manner of the seizure, custody obtained by executing an arrest warrant is not invalidated because of the use of excessive force, even though the *defendant might have a suit for damages against the government agents* involved. (Emphasis added)[246]

In *DiLorenzo v. United States*,[247] a DEA agent arranged for the arrest of the defendant in Panama. Panamanian authorities subsequently were alleged to have tortured the defendant, although their actions were never imputed to the DEA. The court noted in its opinion that the DEA's direct role in the "abduction" from Panama to the United States could subject the individual agents to suit.

Actions brought against government personnel in their own individual capacity for alleged violations of the defendant's constitutional rights are likely to be based upon the Bivens doctrine, which resulted from the case of *Bivens v. Six Unknown Named Agents of the Federal Bureau of Narcotics.*[248] *Bivens* held that a federal agent who had violated the command of the Fourth Amendment could be held liable in damages despite the absence of a federal statute authorizing such a remedy.[249] The *Bivens* decision represented a bold judicial initiative to fabricate a remedy based on the Constitution. The Court in *Bivens* effectively sidestepped the doctrine of sovereign immunity in crafting a remedy for the plaintiff. The Bivens doctrine stands for the proposition that constitutional rights have a self-executing force that not only permits but requires the courts to recognize remedies appropriate for their vindication.[250]

The doctrine has now been extended in *Carlson v. Green* and *Davis v. Passman*[252] to violations of the Fifth and Eighth amendments. In *Carlson*, the U.S. Supreme Court found a cause of action in damages against federal prison officials under the Eighth Amendment even though the plaintiff could have recovered damages under the FTCA directly from the federal government.[253] In *Davis*, the Court held that a woman discharged from her job as a congressional aide because of her gender could sue the congressman for damages under the Fifth Amendment.

In the event U.S. government personnel are sued in their individual capacity, there is no automatic right of indemnification in the absence of a statute. Congress has chosen to provide for indemnification of federal employees in only a narrow category of cases, none of which covers the types of activities likely to be related to extraterritorial apprehensions.[254] While paying judgments for federal officials in such actions has been ruled by the Department of Justice to be an unauthorized expenditure of funds, legal representation is generally provided in litigation that challenges the propriety of the employee's authorized conduct.[255]

In practice, the Bivens doctrine has been applied successfully against U.S. government employees in only a very limited number of cases. A study completed in early 1982 indicated that out of over 2,200 Bivens actions filed in district courts against federal officers, only twelve suits had resulted in actual damage awards.[256] While the doctrine has been expanded to cover additional amendments, the Supreme Court in two 1982 decisions imposed a greater evidentiary burden upon plaintiffs bringing actions against high government officials. In *Nixon v. Fitzgerald*,[257] the Supreme Court held that the president, because of his unique position in the constitutional scheme, is entitled to absolute immunity for official acts. In *Harlow v. Fitzgerald*,[258] the Court lowered a presidential aide's burden of establishing a good-faith defense to liability for discretionary functions. The Court ruled that an official no longer has to establish both "subjective" and "objective" good faith, as had been previously required. Government officials need only show the "objective reasonableness" of their conduct under the new Harlow rule.[259]

Although there is little to prevent an apprehended terrorist from bringing civil action against the government or its agents, the prospects for recovery are remote unless the seizure involves brutality or force far in excess of what is reasonably required under the circumstances. As long as the apprehension is carried out using such force as may be necessary to establish and maintain positive control over the defendant and the immediate area in which he or she is located, it is likely the apprehended terrorist will be without a valid claim or cause of action. Detailed planning, the development of appropriate rules of engagement based upon individual self-defense, and sufficient training in advance of execution should effectively preclude any real chance of civil recovery against either the government or its agents arising out of an extraterritorial apprehension of international terrorists.

Decision Making, Planning, and Execution

If extraterritorial apprehension is adopted as a counterterrorism measure, its success will greatly depend on the development of an effective system of decision making, planning, and execution. With an understanding of the principal legal, policy, and operational considerations that will play a role in this proactive counterterrorism measure, it remains to identify the key participants and describe the functions they must perform in this system.

A System for Decision Making, Planning, and Execution

Implementation of extraterritorial apprehension can be best understood in terms of the chronological steps that will have to be undertaken by decision makers, planners, and operational personnel. Figure 13–1 provides a diagram of a chronologically based decision-making, planning, and execution system applicable to extraterritorial apprehension as a U.S. government counterterrorism measure. The diagram depicts the principal steps in decision making and planning in terms of the sequence of tasks to be performed. It also identifies the government departments or agencies most likely to have cognizance or serve as active participants in the various phases of the system. The system proposed in this diagram generally conforms to the existing U.S. government counterterrorism decisional and planning structures. Although changes could result from congressional action (such as creation of a czar or cabinet-level official whose sole responsibility would be to manage U.S. government counterterrorism policy), the proposed system incorporates both the principal participants and functions required to develop, plan, and execute this counterterrorism measure.

The initial steps to be undertaken would be the principal responsibility of elements of the NSC staff. As a result of recommendations made by the Vice President's Task Force on Combatting Terrorism in December 1985, permanent staff elements have been established within the NSC to manage and coordinate counterterrorism policy and strategy on a full-time basis. Previously this function was accomplished through NSC general staff elements supporting three organizational units subordinate to the council itself: the Senior Interdepartmental Group, the Interdepartmental Group on Terrorism (IG/T), and the Advisory Group on Terrorism.[260]

Function	Participants
Propose Extraterritorial Apprehension (E/A) as Counterterrorism (CT) →	MSC Interdepartmental Group on Terrorism (NSC IG/T)
Staff and Evaluate Proposal →	State, Defense, Justice, CIA, FBI
Formulate Recommendation →	NSC IG/T
Decision to Adopt/Not Adopt →	President via NSC principals
Establish Management and Implementation System and Structure →	NSC IG/T and permanent NSC staff
Establish E/A Working Group →	
Subworking Group on Targeting -Intelligence review & coordination → -Prosecution case development → -Selection of areas subject to E/A →	Justice, State, CIA, NSA, DIA Justice and U.S. attorney State and Defense
Subworking Group on Resources and Operations → -Survey and development resource capability → -Congressional liaison → -Detailed planning and execution →	JCS, CIA, FBI, Marshal's Service Office of President, JCS, CIA JCS, CIA JCS, CIA, unified commanders, others
Apprehension Options Identified →	E/A working group
Staff and Evaluate Options →	NSC IG/T
Develop E/A Operational Plan(s) →	E/A working group (Justice, JCS, CIA, State, others)
Formulate Recommendation(s) →	NSC IG/T
Decision to Execute Proposed Plan(s) →	President via NSC principals

Plan Implementation ..... E/A working group (coordinates)
-Obtain indictment/warrant ..... Justice and U.S. attorney
-Congressional consultation ..... Office of President, JCS, CIA
-Simulation exercising, deployment ..... JCS, CIA, U.S. Marshal's Service
-Advanced consultation with allies ..... State and executing agency/department
-Establish command and control network ..... Executing agency and JCS
-Prepare for countervailing responses ..... State and Defense (JCS)
-Stage law enforcement receiving units ..... FBI and Marshal's Service
-Upgrade physical security surrounding trial ..... U.S. Marshal's Service

Explain U.S. Policy and Strategy ..... NSC IG/T and Office of President
-U.N. General Assembly and Security Council ..... U.S. ambassador to U.N.
-Additional consultations with allies and friendly states ..... State
-Continued dialogue with Congress ..... Office of President and others
-Media and general public ..... Office of President and Justice and others
-Foreign publics ..... USIA and State

Prosecution
-Arrest, rights administered, arraignment ..... FBI, U.S. Marshal's Service
-Pretrial proceedings (CIPA, venue, other) ..... U.S. attorney
-Jury selection ..... U.S. attorney
-Trial ..... U.S. attorney
-Sentencing if guilty ..... U.S. attorney
-Appeal ..... U.S. attorney

Prepare After Action Report, Review and Revise E/A System, Plans, etc. ..... E/A working group

Adjustment to Countervailing Threat Status ..... State and Defense/JCS

Feedback Loop to E/A Working Group to Repeat Application of Measure ..... E/A working group

Figure 13-1. Extraterritorial Apprehension Decision-Making and Planning Diagram

Although counterterrorism and anti-terrorism policy and strategy have been the principal responsibility of the NSC IG/T, this coordinating group comprised of relatively senior representatives of cognizant government departments has not operated on a full-time or continuous basis. The permanent NSC staff organization now provides the needed continuity. In all probability, this element would be an important point of coordination for decision making, planning, and execution of the extraterritorial apprehension measure. The NSC counterterrorism staff element would presumably report to, and receive coordinating instructions from, the NSC IG/T, the president's special assistant for national security affairs, and the vice-president, who, within the Reagan administration, has substantial responsibility for overseeing executive branch policy on counterterrorism. Figure 13–2 provides a diagrammatic depiction of the overall U.S. government structure for anti-terrorism, planning, coordination, and policy formation.

A proposal to adopt extraterritorial apprehension as a proactive counterterrorism measure would be staffed through the NSC IG/T to at least those departments and agencies most likely to have an organizational role or interest. Although the total composition of the IG/T is somewhat larger, it is likely that staffing would entail review by, and clearance from, the Office of the Vice-President, the NSC staff itself, the CIA, and the departments of Defense, Justice, and State. Within the Department of State, particularly close examination of the proposal would be required by the Office of the Legal Adviser, the Office of the Ambassador-at-Large for Counterterrorism, the Bureau of Diplomatic Security, and the Bureau of Intelligence and Research. Within the Department of Defense (DOD), the proposal should be considered by the Office of General Counsel for the Secretary of Defense, the Joint Chiefs of Staff (JCS), the deputy assistant secretary of defense for counterterrorism, the DIA, and the National Security Agency (NSA). At a minimum, key operational personnel and legal counsel providing support to these organizations and officials should review and comment on the proposal.

Department of Justice (DOJ) staffing would most likely include the assistant attorney general for the criminal division, the director of the FBI, and possibly the director of the U.S. Marshal's Service. Staffing within the CIA should include both the Office of General Counsel and appropriate planning, research, and operational divisions having responsibility for counterterrorism matters. During this staffing of the concept throughout the agencies and departments, it may be appropriate to apply the EO 12333 executive branch intelligence oversight review process to confirm the legal, policy, and operational reliability of the concept.

With comments and recommendations received from cognizant IG/T representatives, the NSC staff may find it necessary to revise the proposal and present it through the Senior Interdepartmental Group to the NSC principals for presentation to the Office of the President. The proposal might go forward as a presidential decision memorandum accompanied by a draft presidential directive. If the president elects to adopt this option as a proactive measure available to the United States, the directive would presumably provide broad guidelines to the NSC IG/T to

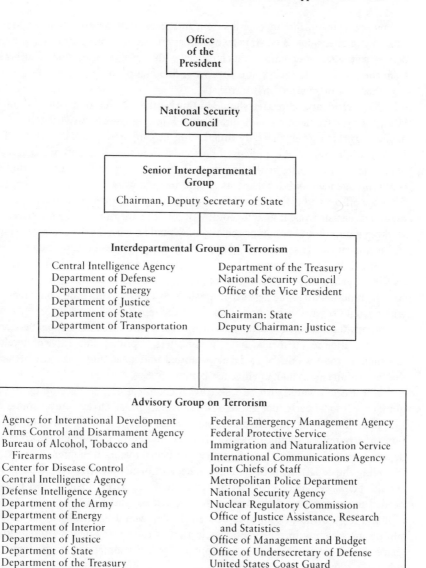

"Combatting Terrorism: American Policy and Organization," *Department of State Bulletin*, (Washington, D.C.: U.S. Department of State, August, 1982), p. 6.

Figure 13–2. U.S. Government Organization for Anti-Terrorism, Planning, Coordination, and Policy Formulation

commence formal planning, coordination, and preparation for execution of extraterritorial apprehensions. The strategy option as envisioned would require the president or a very senior executive branch official with a specific delegation of authority from the president to review and approve individual proposals for extraterritorial apprehension of international terrorists.

The presidential directive should authorize the creation of a unit that might be entitled the Extraterritorial Apprehension Working Group (EAWG) to be added to those working groups already functioning in support of the NSC IG/T. The EAWG would consist of experienced personnel from the NSC staff, CIA, and the departments of Defense, Justice and State. As noted in figure 13–1, at a minimum, cognizant agencies and departments should include working-level representatives from key offices and divisions who would directly participate in the development, planning, decision making, and coordination of this measure. To be effective, the working group should be comprised of representatives with the needed professional and technical expertise to contribute actively in this intense interagency process.

The EAWG would function to establish an effective mechanism for comprehensive intelligence review to assist in targeting terrorists to be apprehended. This specific function might be best accomplished by a subworking group on targeting, which would serve to bring prosecutors and the representatives of the intelligence community together on a routine basis to evaluate intelligence information, necessary case formulation requirements, and related matters. A principal objective of developing such a group would be to develop mutual understanding and trust between the law enforcement and intelligence communities.

The EAWG would also be tasked with coordinating and developing the required operational personnel and resource capability needed to execute an apprehension plan. To address this and other issues, a second subworking group on operations and resources should be established, composed of representatives from the departments and agencies that could play a principal role in the apprehension itself, including the departments of Defense, State, and Justice and the CIA. This group should review available personnel and equipment resources, analyze what may be needed in various probable apprehension scenarios, and direct materiel acquisition and force or unit training as needed. It also would have substantial responsibility for assisting in the eventual selection of the agency or department to be charged with executing a particular apprehension recommended by the targeting subworking group.

The overall functions of the EAWG would be to manage and coordinate the entire governmental process related to extraterritorial apprehension. Once one or more terrorist leadership or operational elites had been identified by the targeting subworking group and the operations and resources subworking group determined the necessary capability was in place, the EAWG would prioritize target options and submit a proposal to the NSC IG/T for review. The proposal would provide a broad outline of the means by which the apprehension would be accomplished. If the IG/T considered that department or agency staffing would be appropriate at this point, its members would refer the proposal on an expedited basis to their respective organizations for comment and recommendations. As soon as feasible, the IG/T would reach a decision regarding whether to recommend adoption of any of the proposed options.

For any options approved by the IG/T, the working group could proceed to develop a detailed operational plan. Planners would engage in an iterative process with one another and their constituent departments or agencies to ensure that necessary interests and considerations regarding policy, law, operational, and political concerns are taken into account. At this juncture, it may be advisable for the State Department to consult in confidence with its country team if one exists for the sanctuary state or stateless area while the JCS enters into a dialogue with the unified commander for the geographical area where the apprehension is to occur. The completed and fully staffed plan would be provided to each of the principal departments or agencies for approval and comment before being forwarded to the NSC IG/T for final consideration. Obviously this staffing can be more centrally accomplished in the interest of increasing operational security, although there would be some risk that important interests and concerns will not be exposed and addressed.

NSC IG/T-approved plans would go forward to the NSC itself and ultimately to the president for a decision to approve or disapprove one or more apprehension positions. The presidential decision would be implemented by the NSC staff organization authorizing appropriate offices, agencies, and departments to proceed with the execution phase on a coordinated basis. The functions identified in figure 13–1 are not intended to represent an exhaustive listing of tasks that would have to be accomplished immediately prior to and during the execution of the apprehension. However, during this phase, it would be necessary for the Department of Justice to perfect its case to the extent possible and to have obtained the necessary indictments or arrest warrants if prosecutors had not already done so.

The department or agency selected to execute the actual apprehension would perform scenario-specific exercising attempting to simulate the apprehension and expected conditions at the apprehension site to the extent possible. When the apprehension unit or force was determined to be ready operationally, it would be deployed in preparation for entry into the sanctuary state or stateless area. The NSC would undertake to complete the necessary congressional liaison, pursuant to the WPR, the Intelligence Oversight Act of 1980, or some alternative mechanism, depending on the apprehension scenario and the forces involved. The Department of State would be tasked with accomplishing limited consultations with principal Western allies. In the event specific foreign support was needed to assist in the apprehension operation, the responsible agency or department and the Department of State would negotiate the detailed arrangements. Press guidance should be coordinated between the Office of the President, the Department of State, and the Department of Justice. Since the operational details of the extraterritorial apprehension should remain classified, the agency or department charged with execution should not have the responsibility for discussing its actions with the media.

The actual execution of the apprehension would in most cases be managed by existing command and control structures for the departments or agencies involved. During at least the actual execution phase, there should be active participation by the appropriate JCS unified military commander for the geographical region, as well as the cognizant country team, if one exists. As the apprehension occurs and is publicly reported, U.S. government departments, particularly Defense and State, with major overseas interests should direct their personnel and facilities to increase physical security readiness in anticipation of possible countervailing action from sympathetic terrorists and sanctuary states or their allies. Under some circumstances, it may be necessary to provide travel advisories or discuss the increased threat with private U.S. and allied interests operating in high-risk areas. The nature and scope of the threat would continue to be monitored up to and after the terrorist trial if appropriate.

Finally, the Department of State and the U.S. ambassador to the United Nations would have the substantial responsibility of explaining U.S. actions to the world community at large. These actions should be explained not only in terms of the justification for proceeding under international law but in terms of overall U.S. counterterrorism policy. Particular emphasis should be placed on the narrow application of the extraterritorial apprehension option, the fact it was used in the absence of any evidence that the sanctuary state or stateless area would either prosecute or extradite, and that the apprehended terrorist leadership or operational elites were considered a serious, continuing, and imminent threat to the vital interests of the United States, its institutions both public and private, and its nationals. The world community, and in particular the terrorist sanctuary states, should be made to understand that the United States or some other apprehending state is prepared to repeat the use of this proactive measure in other appropriate cases. The message should be to extradite, prosecute in good faith, or be prepared to have nations threatened do it instead.

Decision-Making Criteria

Adoption as a Proactive Measure. The many and often conflicting interests involved in developing counterterrorism policy make governmental decision making in this area extraordinarily difficult. As in any other area of governmental decision making, counterterrorist actions must be closely examined for both benefits and costs. The cost-benefit analysis must be compared against similar analyses for other potential counterterrorist measures, as well as the decision to take no action and endure some level of terrorist violence.

The difficulties inherent in the counterterrorism decision-making process were addressed in the Vice President's Task Force on Combatting Terrorism.[261] Recommendation 5 of the final report included sample criteria for developing response options:

Adequacy of information

Reliability of intelligence

Status of forces for preemption

Ability to identify the target

Host country cooperation or opposition

International cooperation

Legality in both domestic and international terms

Risk analysis: What is acceptable risk?

Probability of success (including definition of "success")

Proportionality of forces and damage to the terrorist act

Political reaction of allies

U.S. public attitude

Probable media reaction

Potential for collateral injury to those other than the terrorists

Conformance with national standards of morality and ethics

Timeliness of the response[262]

These criteria, not necessarily exhaustive, should prove useful in examining and comparing extraterritorial apprehension as a counterterrorism measure. This study provides an analysis of many of these very considerations. Recommendation 5 of the report charges the NSC IG/T with preparing a "realistic set of criteria within which the key decisions on the use of force in preemption, reaction, and retaliation can be formulated." Until final criteria are adopted, these sample criteria should prove useful in evaluating the costs and benefits of extraterritorial apprehension as a proactive counterterrorism measure.

Site Selection and Targeting. The task force's sample criteria should also be rigorously applied in the decision making related to the selection of the countries or areas that are to be made subject to the measure. For purposes of these specific decisions, decision makers should take a number of additional factors into account. Countries and stateless areas subject to extraterritorial apprehension should be those that clearly demonstrate an inclination to harbor terrorists who particularly threaten the vital or major interests of the apprehending state and show little or no prospect of increasing the level of their cooperation in international counterterrorist initiatives. Prime candidates at the present would be Libya, Iran, and Lebanon. There may be cases in which the United States has been unable to secure the extradition of defendants it considers international terrorists because the asylum state has honored the political offense exception. However, the erection of this bar to extradition in the absence of a showing that the asylum state is itself supporting or actively condoning the protected terrorist would not justify intervention under the right of extraterritorial apprehension as envisioned in this study. The measure should be reserved for only those countries and areas that have exhibited protracted and continued bad faith in their support for international terrorism.

Since the political as well as resource costs necessary to plan and execute extraterritorial apprehensions may be significant, the selection of those to be apprehended must be done with great care. Decision makers and planners may wish to consider the following factors in the targeting process:

Threat to U.S. national security and other U.S. interests.

Gravity of the crime(s) committed.

Number and nationality of persons victimized.

Strength of prosecution case (admissibility, relevance, credibility, utility, and probative value of evidence).

Difficulties in providing terrorists a fair trial while protecting sensitive classified information.

Probability of countervailing action.

Impact apprehension will have on accused terrorist's organization (greater cohesion or cause for disorientation within the ranks).

Impact apprehension will have on other terrorist organizations.

Impact apprehension will have on sanctuary state or stateless area (stabilizing or destabilizing effect).

These factors, when considered with the sample criteria suggested in the Vice President's Task Force Report, will generally limit targeting to key leadership and operational elites within international terrorist organizations. The cost attendant to using this measure is sufficiently high that decision makers and planners will generally wish to apply it for the purpose of striking a meaningful blow designed to eliminate key figures, such as Mohammed Abbas, Abu Nidal, or Carlos. Assuming a prosecution case can be made, extraterritorial apprehension may even prove a means of holding key government leaders in states sponsoring terrorism accountable under the law for their criminal conduct. The political reaction to employing extraterritorial apprehension in this manner would have to be evaluated carefully, but such an approach should not be automatically ruled out, particularly when proactive measures are considered that necessitate the greater use of force or the increased chance of collateral injury or damage to innocent persons.

Principal Operational Concerns

Selection of Apprehension Unit. Legal and policy considerations will play some role in the selection of a department or agency to conduct the actual extraterritorial apprehension; however, the key consideration in selection should be the type of capability required to accomplish the mission at an acceptable cost. Statutory limitations on CIA and military involvement in law enforcement activities militate strongly in favor of these organizations operating at the express request of the U.S. attorney general. However, once the target for apprehension and his or her location are clearly identified, the selection of the organization or unit to conduct the apprehension should be driven by the anticipated threat that the terrorist and sanctuary state or stateless area local forces may pose and those means considered most effective in addressing this threat.

One possibility remains the use of either U.S. or foreign national surrogate agents to conduct the apprehension. A review of the recent *Ker-Frisbie* line of cases demonstrates the advantages and the disadvantages of conducting the apprehension with the use of surrogate agents. While surrogate apprehensions under the auspices of an apprehending state agency may be successful, some of the *Ker-Frisbie* cases demonstrate the difficulty in ensuring that apprehended persons are properly treated. *Toscanino*[263] serves as an example of a surrogate apprehension in which proper control was not maintained over foreign agents acting at the behest of the U.S government and where the result was the alleged mistreatment of the apprehended person. In *Toscanino*, the absence of sufficient control over the surrogates directly interfered with the government's ability to prosecute its case.

In the event surrogate forces or agents are employed, they must be of proved reliability and be thoroughly briefed on the absolute necessity of affording the apprehended defendant reasonable treatment under the circumstances. An apprehended terrorist who is able to claim persuasively that he or she was brutalized in connection with apprehension and before being formally placed in the hands of U.S. law enforcement authorities will embarrass the U.S. government. Of far greater import, such terrorist defendant may be able to persuade the trial court that it must divest itself of in personam jurisdiction over the case under an application of the *Toscanino* ruling. Such an occurrence would clearly have an adverse long-term effect on extraterritorial apprehension as a counterterrorism measure.

One of the principal reasons for using surrogates in a covert operation is to ensure that the principal may plausibly deny involvement. In the case of extraterritorial apprehension, plausible denial will generally be irrelevant, at least when the mission is successful. However, if planners consider the use of surrogates is advisable under particular circumstances, the U.S. government agency best able to train and manage such a unit or force would be the CIA.

In most instances, the preferable plan will be to employ forces or agents of the apprehending state itself. Four organizations within the U.S. government appear suited to provide this capability: the Department of Defense, the CIA, the FBI, and the U.S. Marshal's Service. The central problem with the FBI's conducting the actual in-country apprehension is that it must maintain its relatively unblemished reputation as a law enforcement organization that operates within overt, formal channels.[264] Although its jurisdiction has expanded with the extension of U.S.

extraterritorial jurisdiction, its overseas activities are principally investigatory and are carried out with the consent of the host nation. To facilitate investigatory access to foreign nations, it is essential that the FBI foster and maintain a high level of credibility with a substantial number of foreign states. Its active involvement in extraterritorial apprehension may jeopardize the credible image it has developed among foreign law enforcement and judicial authorities.

The CIA and the U.S. Marshal's Service do not operate under the same practical constraints and may be suitable alternatives, particularly if the apprehension is to be accomplished through covert operations or by means of ruse, lure, or trickery. The U.S. Marshal's Service provided direct and effective support in the apprehension of former CIA agent Edwin Wilson who was lured out of Libya in 1981 under false pretenses. Once Wilson crossed U.S. borders and before he was landed, he was apprehended by U.S. marshals.[265] No matter which of these two organizations might be used, specialized training and support capability would be required. In more complicated and high-threat scenarios, it is doubtful if either organization could perform an apprehension without the support of the U.S. armed forces.

The Department of Defense has the greatest potential for the near-term development of a working extraterritorial apprehension capability. The threat from the targeted terrorists and the sanctuary state or stateless area forces is likely to prove significant. Since the primary concern during the extraterritorial apprehension itself is the military threat and not the correct application of law enforcement procedures, the direct employment of U.S. military forces will generally prove the desired option. The command and control structure, number of forces, type, deployment, and support should remain a matter within the purview of the JCS, the appropriate unified commanders, and the on-scene military commander.

In the event extraterritorial apprehension is approved as a counterterrorism measure for general application and it is anticipated that U.S. military forces would be directly used in conducting the apprehensions, training should be provided to one or more identified DOD units. Included in such training would be the special concerns of the Department of Justice prosecutors that apprehended terrorists be afforded reasonable treatment under the circumstances and that particular attention be directed toward avoiding direct or collateral injury that might give rise to due process objections in a *Toscanino* defense. Such training might also focus on basic legal requirements related to search and seizure or other investigative functions a military force may be asked to support.

The selection of particular military units to conduct extraterritorial apprehensions must take into account the unique characteristics of this counterterrorism measure. In extraterritorial apprehension, unlike in other counterterrorism missions, the priority will be placed on apprehension force or unit safety followed by securing effective custody over targeted terrorists. If at all possible, such custody must be secured with minimum force and minimum injury. Securing custody under these circumstances will not always be easy as an operational matter; units or forces would have to be specially trained to perform the mission.

Maintaining Mission Integrity. While an extraterritorial apprehension operational plan would have to reflect law enforcement considerations, mission execution must remain the subject of the tested doctrine and practices of the agency or department tasked. The mission objective will be to conduct the apprehension with no injury to the apprehending agents or force and with minimum collateral injury or damage to the targeted terrorist and surroundings. No legal requirements exist for the apprehending force to concern itself with the details of advising the apprehended terrorist of his or her rights under U.S. or some other apprehending state's law. Once the apprehended terrorist is transferred to a platform or area clearly subject to the apprehending state's exclusive control, qualified law enforcement personnel, supported if necessary by interpreters, may advise him or her of the circumstances of the apprehension, the general nature of the charges, and that he or she is under the custody of the apprehending state for law enforcement purposes.

Intelligence interviews of the apprehended terrorist should be avoided until law enforcement agents can be present. The advantage of this procedure is that once the terrorist provides a statement, that which is taken by law enforcement officers would be available and sufficient for defense examination at trial. Under this arrangement, there would be no cause for the defense to demand later a Jencks' Act production of the statement taken by intelligence officers that could be protected from disclosure.[266]

Once the apprehended terrorist is transferred to a secure location, he or she can be formally arrested by on-scene U.S. marshals or FBI agents, who would then assume custody with such continuing military support as may be required. The apprehended and now arrested terrorist should be expeditiously returned to the United States for immediate arraignment before a U.S. magistrate. If such expeditious transfer is not feasible, a specially designated U.S. military judge advocate may be granted temporary magisterial authority and conduct an on-scene arraignment (for example, if the terrorist is taken to a U.S. naval vessel and is awaiting air transportation to the United States).

Mission planning should also include contingency planning to account for an unforeseen emergency or failure. In the light of the threat posed to the apprehending unit or force in case of attack or capture by local forces or terrorists, effective contingency planning should provide alternative means of exfiltrating personnel from the area in which the apprehension is staged in the event major complications occur. This facet of the operation more than any other will dictate that strict operational security surround all extraterritorial apprehension missions.

Conclusion

If Karl von Clausewitz was right, Western democracies will win the war against international terrorism only by finding effective means of eliminating the elements that compromise its center of gravity. The challenge is to devise counterterrorism policies and strategies in a manner consistent with fundamental democratic values. One need only recall the unfortunate French experience in Algeria to be reminded of the ill effects of a democratic state that attempts to attain a desired end by means that violate its fundamental political and social values.

Extraterritorial apprehension can be an effective option among the proactive counterterrorism measures available to the United States and Western allied governments. It is designed to attack and undermine the leadership and operational elites as well as the state sponsorship elements of international terrorism—the components that together form the enemy's Clausewitzian center of gravity. By identifying the elites, removing them from their followers and protected sanctuaries, and undermining the sovereignty of their state sponsors, extraterritorial apprehension has the potential for striking a decisive blow at the heart of one of the West's most dangerous enemies.

To be certain, this measure must be applied only when national or collective self-defense is at stake and when less coercive measures to gain prosecution or extradition prove ineffective. Its use must be weighed against the threat posed to the apprehending force, the possibility of collateral injury to innocent persons, and the impact of countervailing actions mounted by sympathetic terrorists and the sanctuary state. Nor will extraterritorial apprehension be effective in every case. Once it is instituted, terrorist elites can be expected to be even more secretive as to their location, more concerned for their physical security, and more unpredictable in their movements in an effort to frustrate apprehension operations.

But even with these limitations, extraterritorial apprehension offers an option that, perhaps more than any other proactive counterterrorism measure, is consistent with democracy's genuine commitment to the preservation of civil liberties and human rights. Unlike most other proactive measures, overt or covert, the objective of this option is a nonviolent end product.

By openly trying apprehended terrorists in a legal system that functions subject to well-established constitutional and common law constraints on state action, the strength of the democratic form of government is reinforced for the world to see. The trial of the apprehended terrorist may be seen as a reaffirmation by the United States and the other Western democracies as confidence in, and dedication to, their systems of government. Moreover, extraterritorial apprehension can be applied in a manner that serves to advance the cause of nationally and internationally recognized human rights.

Extraterritorial apprehension and the subsequent application of the criminal law in judicial proceedings is a strategy option wholly consistent with open democratic processes and human rights values fundamental to the United States and its allies. It is precisely this quality that makes extraterritorial apprehension an attractive counterterrorism measure for the United States. As a proactive measure, it does not subvert and undermine the fundamental values of society; rather, it tends to reinforce those values in direct opposition to the objectives of international terrorism.

A close examination of this option also demonstrates that far from undermining efforts to expand international cooperation in law enforcement, it complements U.S. and Western allied policy. The proposed measure imposes a meaningful sanction on those few states that consistently resist the anti-terrorist conventions and efforts to improve cooperation through bilateral or multilateral extradition agreements. Moreover, it underscores that the sovereign's rights are counterbalanced by its obligation to other states and to the minimum world public order system itself. The message delivered is to act responsibly to support the minimum world public order system or have one's rights as a sovereign challenged by those threatened through inaction.

If extraterritorial apprehension is to strike a decisive blow against international terrorism, as suggested by this study, it must be applied aggressively over a period of time to offer the United States and its allies some element of retribution for the heinous crimes perpetrated against their institutions and nationals. Far more important, the aggressive application of extraterritorial apprehension and concomitant criminal prosecution stand a good chance of deterring state sponsorship of terrorism while directly interdicting the activities of the terrorists' networks. If this measure does nothing more than cause concern to the sponsors of terrorism and undermine the self-confidence of the terrorist movement, it will have been of significant value. In all probability, it will accomplish far more.

Undertaking such a strategy will not be an easy task, but its potential benefits may be well worth the investment of time and resources. The extraordinarily difficult job given to the intelligence community in dealing with international terrorism will become more difficult if the end product is criminal prosecution. Government agencies and departments with varied missions and conflicting doctrines will be required to rise above bureaucratic interests for a common goal. Doubtful allies will have to be persuaded or led. But the strength of the American people and their government is the ability to seize the initiative and stay the course. The American people and their Congress have signaled their strong support for proactive counterterrorism measures. The NSC must now give serious consideration to recommending that the president adopt extraterritorial apprehension as one of those measures.

Notes

1. Vice President's Task Force on Combatting Terrorism, *Public Reports of the Vice President's Task Force on Combatting Terrorism* (Washington, D.C.: Government Printing Office, February 1986), introductory letter of the vice-president.

2. Ibid., p. 26.

3. Michael Howard, *Clausewitz* (Oxford: Oxford University Press, 1983), p. 39.

4. Penal Law Amendment (Offenses Committed Abroad) (Amendment No. 4) Law, 5732-1972, *Laws of the State of Israel* No. 25 (1971-1972).

5. "Affaire Abu Daoud," France, Court of Appeals of Paris, 1977, in *Journal du droit international,* 104 (1977): 843.

6. American Law Institute, Restatement of the Law Second, *Foreign Relations Law of the United States (Revised)* (1985), Tentative Draft n. 6, v. 1, sec. 402, p. 188.

7. U.S. Treaties, etc., Convention for the Suppression of Unlawful Acts against the Safety of Civil Aviation, done at Montreal, September 23, 1971 [1973], 24 *U.S.T.* 565, *T.I.A.S.* 7570, 10 *I.L.M.* 1151 (1971); International Convention against the Taking of Hostages, 34 U.N. GAOR Supp. (No. 39) at 23, U.N. Doc. A/34/49 (1979), reprinted in 18 *I.L.M.* 1456 (1979); implemented by Comprehensive Crime Control Act of 1984, *U.S. Code, Title 18*, sec. 1203 *et seq. See* Public Law 98–473, 98th Cong., signed into law October 12, 1984.

8. International Convention against the Taking of Hostages.

9. U.S. Treaties, etc., Convention on Offenses and Certain Other Acts Committed on Board Aircraft, done at Tokyo, September 14, 1963 [1969], 20 *U.S.T.* 2941, *T.I.A.S.* 6768, 704 *U.N.T.S.* 219.

10. John F. Murphy, *Punishing International Terrorists* (Totowa, N.J.: Rowman & Allanheld, 1985), p. 36.

11. George P. Shultz, "Terrorism and the Modern World" (address before the Park Avenue Synagogue, New York City, October 25, 1984), reprinted in *Department of State Bulletin* 84, n. 2093 (1985):16.

12. U.S. Laws, Statutes, etc., Comprehensive Crime Control Act of 1984, *U.S. Code, Title 18*, sec. 1203 *et seq*. See Public Law 98–473, secs. 2001–2002, 98th Cong., signed into law October 12, 1984, implementing International Convention against the Taking of Hostages.

13. Andreas F. Lowenfeld and Robert B. Glynn, "Analyzing the Applicable Laws in the *Achille Lauro* Aftermath," *New York Law Journal*, November 1, 1985, p. 3, col. 1.

14. Ibid.

15. U.S. Treaties, etc., Convention for the Suppression of Unlawful Acts against the Safety of Civil Aviation.

16. Richard B. Bilder, "Control of Criminal Conduct in Antarctica," *Virginia Law Review* 52, nos. 1–4 (March 1966):251.

17. Daniel P. Finn, "Some Congressional Perspectives on Security in the Mediterranean" (address to Turkish Institute of Foreign Policy, Turkish Foreign Policy Institute, Istanbul, November 13–15, 1985); p. 7.

18. Stephen Engelberg and Jeff Gerth, "U.S. Is Said to Weigh Abducting Terrorists Abroad for Trials Here," *New York Times*, January 19, 1986, p. 10. See "Abducting Terrorists to Try Them in U.S. Considered by Government," *Providence Sunday Journal*, January 19, 1986, p. A–3.

19. "Terrorist Prosecution Act," *Congressional Record*, February 19, 1986, p. S1383.

20. Senator Specter remarks in support of "S. 871. A Bill to Prohibit Trade with Libya; to the Committee of Finance," *Congressional Record* 3 (April 1985): S6178; see "S. 3018—Prosecution of Terrorists," *Congressional Record*, September 25, 1984, pp. S11774–S11776; see also "Senate Resolution 473—Expressing the Sense of the Senate with Respect to International Terrorism," *Congressional Record*, October 3, 1984, pp. S13201–S13202; see also "S. 1373, A Bill to Amend Title 18, United States Code, to Authorize Prosecution of Terrorists and Others Who Attack U.S. Government Employees Abroad, and for Other Purposes; to the Committee on the Judiciary," *Congressional Record*, June 27, 1985, pp. S8960–S8961; see also "Terrorist Prosecution Act," *Congressional Record*, February 19, 1986, pp. S1382–S1387.

21. Arlen Specter, "Terrorist Prosecution Act," *Congressional Record*, February 19, 1986, p. S1384.

22. Patrick Leahy, "Terrorist Prosecution Action," *Congressional Record*, February 19, 1986, p. S1386.

23. Interview with Joel Lisker, chief counsel to Senate Judiciary Committee's Subcommittee on Terrorism and Security, U.S. Senate, Washington, D.C., April 11, 1986. See interview with Paul Michel, administrative assistant to Senator Arlen Spector, U.S. Senate, Washington, D.C., April 11, 1986.

24. Murphy, *Punishing International Terrorists,* p. 89.

25. *Ker v. Illinois,* 119 U.S. 436 (1886).

26. Ibid., p. 440.

27. Ibid.

28. *Frisbie v. Collins,* 342 U.S. 519 (1952).

29. Ibid., p. 552.

30. *United States v. Toscanino,* 500 F.2d, 267, *rehearing denied,* 504 F.2d 1380 (2d Cir. 1974) (hereinafter *Toscanino*).

31. *Rochin v. California,* 342 U.S. 165 (1952).

32. *Mapp v. Ohio,* 367 U.S. 643 (1961).

33. *Rochin,* p. 166.

34. *Mapp v. Ohio,* 367 U.S. 643.

35. *Toscanino,* p. 273.

36. Ibid., pp. 174–175. See Randall L. Sarosdy, "Jurisdiction Following Illegal Extraterritorial Seizures: International Human Rights Obligations as an Alternative to Constitutional Stalemate," *Texas Law Review* 54, no. 7 (November 1976):1439–1470.

37. *United States v. Toscanino,* 398 F. Supp. 916, 917 (E.D.N.Y. 1975). On remand, the district court considered an eleven-page affidavit submitted by Toscanino alleging the specifics of his abduction. The court, however, determined that the defendant had submitted no credible evidence of U.S. participation in the alleged abduction or torture and as a result declined to hold a further evidentiary hearing. *Accord United States v. Sorren,* 605 F.2d 1211, 1215 (1st Cir. 1979) where court of appeals recognized that review of decision not to hold evidentiary hearing is merely a review of exercise of discretion dependent upon particular facts before the district court.

38. *Toscanino,* 500 F.2d 280.

39. *Katz v. United States,* 389 U.S. 347 (1967); compare *United States v. Pink,* 315 U.S. 203 (1942), with *Au Yi Lau v. United States Immigration & Naturalization Serv.,* 445 F.2d 217 (D.C. Cir.), *cert. denied,* 404 U.S. 864 (1971). See Sarosdy, "Jurisdiction Following," pp. 1450–1451.

40. Sarosdy, "Jurisdiction Following," pp. 1450–1451. See *Balzac v. Puerto Rico,* 258 U.S. 298, 312–313 (1922).

41. Sarosdy, "Jurisdiction Following," pp. 1450–1452. See *Harisiades v. Shaughnessy,* 343 U.S. 580, 586 and n. 9 (1952); *Home Ins. Co. v. Dick,* 281 U.S. 397, 411 (1930). See also *Saipan v. Department of Interior,* 365 F. Supp. 645, (D. Hawaii 1973).

42. *United States ex rel. Lujan v. Gengler,* 510 F.2d 62 (2d Cir. 1975), *cert. denied,* 421 U.S. 1001 (1975).

43. Ibid., p. 65.

44. Ibid., p. 66.

45. Ibid., p. 67 n. 8.

46. *United States v. Lira,* 515 F.2d 68 (2d Cir. 1975), *cert. denied* 423 U.S. 847 (1975).

47. Ibid., pp. 70–71.

48. Ibid., p. 71.

49. *Ex parte Lopez,* 6 F. Supp. 342 (D.C. TX, 1934).

50. Perry John Seaman, "International Bountyhunting: A Question of State Responsibility," *California Western International Law Journal* 15, no. 2 (Spring 1985):397–399. See Wade A. Buser, "The *Jaffe* Case and the Use of International Kidnapping as an Alternative to Extradition," *Georgia Journal of International and Comparative Law* 14, issue 2 (1984):357–62.

51. Buser, "*Jaffe* Case," pp. 358–362, 373–375.

52. Ibid., pp. 374–375. See Seaman, "International Bountyhunting," p. 414.

53. *United States v. Reed,* 639 F.2d 896 (2d Cir. 1981), 64 ALR Fed. 276.

54. Ibid., p. 902.

55. Ibid.

56. Ibid., p. 903.

57. Ibid.

58. Ibid.

59. United Nations Charter, signed San Francisco, June 26, 1945, U.S. Department of State, Facsimile of Charter (US, DOS, Pub. 2368), pp. 1–20, reprinted in Louis B. Sohn, ed. *Basic Documents of the United Nations,* 2d ed. (Brooklyn: Foundation Press, 1968) pp. 1–25 (hereinafter U.N. Charter).

60. Ibid., Art. 2(4).

61. *The Paquete Habana,* 175 U.S. 677 (1900).

62. Ibid., p. 700.

63. Ibid.

64. *Over the Top,* 5 F.2d 838, (D. Conn. 1925) p. 842.

65. H. Kelsen, *Principles of International Law* (1966), p. 317. See Seaman, "International Bountyhunting," pp. 399–400.

66. Kelsen, *Principles,* p. 317.

67. T. Lawrence, *The Principles of International Law* (1923), p. 199. See Seaman, "International Bountyhunting," p. 400.

68. M. Whiteman, *Digest of International Law* 5 (1965):7. See Seaman, "International Bountyhunting," p. 400.

69. Whiteman, *Digest,* p. 216.

70. Ibid., p. 7.

71. U.N. Charter, Art. 2(4).

72. *Toscanino,* p. 277.

73. U.S. Treaties, etc., Charter of the Organization of American States (OAS), 2 *U.S.T.* 2394 (April 30, 1948) *T.I.A.S.* 2361, 119 *U.N.T.S.* 3, done April 30, 1948.

74. Peter Papadatos, *The Eichmann Trial* (New York: Frederick A. Praeger, 1964), pp. 53–62.

75. United Nations, Security Council, U.N. Doc. SCOR Supp. (New York: April–June 1960) at 31, U.N. Doc. S/4342 (1960). See Matthew Lippman, "The Trial of Adolf Eichmann and the Protection of Universal Human Rights under International Law," *Houston Journal of International Law* 5, no. 1 (Autumn 1982):7.

76. United Nations, Security Council, U.N. SCOR Supp. v. 15 (New York: April–June 1960) at 27, U.N. Doc. S/4336 (1960). See Lippman, "Trial of Adolf Eichmann," p. 8.

77. United Nations, Security Council, U.N. SCOR v. 15 (865th mtg.) at 3–5, U.N. Doc. S/P.V. 865 (New York: 1960). See Lippman, "Trial of Adolf Eichmann," pp. 8–9.

78. United Nations, Security Council, U.N. SCOR v. 15 (865th mtg.) at 22, U.N. Doc. S/P.V. 865 (New York: 1960). See Lippman, "Trial of Adolf Eichmann," p. 9.

79. United Nations, Security Council, U.N. SCOR v. 15 (866th mtg.) at 21, U.N. Doc. S/P.V. 866 (New York: 1960). See Lippman, "Trial of Adolf Eichmann," p. 10.

80. United Nations, Security Council, U.N. SCOR v. 15 (868th mtg.) at 31–40, U.N. Doc. S/P.V. 868 (New York: 1960). For the text of the resolution, *see* U.N. SCOR Supp. v. 15 (New York: April–June 1960) at 35, U.N. Doc. S/4349. See Lippman, "Trial of Adolf Eichmann," p. 11.

81. M. Pearlman, *The Capture and Trial of Adolf Eichmann* (1963), p. 79. See Lippman, "Trial of Adolf Eichmann," p. 11.

82. U.N. Charter, Art. 2(4).

83. Ibid., Art. 1.

84. I. Oppenheim, *International Law* (H. Lauterpacht ed. 1948), pp. 254–256. See Gregory F. Intoccia, "International Legal and Policy Implications of an American Counter-Terrorist Strategy," *Denver Journal of International Law and Policy* 14, no. 1 (1985):127–130.

85. Bernard Wientraub, "U.S. Got Alert on Berlin, Ties Plot to Libya," *Providence Journal-Bulletin,* April 11, 1986, pp. A-1, A-20. See Doyle McManus, "American Strike Signifies a New Attitude toward Use of Lethal Force," *Providence Journal-Bulletin,* April 15, 1986, p. 8.

86. "Can Reagan Make Qadhafi Cry Uncle?" *U.S. News & World Report,* April 21, 1986, p. 6.

87. Gross, "The Legal Implications of Israel's 1982 Invasion into Lebanon," *California Western International Law Journal* 13 (1983): pp. 468–470. See Intoccia, "Counter-Terrorist Strategy," p. 128.

88. United Nations, General Assembly, The Declaration of Principles of International Law Concerning Friendly Relations and Cooperation among States in Accordance with the Charter of the United Nations, General Assembly Res. 2625, U.N. GAOR Supp. v. 25 (no. 28) at 121, U.N. Doc. A/8028 (New York: 1970). See Intoccia, "Counter-Terrorist Strategy," p. 128.

89. Intoccia, "Counter-Terrorist Strategy," pp. 128–130.

90. W. Levi, *Contemporary International Law: A Concise Introduction* (1979), pp. 242–243. See Intoccia, "Counter-Terrorist Strategy," p. 128.

91. Hague International Court of Justice, Corfu Channel Case (U.K. v. Albania) [1949] I.C.J. Rep. 4, reprinted in *Yale Law Journal* 58 (1948):187.

92. Intoccia, "Counter-Terrorist Strategy," pp. 128–129. See Part 1 of Draft Articles on State Responsibility [1980] *Year Book on International Law and Commerce,* v. 2, art. 8, at 31, U.N. Doc. A/CN.4/SER.A/1980/Add.1 (Part 2).

93. Intoccia, "Counter-Terrorist Strategy," pp. 128–129.

94. Levi, *Contemporary,* p. 235; Intoccia, "Counter-Terrorist Strategy," p. 129.

95. Intoccia, "Counter-Terrorist Strategy," p. 132.

96. Ibid., p. 132. See Gross, "Legal Implications," p. 479.

97. I. Oppenheim, *International Law,* 8th ed. (1955), p. 301; I. Hyde, *International Law* (2d. 1945), pp. 239–240, 821–822. See W.T. Mallison, Jr., "Limited Naval Blockade or Quarantine-Interdiction: National and Collective Defense Claims Valid under International Law," *George Washington University Law Review* 31 (December 1986):347.

98. Ibid.

99. U.N. Charter, Art. 51.

100. Kunz, "Individual and Collective Self-Defense in Article 51 of the Charter of the United Nations," *American Journal of International Law* 41 (1947):873. See Mallison, "Limited Blockade," p. 361.

101. Ibid. See Mallison, "Limited Blockade," p. 361 n. 118.

102. Intoccia, "Counter-Terrorist Strategy," p. 134.

103. Mallison, "Limited Blockade," pp. 362, 363.

104. Ibid.

105. Intoccia, "Counter-Terrorist Strategy," pp. 135–136. See Gross, "Legal Implications," p. 485.

106. Intoccia, "Counter-Terrorist Strategy," pp. 136–137.

107. Ibid., p. 137.

108. Ibid. See Bowett, "Reprisals Involving Recourse to Armed Force," *American Journal of International Law* 66, (1972):1.

109. Shultz, "Terrorism," p. 3. See Don Oberdorfer, "Some Experts Contradict Shultz on Retaliation," *Washington Post,* January 26, 1986. See also text of President Reagan's televised address to nation April 14, 1986, reprinted in "Text of Reagan's Talk Details Provocations by Libyan Terrorists," *Providence Journal-Bulletin,* April 15, 1986, p. A-9.

110. President's address, April 14, 1986.

111. Ibid.

112. *United States v. Reed,* 639 F.2d 896 (2d Cir. 1981), 64 ALR Fed. 276.

113. Sarosdy, "Jurisdiction Following Illegal Extraterritorial Seizure," pp. 439–471. See Martin Feinrider, "Extraterritorial Abductions: A Newly Developing International Standard," *Akron Law Review* 14, no. 1 (September 1980):27–47.

114. Sarosdy, "Jurisdiction," p. 1473 n. 188. See L. Sohn and T. Buergenthal, *International Protection of Human Rights* (1973), pp. 1–21; Bassiouni, "The Human Rights Program: The Veneer of Civilization Thickens," *DePaul Law Review* 21 (1971):292.

115. Sarosdy, "Jurisdiction," p. 1463 n. 190.

116. U.N. Charter, Art. 1(3).

117. Ibid., Arts. 55, 56.

118. United Nations, General Assembly, International Covenant on Civil and Political Rights, adopted December 19, 1966, General Assembly Res. 2200, U.N. GAOR, Supp. v. 21 (No. 16) 52, U.N. Doc. A/6316 (New York, 1966).

119. Treaties, etc., American Convention on Human Rights, signed November 22, 1969, *O.A.S. Treaty Series,* v. 36, o, O.A.S. Off. Rec. OEA/Ser. L/V/1123 doc. rev. 2.

120. United Nations, General Assembly, Universal Declaration of Human Rights, General Assembly Res. 217A, U.N. Doc. A/810, (1948), p. 71. See generally Feinrider, "Extraterritorial Abductions," pp. 37–42.

121. Hague, International Court of Justice, Advisory Opinion on the Legal Consequences for States of the Continued Presence of South Africa in Namibia (Southwest Africa), notwithstanding Security Council Resolution 276 (1970), [1971]. I.C.J. 16, 57, reprinted in *American Journal of International Law* 66 (1972):180–181. See Sarosdy, "Jurisdiction," pp. 1464–1465.

122. Ibid. See Feinrider, "Extraterritorial Abductions," p. 39.

123. Feinrider, "Extraterritorial Abductions," p. 40. See President J. Carter, March 17, 1977, *Department of State Bulletin* 76 (1977):332–333; Secretary of State C. Vance, April 30, 1977, *Department of State Bulletin* 76 (1977):505–508.

124. U.S. Laws, Statutes, etc., Section 502B of Foreign Assistance Act of 1961, *U.S. Code, Title 22—Foreign Assistance,* sec. 2304 (Supp. III, 1976), amending *U.S. Code, Title 22,* sec. 2304 (Supp. IV, 1974).

125. United Nations, Universal Declaration of Human Rights. See Feinrider, "Extraterritorial Abductions," p. 43.

126. Sarosdy, "Jurisdiction," p. 1468.

127. United Nations, Universal Declaration of Human Rights.

128. Ibid., Art. 3.

129. Ibid., Art. 9.

130. Ibid., Art. 12.

131. Ibid., Art. 3.

132. Ibid., Art. 8.

133. Ibid., Art. 5.

134. Interview with E. Lawrence Varcella, assistant U.S. attorney for the District of Columbia, Washington, D.C., April 9, 1986. *Also* interview with Karen Morrissette, chief, Litigation Section, Criminal Division, and Steve Weglian, U.S. Department of Justice, Washington, D.C., April 10, 1986.

135. U.S. Laws, Statutes, etc., Comprehensive Crime Control Act of 1984, *U.S. Code, Title 18* sec. 1203 et seq. See Public Law 98–473, secs. 2001–2002, 98th Congress, signed into law October 12, 1984.

136. U.S. Constitution, V Amend.

137. "The U.S. Sends a Message," *Time,* October 21, 1985, p. 24. See "The Voyage of the *Achille Lauro,*" *Time,* October 21, 1985, pp. 30–31, 33.

138. "White House Statement, Oct. 13, 1985," *Department of State Bulletin* 85, no. 2105 (December 1985):77–78. See "This Week with David Brinkley," interview with Abraham D. Sofaer, Department of State legal adviser, October 13, 1985, and "Terrorists Seize Cruise Ship in Mediterranean," various statements, both in *Department of State Bulletin* 85 (December 1985):79–80, 74–77.

139. International Convention against the Taking of Hostages.

140. "The U.S. Sends a Message," pp. 22–29.

141. Ibid.

142. Stephen Engelberg and Jeff Gerth, "U.S. Is Said to Weigh Abducting Terrorists Abroad for Trials Here," *New York Times,* January 19, 1986, p. 10, col. 3.

143. Ibid.

144. U.S. Constitution, Art. 1, sec. 8.

145. U.S. Laws, Statutes, etc., War Powers Resolution, *U.S. Code, Title 50,* secs. 1541–1548 (1976), (H.R.J. Res. 542 adopted over presidential veto of Nov. 7, 1973); Public Law 93–148 (93d Cong., 1973).

146. War Powers Resolution, sec. 2(a); 50 U.S.C. sec. 1541(a).

147. Ibid., sec. 2(c), 50 U.S.C. sec. 1541(c).

148. Senator Eagleton, *U.S. Congressional Record* 119, (1973):18, 992. See Newell L. Highsmith, "Policing Executive Adventurism: Congressional Oversight of Military and Paramilitary Operations," *Harvard Journal on Legislation* 19, no. 2 (Summer 1982): 339 n. 47.

149. War Powers Resolution, sec. 3, 50 U.S.C. 1542.

150. Ibid., sec. 4, 50 U.S.C. 1543.

151. Allan S. Nanes, *Anti-Terrorist Activities: Issue Raised by the Reagan Administration's Proposals* (Washington: Congressional Research Service, Library of Congress, Rept. 84–165F, September 27, 1984), pp. 9–12.

152. Ibid., pp. 10–11.

153. Ibid., p. 11.

154. Ibid. See U.S. Congress, House of Representatives, Committee on Foreign Affairs, Subcommittee on International Security and Scientific Affairs, *The War Powers Resolution, Relevant Documents, Correspondence, Reports*, Committee Print, 98th Cong., 1st sess. (Washington: U.S. Govt. Print. Off., December 1983), p. 47.

155. "Reagan's Decision Was Cloaked in Secrecy," *Providence Journal-Bulletin*, April 15, 1986, p. A-9. See Don Edwards, "Views of the Strike against Libya—Consult Congress," *New York Times*, April 23, 1986. See also "Hitting the Source," *Time*, v. 127, no. 17, 28 April 1986, pp. 26–27.

156. "Hitting the Source," p. 27.

157. Nanes, Anti-Terrorist Activities, p. 12.

158. U.S. Laws, Statutes, etc., Intelligence Oversight Act of 1980, *U.S. Code Title 50*, sec. 413, Public Law 96–450, Title IV sec. 407(b)(1), 94 Stat. 1981; Title V of the National Security Act of 1947, sec. 501(a).

159. U.S. Laws, Statutes, etc., Intelligence Authorization Act of 1981, *U.S. Code, Title 50*, sec. 401 et seq. Public Law 96–450. See "Intelligence Authorization Act of 1986," Public Law 99–169.

160. Intelligence Oversight Act of 1980.

161. U.S. Laws, Statutes, etc., "Hughes-Ryan Amendment," *U.S. Code, Title 22— Foreign Relations*, sec. 2422. As amended Public Law 96–450, Title IV sec. 407(a), October 14, 1980, 94 Stat. 1981.

162. Working Group on Intelligence Oversight and Accountability, *Oversight and Accountability of the U.S. Intelligence Agencies: An Evaluation*, Standing Committee on Law and National Security, American Bar Association, 1985, pp. 11–12 (hereinafter "Working Group").

163. Ibid., pp. 7–14. See Intelligence Oversight Act of 1980.

164. 50 U.S.C. 413(a). See Working Group, pp. 7–14.

165. 50 U.S.C. 413(e).

166. Working Group, pp. 12–13. See 50 U.S.C. 413(b).

167. *United States v. Nixon*, 418 U.S. 683 (1974).

168. *United States v. Reynolds*, 345 U.S. 1 (1952).

169. Hughes-Ryan Amendment, 22 *U.S.C.* 2422.

170. Ibid.

171. Nanes, *Anti-Terrorist Activities*, p. 7.

172. Interview with undisclosed source within U.S. intelligence community, Washington, D.C., April 1986.

173. Senator Dave Durenberger, "When the Frameworks Won't Fit: Can the War Powers and Intelligence Oversight Process Cope with Counterterrorist Operations and Overt Covert Actions?" (address before Johns Hopkins School of Advanced International Studies, Baltimore, October 21, 1985), p. 7.

174. "GOP Lawmakers Try to Broaden Reagan's Powers," *Providence Journal-Bulletin*, April 18, 1986, p. A-9.

175. Interview with Joel Lisker, chief counsel to Senate Judiciary Committee's Subcommittee on Terrorism and Security, U.S. Senate, Washington, D.C., April 11, 1986.

176. Working Group, pp. 14–15.

177. Ibid., p. 15. See Foreign Intelligence Surveillance Act of 1978, *U.S. Code, Title 50,* sec. 1801 et seq.

178. U.S. President, Executive Order No. 12334, "President's Intelligence Oversight Board," *Federal Register,* December 4, 1981, p. 59955.

179. Working Group, p. 18.

180. U.S. President, Executive Order No. 12333, "U.S. Intelligence Activities," *Federal Register,* signed December 4, 1981, pp. 59941–59948, subpara 3.4(h). See *U.S. Code Service, Title 50—Executive Orders,* n. 401 (hereinafter Executive Order 12333).

181. Peter Phipps, "Sen. Dole Stumps for Covert Operations," *Providence Journal-Bulletin,* April 16, 1986, p. A–3.

182. U.S. Laws, Statutes, etc., National Security Act of 1947, *U.S. Code, Title 50,* sec. 403(d)(3).

183. Executive Order 12333, subpara. 2.6.

184. *United States v. Reed.*

185. U.S. Laws, Statutes, etc., The Posse Comitatus Act, *U.S. Code, Title 18,* sec. 1385. See *U.S. Code, Title 18,* sec. 112, and *U.S. Code, Title 10,* secs. 331–334 for statutory exceptions to prohibition against the use of military forces in law enforcement.

186. *U.S. Code, Title 18,* secs. 371–378.

187. *United States v. Cotten,* 471 F.2d 744 (9th Cir. 1973), *cert. den.* 411 U.S. 936, 36 L. Ed 2d 396, 93 S. Ct. 1913.

188. "Summit Leaders Condemn Libya," *Providence Journal-Bulletin,* May 6, 1986, pp. A–1, A–2.

189. Ibid.

190. Martin Feinrider, "Extraterritorial Abductions: A Newly Developing International Standard," *Akron Law Review* 14, no. 1 (Summer 1980):28. Note cites *Attorney General of Israel v. Eichmann,* 36 I.L.R. 5 (Disctrict Court of Jerusalem, 1961), *aff'd* 36 I.L.R. 277 (Supreme Court Israel, 1962): *Ex parte Susannah Scott,* 109 Eng. Rep. 166 (King's Bench 1829); *Ex parte Elliott,* 1 All. E. R. 373 (King's Bench 1949); *Abrahams v. Minister of Justice,* 4 South Africa Law Reports 542 (1963); *Ajouneh v. Attorney General,* [1941–42] Ann. Dig. 327 (No. 97) (Supreme Court of Palestine sitting as a Court of Criminal Appeal, 1942); *Geldof v. Meulemeester and Steffen,* 31 I.L.R. 385 (Cour de Cassation, Belgium, 1961); Extradition (Jurisdiction) Case, [1935–37] Ann. Dig. 348 (No. 165) (Supreme Court of Reich, Germany, 1936); *Re Argoud,* 45 I.L.R. 90 (Cass. Crim., France, 1964); *R. v. Walton,* 10 C.C.C. 269 (Ontario Court of Appeals, Canada, 1905).

191. United Nations, General Assembly, Measures to Prevent International Terrorism, *Official Records: Resolutions and Decisions Adopted by the General Assembly during its Thirty-Eighth Session, 101st Plenary Mtg. 19 December 1983,* Res. 38/130, (New York: 1983), pp. 266–267.

192. United Nations, General Assembly, Measures to Prevent International Terrorism, *U.S. Mission to United Nations Advanced Datafax Copy, Fortieth Session, Plenary Mtg. 108,* December 9, 1985, Res. 40/61 (New York: 1985), A/40/1003, pp. 12–15.

193. United Nations, Security Council, Resolution 579 (1985), *U.S. Mission to the United Nations* advanced copy, adopted at 2637th Mtg., December 18, 1985, S/RES/579 (1985).

194. Ibid. See Resolutions supra notes 59 and 60.

195. U.S. Laws, Statutes, etc., Classified Information Procedure Act of 1980, *U.S. Code, Title 18,* app. (Supp. V 1981); Public Law No. 96–456, 94 Stat. 2025 (1980) (hereinafter referred to as CIPA).

196. Standing Committee on Law and National Security, American Bar Association, *Litigating National Security Issues,* proceedings of workshop held August 9, 1982 (Washington; American Bar Association 1983), p. 1.

197. CIPA, sec. 1.

198. *Federal Rules of Criminal Procedure* 16(d)(1) *reprint U.S. Code Service—Court Rules* (Rochester, N.Y.: Lawyers Co-operative Publishing, 1978) provides: "(1) *Protective and Modifying Orders.* Upon a sufficient showing the court may at any time order that the discovery or inspection be denied, restricted, or deferred, or make such other order as is appropriate. Upon motion by a party, the court may permit the party to make such showing, in whole or in part, in the form of a written statement to be inspected by the judge alone. If the court enters an order granting relief following such an ex parte showing, the entire text of the party's statement shall be sealed and preserved in the records of the court to be made available to the appellate court in the event of an appeal."

199. U.S. Congress, Senate, Senate Report no. 96–823, 96th Cong., 2d sess. (1980), reprinted in *U.S. Code Congressional & Administrative News* (St. Paul, Minn.: West Publishing, 1980), pp. 4299–4300 (hereinafter Senate Report no. 96–823).

200. *United States v. Pringle,* 751 F.2d 419 (1st Cir. 1984).

201. *Roviaro v. United States,* 353 U.S. 53 (1957).

202. *Brady v. Maryland,* 373 U.S. 83 (1963).

203. *United States v. Pringle,* 427–428. See *United States v. Porter,* 701 F. 2d 1158, 1162–63 (6th Cir. 1983) (upholding denial of discovery by defendant under section 4 of CIPA).

204. *Roviaro v. United States,* 353 U.S. at 62.

205. Senate Report No. 96–823, p. 4300. See CIPA, sec. 6.

206. Ibid., p. 4301.

207. Ibid.

208. U.S. Congress, House of Representatives, *House Conference Report No. 96–1436,* 96th Cong. 2d sess., 12–13, reprinted in *U.S. Code Congressional and Administrative News* (St. Paul, Minn.: West Publishing, 1980), pp. 4310–4311.

209. *United States v. Porter,* 701 F.2d 1158 (6th Cir. 1983), pp. 1162–1163, where court held even if the defendants may have been hampered to some degree by inability to inspect the surveillance equipment in their defense against narcotics charges, sec. 6(e)(2) of CIPA did not require dismissal of the indictment.

210. CIPA, sec. 7(a).

211. U.S. Laws, Statutes, etc., The Federal Rules of Evidence, *U.S. Statutes at Large,* Public Law 93–595, 93d Cong., Rule 106. See *U.S. Code Service, Title 28—Appendix Rules of Evidence. American Jurisprudence 2d,* v. 32B (New York: Lawyers Co-operative Publishers, 1982), p. 371.

212. Senate Report No. 96–823, p. 4304. See CIPA, sec. 8(b).

213. *United States v. Smith,* 750 F.2d 1215 (4th Cir. 1984) 1220, *reh'g en banc* granted (argued June 6, 1985).

214. *United States v. Collins,* 720 F.2d 1195 (11th Cir. 1983), 1199.

215. Interviews with Barcella, Morrissette, and Weglian. 10 April 1986.

216. *United States v. Felt-Miller,* discussed without citation ABA, *Litigating National Security Issues,* pp. 10–20.

217. Ibid., p. 13.

218. Telephone conversation with John Nields, former special prosecutor (*United States v. Felt-Miller*), U.S. Department of Justice, Miami, April 18, 1986.

219. *United States v. Felt-Miller* discussed without citation ABA, *Litigating National Security Issues*, pp. 16–19.

220. Pearlman, *Capture and Trial of Eichmann*, pp. 567–568. See Lippman, "Trial of Eichmann," p. 25.

221. Lippman, "Trial of Eichmann," p. 25 n. 143.

222. Ibid., p. 26 n. 144.

223. Ibid., n. 145.

224. Ibid., n. 148.

225. Ibid., p. 27 n. 151.

226. Ibid., n. 153.

227. Ibid., p. 28 n. 159.

228. *United States ex rel. Lugan v. Gengler*, 510 F.2d 62 (2d Cir. 1975).

229. *United States v. Quesada*, 512 F.2d 1043 (5th Cir. 1975).

230. *United States v. Herrera*, 504 F.2d 859 (5th Cir. 1974).

231. "Nearly All Together Now," *Time*, May 5, 1986, pp. 28–29. See "Bomb Hits 2 U.S. Firms in France; 1 Injured," *Providence Sunday Journal*, April 27, 1986, p. A–16. See also Al Webb, "Moammar Khadafy: Madman and Genius Rolled into One," *Newport Daily News*, April 25, 1986, p. 19.

232. Interview with Barcella.

233. See, e.g., *United States v. Testan*, 424 U.S. 392 (1976) 399. For the Supreme Court's rationale for the doctrine, see *Kawananakoa v. Polybank*, 205 U.S. 349 (1907) 353.

234. U.S. Laws, Statutes, etc., Federal Tort Claims Act, *U.S. Code, Title 28*, sec. 1346(b), 2671–2680 (hereinafter "FTCA").

235. U.S. Laws, Statutes, etc., Foreign Claims Act, *U.S. Code, Title 10*, sec. 2734 (hereinafter "FCA").

236. U.S. Laws, Statutes, etc., Military Claims Act, *U.S. Code, Title 10—Armed Forces*, sec. 2733 (hereinafter "MCA").

237. FTCA, sec. 1346(b) (1976).

238. Ibid., sec. 2680.

239. Ibid., sec. 2680(h), 1974 amendment, Public Law 93-253, sec. 2, 88 Stat. 50, adopted 16 March 1974.

240. FCA, sec. 2734.

241. Ibid.

242. Ibid.

243. MCA, sec. 2733.

244. *Barr v. Matteo*, 360 U.S. 564 (1959); *Bates v. Carlow*, 430 F.2d 1331 (10th Cir. 1970); *Willingham v. Morgan*, 424 F.2d 200 (10th Cir. 1970).

245. *United States v. Reed*, 639 F.2d 896 (1981) 902.

246. Ibid.

247. *DiLorenzo v. United States*, 496 F. Supp. 79 (S.D.N.Y. 1980).

248. *Bivens v. Six Unknown Names Agents of the Federal Bureau of Narcotics*, 403 U.S. 388 (1971).

249. Ibid., p. 390. "The right of the people to be secure in their persons, houses, papers, and effects, against unreasonable searches and seizures, shall not be violated." U.S. Const.

Amend. IV. Bivens alleged that federal drug enforcement agents, acting without a warrant and without probable cause, entered his apartment, manacled him, threatened his family, and arrested him. 403 U.S. 389. He sought $15,000 damages from each agent.

250. "Rethinking Sovereign Immunity after Bivens," *New York University Law Review* 57, no. 3 (June 1982):597–668.

251. *Carlson v. Green,* 446 U.S. 14 (1980).

252. *David v. Passman,* 442 U.S. 228 (1979).

253. FTCA, sec. 2680(h) (1976).

254. For examples of indemnification statutes, see *U.S. Code, Title 10,* sec. 1089(f) (1976) (optional indemnification for damages paid by certain government medical personnel); *U.S. Code, Title 38,* sec. 4116(e) (1976) (optional indemnification of Veterans' Administration personnel). See generally Bermann, "Integrating Governmental and Officer Tort Liability," *Columbia Law Review* 77 (1977): 1175.

255. Berman, "Integrating Governmental and Officer Tort Liability," pp. 1191–94.

256. "The Suits That U.S. Aides Fear," *National Law Journal,* January 18, 1982, pp. 1:4, 28:1.

257. *Nixon v. Fitzgerald,* 102 S. Ct. 2690 (1982).

258. *Harlow v. Fitzgerald,* 102 S. Ct. 2727 (1982).

259. Ibid., p. 2739.

260. William R. Farrell, "Organized to Combat Terrorism," in Neil C. Livingstone and Terrell E. Arnold, eds., *Fighting Back: Winning the War against Terrorism* (Lexington, Mass.: Lexington Books, 1986), pp. 53–56.

261. Vice President's Task Force on Combatting Terrorism, *Interdepartmental Report on Combatting Terrorism (U),* p. 65.

262. Ibid.

263. *United States v. Toscanino,* 500 F.2d 267, rehearing den'd, 504 F.2d 1380 (2d Cir. 1974).

264. Interview with John Harley, chief, Terrorist Research and Analytical Center, Federal Bureau of Investigation, Washington, D.C., April 10, 1986.

265. Interview with Barcella. See *United States v. Wilson,* 586 F. Supp. 1011, (S.D.N.Y. 1983) *aff'd* 750 F.2d 7 (2d Cir. 1984).

266. Ibid.

INDEX

About the Contributors

Nancy Rodriguez Asencio writes and speaks on the effects of hostage situations on family members. She is married to Ambassador Diego Asencio. Accompanying him on his appointment as ambassador to Colombia in 1980, she found herself suddenly in the role of hostage family member when her husband and fifteen other foreign diplomats were taken hostage in Bogotá by the M-19 terrorist group. She is coauthor with her husband of *Our Man Is Inside*.

Parker W. Borg is a senior foreign service officer of the U.S. Department of State. Since entering the U.S. Foreign Service in 1967 he has served with the U.S. Agency for International Development in Vietnam; as a member of the staff of the secretary of state; as principal officer in Lubumbashi, Zaire; as the State Department director of West African affairs; and as ambassador to the Republic of Mali. During 1984–86 he served as principal deputy to the ambassador at large for counterterrorism, U.S. Department of State. Mr. Borg is a graduate of Dartmouth College (A.B.) and Cornell University (M.P.A.). He is currently a senior fellow of the Center for Strategic and International Studies in Washington, D.C.

Peter J. Brown is a writer on defense and security-related issues whose articles have appeared in *Security Management,* the *Proceedings of the U.S. Naval Institute,* and other publications. He specializes in corporate and educational information networks that use satellite communications. He has worked with the United States Information Agency and the U.S. Postal Service. A graduate of Connecticut College, he has taken part in security exercises, drills, and presentations in several states since 1979.

William R. Farrell is a professor in the National Security and Decision Making Department at the U.S. Naval War College, Newport, Rhode Island. Additionally, he is an associate of the U.S.-Japan Program, Center for International Relations, Harvard University, and on the board of advisers of the U.S.-Japan Society of Rhode Island. He is the author of *The U.S. Government's Response to Terrorism* and a contributing author to *Fighting Back: Winning the War against Terrorism, Foundations* *of Force Planning*, and *Legal Responses to International Terrorism*. He also has written several articles on the topic of terrorism and decision making.

E. Anthony Fessler is a captain (select) of the U.S. Navy Judge Advocate General's Corps and holds a professional specialty designation in international law. He was awarded a master of laws in international law with highest honors from George Washington University in 1978. He is the author of *Directed Energy Weapons—A Juridical Analysis*. Captain Fessler has served extensively throughout the Pacific and as head, Security Assistance and International Agreements Branch, for the International Law Division of the Office of the Judge Advocate General of the U.S. Navy. In July 1986, he was assigned as negotiations representative and chief counsel for the renegotiation of the U.S.–Philippines Military Bases Agreement on the staff of the representative of the commander in chief, U.S. Pacific Command in the Philippines.

Ross S. Kelly is a national security operations consultant specializing in the theory and practice of unconventional warfare, low-intensity conflict, counterterrorism, and other areas involving special military and paramilitary operations. His military experience includes command, intelligence, and operations positions in special operations force units and staffs. He wrote the "Special Operations Report" columns from August 1984 to May 1987 in *Defense and Foreign Affairs*, speaks regularly in conferences addressing special operations and low-intensity conflict, and has appeared as an expert on Capitol Hill and in news programs and articles.

W.D. Livingstone is press secretary for U.S. Senator Pete Wilson of California. He previously served as press secretary for U.S. Senator Jim McClure, press secretary for the Jim McClure Reelection Campaign in 1984, and for the U.S. Senate GOP Conference as a writer and director of video programming.

J. Robert McBrien, a visiting scholar at the Center for Strategic and International Studies (CSIS), has been involved in the U.S. government's anti-terrorism campaign since it began fifteen years ago. As an attorney and senior law enforcement official in the Treasury Department, he has had responsibility for a wide range of issues involving law enforcement and the national security and has worked intimately with ATF, Customs, and the Secret Service. He is currently involved in projects at CSIS dealing with terrorism and unconventional conflict, a new anti-drug strategy, and the national security decision process. He has served in many special assignments, including the Senior Review Group of the Vice President's Task Force on Combatting Terrorism, security planning for the 1984 Olympics in Los Angeles, and the review of the 1981 assassination attempt on President Reagan.

Robert K. Mullen, an independent consultant, has been engaged by private industry and by a variety of central and local government bodies to assess the technological and tactical aspects of actual and potential subnational adversarial activies, domestic and foreign.

Yagil Weinberg is a senior partner in Minerva Associates, an international consulting firm. He is a former member of the Israeli defense establishment and received his Ph.D. from Yale University. A senior MacArthur Fellow at the Maryland Center for International Security, Dr. Weinberg is a former Fulbright Fellow. His book on U.S.–Israeli relations is forthcoming in 1988.

About the Editors

Neil C. Livingstone is a well-known Washington-based consultant, writer, and television commentator on terrorism and national security subjects. He also serves as president of the Institute on Terrorism and Subnational Conflict, as an adjunct professor in Georgetown University's National Security Studies Program, and as editor-in-chief of Lexington Books' Low-Intensity Conflict series. Livingstone is the author of *The War against Terrorism; Fighting Back: Winning the War against Terrorism*, with Terrell E. Arnold; and *America the Vulnerable: The Threat of Chemical/Biological Warfare*, with Joseph D. Douglass, Jr. He is also the author of two forthcoming books: *The Complete Businessman's Security Guide* and *The Cult of Counterterrorism*.

Terrell E. Arnold is a consultant to the Department of State on terrorism and crisis management, as well as a consultant to several private firms. During 1983–1984 he served as principal deputy director of the Office of Counterterrorism, Department of State. He is a former career foreign service officer of the Department of State with extensive background in the Middle East, Latin America, East and Southeast Asia, and Africa. In 1984 he helped draft the legislation and appeared as a witness before congressional committees on four major Reagan administration anti-terrorism bills. In 1985 he served as a consultant to the Vice President's Task Force on Combatting Terrorism. He is coauthor with Neil Livingstone of *Fighting Back: Winning the War against Terrorism*; coauthor with former Iran hostage Moorhead Kennedy of a high school textbook, *Terrorism: Motivations, Methods and Responses*; and the author of *The Violence Formula: Why People Lend Sympathy and Support to Terrorism*.